The Future of Petroleum in Lebanon

The Future of Petroleum in Lebanon

Energy, Politics and Economic Growth

Edited by
Sami Atallah and Bassam Fattouh

I.B.TAURIS
LONDON · NEW YORK · OXFORD · NEW DELHI · SYDNEY

I.B. TAURIS
Bloomsbury Publishing Plc
50 Bedford Square, London, WC1B 3DP, UK
1385 Broadway, New York, NY 10018, USA
29 Earlsfort Terrace, Dublin 2, Ireland

BLOOMSBURY, I.B. TAURIS and the Diana logo are trademarks of
Bloomsbury Publishing Plc

First published in Great Britain 2019
Reprinted 2019
This paperback edition published in 2021

Copyright © Sami Atallah and Bassam Fattouh 2019

Sami Atallah and Bassam Fattouh have asserted their right under the Copyright,
Designs and Patents Act, 1988, to be identified as the Editors of this work.

Cover design: Charlotte Daniels
Cover image © Nora Denes / EyeEm / Getty Images

All rights reserved. No part of this publication may be reproduced or transmitted
in any form or by any means, electronic or mechanical, including photocopying,
recording, or any information storage or retrieval system, without prior permission
in writing from the publishers.

Bloomsbury Publishing Plc does not have any control over, or responsibility for, any
third-party websites referred to or in this book. All internet addresses given in this
book were correct at the time of going to press. The author and publisher regret
any inconvenience caused if addresses have changed or sites have ceased to
exist,but can accept no responsibility for any such changes.

A catalogue record for this book is available from the British Library.

A catalog record for this book is available from the Library of Congress.

ISBN: 978-1-7883-1171-7
PB: 978-0-7556-4371-4
eISBN: 978-1-7883-1850-1
ePDF: 978-1-7883-1849-5

Series Library of Modern Middle East Studies

Typeset by RefineCatch Limited, Bungay, Suffolk

To find out more about our authors and books visit www.bloomsbury.com
and sign up for our newsletters.

*This work was carried out with the support of the International Development
Research Centre, Ottawa, Canada. The views expressed herein do not
necessarily represent those of IDRC or its Board of Governors.*

Contents

List of Illustrations	vii
List of Contributors	xi
Acknowledgments	xv
Introduction	1

Size of the Reserves

1	Estimating the Size of the Levantine East Mediterranean Hydrocarbon Basin *Ata Richard Elias*	15

Governance of the Sector

2	Carving Out a Role for Parliament in the Lebanese Oil and Gas Sector *Sami Atallah and Nancy Ezzeddine*	37
3	Spoils of Oil? Assessing and Mitigating the Risks of Corruption in Lebanon's Emerging Offshore Petroleum Sector *Reinoud Leenders*	63
4	Establishing a National Oil Company in Lebanon *Valérie Marcel*	97

Management and Licensing

5	Licensing and Upstream Petroleum Fiscal Regimes: Assessing Lebanon's Choices *Carole Nakhle*	121
6	Lebanon's Gas Trading Options *Bassam Fattouh and Laura El-Katiri*	155
7	Managing Oil and Gas Revenues in Lebanon *Bassam Fattouh and Lavan Mahadeva*	173
8	Investing Resource Wealth in a Sovereign Development Fund *Sami Atallah, Adeel Malik and Alexandra Tohme*	197

Impact and Implications

9	Macroeconomic Implications of Windfall Oil and Gas Revenues in Lebanon *Jad Chaaban and Jana Harb*	223

vi   *Contents*

10   How Will Oil Affect Lebanon's Export Opportunities?
     Zeina Hasna   245

11   Strengthening Environmental Governance of the Oil and Gas Sector
     in Lebanon *Ricardo Khoury and Dima Al Haj*   275

Public Input

12   What Do Lebanese Citizens Want from Oil and Gas Revenues?
     Sami Atallah, Daniel Garrote Sanchez, Zeina Hawa, Leslie Marshall
     and Laura Paler   305

Index   359

Illustrations

Figures

1.1	Expectation curves for the volume of hydrocarbons in a reservoir	18
1.2	The two-axis Petroleum Resources Management System classification	20
1.3	Map of the Mediterranean Sea showing its main geographic provinces and basins	20
1.4	Map of the Levantine Basin	22
1.5	Mean undiscovered gas in BCFG for the Levantine Basin	27
1.6	Mean undiscovered oil in MMBO for the Levantine Basin	28
1.7	Mean undiscovered natural gas in BCFG for different petroleum provinces of the Middle East	28
2.1	Frequency of themes debated in the parliamentary committee in comparison with the frequency of their mention in the OPRL Law	44
2.2	Opinions of MPs on authorities assigned to the LPA	50
2.3	Oil revenue allocation	53
2.4	MPs' knowledge of the number of pre-qualified companies and number of blocks	55
2.5	How MPs allocate their time	56
5.1	R-factor and windfall tax rate	147
6.1	EdL deficit increases relative to rising fuel costs (in $ million)	157
6.2	Projected natural gas demand in the Middle East (bcf), 2010–40	163
6.3	Projected natural gas demand growth in the Middle East (%), 2010–40	163
6.4	Lebanese natural gas trading option	164
8.1	Transparency rankings for natural resource funds	201
8.2	Financial assets of sovereign wealth funds in Arab countries, 2007–9	202
9.1	Annual variation in real exchange rate (RER), inflation, and real GDP	230
9.2	Annual variation in non-resident deposits, remittances, FDI, and trade deficit	230
9.3	Annual variation in M2, revenues, expenditures, and public deficit	231
9.4	Annual variation in sector-level value added	232
9.5	Cumulative Impulse Response of an increase in budget deficit	236
9.6	Cumulative Impulse Response of an increase in money supply	237
9.7	Cumulative Impulse Response of an increase in real GDP	238
10.1	Cross-country comparisons of the Theil index from 1990 to 2007	252
10.2	Extensive and intensive margins for Italy, Norway, Lebanon, and Saudi Arabia	253–4
10.3	Lebanon's ECI evolution from 1995 to 2014	260
10.4	Lebanon's product space in 2012	260

11.1	Sources of potential environmental effects from production operations	277
11.2	Fate and behavior of spilled oil at sea	282
12.1	Citizens' perceptions of the net impact of oil revenues	310
12.2	Regional variations in citizens' perceptions on the net impact of oil rents on their households	313
12.3	Where do Lebanese want to allocate oil revenues?	317
12.4	Regional variations in citizens' preferences regarding to which government function more rents should be distributed	320–1
12.5	Where do citizens want to allocate oil rents?	321
12.6	Regional variations in citizens' preferences regarding to which sectors the government should distribute more oil rents	324–6
12.7	Regional preference for spending on health and the supply of clinics per capita	327
12.8	Supply of health centers by district and type of institution	328–9
12.9	Supply of different types of healthcare and regional variations on preference for health	330
12.10	Average allocations (percent of total oil and gas revenue) to each district (weighted)	331
12.11	Poverty and development levels of administrative districts	332
12.12	Average allocations (percent of total oil and gas revenue) to each district divided by population size (weighted)	334

Tables

1.1	Undiscovered oil and gas resources in some Middle East provinces	27
1.2	Summary of discovered gas reserves in the Levantine Basin as updated in May 2014	29
4.1	State participation options	108
5.1	Lebanon pre-qualification criteria	128
5.2	Main natural gas discoveries in the Eastern Mediterranean region (1999–2017)	131
5.3	Duration of petroleum rights in Cyprus, Israel, and Lebanon	135
5.4	Size of block areas in km^2	136
5.5	Key features of concessionary and contractual arrangements	141
5.6	Sliding scale royalty on oil	142
5.7	R-Factor and profit sharing rates	142
5.8	Summary of economic terms	148
7.1	Selected macroeconomic indicators for Lebanon	185
7.2	Lebanon government debt, 2009–14 ($ millions unless otherwise indicated)	186
7.3	Central government overall deficit and financing, 2009–14 (% of GDP, unless otherwise specified)	187
7.4	Quality of Lebanon's infrastructure (rank out of 144 countries)	187
9.1	Macroeconomic correlation matrix	231

9.2	Correlation matrix real exchange rate (RER), inflation, M2, and public deficit	232
9.3	Correlation matrix real exchange rate (RER) and value added by sector	232
9.4	Summary statistics for main macroeconomic variables used in the analysis	234
9.5	Selection-order criteria	241
9.6	Johansen tests for cointegration	242
9.7	Vector error-correction model	242
10.1	Summary statistics for Theil index, extensive and intensive margins obtained with SITC-4 data	251
10.2	Summary statistics for Theil index, extensive and intensive margins obtained with SITC-4 data in 2007	251
10.3	Summary statistics for oil abundance for 53 and 95 oil-rich countries	255
10.4	Functional forms	257
10.5	Functional forms continued	258
10.6	More functional forms	263–5
10.7	Fixed and random effects	266
10.8	Instrumental variables	267
10.9	All countries in the sample	269
10.10	Sample of countries empirically investigated	270
10.11	Description of variables	271–2
12.1	Descriptive statistics of the sample and the Lebanese population	308
12.2	Interactions between political connections and economic values on the net impact of oil rents	312
12.3	District-level determinants of geographical variations in citizens' perceptions	315
12.4	Oil revenue allocation to cash transfers: interactions between sect, income, and political networks on preferences over cash transfers	318
12.5	Districts categorized by majority sect and development and poverty level	336
12.6	The effect of various individual and regional characteristics on respondents' likelihood to allocate to certain types of districts	336
12.7	Non-co-sectarian districts available for allocation as a respondent from a particular sect	337
12.8	Extreme allocators according to district type	338
12.9	Population demographics before and after weights are applied	344
12.10	Summary of multivariate regressions with dependent and independent variables	345
12.11	Regression results for perceptions on impact	348–9
12.12	Regression results on revenue allocation by function	350–1
12.13	Regression results on revenue allocation by sector	352
12.14	Multivariate binomial regression results on allocations to particular example districts and the independent factors that affect these allocations	353

12.15	Multivariate binomial regression results on allocations to districts according to their majority sect	354
12.16	Multivariate binomial regression results on allocations to districts according to their levels of poverty and development	355
12.17	Multivariate binomial regression results on allocations to districts whose majority sect is different from theirs	356

Contributors

Dima Alhaj is Senior Environmental Engineer with more than ten years of experience conducting environmental studies including institutional and legal framework assessments, strategic environmental assessments, and environmental impact assessments for onshore and offshore petroleum activities for major oil companies including Total, Petro Canada, Ina, SNG EastMed, PetroChina, CNOOC, and others.

Sami Atallah is Director of the Lebanese Center for Policy Studies (LCPS). He is currently leading several policy studies on the governance of the Lebanese oil and gas sector, economic diversification, electoral behavior, political and social sectarianism, and the role of Lebanese municipalities in addressing with the Syrian refugee crisis. Prior to joining LCPS, Atallah served as a consultant for the World Bank, the European Union, and the United Nations Development Programme in Syria and Saudi Arabia. He holds two master's degrees, in international and development economics from Yale University and in quantitative methods from Columbia University.

Jad Chaaban is Associate Professor of Economics at the American University of Beirut. Previously, he worked as an economist at the World Bank's Middle East regional office, where he conducted research related to poverty reduction and economic management in Lebanon, Syria, Jordan, and Egypt. Dr. Chaaban holds an MBA from the European School of Management, and a master's degree in Agricultural, Environmental and Natural Resources Economics and a PhD in Economics from the Toulouse School of Economics (TSE) in France.

Ata Richard Elias is Assistant Professor of Geology at the American University of Beirut specializing in the geology of the Eastern Mediterranean. His work includes detailed geophysical exploration of the Levantine Basin. He has worked for Lebanese governmental institutions on offshore petroleum exploration projects and since 2008 has frequently lectured on regional geology both locally and abroad. Dr. Richard Elias holds a PhD in Geophysics from the Institut de Physique du Globe de Paris.

Nancy Ezzeddine is Economic Researcher at the Lebanese Center for Policy Studies working on issues related to socioeconomics. Prior to joining LCPS, she worked at the Economic and Social Commission of Western Asia in Lebanon in the field of social, economic, and sustainable development. Ezzeddine holds a master's degree in finance and development from the School of Oriental and African Studies at the University of London as well as a BA in Economics from the American University of Beirut.

Bassam Fattouh is the Director of the Oxford Institute for Energy Studies; a research fellow at the Lebanese Center for Policy Studies (LCPS) and at St Antony's College, Oxford University; and Professor at the School of Oriental and African Studies (SOAS). His work has been published broadly and covers topics such as international oil markets, the oil pricing system, and natural gas markets in the MENA region. Dr. Fattouh holds a PhD in economics from SOAS, University of London.

Jana Harb is Economic Analyst at the World Bank who previously worked as a researcher at LCPS. Prior to joining LCPS, she held research assistant positions at the American University of Beirut (AUB) and worked for the World Bank funded Fiscal Management Reform Project at the Lebanese Ministry of Finance. Harb holds a master's degree in development economics and public policy from the Toulouse School of Economics and a BA in economics from AUB.

Zeina Hasna is a PhD candidate in the Faculty of Economics at the University of Cambridge and a research associate at the Lebanese Center for Policy Studies working on macro-economic development and diversification. She is a teaching fellow at Cambridge and a research assistant at the Keynes Fund, where she works on the distributional effects of climate change mitigation policies. Hasna's past research has focused on the spillover effects of oil discoveries on countries' economic structures and diversification statuses using the product space approach.

Zeina Hawa worked as a researcher at the Lebanese Center for Policy Studies on the oil and gas sector and political representation. Prior to that, she worked on projects such as establishing a natural resource governance hub in the MENA region, focused on training, research, and networking; designing a survey to assess the knowledge and positions of parliamentarians in Lebanon; and developing online portals for oil and gas in the MENA and parliamentary monitoring. Hawa has a Master of Engineering in Environmental Engineering from University College London.

Laura El-Katiri is research fellow at the Oxford Institute for Energy Studies. Her research focuses on energy policy and the management of natural resource wealth in resource-rich economies, with a particular focus on the Middle East and North Africa. Katiri has been published widely on issues including oil and development in the Arab world, domestic energy market and pricing reform, and energy poverty. She holds degrees from St Cross College at Oxford University, and Exeter University.

Ricardo Khoury is an environmental engineer with nearly twenty years of experience who has worked for more than twelve years delivering environmental services to the oil and gas sector. As the managing partner and head of the environmental division at ELARD consultancy group, he regularly provides environmental advice and consultancy services to governments, international oil companies, national oil companies, and FEED and EPC contractors. Khoury holds a master's degree in environmental engineering and water resources management from the American University of Beirut.

Reinoud Leenders is Reader in international relations and Middle East studies in the War Studies Department at King's College London, and an LCPS fellow. His research interests and teaching are focused on Middle East politics generally, and on Syria, Lebanon, and Iraq in particular. Dr. Leenders's work focuses on the political economy of corruption, authoritarian governance, refugee issues, and conflict. He authored the book *Spoils of Truce: Corruption and State Building in Post-War Lebanon* (2012) and holds a PhD from the School of Oriental and African Studies (SOAS), University of London.

Valérie Marcel is an associate fellow at Chatham House and has extensive experience in the fields of oil and gas and international relations. As an expert on national oil companies, petroleum sector governance, and emerging oil and gas producers, she led energy research at Chatham House from 2002 to 2007 and authored the book *Oil Titans: National Oil Companies in the Middle East* (2006) as well as the recent Chatham House research paper "The Cost of an Emerging National Oil Company". Dr. Marcel holds a PhD from Sciences Po, Paris.

Leslie Marshall is a PhD candidate in Political Science at the University of Pittsburgh and a graduate student affiliate with the Economic and Social Rights Research Group of the University of Connecticut's Human Rights Institute. Her research focuses on the political economy of development, political representation and accountability, and mobilization for economic and social goods provision.

Carole Nakhle is Director of Crystol Energy (UK), an LCPS research fellow, and a scholar at the Carnegie Middle East Center. She has worked in the oil and gas industry (Eni and Statoil), policy making (Special Parliamentary Advisor in the House of Lords), academia (University of Surrey), and as a consultant to the IMF, World Bank, and Commonwealth Secretariat. Dr. Nakhle is program advisor to the Washington-based International Tax and Investment Center (ITIC) and holds a PhD in energy economics from the University of Surrey.

Lavan Mahadeva is senior research fellow heading up macroeconomic research at the Oxford Institute for Energy Studies, with a focus on the interaction of energy markets with macroeconomy and international finance. Prior to joining the Institute, he was an economist at the Bank of England for sixteen years. Dr. Mahadeva has a BA from Trinity College, Cambridge, an MSc from the University of Warwick, and a PhD from the European University Institute.

Adeel Malik is the Islamic Centre lecturer in development economics at the University of Oxford, a fellow of St Peter's College, a Globe Fellow in the Economies of Muslim Societies at the Oxford Centre for Islamic Studies, and an LCPS fellow. His previous research affiliations include the Department of Economics, Oxford University (2004–5); Merton College (Lecturer in Economics, 2002–3 and 2005–6); Center for International Development, Harvard University (Visiting Research Fellow, 2001); and the Mahbub ul Haq Human Development Centre, Islamabad (Senior Policy Analyst,

1997–9). He completed his doctorate in economics from Oxford University as a Rhodes Scholar in 2004.

Laura Paler is an assistant professor in the political science department at the University of Pittsburgh. She specializes in comparative politics and the political economy of development. Dr. Paler's projects examine how different sources of revenue (such as natural resource rents, foreign aid, and taxes) affect political behavior and development, how ex-combatants and civilians transition to peace in post-conflict contexts, and how cross-cutting economic and identity cleavages affect support for ethnic versus programmatic politics. Dr. Paler earned her PhD from Columbia University.

Daniel Garrote Sanchez is a senior researcher at the Lebanese Center for Policy Studies. His work focuses on refugees' access to job opportunities and social services, development of lagging regions in Lebanon, and citizens' preferences on government spending. Prior to joining LCPS, Sanchez served as a labor market and migration consultant for the World Bank and the Ministry of Labor of Saudi Arabia, and worked for six years as an economic researcher at the Central Bank of Spain. He holds a master's degree in Public Administration and International Development from the Harvard Kennedy School of Government.

Alexandra Tohme worked as a researcher at LCPS on oil and gas governance and issues related to the Syrian refugee presence in Lebanon. Prior to joining LCPS, she worked at the Permanent Mission of Lebanon to the United Nations for three and a half years. There, she engaged in negotiations and programming for UN agencies' work in Lebanon in the field of social, economic, and sustainable development. Tohme holds a master's degree in public policy from Columbia University's School of International & Public Affairs as well as a BA in International Affairs & Middle East Studies from George Washington University.

Acknowledgments

LCPS would like to thank the International Development Research Centre (IDRC) for its support, and in particular Roula El-Rifai, IDRC's senior program specialist for the MENA region, for her assistance and encouragement throughout this project. We would also like to thank the Lebanese Petroleum Administration (LPA) and its board members (in alphabetical order): Wissam Chbat, head of the Geology and Geophysics Department; Gaby Daaboul, head of the Legal Affairs Department; Nasser Hoteit, head of the Technical and Engineering Department; Assem Abou Ibrahim, head of the Quality, Health, Safety, and Environment Department; Walid Nasr, head of the Strategic Planning Department; and Wissam Zahabi, head of the Economic and Financial Department, for working toward establishing a forum for policy debate as well as providing input and feedback on policy papers.

We also thank all those who have contributed to debates and discussions during roundtables, workshops, and conferences that LCPS co-organized with the LPA. These include the following (in alphabetical order): Mohamed Alem, managing partner at Alem's Law Firm and LCPS board member; Joseph Al-Assad, energy consultant at the Ministry of Energy and Water; Francisco Cravioto, researcher at Fundar; Farouk Al-Kasim, founder of the Norwegian Petroleum Administration; Joseph D'Cruz, UNDP's Asia-Pacific regional team leader for inclusive growth and sustainable development; Kamal Hamdan, managing director of The Consultation and Research Institute; the late Talal Hassoun, former AUB lecturer in the Department of Chemical Engineering; Diana Kaissy, MENA region coordinator for Publish What You Pay; Shadi Karam, advisor to the prime minister; Walid Khadduri, consultant at the Middle East Economic Survey; Habib Maalouf, journalist and professor of environmental philosophy at the Lebanese University; Adeel Malik, LCPS research fellow and Islamic Centre lecturer in development economics at the University of Oxford; Charles McPherson, a consultant focusing on petroleum and mineral policies and former senior adviser on oil and gas at the World Bank; Carole Nakhle, LCPS research fellow and director of Crystol Energy; Ghilain Pastre, a lawyer and independent consultant specializing in advising governments in developing countries on extractive industries; Mounir Rached, advisor to the minister of finance; and Roula Sheikh, formerly with the Ministry of Environment.

We would also like to thank the Economic and Social Council and the Ministry of Environment for hosting two of our round discussions. Additionally, LCPS thanks Ali Berro for his input and feedback on the development of the sector given that he played an important role in its formation. We also would like to thank the LCPS team for providing research and administrative support throughout the project. To this end, we thank (in alphabetical order): Rania Abi Habib, communication and development officer; Mohammed Armali, former researcher; Michele Boujikian, former researcher;

Georgia Dagher, researcher; Jana Harb, former researcher; Dima Mahdi, researcher; Suzie Massaad, executive secretary; and Ned Whalley, intern. Finally, we would like to thank Ryan Bailey and LCPS Editor John McCabe for compiling and editing this book as well as offering editorial feedback.

Sami Atallah
Bassam Fattouh

Introduction

Sami Atallah and Bassam Fattouh

Lebanon's flirtation with oil is not new. As early as March 1938, Lebanon—under the French mandate—sought to become a petro state as part of the attempt by Britain, France, and the United States to find oil in the Middle East. After the collapse of the Ottoman Empire, those same powers organized the scramble for oil through the 1928 Red Line Agreement. This agreement laid the groundwork for oil development in the Middle East and granted the Iraqi Petroleum Company (IPC)—a consortium of British, French, Dutch, and American oil companies—a license to explore for oil in the vicinity of Jabal Terbol, six miles from Tripoli (Shwadran 1959).[1] In May 1947, the Lebanon Petroleum Company began drilling, a process which spanned 17 months, reaching a depth of 10,060 feet without yielding a discovery (Longrigg 1954). Another unsuccessful attempt was made by the Pacific Western Company in Yohmor in the Bekaa Valley. Despite other attempts in El Qaa, Aarbrine, Tell Znoub, Sohmor, and Aadloun, Lebanon did not become a petro state.

However, Lebanon's relationship with oil did not come to an end. For the next 50 years, Lebanon was a transit state and home to two refineries and port facilities through which Iraqi and Saudi oil passed before moving on to Western markets.[2] Already by 1934, oil had begun to flow from Kirkuk in Iraq to Tripoli through the IPC pipeline.[3] In 1947, Lebanon's transit role was further entrenched when it agreed to host the Trans-Arabian pipeline (Tapline)—funded by the Marshall Plan—to transport Saudi Arabia's oil to Western Europe through the port of Saida. In this way, Lebanon not only served as a bridge between oil-rich countries and energy-hungry states in Western Europe, but also became intimately connected to US policies. In fact, according to Gendzier (1997), 78 percent of Iraqi and Saudi oil that passed through Lebanon

---

[1] IPC was owned by British Petroleum, Royal Dutch-Shell Group, Compagnie Française des Petroles, and the Near East Development Corporation (NED). NED was itself a consortium of five US companies: Standard Oil Company of New Jersey, Standard Oil Company of New York (Socony), Gulf Oil, Pan-American Petroleum and Transport Company, and Atlantic Refining.

[2] Lebanon's first refinery was built in 1940 in Tripoli and the country's second refinery was built in 1955 in Saida.

[3] This was one of two pipelines built during that period from Kirkuk to the Mediterranean. The Lebanon section was part of the pipeline that went through Syria, which at the time was under the French mandate. The second pipeline went through Transjordan and Palestine, which were both under the British mandate.

went to Western Europe and 22 percent to the US and Canada. Lebanon was part of the transport revolution that shifted from tankers to pipelines, cutting costs by 50–75 percent (Gendzier 1997). Domestically, it transformed Lebanon's political economy by boosting the service sector, including the launch of the aviation sector through Middle East Airlines.

Almost 70 years later, hope has been renewed that Lebanon may join the petro-state club. The discovery of petroleum deposits in the Eastern Mediterranean, including in the Cypriot and Israeli offshore reserves, again raised the possibility of Lebanon becoming a petroleum-producing country. By April 2010, geological data released by the United States Geological Survey cited the potential for 122 trillion cubic feet of gas in the Eastern Mediterranean, news that was accompanied by expectations of greater prosperity and the opportunity to secure a brighter future for Lebanon. Some analysts have suggested that gas could reduce the country's energy bill, pay off the country's public debt, and precipitate development.

In response to this, the Lebanese government launched a process to establish the sector. It commissioned the Norwegian Petroleum GeoServices (PGS) and British Spectrum to carry out 2D and 3D seismic surveys in Lebanon's coastal waters and formed a committee tasked with drafting oil and gas laws and decrees.[4] One of the major outcomes of this committee's work was the drafting of the first Offshore Petroleum Resources Law (OPRL), which came into effect in August 2010.[5] The law authorizes offshore oil and gas exploration and drilling in Lebanon and lays out general principles covering the following topics: terms and conditions for participation in licensing rounds, conditions for the award of exploration licenses, content of licensing applications, procedures for the award of production licenses, rules related to any petroleum sale, and health and safety regulations. Moreover, the law states that a new authority will manage the hydrocarbon sector under the aegis of the Ministry of Energy and Water (MEW), with a certain amount of financial and administrative independence.

Following the passage of this law, the Council of Ministers (COM) issued a decree that established a petroleum authority, the LPA, on 21 March 2012 and, by November 2012, it had nominated six of its members.[6] Over the next eight months, the LPA prepared, among other matters, the necessary guidelines to launch the licensing round, including draft decrees that defined biddable items, delineation of blocks, and an Exploration and Production Agreement (EPA). Out of 52 companies, 46 were pre-qualified to submit their bids pending the approval of decrees by the COM.

Despite the early gains made in the process, the sector came to a halt in August 2013, largely due to political paralysis. As a consequence, the COM failed to pass two key decrees, which led to several postponements of the licensing round. In April 2014, then Prime Minister Tamam Salam's government attempted to buy time by establishing

---

[4] The committee comprises representatives from the Ministry of Energy and Water, Ministry of Environment, Ministry of Finance, Office of the Minister of State for Administrative Reform, Presidency of the Council of Ministers, and the parliament.

[5] Lebanese Parliament. 2010. *Offshore Petroleum Resources Law.* Law 132, 24 August.

[6] All laws and decrees are available at the LPA website: http://www.lpa.gov.lb

a ministerial committee to advise the government on how to proceed with establishing the oil and gas sector. This decision raised many doubts about the development of the sector. For one, the work of the ministerial committee seemed to be duplicating the role of the LPA. More cynically, the LPA—whose members mirror the sectarian representation of the country, with a one-year presidential rotation for each of its six members—failed to assuage the elite's fears of losing influence over the sector. Despite this, the committee has only managed to meet a few times since then and has kept the process closed to the public, raising more concerns rather than easing public fears of corrupt activity.

The sector only took off after the political elite agreed to elect Michel Aoun as president, and to form a new government under Prime Minister Saad Hariri, in October 2016. In the first COM meeting, held in January 2017, almost three and a half years from the expected date, the government approved the outstanding decrees. In spring 2017, the groundwork was laid for the award of contracts, which also included pre-qualifying seven additional companies. By the time the bidding was closed, only one consortium, comprising Total, Eni, and Novatek, submitted two bids, one for block 4 and the other for block 9. In January 2018, the government signed contracts with the consortium, effectively launching the exploration process.

The political delay in developing the sector did not come without a cost. During those 40 months the global oil and gas market changed significantly. Oil prices took a sharp dip, meaning Lebanon possibly missed an opportunity to secure a better deal from its first licensing round. Not unrelated to the oil price market, there was little to no competition in the licensing round, as only three out of 53 companies actually expressed interest in winning an exploration license.

Oil could be a curse

Despite the initial excitement and speed with which the government moved forward on the oil and gas sector, the record of many countries that have discovered oil is at best not encouraging. For them, oil turned out to be a curse rather than a blessing. The predominant literature on natural resources argues that countries endowed with oil and gas grow slower in the long term, have higher income inequality, are more corrupt, and end up with authoritarian regimes (Mahdavy 1978, Sachs and Warner 1995, Lam and Wantchekon 2003, and Ross 2001).

More recent literature shows that the resource curse is conditional on two factors: human capital and the quality of institutions. Bravo-Ortega and de Gregorio (2007) argue that the effect of resource abundance on an economy depends on human capital stock in a country. The larger that stock is, the more positive its marginal impact on natural resource growth will be. Also, Mehlum *et al.* (2006) find that the quality of institutions is critical to determining whether countries avoid the resource curse or not. Collier (2007) argues that being democratic does not matter as much as the effectiveness of checks and balances on power. In fact, weak democracies with highly personalized politics that thrive on rent-seeking and patronage-driven electoral competition are highly vulnerable to ill effects associated with extracting natural resources. In sum, resource rents may not be the problem, as capital stock and the quality of institutions in a country determine to a large extent whether a natural resource is a blessing or a curse.

Lebanon's weak institutions make it highly susceptible to the resource curse

Although Lebanon is well endowed with human capital, its institutions are weak. They are unable to govern effectively, accountability mechanisms are absent, and personalized politics driven by patronage and clientelism are rampant, making Lebanon particularly vulnerable to the resource curse.

While the 1989 Taef Accord redistributed power more equally across political institutions—including the president, the speaker of the parliament, and the prime minister—it provided little or no incentive for the elite to serve peoples' needs.[7] In fact, the COM, which became the executive authority under Taef, is more concerned about sectarian representation and personal interest, further undermining the governance system. In addition, the speaker of the parliament has become a participant in intra-executive decisions rather than upholding the legislative and oversight authority of the parliament. In effect, the country has become governed by the logic of partitioning the spoils of public office among political elites using the sectarian quota. Worse, these spoils were not intended to trickle down to all Lebanese citizens, but rather were ticketed to be siphoned off by the elite and their cronies. This effectively ended the decision-making process and encouraged corruption and rent creation to benefit the elite. It was on this basis that the political system was made to function. As a result, when rents dwindle, the political system becomes paralyzed while the political elite scramble to divide the shrinking pie. An example of this paralysis is the inability of the elite to uphold constitutional deadlines to elect a president and hold parliamentary elections (which were postponed three times), in addition to the many months it took to form a government and the failure from 2005 to 2017 to approve a national budget.

The political system is now devoid of accountability. For the last 25 years, successive Lebanese governments and elites have diligently worked to undermine all shapes and forms of accountability in our political system. They have crafted electoral districts in such a way that most seats are distributed by those in power rather than being subjected to any serious competition, rendering elections meaningless. In fact, the Lebanese Parliament has adopted four electoral laws since 1992 to organize five rounds of elections. As a consequence, the parliament has failed to exercise its two crucial roles: legislating and conducting oversight of the government. The judiciary has been largely subservient to political demands, including the Constitutional Council's decision to rubber stamp the illegal extension of the parliament's mandate. Oversight agencies—which are awkwardly housed in the Presidency of the Council of Ministers—remain understaffed and their disclosures of violations are left unheeded. Labor unions, which

---

[7] Lebanese Parliament. 1989. *The Taef Accord*. Approved on 4 November.

Introduction 5

could have challenged the dominant sectarian discourse to highlight differences between the haves and the have-nots, have been largely decimated since the early 1990s. The recent emergence of the Teachers' Union in 2013 to spearhead a drive for public sector salary adjustment managed to incur the wrath of almost every main political party. This was aimed at ensuring the union does not succeed in changing the dominant political discourse from sectarian-based to class-based, and in shifting the national focus to implementing equitable policies. In brief, politicians have shielded the political system from any hint of accountability.

The political elite have managed to maintain power by exploiting electoral mechanisms and instrumentalizing confessional identities. With a majoritarian system in place—up to the parliamentary election of May 2018, when Proportional Representation (PR) was adopted—and districts customized to suit those in power, politicians have resorted to clientelistic strategies to win elections. In other words, they have provided citizens with services and jobs conditional on their political loyalty. To this end, political parties have established large networks of health clinics, dispensaries, hospitals, schools, and social assistance programs. In addition to service provision, clientelism takes other forms, including vote buying on the day of the election. Yet in certain districts, where the population is of one confessional identity, the political elite have resorted to sectarian discourse during elections to woo voters. This clientelistic relationship compels politicians to seek resource rents to generate support through the inefficient allocation of jobs in the public sector at the expense of broader developmental goals.

In brief, Lebanon is particularly vulnerable to the oil curse since its democratic system does not serve peoples' needs, checks and balances are weak, and politics are defined by rampant patronage and clientelism.

A roadmap for institutional and policy reform

Lebanon's prospects of translating offshore gas into higher growth and sustainable development are unlikely given current institutional arrangements. Against this background, the Lebanese Center for Policy Studies (LCPS) has undertaken a project with the support of IDRC—the culmination of which is the present volume—to provide a roadmap for institutional and policy reform. It is our hope that such reform will serve to avert the oil curse and optimize the benefits of potential oil and gas revenues, in addition to informing public discourse on the issue and empowering civil society to better conduct oversight of the sector.

To this end, LCPS has embarked on a two-tier approach. The first tier aims to produce policy knowledge that informs policy makers on how to deal with forthcoming challenges brought on by the discovery of oil and gas. Here, we focus on six themes, which are addressed in the 12 chapters of this book: the size of the resource base; governance of the sector, including roles and responsibilities of key institutions and regulating and contracting gas to foreign companies; finding markets and managing revenue; managing macro-economic effects of the sector coming online; protecting the environment; and determining citizens' preferences concerning oil revenue allocation.

While recognizing that geopolitical factors weigh heavily on the petroleum sector, given the geostrategic nature of the commodity, this book focuses primarily on domestic challenges, for two reasons: first, the institutional and policy challenges within the purview of Lebanese authorities are often overshadowed in public discussions and the media by geopolitical concerns over which Lebanon has effectively little-to-no power; second, this book highlights the importance and complexity of challenges that arise in various phases of the value chain, beginning with the extraction phase all the way through dealing with fiscal, economic, and environmental implications.

The central argument of this book is that, in order for Lebanon to benefit from the discovery of petroleum, it must overhaul its institutions across many phases of the value chain. It must strengthen formal accountability mechanisms through encouraging the parliament to play a more effective role in oversight and enhancing the role of civil society organizations (CSO) in monitoring the sector. To open up the decision making process and foster ownership, there is a need to broaden the consultation process to include more stakeholders. Lebanon must strengthen the Ministry of Environment so it can meet the requirements of the petroleum sector. To manage revenues effectively, Lebanon must establish a development fund with a mandate of upgrading Lebanon's depleted infrastructure according to a suitable institutional framework that takes into account the country's political economy challenges. To counter the negative impact of oil on diversification, the government must establish a public–private dialogue with industrialists to mitigate the risks facing the sector, as well as encourage the development of sophisticated products. In the event that petroleum discoveries are substantial, Lebanon could seriously consider establishing a national oil company (NOC) with a proper governance structure.

At the policy level, this book argues that Lebanon must revise its biddable items and focus on the design rather than on fiscal regime type to ensure a better deal from international oil companies. The government must develop policies and pass new legislation that addresses the management of environmental challenges that arise from offshore petroleum operations. As for how to manage oil and gas revenues, Lebanon may need to increase public investment in infrastructure as well as pay off its short-term foreign debt, since these carry the most risk. To avoid Dutch disease effects, the government must adopt a fiscal policy that is non-expansionary and addresses developmental and poverty challenges. The country must develop an export strategy based on the size of the reserve while beginning to build the necessary infrastructure to utilize gas reserves at home. In addition, there is a need to develop an industrial policy that encourages the production of sophisticated products.

As this book is prescriptive in nature, most chapters examine a specific issue in the value chain and conclude with evidence-based policy recommendations. This is done by identifying a challenge brought about by a potential oil and gas discovery, examining other countries' experiences in dealing with similar scenarios, assessing Lebanon's ability to deal with such a challenge, and offering recommendations that can inform both decision makers and the wider public.

The experts who undertook these projects employed multiple methods using primary and secondary data, including comparative approaches, analytical narratives, qualitative interviews, and quantitative survey analysis. The papers were peer reviewed by steering committee members and several drafts were presented and discussed during a closed workshop in June 2014 with a group of experts, scholars, and CSOs.

While most, if not all, such projects result in policy recommendations, many fail to influence decision makers. Hence, the second tier in this project sought to prevent such an outcome by actively engaging with the LPA early on in the process. After all, the exercise of producing policy knowledge should not be carried out in a vacuum but rather should be aimed at addressing policy issues that are relevant to them as long as the independence and integrity of the research is left intact.

The LPA proved to be a willing partner with LCPS in this process, as the LPA engaged openly in these discussions. This relationship was formalized in a first-of-its-kind memorandum of understanding (MOU) between the two parties. Throughout the project, LCPS and the LPA held six meetings, of which four were closed roundtables addressing the following issues with the participation of international experts. The first focused on the development of the sector with Walid Nasr and Bassam Fattouh, in July 2013. The second addressed environmental considerations related to the development of the petroleum sector with Assem Abou Ibrahim, Roula Sheikh, and Habib Maalouf, in November 2013. The third roundtable examined the economic and fiscal dimensions of the exploration and production agreement with Wissam Zahabi and Carole Nakhle, in March 2014. The fourth meeting, which was held over the course of a full day, assessed the governance of the petroleum sector with Walid Nasr and Charles McPherson and examined transparency measures in the bidding process with Wissam Zahabi and Ghilain Pastre, in October 2015. A one-and-a-half-day workshop was held on 19 and 20 June 2014, at which policy paper drafts were presented by authors to a group of experts and scholars, with direct comments and feedback from (in alphabetical order) Joseph Al-Assad, Sami Atallah, Wissam Chbat, Bassam Fattouh, Kamal Hamdan, Farouk Al Kasim, Walid Khadduri, Adeel Malik, and Wissam Zahabi. Finally, LCPS organized a panel on the role of CSOs in the governance of the oil and gas sector in October 2014, as part of a larger conference led by the LPA with the participation of Sami Atallah, Francisco Cravioto, Joseph D'Cruz, and Diana Kaissy.

These meetings provided a much-needed policy platform for discussion among key stakeholders, who normally do not meet to discuss and debate important policy issues. Through such gatherings, LCPS and the LPA have managed to open up the decision making process to those who have no platform to express their policy opinions and concerns. In fact, the roundtables provided the LPA with the opportunity to share its work with experts and CSOs, while international experts were able to present their knowledge as well as reflect on the LPA's work. Additionally, Lebanese experts and CSOs were informed about the latest developments in the sector and raised their own concerns about the direction of the sector.

The two tiers reinforced and complemented each other. The roundtable provided a platform for policy ideas to be presented and debated, and policy dialogues during the roundtables helped identify key policy questions that need to be researched further. Additionally, regular interaction at these meetings has served to narrow the gap between decision makers on the one hand and experts and CSOs on the other. This, by itself, is an important contribution in building much-needed trust between state institutions and citizens.

In order to ensure that policy knowledge remains timely and accessible, LCPS released most policy papers as soon as they were completed. In this way, decision makers and the general public were (and continue to be) able to benefit from the knowledge produced, as soon as it was available, rather than wait for all the chapters to be completed and compiled into a single volume.

Yet it was recognized that the general public might find the papers to be either too long or too technical. To address this, LCPS used the key ideas and recommendations in policy papers to produce policy briefs and articles, in both Arabic and English. A series of policy briefs of 2,500 words each was produced to synthesize the key arguments, including a diagnosis as well as recommendations targeted toward policy advisors and senior government officials.

To optimize dissemination, LCPS also produced short articles (1,000 words each) that synthesize key arguments in a journalistic style and are often published in Arabic and English newspapers. In order to reach out to a larger audience, LCPS chose to rotate the publication of articles across three main Arabic newspapers: *An-nahar*, *As-Safir*, and *Al-Akhbar*. The English versions of the articles were published in the *Daily Star*, the only English-language newspaper in Lebanon. LCPS also posted these articles on its website and shared them on social media to ensure utmost exposure.

Plan of the book

The five themes are fleshed out in 12 chapters. The first theme tackles a fundamental question, which is the size of the petroleum reserve, a factor that will dictate to a large extent how the sector progresses.

In the first chapter, Ata Richard Elias, a professor of geology at the American University of Beirut, argues from a geological perspective that much remains unknown about petroleum deposits in the Levantine Basin, of which Lebanon's coastal waters are part. Elias recommends that estimates of petroleum reserves should be understood as speculative in nature, since exploratory drilling has yet to be conducted and only a few independent assessments of available data have been carried out. He concludes that a more thorough exploration process will yield adequate information about the potential of reserves in the Lebanese offshore.

The second theme, which examines the governance of the sector, comprises three chapters.

In Chapter 2, Sami Atallah, LCPS director, and Nancy Ezzeddine, LCPS researcher, examine the role and responsibilities of the key institutions that are governing the oil and gas sector, particularly the role of the parliament in legislating and holding the government accountable. Atallah and Ezzeddine examine the quality of parliamentary debates over the OPRL as well as the level of knowledge of MPs and their ability to make decisions that hold the government accountable. To this end, they argue that Lebanon would need to enhance the knowledge and capacity of formal institutions to engage effectively in the sector as well as provide incentives for the parliament to live up to its mandate.

Assuming exploration efforts are successful and production moves ahead, Lebanon will be faced with a range of institutional challenges. In Chapter 3, Reinoud Leenders, professor of politics at King's College London, writes that there is a significant threat of corruption in the country's petroleum sector, particularly as the range of state institutions and agencies that will be crucial to daily petroleum governance are unlikely to cope if they are not drastically reformed. This chapter touches on a number of policy choices that will have to be made if or when Lebanon's petroleum reserves are confirmed, including determining the role and management of a "sovereign fund" and considering different proposals for petroleum revenue expenditure and sharing. To mitigate potential corruption, Leenders recommends that state institutions be reformed to handle the allocation of future petroleum revenues.

In many petroleum-producing states there is an impetus to establish an NOC as the leading institution in the oil and gas sector. In Chapter 4, Valérie Marcel, associate fellow at Chatham House, describes how national oil companies can take on a variety of roles and be organized with or have bestowed upon them varying mandates. Marcel recommends that Lebanon be cautious in the event it decides to establish its own NOC, as the size of a resource base and the ability of the state to hold an NOC to account will dictate whether it can carry out its mandate.

The third theme, which addresses the licensing of the sector as well as the management of its revenue, comprises four chapters.

In Chapter 5, Carole Nakhle, director of Crystol Energy, writes on the fiscal terms and strategies to award oil and gas contracts. She hails the decision to select competitive bidding, and calls for a greater review of biddable parameters. She notes that many have questioned Lebanon's choice of petroleum fiscal regime, and argues that the type of regime is less relevant than its design and how its many instruments affect one another and affect the investment climate, as well as the national economy.

Should Lebanon reach a high enough level of petroleum production, it will be necessary to decide whether and how to pursue an export strategy. In Chapter 6, Bassam Fattouh, director of the Oxford Institute for Energy Studies, and Laura El-Katiri, fellow at the Oxford Institute for Energy Studies, explore whether Lebanon should export some of its hydrocarbon wealth, how much of the country's reserves should be earmarked for export, and how to select markets for natural gas exports.

In the event Lebanon receives a windfall from petroleum revenues, leaders in the country will be tasked with planning how the money should be spent. In Chapter 7, Bassam Fattouh and Lavan Mahadeva, senior research fellow at the Oxford Institute for Energy Studies, highlight major features of the Lebanese economy and argue against creating a large savings or liquidity fund. Instead, they suggest paying off Lebanon's national debt and using what money is left for public investment.

Resource-rich countries across the world establish sovereign wealth funds (SWFs) in order to manage the savings and expenditures of oil and gas revenues based on levels of development, investment needs, and economic characteristics. In Chapter 8, Sami Atallah, Adeel Malik, professor of economics at Oxford University, and Alexandra Tohme, LCPS researcher, examine the rationale for establishing an SWF by looking at global and regional perspectives. Specifically, the chapter examines middle-income countries that utilize SWFs as development vehicles to encourage job creation and infrastructure growth. The chapter then analyzes Lebanon's economic landscape, fiscal policy challenges, and political–institutional structure in order to assess whether and how Lebanon might establish an SWF. It concludes by recommending a design that addresses the particularities of Lebanon's case, in terms of both the mandate of the fund and its institutional design.

The fourth theme examines the economic and societal effects of the petroleum sector coming online, and comprises three chapters.

While petroleum revenues are popularly seen as a potential boon for Lebanon's economy, there is a risk of the country falling under the "resource curse". In Chapter 9, Jad Chaaban, professor of economics at the American University of Beirut, and Jana Harb, former LCPS researcher, use available data on capital inflows to Lebanon to demonstrate that the country is already feeling the symptoms of Dutch disease, and that an expansionary fiscal policy through the rise of the budget deficit could exacerbate those symptoms. To mitigate the risks associated with a resource boom, Chaaban and Harb recommend a non-expansionary fiscal policy that would address developmental needs.

Key to capitalizing on Lebanon's petroleum reserves will be understanding the interplay between oil reserves and export diversification from a global perspective. Using data from 95 countries collected over 17 years, Zeina Hasna, former LCPS researcher, demonstrates in Chapter 10 that oil reserves have a negative and significant effect on export diversification, but the effect decreases with increasing national wealth. In light of the recent oil and gas discovery off Lebanon's coast, Hasna re-examines the industrial sector in Lebanon and recommends boosting the country's sophisticated export basket through a public–private dialogue between the government and industrialists before embarking on a period of resource extraction.

Oil exploration and extraction entail a host of risks that require diligent oversight to prevent damage to the environment. In Chapter 11, Ricardo Khoury, environmental consultant, and Dima Alhaj, environmental engineer, present the main environmental risks facing Lebanon at each stage of production. They argue that, while Lebanon's environmental protection regime is adequate in many ways, it should be strengthened to account for gaps in regulations and that emergency plans should be drawn up in the event of an accidental petroleum spill.

The final theme focuses on what people want to gain from a potential influx of petroleum revenues. In Chapter 12, Sami Atallah, Daniel Garrote Sanchez, LCPS senior researcher, Zeina Hawa, former LCPS researcher, Leslie Marshall, PhD candidate at the University of Pittsburgh, and Laura Paler, assistant professor at the University of Pittsburgh look at Lebanese citizens' preferences regarding the oil and gas sector. The chapter seeks to determine the general attitudes of Lebanese citizens regarding the impact of the oil and gas sector and how they would like future potential revenues allocated, sectorally and regionally. Additionally, it examines variations in attitudes toward oil- and gas-related issues and if so what individual and geographical characteristics would motivate these differences. Finally, the chapter examines whether economic or confessional factors influence people's preferences toward oil and gas revenue allocation.

References

Bravo-Ortega, C. and J. de Gregorio. 2007. "The Relative Richness of the Poor? Natural Resources, Human Capital, and Economic Growth." In *Natural Resources: Neither Curse nor Destiny, the World Bank,* edited by D. Lederman and W.F. Maloney. Stanford University Press.

Collier, P. 2007. *The Bottom Billion: Why the Poorest Countries are Failing and What Can be Done About It.* Oxford University Press.

Gendzier, I.L. 1997. *Notes from the Minefield: United States Intervention in Lebanon, 1945–1958.* Columbia University Press.

Lam, R. and L. Wantchekon. 2003. "Political Dutch Disease." Manuscript. New York University.

Longrigg, S. 1954. *Oil in the Middle East: Its Discovery and Development.* Oxford University Press.

Mahdavy, H. 1978. "The Patterns and Problems of Economic Development in Rentier States: The Case of Iran." In *Studies in the Economic History of the Middle East,* edited by M.A. Cook. Oxford University Press.

Mehlum, H., K. Moene, and T. Ragnar. 2006. "Institutions and the Resource Curse." *Economic Journal* 116: 1–20.

Ross, M. 2001. "Does Oil Hinder Democracy?" *World Politics* 53: 325–61.

Sachs, J. and A. Warner. 1995. "Natural Resource Abundance and Economic Growth." Working Paper 5398, National Bureau of Economic Research.

Shwadran, B. 1959. *The Middle East, Oil and the Great Powers.* Council for Middle Eastern Affairs Press.

Size of the Reserves

1

Estimating the Size of the Levantine East Mediterranean Hydrocarbon Basin

Ata Richard Elias

Introduction

Increased demand for oil and gas resources worldwide has spurred hydrocarbon exploration activities in various ways. Exploration and production companies are motivated and being solicited to search for additional resources. As a result, new, outside-the-box ideas and concepts in geology and geophysics are being tested in the search for new discoveries and higher productivity, pushing the limits of exploration activities into frontier areas that are becoming accessible thanks to the latest technological advancements. Increasingly higher recovery factors are being achieved in many developed petroleum fields, and enhanced oil recovery techniques are key to studying and analyzing the percentage of oil produced worldwide. Remote regions are being explored or prepared for hydrocarbon drilling and exploitation activities, while the relative increase in oil and gas prices over the past decade justifies ventures in higher-than-usual risky investments.

Hydrocarbon resources in the Levant have been exploited throughout history. In Lebanon, the trade of asphalt from the Hasbaya mines survived until the end of the nineteenth century (Connan and Nissenbaum 2004). Around the middle of the twentieth century, a modern phase of exploration for hydrocarbons began in the region. These exploration efforts proved successful in other countries but for various reasons did not lead to a commercial discovery or production activity in Lebanon. Significant amounts of petroleum resources—mostly of natural gas—were in fact discovered during the past two decades in neighboring parts of the Eastern Mediterranean. Large estimates of reserves offshore from the Palestinian, Israeli, and Cypriot coasts have been trumpeted, and the Levantine Basin is now considered a promising petroleum province.

This chapter seeks to understand these developments from a geological perspective and proceeds as follows. In the first and second sections, the concept of petroleum systems is presented, and the key geological parameters and conditions that influence the formation and availability of petroleum resources will be explained. The geology of the Levantine Basin is then explained in section three, emphasizing the basic concepts needed to understand the potential and challenges of petroleum exploration and production activities in the basin. Section four presents information on the geological setting of the area and some of the main parameters needed for resource estimation will be highlighted, including the strong and weak points for Lebanon's case. Section five examines the reliability of estimates which have already been made using geological data and information on neighboring states already extracting petroleum. Section six offers an assessment of the current state of affairs, namely what challenges lie ahead for petroleum exploration in Lebanon, what a relative lack of understanding of the region means for the accuracy of resource estimates in Lebanon at this still early stage of the exploration process, and what will be needed to overcome this shortfall in geographic knowledge of the region. The chapter concludes by considering the prospects of a deeper study of different geological aspects of hydrocarbon resources and their estimates in the region.

Petroleum systems

Petroleum resources are the result of a long chain of natural events occurring within the geological context of a region but at the intersection of two different realms: biology and geology. The formation of petroleum resources begins with the availability of requisite amounts of organic material resulting from biological activity on land or beneath the sea. The transportation and burial of these compounds, mixed with debris and fragments of rocks inside basins, is the next required event. During their burial beneath material of increasing thickness, organic compounds mixed with other rock components are put under increasing pressure and temperature conditions at the bottom of basins. The result is the transformation of the chemical composition of organic chains into that of hydrocarbon resources. This phase of "cooking" can occur at different rates and over different durations depending on the evolution of a basin and its fill. The rocks where these transformations take place are referred to as source rocks.

After the generation process, the more or less fluid hydrocarbon resources, driven primarily by their density, start rising along cracks in the rocks within the basin layers. Migration of these fluids will stop when compounds face a layer with insignificant or no cracks or voids. Such a migration barrier or seal retains the fluids on its lower side. Ultimately, hydrocarbon molecules of different types are trapped within this configuration of layers. The last rock unit under the seal, where they accumulate inside its cavities and pores, acts as a reservoir for petroleum substances, storing the generated and migrated molecules of hydrocarbons, thus forming a resource.

All these processes of burial, cooking, generation, migration, trapping, and accumulation must occur in a specific order, for a specific duration, and at a certain intensity in order to reach the last phase of accumulation of hydrocarbon compounds and formation of petroleum resources. The entire set of processes and elements is called a petroleum system. Any missing step or element will result in the failure to produce a working petroleum system. For example, the absence of a good seal rock in many instances prevents the formation of petroleum resources, as the produced hydrocarbon migrates to the surface and is entirely lost along seeps. Also, the inadequate intensity or timing of a process can significantly alter or prevent the formation of the system. For example, overcooking occurs when organic compounds are exposed to excess heat or prolonged exposure to thermal energy. Induced chemical reactions result in the total modification of the chemical composition of compounds and the loss of their economic value in most cases.

The accumulation of hydrocarbons in a trap with a reservoir rock behind a seal is not the ultimate gauge for the existence of resources. In many instances, the geological processes that keep occurring result in the destruction of a trap and the—slow or sudden—release and loss of compounds, or in the modification of the chemical and physical properties of resources or of hosting rocks, making them less valuable or impossible to exploit.

From resources to reserves

Natural resources which have accumulated in a reservoir or a trap can be exploited if the exploration and production activities reach them in due time. For exploration and production companies to locate these resources, they make use of a variety of indirect tools. For example, a combination of different geophysical methods, such as the use of seismic techniques and measurements of gravitational, magnetic, or electrical fields or other remote sensing methods, is most frequently employed. Such methods are extensively used to explore the subsurface and delineate the lateral and vertical extent of any geological structures. Exploration also entails geological modeling of basins using all known parameters related to the infill and burial of rocks and their source. Among these parameters are type, depth and thickness, chemical composition and organic content, age, transportation history, porosity, density, and water content of different rock units. Moreover, the geological evolution and history of an area are important factors used to assess petroleum potential. Similarly, changes in climatic conditions during the period of basin deposition and burial are accounted for in some cases. For their models, experts also need to estimate the geothermal gradient of an area and its evolution over time, as it greatly influences the cooking time and generation windows of different petroleum products.

In order to identify potential accumulations of resources, geoscientists also look for indicators of the presence of hydrocarbons that can be directly observed in different geophysical datasets acquired from the subsurface of an explored area or sometimes in surface geology. These direct hydrocarbon indicators (DHI) are helpful in guiding companies in their exploration efforts.

In the absence of direct insight into the subsurface of the explored area—such as in the case of a pre-existing exploration well—experts rely on analogues from neighboring and better-known areas in order to constrain the modeling of the petroleum system. Correlations of nearby offshore zones with more advanced exploration phases can also be made. Cuttings and rock samples from rocks exposed on land can be taken as possible analogues for offshore counterparts. These parameters are inputs to the modeling process that virtually reproduces the geological events and conditions of the basin, assesses whether the area has the potential to host a working and viable petroleum system that produces and preserves hydrocarbon resources, and estimates the volume of these resources.

All these required geological parameters should be assessed according to an understanding that petroleum system model results are uncertain. Therefore, petroleum system model results for any exploration activity cannot be more accurate than their input parameters. Consequently, it is clear that the best way to reduce the geological risk associated with petroleum exploration is through improving geological understanding of a given area.

Reserve estimation methods are classified in three different ways: performance-based, analogy-based, and volumetric-based (Demirmen 2007). Performance-based methods allow for estimations of available resources based on the previous performance of a given field. Therefore, it is applicable in fields that have a long history of production. Analogy methods refer to estimating the volume of reserves using known production histories from similar (analogue) geological reservoirs, meaning they can be used in hitherto undrilled areas. Volumetric methods involve knowledge of the volume and physical properties of the reservoir to estimate the volume of available reserves.

Two main approaches can be used in volumetric estimations of these resources: probabilistic and deterministic. In the first case, the uncertainty of each input parameter is taken into consideration and addressed in a statistical manner (Figure 1.1). A resulting probability distribution of the available amounts of resources is then obtained. In the deterministic approach, volumes of resources are calculated using a set of individual values for each of the input parameters, resulting in a single value for resource estimates. The deterministic computation is done three times, with values of each parameter representing successively the low, best (intermediate), and high

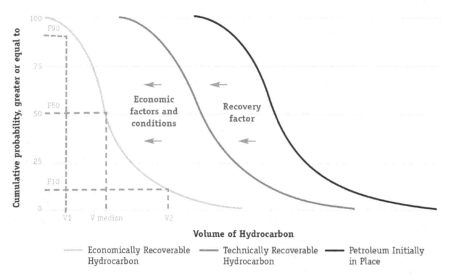

Figure 1.1 Expectation curves for the volume of hydrocarbons in a reservoir.
Source: Compiled by author.

estimates. The low estimation is a conservative one, reproducing the conditions least favorable for resources to exist. However, they are associated with the highest probability of existence. The high estimation is the most favorable for resource accumulation while being the least probable. The intermediate is usually the best probabilistic estimate of a given parameter.

In the petroleum industry, the term "resources" refers to the total estimated volume of hydrocarbons formed and trapped in-place in an explored area before any quantity is removed during the production phase. Of this volume initially in place, exploration and production companies will be physically able to extract only a part. This depends on technological advancements in extracting oil from a reservoir, a parameter known as the "recovery factor," representing the percentage of petroleum extracted from the amount of petroleum initially in a given location. Although this factor is different from one reservoir to another depending on the characteristics of rocks, type of petroleum, and reservoir conditions, on average the worldwide recovery factor is estimated to be about 35 percent at present (Schulte 2005). Future developments in exploration and production activities will no doubt improve this number.

The remaining smaller volume of technically recoverable petroleum, however, is not necessarily commercially exploitable in whole or in part. The portion of petroleum accumulation known to be technically recoverable and commercially viable is termed "reserves". Reserves are further classified as proven (1P), probable (2P), or possible (3P), according to their degree of uncertainty. It is clear that the estimation of reserves is dynamic and can change over time due to technological advancements, changes in economic conditions, or even strategic planning. Discovered amounts of technically recoverable petroleum that are not commercial are considered "contingent resources". In the absence of any discovery, the estimations of potential amounts of accumulated petroleum in the explored area are considered to be "prospective resources" (Figure 1.2).[1]

Geographic framework and geological setting of the Levantine Province within the Eastern Mediterranean

The Mediterranean seafloor and basin is a complex geological zone that can be subdivided into a number of smaller regions or basins based on the geology and the geography of these areas (Figure 1.3). Between the East and West Mediterranean Basins lies a first-order separation due to the presence of an important submarine relief, the Mediterranean Ridge, which is located between the island of Crete in the north and the Libyan shelf to the south. This significantly reduces the depths of the Mediterranean Sea at this location and forms an important submarine divide. The Eastern Mediterranean extends eastward of this ridge and the Libyan offshore, and is surrounded by Egypt, Palestine, Lebanon, Syria, Turkey, and Cyprus. In turn, the Levantine Basin is nestled inside the Eastern Mediterranean region. There are different geographic definitions for this second, smaller basin. In this chapter, it is considered

---

[1] Society of Petroleum Engineers. 2011. "Guidelines for Application of the Petroleum Resources Management System".

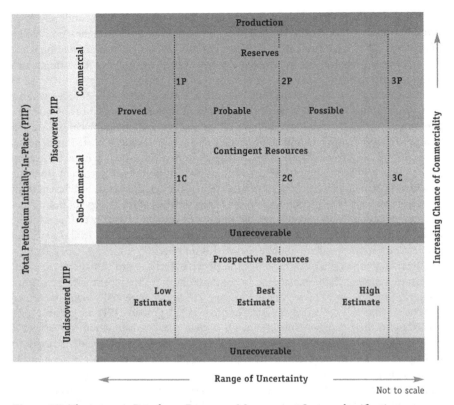

Figure 1.2 The two-axis Petroleum Resources Management System classification.
Source: Society of Petroleum Engineers (2011).

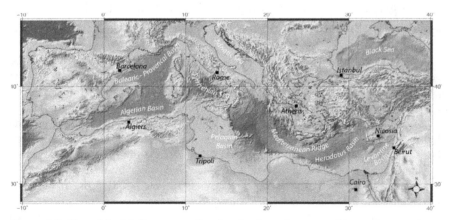

Figure 1.3 Map of the Mediterranean Sea showing its main geographic provinces and basins.
Source: Author.

part of the Eastern Mediterranean bordered by the Nile Delta Cone province in the south, the (Eastern Mediterranean) continental margin to the east, the Latakia (or Tartus) Ridge and basin to the north, and the Cypriot Basin and the Eratosthenes Seamount to the west. In following with our definition, no landmasses are considered part of this basin (Figure 1.4).

Topographically elevated regions surround the Levantine Basin, making it among the deepest and lowest-lying parts of the Eastern Mediterranean seafloor. It is a sink to most of the sediments and particles flowing into the wider Eastern Mediterranean region. This explains the thickness (12–14 kilometers) of deposits under its seafloor, a major attractive feature for hydrocarbon exploration.

In the oil industry, offshore activities are considered "shallow" if they are conducted at depths of less than 400 meters, "deepwater" if between depths of 400 meters and 1,500 meters below sea level, and "ultra-deepwater" if water depths exceed 1,500 meters. The offshore section of the Levantine Basin, as defined above, is approximately 65,000 square kilometers (km^2). The majority of it is located in deep and ultra-deep waters with a maximum depth of about 2,100 meters toward the center of the basin. The shallow areas of the seafloor are essentially restricted to the relatively wide Palestinian and Israeli continental shelf, reaching almost 25 kilometers offshore of central Israel. The shelf narrows northward and is almost absent in the Lebanese offshore between Saida and Tripoli. North of Lebanon, the shelf has a maximum width of 10–15 kilometers offshore of the Akkar coastal plain and narrows down to 5–10 kilometers along the Syrian coast. With such a configuration, few shallow marine sections exist in this basin, and most of the petroleum exploration and production activities will need to operate in deep waters.

Geologic evolution of the Levantine Basin

A number of geological events and processes structured the Levantine Basin as we know it today. Two major events in particular have important implications for the petroleum potential of this area.

The earliest basin floor was created during a Mesozoic rifting phase that occurred over a number of pulses and culminated with the margin formation in the Upper Jurassic to Lower Cretaceous times (Carton *et al.* 2009, Briais *et al.* 2004). Rifting was accompanied by extension and vertical block movements around the basin (Bruner 1991, Garfunkel 1998). It may have resulted in the formation of oceanic-type crusts under a major section of the basin floor, mostly located to the north of a line directed northeast–southwest and joining Saida onshore next to the older continental (or stretched continental) crust offshore of the southern part of the basin (Carton *et al.* 2009). Subsidence accompanied and followed this rifting phase, resulting in the deepening and filling of the basin with thick Mesozoic and Cenozoic sediments.

Later, in the Upper Mesozoic to Cenozoic periods, a geologic episode of contraction occurred. It resulted in an increase in elevation of neighboring landmasses surrounding the basin as well as folding and deformation of the basin fill. The depocenter with the thickest accumulation of sediments was located offshore of the present coastline and appears to have been closer to the center of the basin, between present-day Lebanon

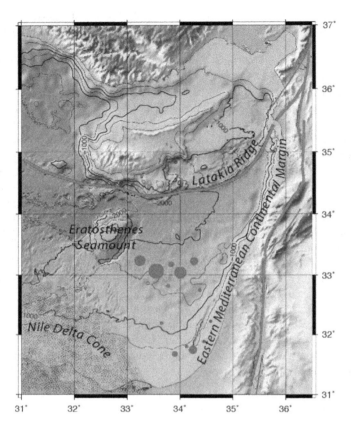

Figure 1.4 Map of the Levantine Basin.
Source: Author.

and the Eratosthenes Seamount to the west (Gardosh *et al.* 2008). The erosion of the growing landmass surrounding the basin resulted in significant amounts of debris being washed out into the deep basin and deposited among sedimentary units in the form of clastic sediments of sand or conglomerates along submarine channels or fans.

In more recent geological times, the Mediterranean Sea level dropped during the Messinian salinity crisis approximately 5.6 million years ago. It resulted in the accumulation of important salt and gypsum layers associated with other special types of evaporitic sediments (Hsu *et al.* 1973). The thickness of these sediments is variable in the basin. They usually thin toward the edges of the basin and are more than 2 kilometers thick at its center. These evaporitic units have very characteristic signatures within the sedimentary deposits of the area and can be used across the basin to correlate the relative age of different sedimentary layers. On account of their physical and mechanical properties, they represent a real challenge to oil exploration campaigns, as they require special exploration techniques in order to be able to explore the underlying structure.

Normal sea conditions resumed with the end of the salinity crisis and re-flooding of the Mediterranean basin. The sea level returned to its previous high stand and water covered the marginal areas of the basin about 5.3 million years ago. Since that time, significant amounts of turbidites with clastics and clays were deposited in the Mediterranean above the Messinian salt. These well-stratified post-salt deposits have a variable thickness (1–2 kilometers) that increases in general toward the edge of the basin where terrigenous input is most important (Carton *et al.* 2009). In some particular locations close to the base of the continental slope, such as offshore of central Lebanon, these sediments are particularly thick, as they are trapped in synclines between growing Messinian salt diapirs and ridges. Material accumulated over the slopes of the continental margin is unstable and ends up falling over west dipping listric normal faults into the deep basin.

In summary, the Levantine Basin is characterized by a relatively thick sedimentary infill easily separated into three groups relative to the Messinian evaporitic unit:

- Pre-salt units
- Salt and evaporitic units
- Post-salt units.

These units can be correlated across the Levantine Basin and the Mediterranean Sea in general. The sedimentary units and associated geological structure (faults and folds) are comparable across the Levantine Basin, although some of their characteristics (thickness, porosity, mineralogy) can be significantly different based on geological conditions. The presence of a thick sedimentary pile of layers in the basin is encouraging for hydrocarbon exploration as these layers are more likely to contain the organic material needed to generate hydrocarbon resources after burial and heating.

Petroleum resources in the Levantine Basin

Exploration for petroleum resources in the Eastern Mediterranean has been taking place for decades. It was successful in discovering oil and gas in onshore Syria, where proven oil reserves are estimated at about 2.5 billion barrels (British Petroleum 2013). Discoveries in Syria were much larger than in other neighboring Eastern Mediterranean countries, meaning Syria has enjoyed a leading position in proven petroleum resources in the Eastern Mediterranean region.

Exploration moved into the shallow part of the Levantine Basin in the mid-1970s. In Lebanon, it concentrated on the structures in near-offshore Tripoli in northern Lebanon. All official petroleum exploration activities were halted during periods of instability in the country, mainly from 1975 to 1991. They resumed only at the beginning of the twenty-first century with offshore 2D and, later, 3D seismic exploration that covered more than 80–85 percent of the Lebanese exclusive economic zone (EEZ). The Lebanese EEZ, which extends to 22,000 km^2, is the central area of the Levantine Basin and represents about 33 percent of its extent. No exploration wells have been drilled in the Lebanese offshore as of the time this book was published.

24 *The Future of Petroleum in Lebanon*

Onshore exploration in Lebanon prior to 1975 led to the drilling of seven wells that did not result in commercial discoveries, although some shows of bitumen and quantities of gas were discovered (Beydoun 1977).

Exploration in the southern Levantine Basin

Sustained exploration activity in the southern Levantine Basin began in the 1960s and produced modest results. After many unsuccessful attempts, oil and gas were discovered in very limited commercial quantities in shallow targets offshore of the Sinai Peninsula. The 1990s resulted in the first oil discoveries in the Yam and Yafo wells near southern Israel's offshore. The reservoir rocks where oil was found are the pre-salt mid-Jurassic to early Cretaceous layers. The source of the oil was not identified and may be the deeper Triassic to Lower Jurassic carbonates (Gardosh and Tannenbaum 2014). The discovered oil resources were not commercially significant.

With technological advances, offshore exploration was made possible in deeper waters and the first gas discoveries in the Levantine Basin were made in supra-salt layers in the Israeli and Palestinian offshore by the late 1990s and early twenty-first century. The discovered gas is of bacterial origin, produced from organic-rich layers in the sub- and post-salt layers, and accumulated in the upper, shallow beds of post-salt layers. Large quantities of this gas were discovered, mostly confined to sand deposits from old submarine canyons and fans resulting from erosion of nearby landmasses in the south-east. About 4 trillion cubic feet (Tcf) of gas was discovered in the earliest wells drilled. A number of discoveries followed and confirmed the presence of shallow gas reserves of the same petroleum system in this province.

Another technical challenge that was overcome in 2003 entailed drilling in deeper sub-salt layers. First, a dry hole discouraged exploration activities, but six years later, in 2009, the oil company Noble Energy successfully drilled and discovered a working petroleum system in the Tamar well offshore of Haifa. This contained about 10 Tcf of gas and paved the way for a series of giant gas discoveries in the southern Levantine Basin. The discovered gas, very likely of biogenic nature, was found in sub-salt sand accumulations, also associated with submarine river channels and fans transporting material eroded from neighboring relief areas. The source of this eroded material could be from Egypt or Sinai, Palestine, Lebanon, or Syria (Gardosh and Tannenbaum 2014). The relatively important thickness of these sands was uncovered in the Tamar Well (and therefore termed the Tamar sands) and estimated at about 250 meters of gross pay, with good porosity and permeability conditions, making them a very good and promising reservoir and petroleum system (Needham *et al.* 2013).

A number of similar discoveries followed in the same area (southern Levantine Basin) targeting plays and systems similar to the Tamar sands. Giant gas discoveries were made from 2009 to 2013, among them the Leviathan field, with estimated gas reserves of 18 Tcf found in a number of sub-salt Miocene sand intervals. The field was drilled from 2010 to 2012, where there are a number of wells located more than 100 kilometers west of Haifa and in more than 1,600 meters of water column. It is noteworthy that estimates for the Leviathan field reserves changed significantly during the exploration process. The first estimates of the volume of reserves announced by Noble Energy, which is responsible for operating the field, were about 25 Tcf but decreased on a consistent basis afterward. In March 2013, the operator announced reserve estimates of 18 Tcf of biogenic methane (United States Energy Information Administration 2013).

An additional 600 million barrels of oil are thought to exist at deeper levels below the gas units but have not been tested due to a number of technical drilling problems related to an increase in well pressure and drilling depth. However, the search for oil did not completely stop after the new gas discoveries. Reports in 2013 indicated the discovery of about 128 million barrels of recoverable oil in one of the shallow coastal wells, Yam-3, near Ashdod (Amiran 2013).

Exploration in Cyprus

After a first successful licensing round in Cyprus in 2008, Block 12 was awarded to Noble Energy. Exploration activities there resulted in another discovery by the same exploration and production company on the Cypriot part of the western Levantine Basin in Block 12, not far from the Israeli EEZ. The discovery was drilled in a water column greater than 1,600 meters and the field lies at a total depth greater than 7,000 meters. The producing geological levels are the same sub-salt sand layers as the Tamar sand. First estimated at about 9 Tcf, the reserves were cut to 4.1 Tcf due to refined appraisal results of thickness of target layers. Since its announcement in March 2012, the estimated size of this discovery was reviewed many times, but always to lower values. In October 2013, it was announced that commercial amounts of condensates estimated at about 8 million barrels were also discovered in this well (Delek 2013). In October 2012, a second licensing round was completed and four additional blocks located within or at the edge of the Levantine Basin were awarded.

Exploration in Syria

The Syrian offshore spreads over a wide zone, of which only a small part is located south of the offshore Latakia ridge inside the Levantine Basin. North and west of the ridge lay the Latakia, Iskenderun, and Cyprean basins respectively. Little exploration activity has taken place in this offshore area. Exploration in the Turkish offshore to the north made one oil discovery out of about thirteen exploration wells (Bowman 2011). A first licensing round for the Syrian offshore in 2007 was not successful in attracting bids. A second licensing round was announced in 2011 but was later postponed. Onshore exploration in coastal Syria within the limits of the extended Levantine Basin uncovered the presence of some oil and gas, though not of commercial quantities.

Estimates of petroleum resources in the basin

The Levantine Basin is an underexplored province that became attractive for petroleum exploration and production activities primarily after the major discoveries of the past decade. Few efforts have been made to assess its overall petroleum potential, and very little—if none—of the results were made public.

In an attempt to assess the distribution of energy resources worldwide, the United States Geological Survey (USGS) World Energy Project conducted geologic studies of a number of "priority petroleum basins" around the world. This information—which was provided to the general public—contains scientific and comprehensive information on the distribution of world oil and gas resources (Unites States Geological Survey 2010). The assessment is based on a probabilistic approach strategy, which estimates the amount of petroleum that is likely to be produced and added to reserves over a 30-year time span. It is based on a gross delineation of sub-units considered homogeneous (the "Assessment Units" [AU]), where the potential of undiscovered oil or gas is assessed individually. The project assessed a large number of provinces, making use of available exploration and production data and known geology. An assessment of the Levantine Basin was published in March 2010. It is likely the only assessment of the petroleum potential of the entire province to date, and certainly the only one made public.

The assessment of undiscovered resources for the Levantine Basin was subdivided over three assessment units:

- The Levantine Margin (mostly on land masses, bound by the plate margin to the east)
- The sub-salt units of the Levantine Basin (Levant Sub-salt AU)
- The supra-salt unit of the Levantine Basin (Plio-Pleistocene AU).

For each of these three units, the estimated undiscovered resources are presented with three different fractiles, F95, F50, and F5. These represent respectively the 95 percent, 50 percent, and 5 percent chances of discovering at least the corresponding amounts of resources, for oil, natural gas, and natural gas liquids (NGL) (Table 1.1).

The estimated volumes should be considered an indicator of the prospectivity of the province compared to others where the same method has been applied, and not as a real value, or proof of the existence of stated amounts. These results suggest that the Offshore LB (the sum of the two offshore AUs of the Levantine Basin) has a higher potential for petroleum resources, compared with the onshore Levant Margin AU, for both natural gas and NGL, and similar prospectivity for oil resources (Figures 1.5 and 1.6). The LB sub-salt layers present the highest prospectivity for gas of all the assessment units of the Levantine Basin.

These results for the Levantine Basin were compared to similar results for other petroleum provinces in the Middle East obtained by the Unites States Geological Survey using the same approach. For that purpose, two other provinces from the Mediterranean Sea were selected (the Nile Delta in Egypt and the Sirte Basin in Libya), in addition to the Zagros province from outside the Mediterranean (Unites States Geological Survey fact sheets 2010–3027, 2011–3105, and 2012–3115). These three provinces are known to be prolific in petroleum resources and have a long and well-established history in petroleum exploration and production. The Nile Delta province is primarily a gas province and is where most of Egypt's gas reserves are located (Estimated 72 Tcf, British Petroleum 2013). For the purpose of the assessment, it was divided into two assessment units: the Nile Cone and the Nile Margin. The results suggest that the mean volume of undiscovered technically recoverable gas in this province is about 223 Tcf and is located primarily in the Nile Cone unit. It also estimated there is a mean amount of undiscovered, technically recoverable oil resources of 1.7 billion barrels of oil (BBO).

Table 1.1 Undiscovered oil and gas resources in some Middle East provinces

Basin (or AU)	Oil mean in MMBO		Oil minimum (F95)	Oil maximum (F5)	Gas mean in BCFG
Nile Delta	1763		491	4266	223242
AU-Nile Cone	475				219071
AU-Nile Margin	1288				4171
LB	1689	% of LB	483	3759	122378
AU- Levant Margin	857	51%	278	1765	6197
AU- LB sub-salt	548	32%	148	1242	81437
AU- LB Plio-Pleistocene	284	17%	57	752	34744
Offshore LB	832	49%	205	1994	116181
Offshore Sirte Basin	2267				2569
Sirte Basin	3545				32451
Zagros	38464				191790

Basin (or AU)		Gas Minimum (F95)	Gas maximum (F5)	NGL mean in MMBNGL	
Nile Delta		92614	425935	5974	
AU-Nile Cone				5862	
AU-Nile Margin				112	
LB	% of LB	500614	227430	3075	% of LB
AU- Levant Margin	5%	2018	12796	182	6%
AU- LB sub-salt	67%	32641	152132	2533	82%
AU- LB Plio-Pleistocene	28%	15428	62502	360	12%
Offshore LB	95%	48069	214634	2893	94%
Offshore Sirte Basin					
Sirte Basin					

Source: United States Geological Survey World Energy Project (2010).

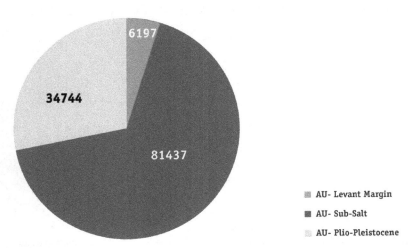

Figure 1.5 Mean undiscovered gas in BCFG for the Levantine Basin.
Source: United States Geological Survey Fact Sheet (2014).

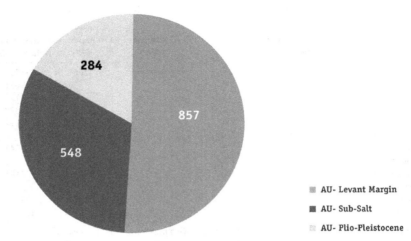

Figure 1.6 Mean undiscovered oil in MMBO for the Levantine Basin.
Source: United States Geological Survey Fact Sheet (2014).

The Unites States Geological Survey fact sheet 2011–3105 assessing undiscovered oil and gas potential for two provinces in Libya and Tunisia estimated resources of 32 Tcf of gas and 3.5 BBO of oil within the Sirte Basin in Libya. The Sirte Basin accounts for about 80 percent of Libya's 47-BBO proven oil reserves as well as a significant amount of its 53 Tcf of gas reserves (United States Energy Information Administration 2012). Finally, the undiscovered resources of the Zagros province—which hosts many giant fields and is one of the largest petroleum provinces in the world—were assessed in the United States Geological Survey fact sheet 2012–3115. The study suggested estimates for a mean of 191.7 Tcf of undiscovered gas resources and a mean of 38 BBO of undiscovered and technically recoverable oil. Taken at face value, the Unites States

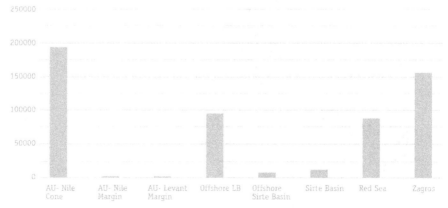

Figure 1.7 Mean undiscovered natural gas in BCFG for different petroleum provinces of the Middle East.
Source: Compiled by author.

Geological Survey estimates of undiscovered reserves confer to the offshore Levantine Basin an advanced position compared to the well-established gas provinces of the Mediterranean basin. The importance of estimated resources is also clear from the relatively high values of minimal undiscovered gas volumes—F95—for the Levantine Basin offshore units, estimated at about 48 Tcf, still a high figure compared with estimates for other provinces. Considering the total of 219 provinces throughout the world assessed by the Unites States Geological Survey, the estimated mean of undiscovered gas resources in the Levantine Basin puts it in tenth place on the list of most promising gas provinces in the next 30 years worldwide, surpassed by the Nile Delta Basin, South Caspian Basin, and Zagros Fold Belt provinces in the Middle East region, respectively in the fourth, seventh, and eighth positions (Figure 1.7).

Petroleum systems and prospectivity of the Levantine Basin

Many lessons about the Levantine Basin's prospectivity were learned from different phases of petroleum exploration and production in the area. The Levantine Basin proved to have working petroleum systems at different levels within the sedimentary sequence. Gas has been easier to find so far, and in larger quantities. This reflects the abundance of resources but also the difficulty in locating working oil systems in this geologically complex area. Of the nearly 50 exploration and appraisal wells drilled offshore in the Levantine Basin through 2013, only ten resulted in gas discoveries, with three giant fields that count among the largest gas discoveries of the decade worldwide. By mid 2014, about 40 Tcf of gas reserves were proven solid in this province (Table 1.2). This number does not necessary coincide well with the original estimates of different petroleum operators and stakeholders, but it clearly confirms the Levantine Basin as a gas province.

A number of estimates for hydrocarbon resources done at early stages of exploration proved to be very optimistic and sometimes speculative. The cases of the Myra and Sarah drilling licenses in offshore occupied Palestine illustrate well these overestimates.

Table 1.2 Summary of discovered gas reserves in the Levantine Basin as updated in May 2014.

Date	Field name	Estimated reserves
1999	Noa	0.04
2000	Gaza Marine	1
2000	Mari-B	1.5
2009	Dalit	0.5
2009	Tamar	10
2010	Leviathan	18
2011	Aphrodite	7→ 5→ 4.1
2012	Shimshon	0.3
2012	Tanin	1.2
2013	Karish	1.8
Total		~40 (Tcf)

Values given for the Aphrodite Field highlight the changes in reserves estimates
Source: United States Geological Survey (2014).

Based on geological and geophysical surveys, the fields were initially estimated in 2010 to contain 6.5 Tcf of gas (Yeshayahou and Koren 2011). Netherland Sewell & Associates Ltd (NSAI) had announced that these two fields, taken together, have a high geological probability of success—about 54 percent—for the announced 6.5 Tcf of gas and 18 percent geological probability of success for approximately 150 million barrels of oil. The two fields located not far from the major Dalit discovery were targeting the proven Tamar sands for gas resources. Compared to other successful discoveries, their prospects seemed very positive. However, the two wells drilled under these licenses from 2012 turned up dry.

Another similar case of unsuccessful estimates came from the Ishai license. This acreage seemed promising as it is located between the 4.1 Tcf Aphrodite discovery in the Cyprus Block 12 to the west and the 18 Tcf Leviathan field to the east. The discovery of 6.7 Tcf of unrisked gas resources in the upper part of the prospect and a less probable 13.5 Tcf of gas and 1.4 BBO at a greater depth was first announced in June 2012. The results were very disappointing for the market and the industry in January 2013, when Israel Opportunity Energy Resources LP announced that the drilling at the Aphrodite-2 well in the Ishai license would be stopped without carrying out any production tests (Amiran 2013). Although significant signs of gas were discovered, the encountered net-pay gas interval was much thinner than expected. The total amounts of resources found were less than 1 Tcf (Hydrocarbon Exploration and Production 2013) and not deemed worth further developing the field.

In light of these examples, one can never be cautious enough when dealing with figures and numbers of resource estimates resulting from prospectivity reports not supported by appraisal tests. Such is the case with the 40 Tcf gas resources estimates within six licensed blocks offshore Cyprus, the 60 Tcf of gas resources estimated for the entire Cypriot EEZ announced by the Cyprus National Hydrocarbon Company (Ellinas on Cyprusprofile.com, Kassinis 2013), or the 95.9 Tcf of gas estimated for about 45 percent of the Lebanese offshore with a probability of 50 percent as announced by the Lebanese Ministry of Energy and Water (MEW) (Bassam 2013).

The Tamar sands concept is currently the most productive gas system in the southern Levantine Basin. The sand in alluvial fans and river channels represents a high-quality reservoir that has been targeted in different licenses of the southern Levantine Basin on account of the net exploration and production advantages that it represents. Other plays present in the basin may also be as productive (Roberts and Peace 2007, Nader 2011, Lie *et al.* 2011).

Research findings suggest that for many geological reasons the prospectivity of the northern Levantine Basin (offshore Cyprus and Lebanon) may be higher than that of the southern part (offshore Palestine and Israel), with higher probability for oil than in the south.

For example, results from geophysical surveys show that the geological layers containing equivalents of the Tamar sands are thicker in the central basin, which hints at possibly larger reservoirs and bigger plays in the area compared to the southern counterpart. The greater burial and thickening of the sedimentary infill in the central basin increased the cooking of sediments and the maturity of tertiary source rocks that may have started expelling oil and could be charging thick reservoirs and traps located above (Hodgson 2012). Therefore, some of the source rocks in the central Levantine Basin are likely to be more mature and in more favorable hydrocarbon generation windows than in the southern part. This maturity and charging issue may explain the relatively very small amounts of oil discovered in the south. Moreover, in the central basin, the trapping structures are more abundant and diverse in age and style due to the more complex geological setting and deformation phases of the central and northern Levantine Basin (Elias *et al.* 2007, Carton *et al.* 2009). This signals better chances at finding a functioning petroleum system in the central basin, where mature oil generated at depth migrated along numerous fractures and faults and was entrapped and sealed in a rock unit with mechanical properties suitable for storing and production of the resource.

Conclusion and recommendations

Over the past 14 years, a significant amount of seismic data has been acquired about the Lebanese offshore. Since 2007, Lebanon has acquired 3D seismic data on more than 85 percent of its EEZ, placing it far ahead of all neighboring countries, while also possibly making it one of the rare countries worldwide with such a high percentage of 3D coverage. These exploration lines served well for executing assessment reports and establishing the framework for the offshore licensing round. They represent an important asset for the country's capacity to execute a volumetric assessment of resources and direct exploration activities.

Despite the amount of 2D and 3D seismic data collected over the entire Lebanese EEZ, the absence of any exploration well drilled in the central part of the Levantine Basin corresponding to the Lebanese and Syrian offshore makes all attempts and issued reports on the estimate of the volumes of resources in the area non-reliable, if not speculative. No discoveries have been made thus far in the Lebanese offshore and the numbers and estimates suggested by the different studies reported in the media such as the Unites States Geological Survey or the Lebanese MEW are—at best—for "prospective resources," and do not represent actual volumes of petroleum. The essential physical and chemical parameters needed to perform the basin modeling and analysis that characterize the geological units and formations in the central part of the basin might be very different from their counterparts in the southern basin. The analogy with similar fields or prospects in the southern basin is not reliable enough given the differences in geological settings that may exist over such a small area, as discussed above. Exploratory wells are crucially important to obtaining reliable geophysical and geochemical 1D and 2D data before attempting any serious assessment of resource potential.

Increased exploration activity in the basin has gathered large amounts of geological and geophysical information about the area and has led to a much better understanding of its hydrocarbon potential. The discoveries made in other parts of the basin have significantly decreased the risk in petroleum exploration within the central region of offshore Lebanon. It should be recognized, however, that geologists' understanding of some parts of the basin remains limited and depends on exploration activity, while most scientific reports and studies related to the basin are designed to answer industrial purposes and needs. Very little scientific work is being done independently of industrial control, which introduces a bias in the assessment of the geological setting and in guiding exploration activities. The majority of published material and data on available resources result from studies done in association with, or completely by, scientists from exploration companies. These reports or publications serve the purpose of promoting a company's dataset or assets. Scientific research should be encouraged in order to improve the geological understanding of this province and better assess its prospectivity. Governments should empower research institutions to access or acquire needed data in order to perform independent research and publish their results. Academic- and research-oriented exploration of the Levantine Basin is needed to encourage and develop groups of informed experts and produce public information that can be used to inform policy makers and public opinion, as well as monitor the process of exploration and production of this national resource, in addition to increasing awareness about it.

Exploration and production activities face many challenges in the Levantine Basin in general and the Lebanese offshore in particular. The determining and critical factor is likely to be the important water depths—mostly below 1,500 meters—associated with the presence of a shallow, thick evaporitic unit. The ultra-deep environment adds serious technical complications for exploration and production activities (Boesch 2012) and requires additional investments in security, infrastructure, and technical skills during the design, implementation, and operation phases. With these extra investments, production cost will increase, preventing some proven resources from becoming a viable economic discovery or reserve. In these conditions only large or giant discoveries will be of commercial interest or attraction. As great water depths will favor large-scale field development, parts of the resources in the basin will lose their attraction.

Finally, the scarcity of reliable and publicly available estimates of resources in different parts of the Levantine Basin contradicts the large number of related political and commercial communications that accompanied this activity in past years. The high frequency of media releases and other published material related to oil exploration in the offshore reflects the importance that different public and private stakeholders place on this sector and their political, economic, or environmental concerns. In the absence of reliable data regarding the availability of resources and size of reserves, false or exaggerated expectations are not only misleading but also dangerous, as they will only serve to place pressure on the national economy and democratic process.

References

Authored references

Amiran, B. 2013. "Ishai Well Disappoints." *Globes*, 3 January.
Bassam, L. 2013. "Lebanon Says Gas, Oil Reserves May be Higher than Thought." *Reuters*, 27 October.

Beydoun, Z.R. 1977. "Petroleum Prospects of Lebanon: Re-evaluation." *AAPG Bulletin* 61: 43–64.

Boesch, D. 2012. "Deep-Water Drilling Remains a Risky Business." *Nature* 484: 282–9.

Bownman, S. 2011. "Regional Seismic Interpretation of the Hydrocarbon Prospectivity of Offshore Syria." *GeoArabia* 16: 95–124.

Briais, A., P. Tapponnier, S.C. Singh, and E. Jacques. 2004. "Neogene and Active Shortening Offshore the Reactivated Levant Margin in Lebanon: Results of the Shalimar Cruise." *Transactions AGU*: 85.

Bruner, I. 1991. "Investigation of the Subsurface in the Northern Negev, Israel, Using Seismic Reflection Techniques." PhD diss., Tel Aviv University.

Carton, H., S.C. Singh, P. Tapponnier, A. Elias, A. Briais, A. Sursock, R. Jomaa, G. King, M. Daeron, E. Jacques, and L. Barrier. 2009. "Seismic Evidence for Neogene and Active Shortening Offshore of Lebanon (Shalimar Cruise)." *Journal of Geophysical Research*: 114.

Connan, J. and A. Nissenbaum. 2004. "The Organic Geochemistry of the Hasbeya Asphalt (Lebanon): Comparison with Asphalts from the Dead Sea Area and Iraq." *Organic Geochemistry* 10: 775–89.

Demirmen, F. 2007. "Reserves Estimation: The Challenge for the Industry." *Journal of Petroleum Technology*, May: 80–9.

Elias, A., P. Tapponnier, S.C. Singh, G. King, A. Briais, M. Daeron, H. Carton, A. Sursock, E. Jacques, R. Jomaa, and Y. Klinger. 2007. "Active Thrusting Offshore Mount Lebanon: Source of the Tsunamigenic, 551 A.D. Beirut–Tripoli Earthquake." *Geology* 35: 755–8.

Gardosh, M., Y. Druckman, B. Buchbinder, and R. Calvo. 2008. "The Oligo-Miocene Deepwater System of the Levant Basin." *Geophysical Survey of Israel* 33: 1–73.

Gardosh, M., and E. Tannenbaum. 2014. "The Petroleum Systems of Israel." In *Petroleum Systems of the Tethyan Region*, edited by L. Marlow, C.G.C. Kendall, and L.A. Yose. American Association of Petroleum Geologists.

Garfunkel, Z. 1998. "Constraints on the Origin and History of the Eastern Mediterranean Basin." *Tectonophysics* 298: 5–35.

Hodgson, N. 2012. "The Miocene Hydrocarbon Play in Southern Lebanon." *First Break* 30: 93–8.

Hsu, K.J., M.B. Cita, and W.B.F. Ryan. 1973. "The Origin of the Mediterranean Evaporites." Initial Report 13, the Deep Sea Drilling Project.

Kassinis, S. 2013. "Developments and Opportunities in Cyprus Offshore Exploration." Paper presented at the 4th Annual Mediterranean Oil & Gas Conference, Athens, 13 June.

Lie, O., C. Skiple, and C. Lowrey. 2011. "New Insights into the Levantine Basin." *GeoExPro* 8: 24–7.

Nader, F.H. 2011. "The Petroleum Prospectivity of Lebanon: An Overview." *Journal of Petroleum Geology* 34: 135–56.

Needham, D., J. French, M. Barrett, B. Bruce, V. O'Brien, G. Romero, M. Bogaards, J. Van Horn, G. Franco, S. Fenton. 2013. "Exploration Success in the Eastern Mediterranean: Levant Basin Gas Discoveries." Paper presented at the AAPG Annual Convention and Exhibition, Pittsburgh, 20 May.

Roberts, G., and D. Peace. 2007. "Hydrocarbon Plays and Prospectivity of the Levantine Basin, Offshore Lebanon and Syria from Modern Seismic Data." *GeoArabia* 12: 99–124.

Schulte, W. 2005. "Challenges and Strategy for Increased Oil Recovery." Paper presented at the International Petroleum Technology Conference, Doha, Qatar, 21–23 November.

Yeshayahou, K. 2013. "Shemen Finds Oil at Yam 3." *Globes*, 8 September.

Yeshayahou, K. and H. Koren. 2011. "Licensees Confirm 6.5Tcf Gas at Myra and Sarah." *Globes*, 30 June.

Non-Authored References

British Petroleum. 2013. "BP Statistical Review of World Energy 2013."
Cyprus Profile. 2013. "Dr. Charles Ellinas—Cyprus Profile." Interview by *Cyprus Profile.* 29 May.
Hydrocarbon Exploration and Production. 2013. "Israel's Aphrodite-2 Well in Ishai License Proves Disappointing."
United States Energy Information Administration. 2012. "Country Analysis Briefs: Libya."
United States Energy Information Administration. 2013. "Overview of oil and natural gas in the Eastern Mediterranean region." August.
United States Geological Survey. 2010. "Assessment of Undiscovered Oil and Gas Resources of the Levant Basin Province, Eastern Mediterranean." Petroleum Resources Project. Fact Sheet 2010–3014, March.
United States Geological Survey. 2010. "Assessment of Undiscovered Oil and Gas Resources of the Nile Delta Basin Province, Eastern Mediterranean." Petroleum Resources Project. Fact Sheet 2010–3027, May.
United States Geological Survey. 2011. "Assessment of Undiscovered Oil and Gas Resources of Libya and Tunisia, 2010." Petroleum Resources Project. Fact Sheet 2011–3105, September.
United States Geological Survey. 2012. "Assessment of Undiscovered Conventional Oil and Gas Resources of the Arabian Peninsula and Zagros Fold Belt." Petroleum Resources Project. Fact Sheet 2012–3115, September.

Governance of the Sector

2

Carving Out a Role for Parliament in the Lebanese Oil and Gas Sector

Sami Atallah and Nancy Ezzeddine[1]

Introduction

The Lebanese government's signing of a licensing agreement with the Total-Eni-Novatek consortium for two blocks off the coast of Lebanon has brought the country one step closer to reaping the benefits of oil and gas extraction. Despite the fanfare accompanying this agreement, the weakness of Lebanon's institutions—particularly those that ensure checks and balances—may very well deny citizens the opportunity to realize the benefits of this natural resource.

Although the licensing agreement was reached one year after the passage of two decrees covering the delineation of blocks and the Exploration and Production Agreement (EPA), these decrees were effectively blocked by the Council of Ministers (COM) for over 40 months—a delay for which no official explanation was given. In turn, this delay has cast a shadow over Lebanon's national legislative body on account of the parliament neglecting its oversight duties and its apparent inability or unwillingness to query the government about delays in the development of the oil and gas sector.

The world over, countries endowed with strong institutions that contribute to decision making processes have managed to turn oil rents into a blessing. The Lebanese Parliament, through its legislative and oversight authorities, is a central institution and should play a key role in the development of the national petroleum sector. On the legislative side, parliamentarians are tasked with setting the policy framework for the oil and gas sector by debating and approving key laws. Also, they are responsible for holding the government accountable in its compliance with laws and policies regarding the development and management of the sector.

This chapter assesses the ability of the Lebanese Parliament to properly govern the oil and gas sector through its legislative and oversight authorities. The offshore law of 2010[2] and parliamentary committee deliberations concerning the law, as well as the

---

[1] The authors would like to thank Michele Boujikian for assisting in the coding and analysis of parliamentary committee deliberations.

[2] Lebanese Parliament. 2010. Offshore Petroleum Resources Law. Law 132, 24 August.

parliament's response to paralysis in the sector from August 2013 to January 2017, provide an opportunity to examine the parliament's ability to establish an enabling framework and perform its designated role. Based on this, we argue that the parliament has failed to incorporate into the law any significant role for it to regulate or shape the outlook of the national petroleum sector. Additionally, the process by which the offshore draft law became law has further undermined any effective role the parliament—as a democratic institution—can play in regulating the sector. In some instances, the voices of a majority of MPs were overshadowed by a few powerful MPs. Finally, the parliament failed to exercise its oversight role concerning the government's long delay in signing the two decrees covering the delineation of blocks and the EPA.

Accordingly, this chapter concludes that reform and rehabilitation within the parliament is necessary and must be preceded by political and institutional reform that supports democratic accountability across and within institutions. This should be preceded by (vertical) accountability between elected officials and voters, reforming election processes, and embracing programmatic representation. Subsequently, the parliament must enhance its role within the oil and gas sector by bolstering its legislative and oversight capacity through greater access to knowledge, expertise, and information.

This chapter proceeds as follows. The first section provides a brief analytical framework on the role of institutions, particularly the parliament, in governing the oil and gas sector across the resource value chain. Section two describes the data used to make inferences about the role of the parliament. In section three, we evaluate parliamentary work across its two core functions by reviewing key practices within the oil and gas sector. Section four concludes by presenting key institutional and capacity building recommendations to foster accountability, promote political representation, and equip legislators with technical knowledge to better enable parliamentary institutions to perform their critical functions.

Parliament's mandate to play a crucial role in governing the oil and gas sector

At their most basic level, parliaments are established to represent citizens, and members of parliament (MPs) are elected to give voice to the concerns of constituents (Chohan 2015). Accordingly, many oil-producing states such as Canada and Norway have legislative bodies that play an active role in shaping objectives, targets, and regulations, or seek to influence the decision-making process in the petroleum sector (Lahn *et al.* 2007). If properly conducted, parliaments can provide opportunities for more open and participatory governance. The patronage model of Robinson *et al.* (2006), for example, emphasizes the role that institutions play in public sector accountability. Collier (2007) complements Robinson's work by supporting the establishment of institutions that are endowed with robust checks and balances on authority. Without these checks and balances, competition for natural resource rents can lead to the breakdown of democratic institutions. Furthering this point, Collier (2007) argues that oil revenues lessen the need to tax—thus contributing further to the weakening of checks and balances by reducing public calls for sound policies and responsiveness to citizen needs.

Parliamentary accountability requires clear delegation of authority, capable institutions, and mechanisms of enforcement. Ross (2001), Sala-i-Martin and Artadi (2002), and the World Bank (2003) find that, controlling for incomes and population size, oil rents have explanatory power for weak governance in the Middle East. These studies show that there is little difference in the quality of administration between oil- and non-oil countries, but that public accountability in oil-reliant countries is systematically lower than in non-oil-reliant countries. This is consistent with the conclusion of Robinson *et al.* (2006), namely that effective institutional safeguards against political patronage are a key characteristic of political regimes that manage to resist the pressures associated with resource rents.

Accordingly, the rapid growth of transparency and accountability initiatives in the petroleum sector over the past decade reflects attempts to devise and implement institutional mechanisms aimed at holding governments accountable for their actions regarding extraction, allocation, and use of revenues. In practice, resource governance norms have evolved at multiple levels to counter resource curse effects by mainstreaming transparency and accountability throughout the resource value chain. The resource value chain analysis, as popularized by Paul Collier (2007), focuses on the sequence of consecutive activities that are required to bring resources from extraction, to their processing and sale, all the way through to the ultimate use of revenues. The resource value chain was developed to ensure that the best decisions are made at each stage of the sector's development. These stages include: deciding to extract resources, negotiating the best deals for resources, ensuring revenue transparency, managing and sharing revenues, and achieving sustainable development.[3]

As broadly noted earlier in this section, legislators are responsible for promoting an enabling environment for the sustainable and accountable management of a petroleum sector by drafting and reviewing bills and legislation that govern the sector. Additionally, in some countries, parliaments are bestowed with the responsibility of amending and approving agreements and contracts within the sector (AGORA 2009). Also, parliaments are responsible for passing laws to institute and promote appropriate economic and fiscal policies that complement the petroleum sector. As a result, all decisions concerning the course of the sector are subject to parliamentary approval in some form or another—whether through the approval of legislation, policies, agreements, or budgets. Through legislation, parliaments are also responsible for the development of regulatory frameworks regarding the management of natural resources and revenues. It is only within such an existing framework that effective oversight of the sector—the second parliamentary function—can be carried out (AGORA 2013).

Once legislative and regulatory frameworks are in place, contracts and agreements are approved and signed, and operations are underway, the parliament plays a role in

---

[3] Natural Resource Governance Institute. 2010. "The Value Chain". https://resourcegovernance.org/analysis-tools/publications/value-chain

40   *The Future of Petroleum in Lebanon*

overseeing revenue distribution and governance of the sector. Through their oversight function, legislators act as the "national watchdog" of the sector (AGORA 2009). Parliaments should ensure that the implementation of laws, programs, and policies by governments are carried out in an effective and legal manner (Whitton, 2001). Strong parliaments in resource-rich countries closely evaluate the government's work through field visits and engagement with governmental actors, companies, and civil society organizations (AGORA 2009). Parliaments employ different tools to monitor the sector, such as question periods, committee hearings, investigations, and the design and presentation of recommendations for reform (AGORA 2013).

Methodology

To assess the performance of the Lebanese Parliament in governing the oil and gas sector, we confined our study to the period from 2010 to 2017 for two reasons. First, the oil and gas offshore law approved in August 2010 provides us with an opportunity to examine not only the content of the law but also the debate that took place in the joint committee tasked with reviewing it. This was made possible after LCPS officially requested and obtained the minutes of the meetings of the joint committee.[4]

To this end, we reviewed and analyzed the hand-written minutes of seven committee meetings and ten general sessions that were held from June 2010 to March 2014.[5] To ensure consistency in analysis, two LCPS researchers reviewed and separately coded the minutes of the parliamentary committee meetings along the following themes: governance of the sector, operational activities, emergency measures, environmental assessment, onshore resources, Israeli offshore threat, and the sovereign wealth fund. In this way, we are able to avoid any inconsistencies in the coding.

In addition to the committees' work, LCPS examined oversight sessions—specifically from August 2013 to December 2016—and assessed the positions of individual MPs. This provided us with the opportunity to assess how the parliament and its members chose to exercise their oversight role when the COM failed to pass two decrees that were central to launching the sector. To do so, we resorted to two sources of data. The first comprises minutes of oversight sessions that were held during this period. This allowed us to assess the substance of discussions and the extent to which MPs who participated in the five sessions held during this period addressed the delay in the oil and gas sector. The second source is unique survey data developed and collected by LCPS on 65 out of 128 MPs. Comprising 52 questions, the questionnaire aims to offer insight into MPs' priorities, the way they spend their time, their positions on various public policy issues including oil and gas activities, and general knowledge of the sector.

---

[4]   Records of the seven parliamentary committee meetings total more than 350 pages. Meetings were held on 22/6/2010, 28/6/2010, 12/7/2010, 26/7/2010, 29/7/2010, 2/8/2010, and 12/8/2010.

[5]   The general assembly legislative sessions were held on: 15/6/2010, 15/7/2010, 10/8/2010, 3/8/2011, 4/8/2011, 17/8/2011, 22/2/2012, 23/2/2012, 19/3/2014, and 20/3/2014.

Lebanon's parliament: strong but untapped authorities

The Taef Accord strengthened the role of the parliament, particularly in the realm of governance and national decision-making.[6] In addition to equalizing Christian–Muslim representation in Article 24, it extended the term of the speaker of the parliament, whose position is designated to the Shia community (Article 44). The parliament is also entrusted with electing the president (Article 49) as well as nominating the prime minister (Article 53).

The parliament has broad legislative power according to Article 18, which ensures that "No Law shall be promulgated until it has been adopted by the chamber." Other provisions consolidate its law-making authority, such as Article 51, which states that the "president shall promulgate laws after they have been approved by the chamber." Furthermore, Article 58 limits the ability of the executive body to bypass the parliament in urgent matters and Article 57 weakens the president's ability to obstruct the parliament's legislative power, since any law that is not issued or returned by the president "shall be considered legally operative and must be promulgated."[7]

Concerning the parliament's oversight role, Article 37 gives parliamentarians "the absolute right to raise the question of no-confidence in the government during ordinary or extraordinary sessions." The parliament's oversight roles are subsumed in the third section (parliamentary oversight) of its bylaws (Articles 124–143)[8] including questions (chapter one), interrogations (chapter two), and parliamentary inquiry (chapter three). For example, Article 124 states that "A parliamentarian may present oral or written questions to the government as a whole or to a minister. The government is requested to reply within fifteen days from the date of receipt of the question." This section of the bylaws provides several oversight tools and mechanisms that the parliament can use to hold the government and other public administrations accountable.

In practice, the parliament has not assumed its duties or exercised the authorities granted to it. On the legislative side, although the parliament passed 352 laws from

---

[6] Lebanese Parliament. 1989. The Taef Accord. Approved on 4 November.

[7] Article 58 states the following: "Every bill that the COM deems urgent and in which this urgency is indicated in the Decree of Transmission to the Chamber of Deputies may be issued by the president within forty days following its communication to the Chamber and after including it on the agenda of a general meeting, reading it aloud before the Chamber, and after the expiration of the time limit without the Chamber acting on it." Article 57 is as follows: "The president of the Republic, after consultation with the COM, shall have the right to request the reconsideration of a Law once during the period prescribed for its promulgation. This request may not be refused. When the president exercises this right, he shall not be required to promulgate this Law until it has been reconsidered and approved by an absolute majority of all the members legally composing the chamber. If the time limits pass without the Law being issued or returned, the Law shall be considered legally operative and must be promulgated."

[8] For the parliament's bylaws, see: https://www.lp.gov.lb/CustomPage.aspx?id=37&masterId=1. Similarly Article 131 states that "Each deputy or more may request to question the government as a whole or a minister on a particular subject. The request for questioning shall be submitted in writing to the president of the council who refers it to the Government." In addition, Article 139 states that "the Parliament may decide to conduct a parliamentary inquiry on any subject on the basis of a proposal submitted to it for discussion or in the course of a question on a particular subject or draft law presented to it."

June 2009 to April 2017, only 22 percent of them have a direct impact on citizens' welfare (Atallah 2018). The remaining 78 percent pertain to administrative and budgetary issues since the parliament failed to pass a national budget from 2005 to 2017. Out of the 22 percent (77 laws in total), only 31 laws directly address peoples' priorities—such as increases in the price of goods, unemployment, education and healthcare costs, and the provision of water and electricity.[9] Moreover, only five of the 31 laws were introduced by MPs. Not only has the parliament failed to pass laws that are pertinent to people's interest, it has not sufficiently discussed their problems during general sessions. After examining almost 5,000 pages of parliamentary deliberations over 37 sessions, the results show that parliamentarians have infrequently conveyed people's concerns. For instance, unemployment or job creation was brought up 90 times over 30 sessions by all 128 MPs, which is, on average, three times per session.

By looking closely at efforts exerted by each parliamentarian, Atallah (2017) measures their performance proxied by the number of sessions attended and number of times they participated in a discussion. Using a composite score from zero and ten, the average score was six.[10] Many MPs attended parliamentary sessions but only a fraction of them contributed to discussions. More problematically, political parties represented in the parliament have no policy coherence among their members, which effectively undermines any effort to put together a legislative agenda (Atallah 2018).

Although the parliament should have held nine oversight sessions from June 2009 to May 2018, it only held five[11] (Atallah 2018). This is particularly troubling given several urgent matters that the country faced during that time period—including the absence of a national budget since 2005, a waste management crisis in the summer of 2015, and paralysis in the oil and gas sector from 2013 to 2016, among other cases of mismanagement. Even when sessions were held, the parliament failed to seriously question the government on its handling of these pertinent issues. Moreover, it did not hold the government accountable for its failure to issue implementation decrees to activate over 33 laws pending since 2000 (Atallah 2018).

Despite its legislative and oversight authorities, the parliament has failed to exercise its power.[12] The parliament's poor performance has not been overlooked by citizens. According to the Arab Barometer Survey, 61 percent of Lebanese reported a complete lack of trust in the parliament in 2013 compared to 49 percent in 2011. The only other institution that fares worse is the national government, to which 69 percent of respondents expressed an absolute lack of trust. Other institutions, such as the judiciary, police, and armed forces, are perceived more positively than the parliament, with 52 percent, 33 percent, and 11 percent of respondents expressing an absolute lack of trust, respectively.[13]

---

[9] LCPS identified peoples' priorities based on a survey of 2,496 citizens conducted in the fall of 2015 and winter of 2016.

[10] This is based on LCPS's calculations according to which attendance and participation were averaged to produce a performance score. While the index would benefit from including the number of draft laws each MP produced, this data is not available.

[11] Based on Article 136 of the bylaws, for every three legislative sessions the parliament must hold one oversight session.

[12] It took 30 months and 35 sessions to elect a president in October 2016.

[13] *Arab Barometer*. 2011–13. "Online Data Analysis Portal." http://www.arabbarometer.org/content/online-data-analysis

Assessing the parliament's four-pillar governance framework for the sector

The parliament managed to pass the 2010 Offshore Petroleum Resources Law (OPRL)—the primary text governing the oil and gas sector in Lebanon. The OPRL governs the planning, preparation, installation, and execution of all activities related to oil and natural gas, in addition to all kinds of gas and other hydrocarbons associated with a sub-sea reservoir within Lebanese territorial waters, the waters of the exclusive economic zone, and the Lebanese continental shelf (all activities defined by the law as "Petroleum Activities").[14] All these issues are detailed in the OPRL in just 77 articles broken down into ten chapters over 34 pages.[15]

Each chapter in the law did not receive equal scrutiny from the parliamentary committee. Based on our review and coding of the parliamentary deliberation committee, three themes dominated the discussion: the governance framework, which is spelled out in chapters 2 and 6 of the law; petroleum activities, which are addressed in chapters 3 to 7; and emergency procedures and environmental assessments, which are both covered in chapter 9.

A comparison of the deliberations over the OPRL draft law and the law that was passed reveals differences concerning two matters. First, the governance framework is a priority for politicians. While just over 20 percent of the articles in the OPRL address governance issues, these accounted for 60 percent of parliamentary deliberations (Figure 2.1).[16] Second, while petroleum activities account for 64 percent of the articles in the OPRL, only 13 percent of the deliberation was devoted to it. In fact, all other issues, such as emergency procedures, onshore exploration, environmental assessments, and local content were lightly—if at all—debated.

In this section, we assess the governance framework, which determines the institutional setup and bylaws of the sector set forth in the OPRL. Through the governance framework, the parliament can guarantee a role for itself in the larger regulatory framework of the sector. To this end, we analyze in the following sub-sections the law and deliberations across four pillars of governance developed by Chatham House (2013) and the World Bank (2013): policies and objectives of the sector, structural and hierarchical organization of the sector, revenue management, as well as monitoring and regulation of activities.

Equally important is the process according to which the law was deliberated in the committee prior to voting, as it sheds light on MPs' priorities and concerns. Accordingly,

---

[14] The OPRL is complemented by a number of decrees approved by the COM. Chief among them are: the Petroleum Activities Regulation (PAR) Decree, the tender protocol including the Exploration and Production Agreement (EPA) and Block Delineation, in addition to other decrees covering various regulatory and environmental issues.

[15] The OPRL covers the following issues: 1. Introductory Provisions; 2. Powers of the Government; 3. Reconnaissance; 4. Award of Exploration and Production Rights; 5. Plans for Petroleum Production and Transportation; 6. Petroleum Entitlements and Fees; 7. Decommissioning; 8. Mortgaging and Registration of Rights; 9. Health, Safety, and Environment; and 10. General Provisions.

[16] In order not to overstate the nature of interventions, we have only counted the type of statements made by each MP in each session once. Put more precisely, an MP who made two or more statements in the same session on the same topic is counted once.

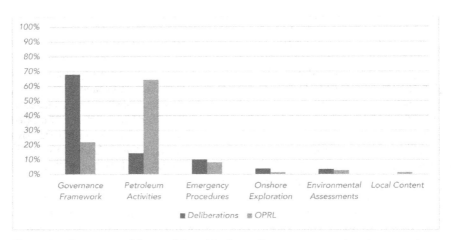

Figure 2.1 Frequency of themes debated in the parliamentary committee in comparison with the frequency of their mention in the OPRL Law.

Note: LCPS researchers script-coded each of the interventions provided by each MP during the committee sessions that discussed the OPRL. Based on the main arguments discussed in the MP's intervention, LCPS researchers would mark a point for the matched theme. The same code count per theme was followed to analyze each article of the OPRL.

Source: Compiled by authors based on parliamentary deliberations and text of 2010 Offshore Petroleum Resources Law.

this assessment arrives at the conclusion that the OPRL, as a piece of legislation, fails to incorporate a robust governance framework as it lacks overarching policies and objectives for the sector, does not clearly distinguish roles and responsibilities in the management of the sector, remains ambiguous concerning revenue management, and does not explicitly mention monitoring or regulatory frameworks. The OPRL—a brief document—leaves details regarding governance of revenue, operational agreements, legislation, and other modalities and parameters to be decided upon by the COM. Notably, the OPRL fails to ensure a role for the parliament, as it omits mention of further parliamentary responsibility in deciding future legislation or monitoring the government's work within the sector. Furthermore, the draft law was rushed through the parliament as MPs refused to wait for feedback from the government following its simultaneous review of the law. Moreover, by evaluating parliamentary deliberations, it is apparent that decisions are often influenced by a few key legislators at the expense of the opinions of the majority of MPs.

Policies and objectives for the sector: no clear vision

The main pillars of a petroleum regime include the policies and objectives set forth in a country's constitution, petroleum policy, petroleum law, and petroleum regulations. While constitutions generally assign the underlying framework for policies and legislation pertaining to natural resources, petroleum policies should estimate the country's energy needs, how that demand will be met, and from which potential markets energy resources can be procured. Based on a petroleum policy, a petroleum law then establishes the legislative framework for how the sector will be managed. A law or code is complemented by decrees and regulations that implement the law's objectives. Hence, the existence of an overarching uniformity among the above components as well as linkages across legislative and regulatory instruments are critical (AGORA 2013 and Nakhle 2017).[17]

Against this framework, Lebanon's constitution affirms state ownership of natural resources and the exclusive right of the state to manage them (Nakhle 2017).[18] However, the government has not articulated its future energy needs and how it plans to meet them. Its energy policies seem incoherent or at best fragmented, and in some cases thin on details. Additionally—as noted at the end of the preceding section—the ability of the majority of MPs to constructively contribute to the decision making process has been constrained by more powerful members, thus undermining the role of the parliament in the legislative process.

One of the Lebanese government's key responsibilities is producing an energy policy that describes the country's energy outlook as well as how it plans to meet them. The last such document was formulated in 2008. Not only has it not been updated to take into account the latest and substantial changes in petroleum markets but the energy policy is also a thin document with little detail on how to meet the country's energy needs. It should have been the foundation of all related energy laws. Instead, the Ministry of Energy and Water (MEW) produced an electricity policy and a renewable energy policy that do not fully take into account such an outlook. Furthermore, the country would have benefited from a coherent petroleum law that encompasses both onshore and offshore operations. Instead, the government decided to address these two areas separately, hence contributing to fragmentation in the legal framework.

The offshore oil and gas law is considered to be short on details[19] and leaves modalities and parameters to be addressed in regulations and contracts,[20] thus undermining the parliament's role in the legislative process and leaving more leeway than necessary for the government to negotiate with oil companies (Nakhle 2017). Although several MPs recognized the need to have a petroleum policy in place before

---

[17] For example, environmental laws and regulations should adequately cater to matters relating to exploration and production activities, otherwise hydrocarbon legislation should incorporate such provisions if they are absent from the environmental legislation (AGORA 2013).

[18] Article 89 of the constitution (Lebanese Parliament. 1926. The Lebanese Constitution. Promulgated on 26 May) confirms that "no contract or concession for the exploitation of the natural resources of the country, or a public utility service, and no monopoly may be granted except by virtue of a law and for a limited period."

[19] In fact, the ORPL passed by the parliament refers to other pieces of legislation that are applicable to the sector, including the Lebanese Law for the Protection of the Environment and the Income Tax Law. However, several details were left to be developed in decrees and agreements. The Petroleum Activities Regulations (PAR) and the Exploration and Production Agreement (EPA) are more detailed documents (nearing 100 and 200 pages respectively).

[20] While it is argued that leaving the modalities to the discretion of the executive authority so the government has leeway in its negotiations with companies, Nakhle (2017) argues that these advantages are not only exaggerated but they could encourage corruption.

46   *The Future of Petroleum in Lebanon*

discussing the OPRL draft law, their calls went unheeded. For instance, MP Ghassan Moukheiber called for a petroleum policy to be submitted by the government and discussed by the parliament.[21] This was again brought up in the next session by MP Alain Aoun, who stated that "the law must be processed within an overarching petroleum policy set forth by the government."[22] However, other MPs could not distinguish between petroleum policy and the petroleum law. Then Minister of Energy and Water Gebran Bassil, who was participating in the parliamentary session on 28 June 2010, went on to state that the law is equivalent to a policy—asserting that petroleum "policy is clear in the rationale accompanying the law but the offshore draft law in its entirety is equivalent to a petroleum policy."[23] Others did not think that time should be wasted on policies, including MP Ghazi Zeitar, who asked "what is there to discuss in a petroleum policy? Do we discuss whether we should extract oil or not?"[24] This snapshot illustrates a broader reality—namely, that some MPs did not realize or appreciate the importance of a petroleum policy.

The law also exclusively covers offshore operations, raising further concerns. This prompted Moukheiber to question the logic of excluding potential onshore operations.[25] He noted that "95 percent of the articles [should] apply to both."[26] Mr Sarkis Hallis, representative of the Minister of Energy and Water, justified the exclusion of the onshore because "it will take a longer [period of] time" as there is a need to deal with land appropriation.[27] To Speaker of the Parliament Nabih Berri, the threat from Israel compelled him to address the offshore first. Bassil admitted that "[the matter of onshore] was the first question he asked when the draft law was presented to him. But there is no technical capability. Offshore extraction is completely different from onshore extraction and that is why it needs a second law."[28] It is not clear on what basis the minister was making his claims as many countries have one hydrocarbon law covering both onshore and offshore. When Moukheiber raised the issue again in the parliamentary session held on 12 July 2010, Berri responded firmly, stating that the "topic is closed, we discussed it in the last session and this law will be for offshore only."[29]

Additionally, the draft law that was submitted to the parliament was concurrently being discussed by the COM. The parliament failed to consolidate the legislative and executive tracks, leading to a duplication of work and confusion among MPs. Several MPs expressed concern over the parallel track. For instance, Moukheiber raised concerns about the duplication of effort, namely the potential of drafting two versions of the law.[30] In the same session, MP Ghazi Yousef reiterated this idea, stating that

---

[21] From the minutes of the parliamentary committee meeting held on 22/6/2010. Minutes of the seven parliamentary sessions cited in this chapter were provided to LCPS by the Lebanese Parliament's administrative office (مكتب المجلس).
[22] Minutes of the parliamentary committee meeting held on 28/6/2010.
[23] Ibid.
[24] Minutes of the parliamentary committee meeting held on 22/6/2010.
[25] Ibid.
[26] Minutes of the parliamentary committee meeting held on 12/7/2010.
[27] Minutes of the parliamentary committee meeting held on 22/6/2010.
[28] Minutes of the parliamentary committee meeting held on 28/6/2010.
[29] Minutes of the parliamentary committee meeting held on 12/7/2010.
[30] Minutes of the parliamentary committee meeting held on 22/6/2010.

parliamentarians should review a modified version of the draft law rather than "deliberate the same topic twice." Other MPs thought it would be useful to seek experts' opinions. MP Samir El Jisr stated in a session on 6 June 2010 that "This law requires a high degree of technical knowledge and expertise. Therefore, we need to wait until the government provides its feedback."[31] Others, like MP Serge Toursakasian, suggested that the parliament should call upon experts to inform the discussion: "Why don't we listen to experts on these issues?"[32] In fact, according to the deliberations, several articles could not be discussed until the parliament received the final version of the draft law from the government. Yousef summarized this by stating: "We postponed the deliberation over articles 8, 9, and 10 but there are many articles in the draft law that are linked to these articles, particularly the petroleum administration and the fund." Berri confirmed Yousef's statement, saying, "every time we are about to deliberate the articles that touch upon those two matters, we end up postponing them until the ministerial committee finalizes its draft. We were promised that in two weeks the draft law would be complete but this did not happen."

Despite these concerns, a few parliamentarians insisted on expediting deliberations out of fear of an "Israeli threat" to extract oil and gas from Lebanon's offshore fields. Berri asserted that the government and the parliament were cooperating and would expedite the process to address "Israel's attempt to steal oil from the common economic zone [with Lebanon], which seems to contain the highest quantities of oil." During the same session, MP Hassan Fadlallah emphasized this, suggesting that this law might "send a message to the Israelis." The speaker of the parliament went on to reassure MPs that the draft law submitted to the parliament by MP Ali Hassan Khalil is the same as the one discussed by the government, since they both have a common origin, which is input by the Norwegian government. He stated that the Norwegian government "donated this law that is being currently reviewed in the parliament."[33]

His statement exposed three sets of issues regarding the policy making process. First, a proper policy making process according to which MPs raise concerns is secondary to an agreement between the head of the executive and head of legislative institutions. Second, an assumed Israeli threat justifies hijacking the process. Third, the fact that the law originated with the Norwegian government raises important questions about how proactive the government has been in assuming its duties and responsibilities vis-à-vis the petroleum sector.

Contrary to the convictions of a majority of MPs, the draft law was deliberated in the parliamentary committee. While 56 percent of MPs thought that they should take their time in studying the law—out of whom 44 percent wanted to wait for the government's final draft and 12 percent thought the parliament should consult with experts—the remaining 44 percent were in favor of pushing the draft law through the parliament even though the final version of the law was still being discussed in the COM.

---

[31] Minutes of the parliamentary committee meeting held on 6/6/2010.
[32] Minutes of the parliamentary committee meeting held on 12/7/2010.
[33] Minutes of the parliamentary committee meeting held on 28/6/2010.

Examining the debate in parliament, MP Ali Fayad stated that

[T]he approach that we have adopted is to quickly deliberate the draft law, knowing that there are many remarks that could improve the text and the future performance of the sector in Lebanon through establishing a special ministry as well as a national oil company. However, in my opinion, all that may delay or place a hurdle in approving this law must be postponed and discussed at some point in the future. I remind parliamentarians about the importance of quickly addressing this law without compromising on our ability to improve the text.[34]

Compounding matters was the fact that, when the final version of the draft law was being discussed in the legislative session on 17 August 2010, MPs did not have a version to review beforehand. MP Ahmad Fatfat expressed his frustration during this session by stating: "I want to express my objection because I did not have the opportunity to review this law as I just received it this morning [before the session]."[35]

Despite the flaws that were highlighted in the general session, many MPs insisted not only on passing the draft law as written, but also as one article. In fact, MP Robert Ghanem summarized this by stating the following: "I propose for the national interest, the higher interest, and for Lebanon's interest that we approve it in one article and when we need to amend we shall do so as a proposal or [based on a request] from the government. Let's approve it now because we have discussed it for too long."[36] The speaker of the parliament then put the law up for a vote as a single article by "relying on God."

The structural and hierarchical organization of the sector: a dependent LPA

A key component in managing the sector is the delineation of roles and responsibilities among principal actors (AGORA 2013 and Marcel 2013). Those involved in the decision making process should know who is responsible for providing inputs to make a decision, advise on the decision, approve the decision, implement the decision, and monitor its implementation. Otherwise, a lack of clarity can lead to conflicting agendas, duplication of effort, and policy paralysis. There is no one-size-fits-all model to accomplish this, but the parliament should be responsible for approving major policies and legislation, defining institutional actors, and establishing reporting requirements. In turn, the government has the executive authority to implement and oversee operations.[37]

---

[34] Minutes of the parliamentary committee meeting held on 12/7/2010.
[35] Minutes of the general assembly legislative session held on 17/8/2010.
[36] Ibid.
[37] There are multiple organizational models, including the Norwegian and Malaysian models, which can be seen as different examples that highlight opposite ends of the spectrum. Norway separates policy (ministry), regulation (government-appointed and statutory bodies), and operations (NOC) into different entities. By contrast, the Malaysian model has no ministry. Policy, regulation, and operations are housed in separate departments of a single national oil company whose head reports directly to the prime minister (The World Bank Group 2009).

In Lebanon, there are three key stakeholders and institutions involved in the management and monitoring of the sector: the COM, the MEW, and the Lebanese Petroleum Administration (LPA). Reviewing both the law and parliamentary deliberations, two key issues deserve to be highlighted. The first concerns how the law entrusts authority over the sector to the minister rather than the LPA, thus disregarding the opinion of the majority of MPs involved in the drafting of the law. The second issue is the absence of an effective role for the parliament in the sector beyond its legislative authority.

Concerning the first point, the law emphasizes the role of the COM in formulating a petroleum policy, approving decrees proposed by the minister, and authorizing the minister of energy and water to "sign on its behalf the Exploration and Production Agreements" (Article 8). More specifically, the article states that these decisions "shall be stipulated by a COM Decree made on the basis of a proposal by the minister based upon the opinion of the Petroleum Administration." Effectively, this article relegated the role of the LPA in favor of the COM and minister, hence producing a centralized power structure.

Furthermore, although Article 10 entrusts the petroleum administration with "financial and administrative autonomy," it confines its role by giving the minister "tutelage authority." Moreover, "certain financial and administrative decisions by the petroleum administration shall be subject to the approval of the minister as stipulated by a decree regulating its organization." The law does not state what these instances are, effectively ensuring that the LPA remains under the patronage of the minister.

Looking closely at parliamentary committee deliberations, there were many calls by MPs for both an independent petroleum administration and the inclusion of other ministries in the decision making process. For instance, MP Mohammed Qabbani was concerned that the minister would simply treat the LPA as an advisory council and possibly disregard its advice.[38] Bassil confirmed that the petroleum administration would not be an advisory body to the minister. MP Samir El-Jisr, however, raised the issue and suggested that the opinion of the LPA should be binding on the minister.

While these parliamentarians favored a more assertive role for the LPA, others argued in favor of giving power to the minister. For instance, MP Ibrahim Kanaan argued that the "minister is the head of the administrative authority in the ministry. How could we deprive the minister of his mandate?" Berri emphasized that "we cannot cancel the role of the minister."[39] In the same vein, MP Nicolas Fattoush stated that, "Based on Article 66 of the constitution, the affairs of the ministry are managed by the minister according to rules and regulations. Therefore, if we give the administration binding authority, we are in fact undermining Article 66 of the constitution."[40]

Based on deliberation records, LCPS classified the opinions of MPs in relation to the authority that should be given to the LPA into five categories: 12 percent of MPs supported the idea that the minister should consult with the LPA only when he or she finds it necessary, 26 percent were in favor of the minister making decisions in

[38] Minutes of the parliamentary committee meeting held on 12/7/2010.
[39] Ibid.
[40] Ibid.

consultation with the LPA, 41 percent supported the inclusion of other ministries in decision making, 18 percent supported an increase in the administrative role of the LPA, and 3 percent favored an independent LPA (Figure 2.2).

In effect, these five categories can be grouped into two camps. The first camp, which comprised 38 percent of MPs, advocated a strong decision making role for the minister—arguing that this would reduce bureaucratic inefficiencies and speed up the decision making process. The second camp, made up of the remaining 62 percent of MPs, called for a more independent role for the LPA and wider representation in the decision making process to handle complex environmental, economic, health, safety, and technical dimensions that are related to petroleum extraction. Moreover, these advocates feared that centralized authority under one ministry could result in biased decision making.

Despite the majority of MPs tilting toward the more inclusive power system, the law ended up favoring the minority voices of the first camp.

Berri "authorized" himself during the last committee meeting on 12 August 2010 to negotiate the terms of these provisions on behalf of the committee, prior to the forthcoming legislative session with Prime Minister Saad Hariri.[41] During the legislative session of 17 August 2010, Berri explained to the general assembly that "we do not want to increase the bureaucratic process for the investor by making him refer to several administrations ... it is not easy to persuade investors."[42] He "met with Hariri to discuss the contentious role and responsibilities of key institutions (Articles 9 and 10 in the law) and delegated MP Ali Hassan Khalil to continue this consultation with Hariri to arrive at a fair formulation." This formulation—as presented in the OPRL—was delivered to MPs during the legislative session without prior notice or any further discussion. The

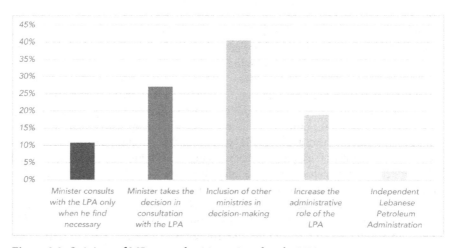

Figure 2.2 Opinions of MPs on authorities assigned to the LPA.
Source: Compiled by authors based on parliamentary deliberations.

[41] Minutes of the parliamentary committee meeting held on 12/8/2010.
[42] Minutes of the legislative session held on 17/8/2010.

arrangement fostered a considerable amount of controversy and frustration among present MPs, as the speaker of the parliament undermined the role of the committee to democratically resolve the controversy over the allocation of responsibilities.

Additionally, the Lebanese Parliament failed to establish its role in the sector across the resource value chain by requiring that decisions be subject to parliamentary approval in some form or another. Indeed, the OPRL makes no mention of the parliament's role within the sector. This was noted by several Lebanese MPs, including five MPs who mentioned this flaw during deliberations about the sector's governance framework. However, their comments were disregarded shortly after. Among them was Fatfat, who stated during the 12 August 2010 committee session that "it is necessary to specify the role of the parliament within this draft law."[43] During the same session, MP Nabil De Freige continued by affirming that "by providing such extensive authority to the minister you are allowing him to take on the structural organization and authority of the legislator." Similarly, other MPs such as Ghassan Moukheiber and Michel Helou argued that the parliament must ensure it takes on a more potent role within the management sector through the OPRL and through ensuring its role in deciding on upcoming pieces of legislation.

Revenue management: obsessed with an SWF

Oil and gas revenues provide an opportunity for developing countries to promote economic and social development, build human capital, and reduce infrastructure gaps. Good governance in revenue management—which encompasses the proper division of roles and responsibilities, effective oversight, and strong accountability mechanisms—is a key prerequisite to reaching these ends (Lahn *et al.* 2007). Norway's success in escaping the resource curse and establishing an exemplary sovereign wealth fund (SWF) is largely due to its institutions that ensure fiscal discipline (Anderson, Curristine, and Merk 2006).[44]

While Lebanon has yet to find oil and gas reserves, it is also still far from establishing the right framework to manage revenues. Although the OPRL references establishing an SWF, this has yet to materialize. Based on committee deliberations, MPs seem to hold opposing views on how its governance structure might be set up.

Article 3 of the OPRL briefly references the allocation of oil and gas revenues to an SWF, stating that "net proceeds collected or received by the government arising out of petroleum activities or petroleum rights shall be placed in a sovereign fund." While the law stops short of dictating how the fund will be managed, leaving the issue to be addressed in a "specific law," it allows for the "capital and part of the proceeds" to be partially invested in an "investment fund for future generations" and another "part to be spent according to standards that will guarantee the rights of the state."

---

[43] Minutes of the parliamentary committee meeting held on 12/8/2010.

[44] Norway's legislature, the *Storting*, has set the framework for the fund in the Government Pension Fund Act. The Ministry of Finance has the formal responsibility of managing the fund. The fund is placed in the form of a Norwegian krone deposit with the Central Bank (Norges Bank) which handles its operational management (Nakhle 2017).

This article alone—one of 77 in the OPRL—was subject to the lion's share of debate in the parliament when the law was voted on. There was major disagreement on how money should be managed, and by which institution. One group of parliamentarians advocated for the establishment of a sovereign fund based on their belief that incorporating revenue into the state's budget would lead to corruption and embezzlement. They contended that an independent fund would guarantee impartiality from political interference as well as sustainability through continuous investment into the fund. For instance, Berri stated that "These revenues transform an offshore resource into a financial resource. Therefore, and in accordance with the Norwegian experience and many other [reputable] countries, we must develop an SWF for our resources to be sovereign. This fund will serve intergenerational purposes through investing money in this fund. Even though it is tempting to use the revenues to repay the debt, a fund will guarantee funds for future generations on the one hand and ensure stability on the other hand."[45] Bassil, on 12 August 2010, stated that "The whole point of the fund is that the resources remain independent and are not channelled in any way through the state budget."[46]

Other MPs had opposing views. They were inclined toward having revenues—at least in part—managed by the Ministry of Finance (MOF), COM, or the parliament. As such, the revenues would feed into the state's budget and be used in part to pay off debt. For instance, Robert Ghanem argued that, "when deciding on the financial parameters and revenue management, we should take into consideration the MOF's opinion. Therefore a representative of the ministry should be taking part in this conversation."[47] MP Assem Kanso raised the bar and suggested annulling the SWF and, "instead, the revenues will feed into the MOF, which is responsible for the state's revenues."[48] However, Moukheiber stated that oil money "should be part of the budget law approved by the parliament. Therefore, the parliament should have full control over the destiny of these resources." In between the two camps, MP Antoine Zahra stated "I am [in favor of] establishing an individual account for resource revenues. However, this account should be situated within the MOF and not in an SWF. The MOF will then invest part of this money for intergenerational purposes. However, it is unconstitutional for "public money" to sit anywhere other than within the MOF." On the same day, MP Ghazi Yousef stated that "We shouldn't commit ourselves to keeping all of the revenues within a fund. On the contrary, we should retain some flexibility, by keeping some of the revenues within the state budget to be used as is needed."[49]

Examining the full transcript of the deliberation, MPs' positions on how to manage oil and gas proceeds could be classified into two groups (Figure 2.3): the first group, comprising 36 percent of parliamentarians, expressed full commitment to channelling all revenues to an SWF. By contrast, the second group—about 64 percent of MPs (the sum of the first three columns in Figure 2.3)—advocated for allocating revenues, at

---

[45] Minutes of the parliamentary committee meeting held on 28/6/2010.
[46] Minutes of the parliamentary committee meeting held on 12/8/2010.
[47] Minutes of the parliamentary committee meeting held on 12/7/2010.
[48] Minutes of the parliamentary committee meeting held on 12/8/2010.
[49] Minutes of the parliamentary committee meeting held on 12/8/2010.

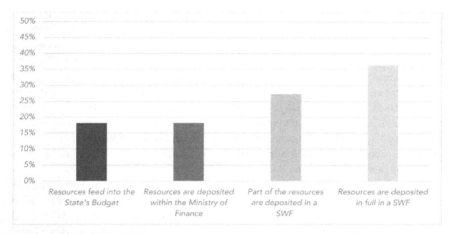

Figure 2.3 Oil revenue allocation.
Source: Compiled by authors based on parliamentary deliberations.

least part of them, to the government or ministry's budget. Within this group, parliamentarians suggested different mechanisms by which the state could control revenues: 18 percent believed that the resources should feed directly into the state budget (column 1), 18 percent believed that resources should be controlled by the MOF (column 2), and 27 percent believed that only part of the funds should be kept in an SWF, with the rest added to the state's budget (column 3).

Lebanon has yet to establish a proper governance structure that clearly identifies the role of the government and governing bodies, as well as who will be responsible for managing an SWF (Atallah et al. 2018 and Nakhle 2017). Although the parliament established a committee to draft legislation on administering an SWF in early 2018, this committee has yet to meet. In the absence of a strong public finance framework including a strong accountability mechanism, the risks of mismanaging oil and gas revenues are real.

Monitoring and regulating the sector: no serious oversight

The monitoring and regulation function provides assurances that policies are being adhered to and national goals are being met (Lahn et al. 2007). This includes parliamentary financial and technical oversight, data auditing, and oversight of government agencies. It may also include adopting rules and standards for the industry, monitoring performance, and ensuring compliance through legislation.[50] Specialist parliamentary committees can be part of the auditing process and special interest NGOs can help communicate society's expectations for the sector (AGORA 2013). In the mid-2010s, for example, the Ghanaian Parliament passed two pieces of legislation—

---

[50] Organisation for Economic Co-operation and Development. 2012. "Best Practice Principles for Improving Regulatory Enforcement and Inspections".

the Petroleum Revenue Management Bill (PMRB) and the Petroleum Bill (Exploration and Production)—which demonstrated commitments to public accountability (Thurber, Hults, and Heller, 2010). In developed countries, including Norway, a petroleum act entails adequate environmental and social regulations as well as the establishment of an independent, competent authority charged with approving and monitoring environmental and social impact assessments and management plans, in addition to enforcing compliance. The OPRL places the responsibility of monitoring and supervising petroleum activities on the minister, but remains mute on who, in turn, should be in charge of monitoring the minister. There is no mention in the law about the parliament's role in holding the COM and the minister accountable for its performance within the sector.

Not only did the parliament fail to develop accountability measures within the law, it did not hold the government accountable when the sector's development was stalled for more than three years. After all, the speaker of the parliament and many MPs called for the parliamentary committee to approve the law quickly in 2010 to deter Israel from "stealing" offshore gas from fields that are near to the border. When the government failed to pass the two decrees necessary to start the bidding process, MPs did not find it imperative to compel it to do so, despite their expressed concerns over the purported Israeli threat.

Some MPs voiced concerns regarding the delay in oversight sessions.[51] However, their concerns fell on deaf ears. For instance, Qabbani stated on 2 August 2011: "Last August we issued, at a marathon pace, the OPRL. Within this law we agreed on establishing a petroleum administration. It is a waste for this country if we do not establish this administration and move forward with the sector." On the same day, MP Ali Fayad stated: "This government managed to put the oil and gas sector on track. But I would like to remind you how Berri pushed for this sector and "obliged" the approval of the OPRL. So now I wonder, with such an important sector related to the economic environment and the future of the country, why has this government failed to move the sector forward?"[52]

While many international companies applied to be part of the qualification round, two concerns emerged. First, two of these companies were established only a few weeks before the deadline and hence had no experience in the oil and gas sector. This raised the possibility that Lebanese businessmen, in possible partnerships with political leaders, may gain access to large rents associated with upstream activities without having the necessary experience (Leenders 2018). The second concern is that several international companies that were pre-qualified are actually co-owned by each other. While this may not be illegal, it does open up the possibility of collusion among firms when they submit their bids. When both issues were raised with the LPA, no satisfactory answers were provided, raising some questions about the credibility of the qualification process. In addition, the ministry and the LPA failed to release full ownership data on pre-qualified companies, reducing the value of what otherwise appears to be a transparent pre-qualification process (Atallah 2017).

---

[51] MPs who expressed concern for the delay include: Mohammad Qabani, Marwan Fares, Ali Fayad, Ghassan Moukheiber, Joseph Maalouf, and Ayoub Hmeid.
[52] Minutes of the parliamentary committee meeting held on 2/8/2010.

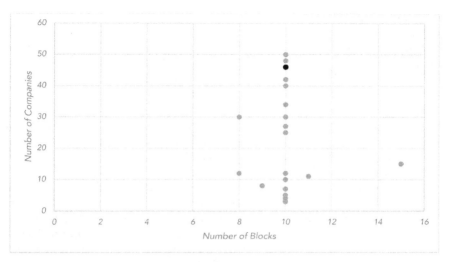

Figure 2.4 MPs' knowledge of the number of pre-qualified companies and number of blocks.

Note: The correct answer is the black marker.

Source: Based on a survey of 65 Lebanese MPs conducted by LCPS in 2016.

As for the parliament's role in monitoring the sector, its work has been confined to reviewing draft laws while largely avoiding reviews of various ministries' activities. For instance, the Public Works, Water and Energy Committee—which is responsible for overseeing activities and operations within the sector—has held 210 meetings in the last four years. However, it has not seriously followed up on or questioned the government's delay in passing the two decrees (Atallah 2018).

Moreover, for parliamentarians to play an effective role in oversight, they need to have some knowledge of the sector. A survey of MPs conducted by LCPS in 2016 indicates that MPs do not know basic information about the oil and gas sector. In fact, out of 65 interviewed MPs, only one MP knew the number of blocks comprising Lebanon's offshore area (which is ten) and the number of pre-qualified companies (which was 46, prior to re-opening the pre-qualification in February 2017) (Figure 2.4). Indeed, it stands to reason that absent basic knowledge of the sector, parliamentarians cannot play an effective role in the oversight of the sector.

Contextualizing the parliament's role in the oil and gas sector

This chapter demonstrates how the Lebanese Parliament has failed to contribute to the proper governance of the oil and gas sector. It fell short in correcting discrepancies in the decision making process caused by the government. For instance, it failed to compel the government to develop an energy policy, based on which the OPRL should have been drafted. While MPs voiced their concern about not having a single petroleum law, they succumbed to pressure to adopt an offshore law, which can be followed by the passage of an onshore law in the future, an action that is contrary to common practice. Despite raising this concern, MPs were unable to consolidate the two unnecessary and simultaneous tracks—legislative and executive—that were simultaneously working on the draft law. Furthermore, MPs did not impose strict parameters and modalities within the OPRL to reduce flexibility and the possibility of corruption that may arise thereafter regarding negotiations with oil companies.

More generally, MPs did not create a role for the parliament in the sector's development as other countries have done. Concerning oversight, the parliament did not hold the government accountable for delaying the licensing round for more than 40 months, nor did the parliament demonstrate interest in allegations of misconduct with respect to the pre-qualification of some companies.

The failure of the parliament to assume its responsibilities has deeper roots. Such practices are not confined to the oil and gas sector. A recent study on the Lebanese Parliament shows that only 9 percent of the laws passed from June 2009 to April 2017 addressed peoples' most pressing concerns (Atallah 2018). The parliament also did not hold the government accountable on issues not relating to the petroleum sector during this period despite many serious challenges facing the country.

Based on an LCPS survey of 65 MPs, parliamentarians—according to their own estimate—spend only 20 percent of their time legislating and 10 percent monitoring the government (Figure 2.5). They spend the remaining 70 percent of their time interacting with fellow MPs, the media, and their constituencies to cement clientelistic relationships.

Moreover, an analysis of the legislative process, captured through deliberation analyses, indicates high levels of political interference that ignored the will of the majority. For instance, while many MPs wanted more time to discuss the OPRL, they were forced by a few MPs to expedite the process. When MPs requested that experts be

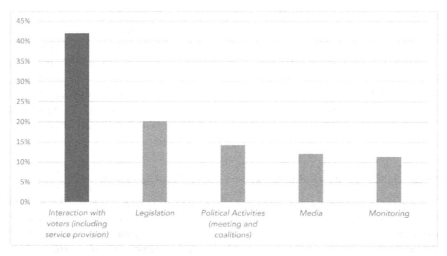

Figure 2.5 How MPs allocate their time.

Source: Based on a survey of 65 Lebanese MPs conducted by LCPS in 2016.

consulted on oil and gas matters, they were ignored. Furthermore, when many MPs called for a decentralized role for the LPA, the speaker of the parliament along with the prime minister imposed their will on the parliament—silencing the majority of MPs. When MPs requested more time to study the draft law before voting on it, they were pushed to approve the law despite flaws in both the process and the substance.[53]

Conclusion and recommendations

Based on the analysis in this chapter, the following recommendations are suggested in terms of enhancing the parliament's role in the oil and gas sector.

Strengthen and reform parliamentary committees and other supporting bodies

The parliament cooperates with many subsidiary organs in carrying out its legislative and supervisory duties (Atallah 2018). The literature highlights how committee work plays a leading role in the management of extractive resources (AGORA 2013). Extractive industry policies are most effective when they are well managed and monitored, and when the results are publicized. Through organized and coordinated committee work, legislators can use their oversight authority to affirm their role in representative and accountable policy implementation. While the Committee on Public Works is responsible for oil- and gas-related activities, including legislation and monitoring of the sector, an independent committee for oil and gas should be established for legislators to organize and coordinate their involvement in the extractive industries sector. This committee could also coordinate with other involved committees, including: budget, anti-corruption, public accounts, and others that have purview over various aspects of the oil and gas sector.

There is an urgent need to intensify the frequency of committee meetings by setting weekly timetables and specific meeting agendas to organize priorities according to the requirements of their legislative duties. Moreover, the parliament should consider establishing a mechanism to assess committees' work periodically in order to measure the pace at which committees conduct their work and scrutinize the type and quality of work being done by each committee.

Fortify accountability channels between the legislative and the executive

Parliamentary oversight of the government's work constitutes a cornerstone of democratic parliamentary systems. Thus, this reality entails close coordination and cooperation between the two bodies, and the intensification of oversight work exercised

---

[53] MP Ahmad Fatfat expressed his frustration during this session by stating "I want to express my objection because I did not have the opportunity to review this law as I just received it this morning [before the session]."

by the parliament. The Lebanese Parliament must adopt new tools to carry out this role in order to enhance communication channels with the government and ministries. For example, MPs could schedule weekly or monthly periodic meetings to hold question-and-answer sessions with different ministries. For such measures to be successful, it is necessary that the parliament tighten oversight regulations clarifying the consequences in the event ministries ignore requests to share information and public officials do not update or respond to MPs' questions.

Increase transparency

This chapter establishes that the principles of transparency and access to information are fundamental to successful governance of the oil and gas sector. Transparent governance entails that information be made available at regular intervals and in a timely fashion upon request. Opportunities for corruption in extractive industries begin at the contracting or procurement phase, something to which Lebanon is particularly susceptible since the decision making process which led to the establishment of the sector lacks transparency. If the rules and terms for bids or concessions are made clear and available to the parliament, detecting and correcting non-compliance with contractual terms would become an easier task.

Although the Access to Information Law was passed in early 2017, the records of parliamentary committee meetings that were held prior to the law's passage are not covered under its provisions. Routine disclosure can also play an important role in addressing a culture of secrecy. Transparency should stem from the parliament, the most representative body. Accordingly, the parliament should update the methods of documenting general records, including meeting minutes, and ensuring that all records are accessible to the public. Moreover, many sessions, particularly oversight sessions, should be open to the public, including media and civil society organizations.

In response to this transparency challenge, many local and international actors are calling for Lebanon to sign up to the Extractive Industries Transparency Initiative (EITI), which aims to enhance transparency in the sector. Despite the best of intentions, EITI is unlikely to solve Lebanon's problems. While EITI procedure succeeds in auditing money transfers into and out of the sector, it is by no means sufficient to hold the government accountable.

Develop an integrated legislative vision to strengthen policies

With the exception of some of the initiatives launched by parliamentary committees to chart a legislative road map for national issues, the parliament rarely follows national policy planning in several sectors, as exemplified in legislation regarding the oil and gas sector. By analyzing the OPRL, it becomes evident that MPs did not indicate their intention or readiness to work on establishing a general framework that harmonizes a coherent vision or strategy for the sector. On the contrary, MPs' discussions were focused on criticizing terminology and challenging political rivals. Within this context, it is necessary for parliamentarians to put forward comprehensive proposals for national strategies concerning the oil and gas sector. This could be supported by forming research teams that review proposals and draft laws, presenting economic and social feasibility studies, and engaging in interdisciplinary research support to bolster the legislative processes.

Consult with different stakeholders, particularly experts and civil society organizations

Parliamentary committees should consult with key experts and civil society organizations for the purpose of gaining insight as well as building consensus on the development of the sector.

Local coordination will make project implementation more effective since resources and time can be saved if best practices are shared. The parliament could engage civil bodies in the legislative process to meet the needs and demands of citizens from different regions and in different sectors. Moreover, the parliament could reintroduce means and procedures, such as petitions and complaints, and develop mechanisms to stimulate continuous and direct communication between legislators and citizens. Finally, it is essential that the parliament intensify meetings and discussions with civil society organizations and media to foster an open process of debate and communication.

Improve knowledge of oil and gas sector governance and operations

For the parliament to be effective in governing extractive resources, it is essential that MPs, support staff, and subsidiary organs be well informed about the oil and gas sector and how it operates. This requires providing intensive training courses for parliamentarians and other staff members working on oil- and gas-related operations to improve their technical understanding of the sector and their skills in legislative drafting and oversight operations. These measures could be complemented by hosting seminars to inform parliamentarians about the experiences of other countries and international standards and approaches.

Parliaments can use various oversight tools to retain this information from concerned public administrations. For example, committees can request that senior government officials provide briefings on a regular basis.

The challenge facing the parliament is much deeper. As argued by Atallah and Geagea (2018), parliament's inability to legislate and hold the government accountable is largely due to the absence of incentives for political parties and their MPs to serve the interests of citizens. Two reasons stand out in this regard. The first pertains largely to the relationship between voters and politicians, as the electoral law and voting behavior have largely undermined the meaning of elections as an opportunity for voters to elect those who serve their interests while holding others accountable. In fact, the clientelistic nature of the relationship between voters and politicians, along with sectarian discourse and fear, has allowed political elites to hold their constituents captive. The second factor concerns the consociational political system, under which the COM and parliament members are represented by different confessional groups. While this system ensures sectarian representation, it undermines accountability since the political system in practice oscillates between political collusion when parties are

60   *The Future of Petroleum in Lebanon*

in agreement, and paralysis when they are in disagreement—leaving little space for accountability mechanisms to be effective, if put in place at all. While this issue does not pertain to the oil and gas sector per se, it will negatively impact the development of the sector due to the weak—or largely non-existent—incentives for MPs to exercise their oversight roles.

References

Authored references

Anderson, B., Curristine, T., and Merk, O. (2006). "Budgeting in Norway." *OECD Journal on Budgeting*, 6 (1).

Arab Barometer. (2011–13). Online Data Analysis Portal.

Atallah, S. (2017). "New Strategy Needed for Lebanon's Oil and Gas Sector." *Executive Magazine*.

Atallah, S. and Helou, Z. (2017). "Lebanon's New Electoral Law: Proportional in Form, Majoritarian at Heart." *Lebanese Center for Policy Studies*.

Chohan, U.W. (2015). *Corporate Leverage in Emerging Markets: Discussing the Implications for Legislative Fiscal Oversight*. University of New South Wales.

Collier, P. (2007). *The Bottom Billion: Why the Poorest Countries are Failing and What Can Be Done About It*. Oxford University Press.

Lahn, G., Marcel, V., Mitchell, J., Myers, K., and Stevens, P. (2007). *Good Governance of the National Petroleum Sector*. Chatham House.

Marcel, V. (2013). *Guidelines for Good Governance in Emerging Oil and Gas Producers*. Chatham House.

Nakhle, C. (2017). *Management and Governance of the Oil and Gas Sector: A Comparative Study between Lebanon, Cyprus, Israel, and Norway*.

NRGI. (2010). *The Value Chain*. Natural Resource Governance Institute: https://resourcegovernance.org/analysis-tools/publications/value-chain

OECD. (2012). Best Practice Principles for Improving Regulatory Enforcement and Inspections.

Offshore Petroleum Resources Law. (2010). http://www.lpa.gov.lb/pdf/OPRL%20-%20English.pdf

Parliament Bylaws. (n.d.). Lebanese Parliament: https://www.lp.gov.lb/CustomPage.aspx?id=37&masterId=1

Robinson, J.A., Torvik, R., and Verdier, T. (2006). "Political Foundations of the Resource Curse." *Journal of Development Economics*, 447–68.

Ross, M. (2001). *Does Oil Hinder Democracy?* Project MUSE.

Sala-i-Martin, X. and Artadi, E.V. (2002). *Economic Growth and Investment in the Arab World*. Columbia University, Department of Economics.

The Taif Agreement. (1989). *https://www.un.int/lebanon/sites/www.un.int/files/Lebanon/the_taif_agreement_english_version_.pdf*

The World Bank Institute. (2013). *Parliamentary Oversight of the Extractive Industries Sector*.

Thurber, M., Hults, D., and Heller, P. (2010). "The Limits of Institutional Design in Oil Sector Governance: Exporting the 'Norwegian Model'." *ISA Annual Convention 2010*.

Whitton, H. (2001). *Implementing Effective Ethics Standards in Government and the Civil Service*. Transparency International.

World Bank. (2003). *Breaking the Conflict Trap: Civil War and Development Policy*. Oxford University Press.

World Economic Forum. (2017). *The Global Competitiveness Report 2016–2017*.

Non-authored references

AGORA. 2009. "Parliaments & Extractive Industries." The World Bank. http://www.agora-parl.org

AGORA. 2013. "Parliamentary Oversight of the Extractive Industries Sector." The World Bank. http://www.agora-parl.org

World Economic Forum. 2016. "The Global Competitiveness Report 2016–2017."

3

Spoils of Oil?

Assessing and Mitigating the Risks of Corruption in Lebanon's Emerging Offshore Petroleum Sector

Reinoud Leenders

Introduction

The discovery of oil and gas deposits off the coast of Lebanon has yet to be confirmed but it has already inspired hope and optimism for the country's future economic viability and development. Significant revenues extracted from producing oil and gas, or "petroleum" to denote both, indeed can become a source of wealth and sustained economic growth if managed properly and in accordance with internationally tested good practices adjusted to Lebanon's political and institutional conditions. However, a large body of literature and international experience shows that the extraction and marketing of oil and gas resources—in addition to associated revenue management and expenditure policies—are exposed to high risks of lacking transparency, discretionary decision making, the absence of accountability, favoritism, rampant corruption, and/or waste. Furthermore, a windfall of natural resource rents, or the expectation thereof, also tends to encourage a scramble for and brings about high competition over resources, while (perceptions of) entrenched corruption and unjust distribution of economic opportunities and revenues may set the stage for new and/or reinvigorated conflicts. Given its own troublesome past and experience of rampant corruption and civil conflict, these general risks are especially pertinent in the Lebanese context. For now, and despite clear efforts to counter corruption and increase transparency and accountability, the country's institutional capacities appear too weak to meet the heightened need for a solid framework that regulating the petroleum sector and expected windfall of revenues typically calls for. At the same time, Lebanon cannot afford oil and gas discoveries that magnify or add to its already high levels of corruption, worsen real and perceived injustice in governance, and fuel conflict.

This chapter proceeds as follows. Section one presents an analytical framework for assessing and mitigating the risks of corruption in Lebanon's nascent petroleum sector. It draws on discussions with Lebanese officials in relevant government institutions, stakeholders in the private oil and gas sector, Lebanon's business community more

64   *The Future of Petroleum in Lebanon*

generally, its civil society, and some foreign diplomats closely following Lebanon's petroleum developments. It was agreed with interviewees, unless stated otherwise, to cite them without attribution in order to encourage a frank discussion about what are often considered highly contentious issues. It should be emphasized that the more critical observations in this chapter do not suggest that corruption or cronyism has occurred or will take place; the chapter merely flags the risks or probabilities of such practices if not addressed properly.

Subsequent sections of this chapter assess the general risks of corruption in connection to Lebanon's emerging oil and gas sector, identify which institutional and regulatory measures and policy tools have thus far been put into place and assess whether these are sufficiently robust to counter or reduce corruption risks, and formulate proposals to help inform a growing debate on how the risks of corruption and malpractice associated with Lebanon's emerging oil and gas sector—across its value chain—can and should be reduced.[1]

The petroleum–corruption nexus

Numerous studies have demonstrated that the extraction of natural resources generally, and oil and gas more specifically, often comes with heightened levels of corruption and malpractice in governance (Ross 2003, 24–6; Marshall 2001; Sachs and Warner 1999, 13–38). This literature, mostly drawing on large-N quantitative methodologies, was developed in an attempt to understand the exact causal mechanisms at work in purported correlations between natural resource abundance, variously defined, and inferior or disappointing levels of sustained economic growth and development. From this perspective, institutions matter in that they are tasked with formulating and carrying out vital policies to counter or prevent a host of harmful economic and financial effects of revenue windfalls from the extraction of natural resources, including "Dutch disease," the volatility of oil and gas prices, and revenue and environmental challenges. While from this perspective the need for solid and sound institutions and policies is particularly underscored and even becomes acute as soon as natural resource rents arrive, many have argued that the relative financial and technical complexity of the oil and gas industry and their state ownership, in combination with large rents controlled by state agencies and a host of political effects ascribed to them, often tend to undermine states' capacity to build and sustain such necessary institutional qualities (Papyrakis and Gerlagh 2004, McPherson and MacSearraigh 2007). A lack of transparency, reduced levels of accountability, patronage substituting for political representation, and the temptation to waste rent windfalls on white elephant projects are in this context variously argued to cause systemic malpractices in governance as failing institutions cause "mother nature to corrupt" (Leite and Weidmann 1999).

---

[1] This chapter does not cover or speculate on current or future developments in Lebanon's expected onshore potential for oil and gas, which—if confirmed—would considerably complicate the analysis and very likely further underscore the risks of both corruption and conflict.

The suggested correlations and causal mechanisms involving the oil–corruption nexus continue to be fiercely disputed in academic debates, as are most other dimensions of the alleged "natural resource curse" (Brunnschweiler and Bulte 2008, John 2007, Ledermann and Maloney 2007). Without intending to comprehensively review this literature, for the purposes of this chapter three observations in this context must suffice, as they will steer this chapter's assessment of the risks of corruption in Lebanon's emerging oil and gas industry and related issues of governance.

First, not all oil- and gas-producing countries suffer from heightened or extraordinary levels of corruption. In this context, it has been commonly observed that it matters a great deal whether the country already has solid institutions in place at the time that petroleum is discovered, in which case it is more likely that appropriate institutional adjustments are made to counter or cushion the perilous effects of the "natural resource curse" (Frankel 2012, Smith 2007, Engen *et al.* 2012). Conversely, "green field" countries with weak pre-existing institutional capacities and already alarming levels of pre-discovery corruption are especially at risk of falling into the oil–corruption trap. Even so, not all countries with modest or even weak institutional capacities entered a spiral of corruption when they found themselves endowed with ample natural resources. Indeed, oil and gas producing countries, even when relatively new to the sector, show varying levels of institutional development and associated corruption. Among these countries one can find an array of institutions and regulatory measures that had variable effects on petroleum-related corruption levels.

Historical institutional antecedents may partly explain such variation, but these and post-discovery institution building relevant to the oil and gas sector do not come about in a vacuum. In common with institutions more generally, oil and gas sector institutions are generated, shaped, and underpinned by public decision making processes and political struggles. This leads to a second observation that, although perhaps sounding self-evident to some, is often neglected in the predominantly economistic literature on the "natural resource curse". To understand and predict whether, why, and how institutions governing the oil and gas sector will be solid enough to withstand corruption, or not, attention should be paid to the "political settlement," or the power constellations and the rules (both written and unwritten) affecting and governing public decision making on creating, sustaining, and reforming relevant institutions. Given countries' specific features in this context, their political settlements should be taken into account in order to both explain their respective existing institutions and prescribe ways in which ensuing levels or risks of corruption can be feasibly mitigated.

Third, economists using large-N studies and operating on highly aggregated levels of analysis involving, inter alia, "natural resource dependency" and "corruption" may have developed a strong nose for "smelling a rat" but they do not tell us much about where, exactly, the rat is hiding. This has repercussions for understanding where, how, and why the risks of corruption manifest themselves, just as it reduces the utility of such studies for proposals to effectively counter more specific risks (Kolstad *et al.* 2008). By contrast, investigative research into corruption in some countries' oil and gas sectors that are most notorious for corruption and malpractices was conducted by such organizations as Global Witness and Human Rights Watch (2010). Such studies have the advantage of identifying relevant bottlenecks in specific contexts, yet they are often highly descriptive in nature to the extent of failing to offer much transferrable knowledge and insights. Others have taken an approach that is perhaps more useful in this context as they propose an assessment of corruption risks along the industry's "value chain," which involves an exploration process, a production process, and a post-production or decommissioning phase (Al-Kasim et al. 2008). Depending on the robustness of regulatory frameworks and institutions tasked with upholding them, opportunities and risks of corruption may flourish variously at all stages in the value chain. Along these lines, Al-Kasim (et al.) focused exclusively on the regulation of the oil industry in its pre-operational and post-operational phases.[2] Building on this approach, one may add the dimension of revenue management and expenditure. As Michael Ross put it succinctly, "the most important political fact about oil—and the reason it leads to so much trouble in so many developing countries—is that the revenues it bestows on governments are unusually large, do not come from taxes, fluctuate unpredictably, and can be easily hidden" (Ross 2012). Depending on what policy choices are made in this context and given the robustness of relevant institutions implementing them, ample opportunities and risks of corruption may arise on the revenue and expenditure side of oil and gas extraction as well.

Using inverse logic, organizations campaigning for good governance in natural resource sectors worldwide have pursued a similarly comprehensive, yet disaggregated approach. For example, Publish What You Pay (PWYP) produced a "chain for change" tracking the need for robust and transparent institutions and policies from the moment of exploration up to dismantling extractive projects (Alba 2009). Together with other organizations, including the Extractive Industries Transparency Initiative (EITI) and Revenue Watch Institute (now the Natural Resource Governance Institute), it designed elaborate recommendations to ensure transparency, accountability, and solid institutional arrangements to govern the natural resource industry in most of its aspects (Ross 2012).[3] However, even when some of these generic recommendations may prove to be highly relevant for Lebanon, they need to be assessed for their appropriateness and feasibility, and tailored to local circumstances. Most importantly from the perspective of this chapter, such recommendations also need to address relevant opportunities and risks of corruption arising from the institutional capacities and underlying political settlement in Lebanon. It is to these conditions that we turn first.

Public institutions, corruption and political settlement in Lebanon

Upon hearing news of a potentially significant petroleum endowment off the country's coast, many Lebanese intuitively sensed the mixed blessing that this may bring. Few do not have some proposal on how to spend the expected revenues in a country that is

---

[2] Supplementary annexes showing risks of corruption throughout the value chain are available on LCPS's website via the following link: https://www.lcps-lebanon.org/publications/1446546839-leenders-paper_eng.qxp_lcps.pdf

[3] A common criticism in this context is that these and other initiatives focus primarily on how revenues accrued from natural resources are collected, not how they are spent.

burdened with public debt, inadequate basic infrastructure and welfare services, and sharp inequalities in terms of income and wealth (Fadlallah 2012). Yet, many commentators, Lebanese and foreign alike, already warned specifically against the risk, and for some even the inevitability, of widespread corruption in Lebanon's emerging petroleum sector. They variously suspect that high levels of corruption will follow from an unhappy mix involving international oil companies not especially reputed for fair and transparent practices; Lebanon's political class that is widely viewed as corrupt, greedy, and looked at with distrust; and a dysfunctional, divided, and gridlocked political process at best geared toward deals "dividing up the cake"[4] (Abu Muslih 2013, Zahi 2013). In short, a windfall of business opportunities and revenues generated by petroleum extraction is widely sensed as carrying serious risks of magnifying these various failings. In response, Lebanese politicians and officials have emphasized that corruption in the emerging governance of the petroleum sector will not be tolerated. Implicitly, legal measures contain a similar pledge. Most importantly, the country's Petroleum Activities Regulations decree (Decree 10289, Article 162) explicitly bans any form of corruption or bribery in the sector, as defined by Lebanese law and international conventions.[5] Furthermore, in May 2017, EITI reported that the Lebanese government expressed its commitment to adhere to its guidelines on transparency (but by February 2018 Lebanon had not yet become a member), which would compel the government to fully disclose its revenues from petroleum activities and establish a multi-stakeholder group to oversee its commitments arising from membership (EITI 2017).

Some may dismiss popularly held views on the risks of corruption in Lebanon's emerging petroleum sector as ill informed (especially on account of the technicalities of the petroleum industry), excessively pessimistic, suffering from unrealistically high expectations, or all of the above. Yet, to the extent that a track record of public institution building and corruption provides a guide to a country's future ability to establish sound and corruption-free institutions governing an emerging petroleum sector, Lebanon's past achievements in this regard constitute a serious source of concern. International indices covering (perceptions of) corruption and bribery levels, in addition to numerous opinion surveys held among the Lebanese population at large and among Lebanese and foreign entrepreneurs, consistently suggest that extremely high corruption levels pervade Lebanon's political system, its public sector, its private sector, and society at large (Transparency International Corruption Perceptions Index 2016 and Global Corruption Barometer 2016, and earlier years).[6] Those indices that have included Lebanon over a longer period of time also alarmingly suggest rising levels of corruption in Lebanon. In comparative terms, they rank Lebanon among the worst affected countries by corruption, both within the Middle East and North Africa (MENA) and worldwide.

---

[4] "In the end everything will be divided up among the main politicians. The people won't get to see anything of it. That's trivial to anyone." Author's interview with Lebanese academic in Beirut, June 2014.

[5] All laws and decrees are available at the LPA website: http://www.lpa.gov.lb.

[6] For a comprehensive overview of Lebanon's scores on such indices and surveys since the early 1990s see Leenders (2012).

Academic research carried out by social scientists and economists, by both international and Lebanese scholars, unanimously confirmed assessments of Lebanon's corruption problem and generally found it to be so engrained as to have become institutionalized in all matters of public life. In my own book, I conducted a qualitative analysis of numerous corruption allegations in the context of a range of public institutions following the signing of the Taef Accord in 1989 until 2012 (Leenders 2012). It detailed how senior policy makers and high-ranking public servants in key sectors of the Lebanese economy and governance, including transportation, healthcare, natural resources and energy, construction, and social assistance programs were implicated in corruption. The study is congruent with the assessments of numerous other scholars that corruption and associated practices of clientelism have permeated Lebanon's state institutions and politicians' relations with the private sector and civil society alike throughout the post-Taef period (Cammet and Issar 2010, Cammet 2011, Chen and Cammet 2012, Stel and Naudé 2013, Baumann 2012, Leenders 2004, Balanche 2012, Gaspard 2004, Kingston 2013, Picard 2000).

None of these dire assessments should be uncritically or automatically applied to forecast what awaits Lebanon in terms of governing the petroleum sector and the management of its revenues. Indeed, key policy makers, highly capable regulators, and civil society activists alike are adamant that with the expected start of petroleum activities and the arrival of their revenues, Lebanon will finally turn its back on inadequate institution building and rampant corruption. As one official at the Ministry of Energy and Water (MEW) stated:

> The governance of the oil sector inevitably will be within the system, whether you like it or not. This leaves two options, forget about it, or create a nucleus that is relatively insulated and does something different. The international oil companies demand quality. In this sense, the petroleum sector provides an opportunity to establish units of new and well-qualified people in several ministries. As there is revenue-making potential, there will be an effort to build sound institutions. Petroleum this way presents an incentive for reform.[7]

Furthermore, the technicalities of the petroleum sector and the institutions created to govern the sector are entirely new, as Lebanon has never embarked on significant petroleum production before. This, one could reason, provides Lebanon with an opportunity to this time create more efficient and less corrupt institutions. Yet, such individual qualities, good intentions, and relatively anomalous features of the petroleum sector should be understood against the systemic causes of widespread institutional failure and corruption in Lebanon generally, which are still far from being addressed. In this context, many rival explanations have been suggested (Leenders 2012). Indeed, it may be argued that an analysis of a complex phenomenon like corruption cannot be mono-causal and, by contrast, will need to be tailored to the specific sector and operations in which it occurs. This offers an additional reason to be cautious about unreservedly juxtaposing Lebanon's overall corruption record to its emerging petroleum sector.

---

[7] Author's interview, Beirut, 20 June 2014.

By comparing the trajectories of various Lebanese sectors and state institutions in which corruption has thrived, one can find clear trends in that they persistently lacked a clear mandate governed by procedures and regulations with robust external checks and controls to ensure accountability, in addition to a separation of public office from private interests (Leenders 2012). Such failings have given way to and become associated with Lebanon's "allotment state" (*dawlat al-muhasasa*) in which fierce struggles over the building of state institutions coexist with an utter disregard for the universal application of institutional rules (Leenders 2012). In this context, the country's political class divides highly prized resources, opportunities, and privileges accrued from the state and its prerogatives among themselves and their allies and, to some extent, they pass it on to their (sectarian) constituencies to ensure their continued political support.

Arguably, Lebanon's political settlement or its post-Taef arrangement to manage multiple conflicts and generate decisions on institutions and policies is at the root of the country's endemic failure to produce robust institutions able to withstand high levels of corruption. One of the major characteristics and indeed flaws of the political settlement was that it converted the political and military stalemate of the late 1980s into a new arrangement for public decision making that was similarly characterized by gridlock and fragmentation of power. In brief, Lebanon's political settlement significantly shaped the process of decision making and institution building in Lebanon's Second Republic (Leenders 2012).[8] Even when the exact manifestations and relative weight of each of its main features have somewhat changed and are likely to change in the future, they by and large have remained the same and jointly constitute the context in which Lebanon's regulatory and institutional framework for its petroleum sector has been designed, will be further developed, and will be enforced.

Assessing Lebanon's first steps in petroleum governance and the risks of corruption

Since 2010, Lebanon reached a number of milestones in its preparations for petroleum sector governance. Overall, stakeholders and observers consider the process to be reasonably transparent and promising, even when frustration has been or was rife about the necessary steps and policies being significantly delayed on account of the country's political gridlock. Within these political constraints, the parliament approved the Offshore Petroleum Resources Law (OPRL) in August 2010,[9] which presents a general framework on how the sector should be organized, regulated, and governed. It was followed in April 2012 by Decree 7968 (7 April 2012) establishing the Lebanese Petroleum Administration

---

[8] It did so by way of an extreme dispersal of power and associated quasi-permanent gridlock in decision making, the predominance of the troika, and the politics of *muhasasa*; continuous attempts to circumvent the built-in stalemates of the political arrangement laid out in the Taef Accord and the constitution; weak popular support for political elites, exposing them to confessionalist strategies and narrow, local agendas; and the overriding role of the interests of external powers in Lebanon, as well as their manipulation of political and social divides in Lebanon.

[9] Lebanese Parliament. 2010. Offshore Petroleum Resources Law. Law 132, 24 August.

70 *The Future of Petroleum in Lebanon*

(LPA), whose members were appointed on 4 December 2012. In February 2013, the Council of Ministers (COM) approved the Petroleum Activities Regulations for Lebanon (Decree 10289), which provides general guidelines for commercial involvement in the sector and their regulation. In accordance with this emerging legal framework, companies were invited in March 2013 to submit their credentials for the purpose of pre-qualification, which, in turn, allowed such companies to submit their bids for the envisaged licensing round. Decree 9882 (13 February 2013) was issued calling on interested companies to apply for pre-qualification by detailing further conditions and required documents. Out of 52 applying companies from 25 countries, 12 applicants pre-qualified as "operators" and 34 companies as "non-operators."[10]

Subsequently, two decrees (one on delineating the ten offshore production "blocks," the other on the model contract, or model Exploration and Production Agreement, EPA) were held up in the COM for approval. After a new cabinet was formed—led by then Prime Minister Tamam Salam—in March 2014, an inter-ministerial committee was set up to study the two draft decrees but no agreement was reached on their exact contents. As a result, the actual invitation for the tender for EPAs faced lengthy delays. The process involving Lebanon's petroleum activities was held up by the country's general political paralysis until, in December 2016, a new government, led by Prime Minister Saad Hariri, was appointed. In January 2017, a model EPA was released and a decree (Decree 42) was issued delineating Lebanon's offshore production blocks.[11] From February to March 2017, a second pre-qualification round was held, as the new Minister of Energy and Water Cesar Abi Khalil explained that some companies may have lost interest while others that did not meet the requirements before may now be able to (Alieh 2017). This time, 53 companies pre-qualified, including 13 operators and 40 non-operators.[12] In September 2017, the parliament approved a law (Law 57) to tax 20 percent on revenues from petroleum operations. Interested companies were given until October 2017 to place their bids in the first licensing round for offshore petroleum exploration. Only one consortium—comprising Total (France), Eni (Italy), and Novatek (Russia)—submitted bids, one for block 4 and another for block 9, and was awarded two licenses in December that year.

The Lebanese Petroleum Administration

The Lebanese media have generally welcomed the establishment of the LPA as a positive step toward competent and responsible institution building in a country that has lacked such qualities for a long time. One MP, a member of the political bloc (the Free Patriotic Movement) to which former Minister of Energy and Water Gebran Bassil belongs, went as far as to claim that "the new petroleum administration is the first proper public institution created since the times of [former President] Fuad Chehab."[13]

---

[10] Lebanese Republic, Ministry of Energy and Water Resources, Petroleum Administration.

[11] Decree 43 dated 1 January 2017 http://www.lpa.gov.lb/pdf/Decree%20%2043%20-%20EPA%20-%20Rev%206%20-%2029-09-2015.pdf.

[12] The model Exploration and Production Agreement is available at http://www.lpa.gov.lb/prequalification.php

[13] Author's interview, Beirut, 3 June 2014.

The OPRL and Decree 7968 essentially mandate the LPA with an overall advisory and supportive role in preparing and applying the technical and financial framework for the country's emerging petroleum sector. Although separate from the MEW, the LPA falls under the ministry's tutelage and, indirectly, is heavily reliant on the COM in making key decisions. As such, the LPA has some of the features of a regulatory body but, arguably, it lacks sufficient institutional independence that is required to perform its hefty tasks without political interference.

In this, the LPA differs from what was initially envisaged. From the mid-2000s onward, draft laws were drawn up, foremost involving advisors at the MEW assisted by experts sent by the Norwegian Oil for Development Program from 2007 onward. These called for a more independent regulator for the petroleum sector by insulating it from political interference, whether by the MEW or the COM.[14] Some of those involved in these early efforts stressed that a fully independent regulator was not considered feasible, and perhaps would even be undesirable, as it would run the risk of simply being sidelined or marginalized by political authorities.[15] However, before adopting the OPRL, objections raised within the COM caused this envisaged independence, even if relative in nature, to be watered down further. Perhaps most importantly, the LPA lacks financial independence as it is stipulated that its budget is to be part of the overall budget of the MEW.

The LPA board consists of six members. On the positive side, they are barred from having any personal interests, directly or indirectly, in the contracts concluded by the LPA or with any company working in the field by being related through any of their relatives (up to the fourth degree). After leaving office former LPA staff are not to engage in any private sector activity pertaining to petroleum in Lebanon for at least two years. Furthermore, the presidency of the board rotates among the six members, which can be read as a measure working against potential abuse of power. Their high salaries, at least by Lebanese public sector standards (Leenders 2016), also can be viewed as mitigating the risk of bribery, provided that one subscribes to the disputed claim that susceptibility to bribery correlates with low or more modest salaries, and vice versa (Abbink 2000).[16]

All LPA board members were appointed by the COM upon the recommendation of the Minister of Energy and Water. In practice, this legally prescribed formula necessitated a grand political bargain involving key sectarian and political leaders backing their preferred candidates from a shortlist based on individual merit and experience. This pre-selection was done by a committee comprising a representative of the Civil Service Board (the state's human resources agency), the minister of state for administrative reform, the deputy governor of the central bank (acting for the office for the minister of state for administrative reform), and the minister of energy and water.

---

[14] Author's interview with Ali Berro, former advisor at the MEW, Beirut, 6 June 2014, and with a foreign oil expert, Beirut, 20 June 2014.

[15] Ibid.

[16] Such reasoning does not seem to have been a prime factor in the decision to place LPA salaries at higher than usual levels. Instead, salary scales prevailing in the worldwide petroleum sector generally were viewed as necessitating higher salaries for LPA staff in order to attract and retain qualified people. Author's interview with MEW official, Beirut, 20 June 2014.

The committee received more than 600 applications, 18 of which were shortlisted and presented to the COM.[17] Most agree that the selection process was unusually rigorous and transparent, and that the six selected candidates were highly capable and experienced, as some were drawn from renowned international petroleum companies. Concerns remain, however, that regardless of their qualifications the board members will be beholden to their political backers, thus making them indirectly vulnerable to such politicians' possible conflicts of interest. Should these fears prove to be founded, the LPA board members risk sharing the fate of many other first grade public servants throughout Lebanon's public administration (Leenders 2012). In addition, there may be a risk that a lack of political agreement on future replacements (following expiration of the LPA board's six-year mandate or after individual dismissals or resignations) may cause the LPA board to sustain vacancies crippling the agency, as happened frequently since the early 1990s in numerous key state agencies and ministries more generally.[18]

Finally, and despite the potential avenues that all these features already hypothetically offer in terms of political interference and influence, the LPA's role is of a mainly advisory nature in relation to the overriding role of the Minister of Energy and Water who, in turn, is to obtain the endorsement of the COM for his/her policies and decisions. In short, within this institutional setup, and despite the rigorous process that resulted in the appointment of individuals with the highest qualifications and right intentions, the LPA runs a significant risk of becoming subjected to political pressure and influence. This vulnerability is underscored by the power of the Minister of Energy and Water to present LPA staff to the state's disciplinary board for alleged violations of the law and neglect of duty, thereby giving the minister, at least hypothetically, a powerful tool to press dissenting staff into compliance.

Officials at the MEW counter that, even when the LPA is not fully independent, it still has important leverage in the power structure involving the MEW and the COM.[19] They point out that the Minister of Energy and Water cannot diverge from the LPA's recommendations regarding key policies or measures in the petroleum sector, just as the minister will have to explain his/her position to the COM if he/she does. Yet, it is doubtful that this will be sufficient, as it does not shield the LPA from possible pressures or overriding powers of the COM, with or without collusion with the Minister of Energy and Water.

In the hypothetical event that the LPA succumbs to political pressure and associated malpractices in regulating and governing the petroleum sector, chances are that with current auditing mechanisms and their administrative capacities this may not be properly detected. External auditing of the LPA's activities is to be carried out a posteriori by the Court of Accounts (CA, *Diwan al-Muhasaba*), the state's financial watchdog (Law 132, Article 10). Unless this agency is dramatically revamped and significantly strengthened—a necessity underscored repeatedly since the early 1990s but never seriously followed up—it will not be able to carry out this task adequately. The CA currently has no expertise on matters related to the oil and gas sector and,

[17] Author's interview with a Ministry of Energy and Water official, Beirut, 12 June 2014.
[18] Ibid.
[19] Author's interview, Beirut, 20 June 2014.

throughout the 1990s to date, it failed to meaningfully monitor the MEW's operations in Lebanon's unruly petroleum imports sector. Its senior staff and auditors lost immunity in the 1970s from dismissal by the president and, under the stipulations agreed to in the Taef Accord, the COM. The CA has consistently suffered from personnel shortages, political bickering over key staff appointments, political interference, and from blatant political maneuvers to suppress the few incriminating reports that under these conditions it was still able to produce (Leenders 2012, As-Safir 2012). These obstacles undermined the CA's operations dramatically, thereby earning it a reputation of being overly legalistic and out of touch with the state's responsibilities.

It is of course too early to say whether or how the LPA's institutional framework will affect its staff's professionalism or integrity in practice. For now, stakeholders including concerned international oil companies (IOCs) say they are impressed with the efficient and transparent way in which the LPA has approached the pre-qualification round, the LPA's first major accomplishment.[20] Others, including Lebanese journalists working on petroleum issues, expressed satisfaction with the LPA's efforts to explain its policies and operations, and answer their questions, at first without attribution and, more recently, by giving high-profile media interviews (Hoteit 2014).[21] Based on this, it seems that the regulation compelling the LPA to first obtain the prior consent of the minister of energy and water before making public statements (Decree 7968, Article 5) is liberally applied in favor of transparency and outreach to the public, although the latter would be fully realized if this stipulation was removed.

Pre-qualification

In terms of transparency and accountability, there remain a number of concerns about pre-qualification rounds. According to Decree 9882, successful companies needed to comply with a strict set of legal, financial, technical, and environmental criteria designed to enable the LPA to identify serious contenders who possess relevant experience in the technically demanding business of deep-water offshore petroleum extraction and who have sufficient financial clout to carry out and sustain their tasks.[22] In this context, a distinction is made between "operating companies" and "non-operating companies," which need to meet different criteria, and which, after being pre-qualified, were eligible to present their joint bids for an EPA as a consortium comprising at least one operator and two non-operating companies. Accordingly, companies first submitted their pre-qualification applications in February and March 2013. After assessing the applications, the MEW and the LPA announced on 18 April 2013 that 12 companies had pre-qualified as operators and 34 as non-operators. The large number of contenders promised to encourage a highly competitive bidding process, which from an anti-corruption perspective could be viewed as placing some checks on unfair practices such as granting contracts at suboptimal terms. Crucially,

---

[20] Author's interviews with IOC officials, May–June 2014.
[21] Author's interviews with Lebanese journalists, May–June 2014.
[22] Republic of Lebanon, Ministry of Energy and Water, Petroleum Administration, Lebanon First Offshore License Round, 15 February 2013. http://www.lpa.gov.lb/pdf/Pre-Qualification%20Results%20Presentation.pdf.

however, no sufficient documentation or explanation was provided about why and how companies had been found to meet the criteria of pre-qualification.[23] The second pre-qualification round, held in March 2017, showed no improvement in this regard. Sources at the MEW told the author that it refrained from publishing such information after receiving strong requests from the companies to maintain confidentiality, especially when it was suggested that data be released on their total capital.[24]

On the surface, for the main pre-qualified operators such sub-optimal disclosure may appear to raise no immediate questions. After all, the 13 large operators that pre-qualified are all internationally and publicly renowned for having many years of relevant experience in offshore petroleum extraction. Also, as all these companies are listed on United States and/or European stock exchanges, since the US Congress passed the Dodd-Frank Act in 2010 and the European Union adopted similar legislation, they are obliged to disclose their capital and assets just as they are normally keen to inform their shareholders about their activities. However, one study found that out of all companies that managed to pre-qualify, eight had been subjected elsewhere to legal action related to corruption, including Total and Eni, the first two awarded operating companies (Lebanon Oil and Gas Initiative 2017).

Concerns about limited disclosure are even more pertinent regarding pre-qualified non-operating companies. As one observer put it, "so, okay, the LPA says it found that these companies have met the criteria and they listed their names, but give me one reason to trust them."[25] This is not to imply that unfair or shady practices did in fact occur. Indeed, MEW officials stress that pre-qualified companies all met the legal, financial, and technical criteria.[26] Yet, the importance of full transparency is underscored by some of the pre-qualified non-operating companies far from reassuring track records in terms of anti-corruption controls. Novatek, the non-operating partner within the awarded consortium, is a Russian company subjected to United States sanctions for its close ties to Russian President Vladimir Putin and for its role in the Ukraine crisis.[27] Russian anti-corruption investigators accused its owners of conflicts of interest involving Russia's minister of natural resources and ecology and of influence peddling involving Prime Minister Dmitry Medvedev (Crime Russia 2017, Bershidsky 2017). In 2009, a leaked US diplomatic cable described Gazprom, which owns 20 percent of Novatek, as "inefficient, politically driven, and corrupt".[28]

---

[23] The information brochure released on the occasion only presented the names of the companies and very general company descriptions provided by the companies themselves. See Lebanese Republic, Ministry of Energy and Water, Petroleum Administration, Lebanon's First Offshore Licensing Round, the prequalified Companies, n.d. However, at the press conference on 18 April 2013, the MEW and LPA explained orally why the companies involved pre-qualified in reference to their capital assets and other qualities. Strikingly, Lebanese media showed no interest in such key data as they failed to include these in their coverage of the event.

[24] "Initially some companies even objected to us printing their logos in the brochure listing all pre-qualified companies." From author's interview at the MEW, Beirut, 6 June 2014.

[25] Author's interview with Lebanese petroleum geologist, Beirut, 8 June 2014.

[26] Author's interview, Beirut, 12 June 2014.

[27] United States Department of the Treasury. 2014. "Announcement of Treasury Sanctions on Entities Within the Financial Services and Energy Sectors of Russia, Against Arms or Related Materiel Entities, and those Undermining Ukraine's Sovereignty." 16 July.

[28] Wikileaks. 2009. "Public Library of US Diplomacy: Gazprom's Reversal of Fortune." 7 October.

Another key concern raised by non-disclosure and lack of transparency involving non-operating companies remains the extent to which Lebanese businessmen, in possible or perhaps even likely partnerships with political leaders, may gain access to large rents associated with upstream activities by winning consortiums. In particular, one non-operating company involving Lebanese nationals drew some suspicion in this regard as its ownership, upon being pre-qualified, was concealed. Listing itself as a Lebanese company during the first pre-qualification round, APEX Oil and Gas Limited turned out to be registered in Hong Kong, a jurisdiction that allowed it to hide its real owners.[29]

From this perspective, the failure to release full ownership data on pre-qualified (non-operating) companies reduced the value of what otherwise seems to have been intended as a fully transparent pre-qualification process. Sources at the MEW objected in this context that such a degree of confidentiality is not uncommon in pre-qualification processes worldwide.[30] Perhaps so, but Lebanon's dismal record of corruption and its endemic blurring of public and private interests arguably calls for extra caution and full transparency.

In terms of transparency, the above can be viewed as a missed opportunity. Arguably, incomplete transparency caused by not disclosing how and why pre-qualified companies met the criteria, and by not identifying their owners, was compounded by a stipulation in Decree 9882 (Article 3). The latter allows non-operators to partner with other companies in their applications for pre-qualification as long as at least the main applicant (and not necessarily its partners) can prove that it meets the pre-qualification criteria, including having relevant experience in the sector and possessing at least $500 million in total assets. One Lebanese lawyer specializing in the petroleum sector argued in this context that this stipulation may be viewed as sitting uneasily with the general principle set out in Law 132, and explicitly mentioned in Decree 9882,[31] that only capable and experienced companies may take part in oil extraction.[32] After all, now companies with no relevant experience whatsoever may join consortiums by partnering with an established company in the sector that jointly pre-qualified.[33] Sources within the MEW explained that the COM had added this option to an earlier draft of the pre-qualification decree, prepared by the LPA, in order to allow for Lebanese participation in the consortiums and promote the country's private sector.[34] In addition, they stressed that the main company that decides to partner with other companies retains full legal responsibility and liability in any joint application for pre-qualification, and that as such the provision contains no risks.[35]

---

[29] In 2014, the owners identified themselves to *Executive Magazine* as Mahmoud Sidani, CEO of Lebanese importer UniGaz, and Mohamed Choucair, president of the Beirut and Mount Lebanon Chambers of Commerce (Lebanon Oil and Gas Initiative 2017).

[30] Author's interview, Beirut, 6 June 2014.

[31] Annex 4, 4.1 "Eligibility criteria" (2).

[32] Author's interview, Beirut, 2 June 2014.

[33] Among the pre-qualified non-operating companies, Geo-Park (active in oil and with activities in South America), partners with Lebanese company Petroleb (owned by the Al Khayat family), which has no experience in the sector. Mohamed Choucair of APEX company is a chocolate manufacturer (Lebanon Oil and Gas Initiative 2017).

[34] Author's interview, Beirut, 6 June 2014.

[35] Ibid.

Yet, if (Lebanese) companies lacking relevant experience in petroleum may still be viewed as desirable partners to other (foreign) companies that do meet these criteria, one may legitimately ask why fully skilled and solvent foreign petroleum companies would want to associate themselves with (Lebanese) companies that cannot or do not necessarily demonstrate a relevant track record. Again, there is no suggestion made here that dishonest practices in this context did occur. Indeed, it is quite conceivable that foreign companies wish to partner with Lebanese partners in order to be better placed, for example, to meet the legally prescribed criterion to employ at least 80 percent Lebanese citizens among its workforce or to better navigate the country's institutional and economic landscape generally by virtue of incorporating local knowledge and expertise. Another conjectural suggestion, and therefore risk, may be that companies this way prepare the ground for gaining *wasta*, or influence peddling judged beneficial or necessary in future dealings with Lebanese authorities.

Of course, there are ample alternatives for foreign non-operating companies to allow for or encourage direct or indirect Lebanese participation, for example by selling stock or by establishing credit relationships with Lebanese banks.[36] None of this is necessarily illegal or even circumspect. On the contrary, there are some good economic and practical reasons to encourage Lebanese participation as much as possible. However, in Lebanon's climate of fundamental distrust involving the relationship between business and politics, the above also points to the imperative that any future access by (Lebanese) businessmen to the consortiums' sizeable royalties and shares of oil revenues should at least be made fully transparent and known to the public. Despite efforts to make the pre-qualification process as transparent as possible, this requirement has yet to be fully met.

Tendering for exploration and production agreements

Evidently, concerns about the transparency of the pre-qualification process become critical in the process of bidding for and signing contracts, or EPAs. In addition, there are some concerns regarding the envisaged confidentiality of these EPAs. The "model contract" was released in January 2017. According to sources within the MEW, this makes it unnecessary to disclose the actual EPAs concluded with the bidding consortium(s), as the final contracts will not significantly differ from the model EPA.[37] Yet, in this context, the difference between production-sharing contracts and the alternative, that of licensing, is of importance. While in the latter case all financial stipulations—such as royalties, taxes, and "profit oil" and "cost oil"—are set by law, production-sharing contracts contain certain "biddable items," i.e. agreements on ways to share petroleum proceeds. For reasons of transparency, the licensing system is generally preferred (if certainly not always practiced, not even in countries subscribing to "best practices") primarily because all financial or fiscal agreements will this way be

---

[36] It is this additional possibility for Lebanese participation that made LPA members decide not to object to the Council of Ministers amending Decree 9882 (Article 3), "even when this was not ideal." Author's interview with an MEW official, Beirut, 20 June 2014.

[37] Author's interviews, Beirut, 30 May and 6 June 2014.

made public and be more difficult to change by way of negotiation.[38] If kept undisclosed, actual production-sharing contracts will cause agreements on such crucial issues to remain unknown to the public. Lebanon has opted for a hybrid system whereby some fiscal items are set by law (taxes and royalties to the state), as was done in September 2017, but others (including "cost oil" to reimburse the right holders, and a percentage of the remaining oil split between the state and the producer) are left to be determined in the final EPAs; the so-called "biddable items".[39] For now there are no legal obligations for the EPA contracts to be made public, although Bassil publicly made a promise to this effect (*Executive* Magazine 2013). Indeed, the EPAs signed in February 2018 have thus far not been released. Sources within the MEW argue that it is the companies who are insisting on confidentiality, as the contracts will contain sensitive geological and production data that will be of great interest to their competitors.[40] This, however, is no good reason for Lebanese authorities to not at least release the fiscal details in the EPAs or to redact sensitive private information to the same effect (Publish What You Pay 2012). If this does not happen, financial disclosure requirements of international oil companies falling under US and European jurisdictions will only be partially helpful in extrapolating what fiscal agreements within the EPAs may have been.[41] International oil companies are not obliged to disclose the contracts they sign, neither would the Lebanese government be under current legislation, not even now that it seems slated to join EITI.

The need for disclosure of Lebanon's EPA contracts and its fiscal details, in addition to full transparency on the ownership of all right holders in the extraction of petroleum, only became more pertinent in the Lebanese context of continuous political bickering that preceded the actual tendering process initiated in 2017. In Lebanese media and in conversations with the author, disagreements in this respect were explained in reference to the preference of former Minister Gebran Bassil to auction only a few blocks (blocks 1, 4, 5, 6, and 9) out of ten delineated, while Berri purportedly preferred to open all of them at once to receive bids. The pros and cons of both proposals are beyond the scope of this chapter, but essentially appeared to come down to different strategies to gain maximum leverage vis-à-vis oil companies or kick-start extraction at maximum levels. However, it is questionable whether such technical details of substance really constituted the core of the disagreement. Indeed, Berri did not seem to argue that all blocks opened for bidding were to be awarded to companies.[42] This reinforced the impression or prompted speculation that Lebanon's political leaders are resorting to their engrained practice of *muhasasa* and that their quarrels are, in fact, about dividing up revenues and/or business opportunities associated with the emerging petroleum sector. Several theories have in this context been suggested. They range from politicians

---

[38] Author's interview with an international diplomat specializing in petroleum finance, 9 June 2014.
[39] LPA, "The Exploration and Production Agreement," n.d. Other biddable items include the royalty rate for other petroleum than crude oil. Decree 10289 (Article 72).
[40] Author's interviews, 30 May and 6 June 2014.
[41] One obstacle in this context may be that, in Lebanon, petroleum companies falling under US or European jurisdiction will partner in their consortium with non-operating companies that may come from jurisdictions that do not require disclosure on their revenues and/or ownership.
[42] Author's interview with MEW official, 6 June 2014.

placing sectarian denominations on the blocks and their respective revenues; them giving priority to blocks that are closest to the territories under their control in order to benefit from onshore petroleum activities; to them striving for access to companies that will take part in the consortiums and/or the upstream operations they will be subcontracting; to geopolitical struggles involving Russia, whose companies were not originally among the pre-qualified operating companies.[43]

None of these theories can be easily substantiated, others sound unlikely, and some may be dismissed as rather fanciful. Yet unfounded speculations are at least partly a result of the fact that transparency in the process thus far could, and perhaps should, have been taken to higher levels, combined with a deeply rooted mistrust of Lebanese politicians. In any case, the severe delay caused by continued political bickering had in itself a harmful effect on the competitiveness of the bidding process. A number of pre-qualified operating companies lost both patience and confidence.[44] The government's decision in 2017 to approve a last-minute change regarding blocks up for auction is also likely to have caused companies to further lose interest because their seismic data no longer matched the areas on offer. Consequently, only one consortium placed its bids and received the contracts for blocks 4 and 9.[45]

Upstream subcontracting

As Lebanon moves further into the exploration phase, large scale subcontracting is expected to take place to service and supply the operators, primarily onshore. Such upstream activities will range from hiring security companies, supplying equipment, and purchasing or leasing land for petroleum installations, to building and servicing them. Operators are in this context legally obliged to give "preferential treatment to the procurement of Lebanese originating goods and services when such goods and services are internationally competitive with regard to quality, availability, price, and performance" (Decree 10289, Article 157). Undoubtedly, this obligation is aimed at ensuring that Lebanese private sector companies receive a much-needed boost. Accordingly, scores of Lebanese companies are already preparing themselves for the petroleum industry.[46] At the same time, it has been rightly noted that in the Lebanese context, and indeed perhaps generally, the risks of corruption and clientelist practices in subcontracting will be significant (Hoteit 2014).[47] Among Lebanese petroleum officials there seems to be an expectation that the operators will be largely self-regulating in this respect as they are assumed to pursue efficiency targets that are at odds with favoritism and corruption, and because as a consortium its members will keep each other in check.[48] In congruence with this, sources within Western oil

---

[43] Author's interviews with Lebanese businessmen, civil society activists, journalists, and foreign diplomats, Beirut, May–June 2014.

[44] Author's interview with Western petroleum company official, 23 May 2014.

[45] Another deterring factor may have been the government's decision to include block 9 adjacent to the disputed Lebanese–Israeli maritime border (Middle East Strategic Perspectives 2017).

[46] Author's interviews with Lebanese businessmen and at the Beirut Chamber of Commerce, June 2014.

[47] Ibid.

[48] Author's interviews with MEW officials, Beirut, 6 and 12 June 2014.

companies that pre-qualified confirm their strong intention to refrain from unfair practices and bribery, calling them "bad business practice" primarily in reference to the potentially escalating nature of bribery or sweetheart deals if given into.[49] It is perhaps against this background that the regulations or mechanisms being put in place or envisaged to mitigate the risks of corruption in upstream subcontracting do not include unusual or overly drastic measures, or place stringent disclosure obligations on the consortiums. On top of the generally phrased legislation banning corruption in all petroleum activities (Decree 10289, Article 162), the operators are expected to subject "major procurement contracts" to public tendering, to submit a list of pre-qualified bidders to the LPA, justify the selection of the supplier, and allow themselves to be scrutinized by an external auditor (Decree 10289, Article 157). As such, these requirements certainly meet international best practices and Lebanese authorities should be lauded for adopting them.

Even when strictly enforced, such legal measures will still not necessarily result in reduced levels of corruption or cronyism. Ironically, one could argue in this context that Lebanon's general conditions of heightened corruption risks call for more drastic measures than are called for by best international practices. For one, the Lebanese market is characterized by strong monopolistic and oligopolistic tendencies, particularly in the petroleum imports and distribution sector that is likely to sweep up many subcontracting opportunities (Leenders 2012, Traboulsi 2014). Sources within the MEW understandably argue that they "are not into the business of market regulation."[50] But, for now, neither is any other Lebanese public agency as attempts to adopt and effectively implement anti-trust legislation have thus far been unsuccessful. In combination with Lebanon's blurred boundaries between business ownership and its political elites (Leenders 2012, Traboulsi 2014, Chaaban 2016), this forms a source of apprehension as far as petroleum subcontracting is concerned. Furthermore, it is not fully clear from existing legislation on the emerging petroleum sector to what extent and how exactly the LPA will monitor and screen the subcontracting process, and what powers it would have if any irregularities were to be detected.[51] The less-than-optimal degree of the LPA's political insulation generally adds to the risk that even when it chooses to be pro-active in this field, as the intention appears to be, it may ultimately not be fully successful in effectively countering corruption in upstream subcontracting. Under existing legislation, public oversight or scrutiny in this respect, by media and/or civil society, does not appear to be on the cards, as neither operators nor the authorities seem to be under any obligation to publicly disclose information on tendering, let alone disclose ownership details of winning companies. Indeed, such details may not be released due to possible confidentiality clauses in the EPAs covering the formalities of subcontracting.

---

[49] Author's interviews, Beirut, May 2014.
[50] Author's interview, Beirut, 6 June 2014.
[51] Decree 10289 (Article 72) obliges operators to disclose their subcontracts to the LPA, but only upon a decree drafted by the Minister of Energy and Water and adopted by the COM. Although this can be positively viewed as acknowledging the need for disclosure of subcontracts, it at the same time points to the possible pitfalls associated with the LPA lacking full independence and the need for public disclosure.

When offshore subcontracting will provide lucrative business opportunities, chances are that it may be subjected to pressures of *muhasasa*. It is possibly the anticipation thereof that constituted one factor in having held back political agreement on the sector until early 2017. After all, depending on the blocks that were and will be put up for auction and that will first start production, onshore locations that are closest to the terminals are likely to witness a boom in construction, services, and business generally. To the extent that drawing analogies provides any guidance, wartime control over several clandestine ports by sectarian militias and illegal seaside properties held by major Lebanese politicians since suggest there is a risk that such onshore locations may be viewed as political-confessional fiefdoms (Leenders 2012, Al-Akhbar 2012). That, in turn, could place serious political and confessional constraints on fair and competitive bidding and fair practices in operators' upstream subcontracting.

The consequences of possible corruption, market concentration, and/or politically induced inefficiencies in subcontracting arrangements cannot be discounted in the context of the "cost oil" arrangement foreseen in the EPAs (Decree 10289, Article 72). This allows operators to be reimbursed for their "recoverable costs" in kind. As explained above, this constitutes a "biddable item" and, hence, if the EPAs are not disclosed, it may never become known to the public what exact arrangements were put in place. Equally, if not strictly monitored, regulated, seriously capped, and publicly disclosed, the "cost oil" provision may challenge the overall assumption that operators will be driven by efficiency concerns in their subcontracting. IOCs and their non-operating partners may ideally seek maximum efficiency and cost savings, but the need to overcome political constraints and boost expediency may at times rival such basic incentives. Indeed, experiences elsewhere, including in India, suggest that operators may at times fail to show self-restraint when their subcontracting is not bound by very strict rules, oversight, and limitations, both by hosting authorities and the public at large (Achong 2009/2010).[52] In short, market concentration, favoritism, corruption, and measures that fall short of drastically regulating, policing, and disclosing "cost oil" provisions would constitute a risk of Lebanon's petroleum revenues being skimmed even before they reach the state's treasury.

There are measures that Lebanon could take to mitigate the risks of corruption and cronyism in petroleum-related subcontracting. Most importantly, all tendering and major subcontracting should be made transparent to both the authorities and the public on a routine basis. Kazakhstan's Contract Agency (KCA), established in 2002 to promote local involvement in petroleum sector activities, could be an object of emulation in this respect.

Daily petroleum operations and settling disputes

State regulation and governance of significant petroleum activities narrowly defined already constitute a significant challenge, but so will the task of building and reforming

---

[52] A report prepared by India's Comptroller and Auditor General investigating excessive recoverable cost declarations by petroleum companies read: "The private contractors have inadequate incentives to reduce capital expenditure—and substantial incentive to increase capital expenditure or 'front end' capital expenditure" (Livemint and The *Wall Street Journal*, 9 September 2011).

a range of state institutions and agencies that are less directly involved in petroleum activities and yet crucial to their daily governance. Given their current capacity and susceptibility to corruption, such secondary institutions in Lebanon are unlikely to cope. Particularly vulnerable to corruption is the Lebanese Customs Authority, which, although having gone through some institutional reforms since the 1990s, is still struck by high levels of corruption and inefficiency (International Monetary Fund 2005). Western IOC officials expressed concern that the import of highly specialized equipment and machinery unknown to Lebanese customs officials (or absent from their inventory lists) would likely cause costly delays in clearances, thereby creating opportunities or, from an importer's perspective, a need for bribery to expedite entry.[53] Hypothetically, politicians with control over customs officials, whether by way of their appointments or otherwise, could use their leverage to press operators into making subcontracting decisions in their favor, as happened in Iraq.[54]

Numerous other state agencies and institutions with currently weak anti-corruption controls will inevitably see their activities and workload augmented when or if routine petroleum-related operations commence. In this context, the risk of "bureaucratic overstretch" is real (Ross 2012). Licenses and permits of all kinds are a domain wherein Lebanese state agencies are frequently very cumbersome to deal with unless bribes are offered to obtain them or to expedite formalities. Similarly, enforcement of environmental regulations is often highly selective when involving private interests of politicians and influential businessmen with sufficient "protection" (*mahsubiya*), as illustrated by largely unsuccessful attempts to put a halt to illegal quarrying (Leenders 2012). Several ministries and state agencies are currently involved in Lebanon's preparations for its emerging petroleum sector and are cooperating with the LPA to put in place appropriate measures and reforms. In this context it should be noted that administrative reforms involving such and other public sector institutions since the early 1990s have been slow, and that tangible results have been disappointingly limited (El Ghaziri 2007). Arguably, this has been largely due to the crippling effects of Lebanon's political settlement and the failure of reformers to take this into account (Leenders 2012). Whether Lebanon's political class will grasp the need for comprehensive administrative reforms in the context of petroleum governance requirements as a way to reinvigorate and bolster administrative reform remains to be seen.

Lebanon's judiciary calls for specific attention in this context. Operators will to a large extent be able to resort to international arbitration clauses in its dealings with the state[55] and with major (sub-) contracts with providers and service companies. It should be noted that Lebanon has a reasonably good reputation in terms of executing international arbitrators' decisions, although at times following long delays (Al-Akhbar 2007).[56] Yet, such international arbitration will to some extent still depend on Lebanon's court system for its execution. Smaller contracts involving Lebanese subcontracting

---

[53] Author's interviews, Beirut, May–June 2014.
[54] Author's interview with IOC official, Beirut, 23 May 2014.
[55] These provisions will be stipulated in the EPAs.
[56] For instance, Paris-based arbitration in a dispute between the Lebanese state and CCC-Hochtief over payments for construction work at Beirut International Airport in 1997 lasted over a decade before resulting in an "amicable agreement".

companies will likely rely on local arbitration whereby in addition to courts' involvement in execution, and in case of a disagreement about the appointment of an arbitrator, a court of first instance will typically assign one.[57] Furthermore, criminal infringements, including violations of environmental laws and corruption, fall under the sole jurisdiction of Lebanese courts. It is in this context that the judiciary's deficiencies in terms of integrity and independence—as suggested by numerous international indices and opinion surveys—will gain pertinence (Freedom House Index 2018 and other years[58]; Transparency International Global Barometer 2016 and other years;[59] World Bank Ease of Doing Business 2017 and other years;[60] World Economic Forum Global Competitiveness Index 2017 and other years; World Justice Project Rule of Law Index 2017–18[61] and other years). If Lebanon is to become a significant producer of oil and gas, its courts' current corruption and inefficiency levels may become amplified by increased workloads, by at times large and complex financial and environmental claims, and on account of blurred public and private interests potentially troubling Lebanon's petroleum industry.

Establishing a national oil company

The OPRL stipulates that, "when necessary and after promising commercial opportunities have been verified, the COM may establish a national oil company (NOC) on the basis of a proposal by the minister based upon the opinion of the petroleum administration."[62] Accordingly, a future option was created for an NOC to operate on the production side of the petroleum sector. Yet, the legally enshrined requirement of such an NOC's commercial viability and the explicit need for the LPA's endorsement appears to be as much designed to prevent its immediate establishment.[63] Regardless, the idea already prompted some controversy as some Lebanese observers suspect that the running of a Lebanese NOC would be riddled with corruption and struck by inefficiencies, akin to the experience with Electricité du Liban (Hasbani 2011, Takieddine 2013, ILPI 2013, Sarkis 2014).[64] They also point out that NOCs worldwide, and especially in the Middle East, have often been prone to corruption (Barma 2012). Lebanese common skepticism vis-à-vis an assertive role of the state, and "statism" more

---

[57] The International Bar Association concluded that arbitration in Lebanon "is not yet at a stage where one could assert that arbitration has become a real alternative to court proceedings." (International Bar Association. 2012. "Arbitration Guide Lebanon." February.)

[58] Freedom House. 2018. "Freedom House Index." https://freedomhouse.org/report/freedom-world/freedom-world-2018

[59] Transparency International "Corruption Perceptions Index 2016." https://www.transparency.org/news/feature/corruption_perceptions_index_2016?gclid=CjwKCAjw4uXaBRAcEiwAuAUz8D5sC-JtdmQArRMbpepahf2eR0NwUhnU7EYY2IjQi3OgUISU1IJW8xoCEY8QAvD_BwE.

[60] World Bank Ease of Doing Business rankings for 2017 and previous years http://www.doingbusiness.org/rankings

[61] World Justice Project. 2017–18. "Rule of Law Index."

[62] By late 2017, a parliamentary committee began studying a bill for the establishment of a NOC (Azar 2017).

[63] "We wanted to prevent the establishment of another redundant public institution, such as the Lebanese railway authority, which continues to have 1,000 staffers while there isn't one train running. And they are still recruiting!" Author's interview with MEW official, Beirut, 20 June 2014.

[64] Author's interviews, Beirut, May–June 2014.

generally, is echoed by international financial institutions and some IOCs who have their own reasons and arguments to counter the worldwide trend toward establishing NOCs and "resource nationalism" (Ross 2012). Analogies with seemingly similar and corruption-ridden institutions, within Lebanon or in other petroleum producing countries, can be as helpful as they are deceptive. With the creation of any new state institution, vested interests and long-established expectations of entitlement will be less ingrained. This does not remove the risks of corruption but it does offer new opportunities to break with "business as usual". In the longer term, an NOC is likely to promote Lebanon's high-end human capital to be employed in the sector while it will allow for higher returns on petroleum production. While aiming for these goals, a Lebanese NOC could cooperate, partner with, and learn from IOCs that have both the capital and expertise to spearhead offshore petroleum activities. From a perspective of corruption control, an NOC's initial and inevitable dependency on IOCs, possibly by way of taking part in a consortium, would generate some important checks and balances on a Lebanese NOC as its partners are unlikely to tolerate systemic and loss-making mediocrity, corruption, and cronyism. In addition, as argued below, an NOC may play an important role on the revenue side of the value chain and help to enhance public accountability vis-à-vis the petroleum sector at large.

Revenue management options, expenditure and risks of corruption

Of course, the more one moves up Lebanon's prospective value chain involving petroleum, the more speculative the analysis will be. This certainly applies to revenue management, spending aims and targets, and procurement and expenditure mechanisms. The complex choices that will have to be made in this respect will and should not only be steered by concerns or efforts to reduce corruption risks, but the latter certainly deserve to receive close consideration. Understandably, since Lebanon's petroleum potential still needs to be confirmed, few concrete steps have been taken in this direction. Accordingly, a public debate on the issue is in order in preparation for the day that petroleum revenues may arrive.

The "sovereign fund" and its management

The OPRL stipulates that net proceeds arising out of petroleum activities or rights will be placed in a "sovereign fund," leaving it to another law to prescribe the fund's specific management.[65] However, it does already specify that the fund as such will be designed for saving purposes, meaning it will keep the capital and part of the proceeds "for future generations," and only make available the dividends from investments for other, current purposes. From the perspective of international best practice, the very mentioning of

---

[65] In November 2017 MP Yassin Jaber presented to the parliament a draft law for establishing a sovereign wealth fund (Redd 2017).

the fund is congruent with the widely accepted notion that petroleum is a depletable resource that has developed over millions of years and that, as such, there is no moral justification for the generation that stumbles upon a resource to spend all revenues garnered from it. However, other motivating factors come into play as well, including policies to counter "Dutch disease" effects and stabilizing sharply fluctuating revenues associated with high price volatility in petroleum prices, intentions to use the dividends for developmental purposes and economic diversification, and attempts to separate the petroleum proceeds from the ordinary state budget to better control their usage ("ring fencing") (World Bank 2014). The idea that such funds can be helpful in insulating revenue management from day-to-day politics and the risk of waste and corruption is most relevant here. Accordingly, since the early 1990s many oil producers have established such special funds. All these considerations have also informed the Lebanese intention to establish a petroleum fund, including a resolution to counter corruption, waste, and the plunder of what may be significant volumes of precious resources.[66]

The problem is that worldwide experience suggests that "sovereign wealth funds" often have done little to advance the goals for which they were established. In fact, they can even worsen the risk of corruption. As a report by Revenue Watch Institute put it: "The rhetorical appeal of natural resource funds as symbols of development and progress has sometimes outstripped their practical value as solutions to specific macroeconomic or budgetary problems. This lack of clarity represents a real danger, as poorly conceived funds can become channels for corruption" (Revenue Watch Institute 2014, Bulte and Damania 2008).

In this context it is of essential importance that there exist strict rules for withdrawals, clear and legally bolstered criteria or earmarks for expenditure, and high levels of transparency and accountability. Even so, more often than not, as one scholar on petroleum governance found, "politicians sweep aside institutional constraints to gain control over how a valuable resource is allocated and regulated—giving them the power to use it for patronage or corruption" (Ross 2012). "Fund raiding," as happened under Muammar Ghadhafi's rule in Libya, is the most striking example of this as billions of dollars were consumed, spent on white elephant projects and other dubious investments, or simply vanished in numerous private bank accounts of the Ghadhafi family and their allies (Global Witness 2012). Another example of this is the expenditure of petroleum proceeds held in such funds on arms in times of extreme political crisis, as happened in Chad where its fund for future generations, even when supervised by the World Bank, was cancelled in 2005 following several coup attempts against President Idriss Déby (Pegg 2009). Yet, even when such excesses cannot be ruled out in non-dictatorships or even (semi-) democracies, it is striking that blatant and massive "fund raiding" appears to be a trademark of heavily centralized and coercive authoritarian regimes.

Given Lebanon's unruly, fragmented, or pluralist political system (or, as one author called it less euphemistically, its "authoritarianism by diffusion") (El Khazen 2003), the probability of fund raiding appears to be less acute except, perhaps, in times of

---

[66] Author's interview with MEW officials, 12 June 2014.

full-scale war.[67] A much greater risk, however, is that by design, or by reflecting the lowest common denominator of the Lebanese political class's demands and preferences, the institutional checks and balances on Lebanon's sovereign fund will be too diluted and too weak to withstand escalating political pressures to make withdrawals, for instance to achieve or restore a "confessional balance," or indeed to create opportunities for grand corruption (Eifer *et al.* 2003).

In the context of Lebanon's crippling political settlement, it is extremely doubtful that, from scratch, a new agency can miraculously emerge that will sustain the solid institutional qualities to withstand political interference and offer guarantees of full transparency and accountability, even when such features remain a necessary precondition for effective corruption controls. However, in this context some Lebanese and foreign observers have already suggested that Banque du Liban (BDL) could be a suitable candidate to manage the fund, which would certainly not be unusual as central banks elsewhere are often the designated manager of sovereign wealth funds given their asset management expertise. Indeed, BDL has by and large preserved its integrity and independence, in sharp contrast with most public institutions (Leenders 2012). In this context, the Norwegian International Law and Policy Institute observed in a report on Lebanon's emerging petroleum sector that "the combination of strong qualitative performance combined with a shared understanding among Lebanese of the importance of [the central bank's] independence ... was part of the explanations informants gave" (International Law and Policy Institute 2013). The report continues that, for its integrity and independence, the central bank should be viewed as a "model" for petroleum governance. Yet, the main reason why the central bank did not succumb to political pressure and *muhasasa* is far from selfless respect for institutional independence; arguably, it was the direct result of the fact that the central bank's independence was and still is the pillar of the lucrative market for treasury bills. Lebanon's private banks rely heavily on this market and political elites are among its key owners (Leenders 2012, Chaaban 2016). One lesson that can be drawn from this, crudely as it may sound, is that Lebanon's political class needs to sustain a private interest in preserving or respecting the sovereign fund's independence and integrity. This hardly offers grounds to see the central bank as a "model," as the circumstances under which its institutional qualities arose are somewhat anomalous and, indeed, not immune to controversy. Perhaps one way to go about this is by placing the fund within the central bank and closely integrating the general management of the central bank with that of the fund (e.g. by granting its governor overlapping roles and responsibilities). This way one would intently connect the country's market for treasury bills (and associated interests of private banks) with the management of petroleum revenues, and thereby help create vested interests among the political class in good governance. In short, the way in which the sovereign fund will be managed and by whom, and how this will relate to the interests of the political elites, will be essential for any rules on withdrawals and technical safeguards for independence, transparency, and accountability to stand a chance of being respected.

---

[67] Even so, during Lebanon's civil war (1975–90), Lebanon's central bank was never fully raided by militias, earning its governor a reputation of "the banker in a bunker" (Al-Ayyash 1997).

Sovereign fund allocations and expenditures

Having an effective fund manager in place, whether this is the central bank or otherwise, will not guarantee that all resources that it releases will be effectively spent without waste, cronyism, and corruption. For one, such will be dependent on implementing agencies including line ministries, especially if at least part of the revenues will be allocated, for instance, to infrastructural projects, initiatives enhancing social welfare provision, and poverty alleviation. Partly due to Lebanon's dismal record of institutional weakness, political interference, *muhasasa*, and corruption in public procurement and public welfare provision, some have already suggested radical alternatives to circumvent this problem. Paying off Lebanon's hefty public debt, and/or re-financing (parts of) it, is one such a proposal (Le Commerce du Levant 2012).[68] From a purely economic and financial point of view there are certainly grounds to argue for this. Moreover, it is believed that this would radically resolve any problem or remove any risk of the country's expected petroleum wealth being squandered. At first sight, and from an anti-corruption perspective, the suggestion sounds appealing. Yet, for a number of reasons it ultimately fails to be persuasive. First, it is highly doubtful that there will be political or indeed popular support for the idea, as spending (most of or all) the proceeds from petroleum will be viewed as financing past corruption and waste while it would have the opportunity costs of ignoring urgent problems such as widespread poverty and sharp regional socio-economic imbalances. Second, without guarantees of fiscal prudence, paying off the public debt may simply improve the state's creditworthiness, which could be an incentive to start the borrowing and spending cycle all over again in a context of still failing or lacking political and administrative reforms. In this sense, paying off the debt now could be tantamount to financing the corruption of tomorrow. Third, by hypothetically removing any opportunities for corruption on the revenue-side via drastic debt repayments, the scramble for access to and *muhasasa* in the production-side of the petroleum sector is likely to be intensified, negatively affecting production performance. Fourth, paying off the entire debt, if indeed the size of petroleum revenues would allow for this, would eradicate the treasury bill market and put the private banks out of business. By implication, this would remove one of the very few remaining pillars of cohesion and collaboration among the political class.

The allocation of significant petroleum proceeds and their expenditure, or that of sovereign fund dividends, is bound to entail a menu of items that will all deserve to be considered and financed, including paying off part of the public debt and refinancing other parts to bring it back to healthier proportions, as well as expenditures on public procurement, social welfare, and poverty alleviation. Judging from Lebanon's past experience with reconstruction, public procurement in particular will run the risk of rampant corruption. However, as the case of Mongolia illustrates, the arrival of revenues from mineral assets could be seized as an opportunity for drastic reforms in this context. In 2013, Mongolia established a new central procurement agency, which

---

[68] In January 2012, former Prime Minister Najib Mikati announced that proceeds from a sovereign fund would be used to bring down Lebanon's public debt from 137 percent of GDP to 60 percent (Le Commerce du Levant 2012).

takes major spending responsibilities for large projects away from line ministries, standardizes procedures, and makes them fully transparent online (Van den Brink 2012). Most strikingly and promisingly, it allows a role for civil society organizations in both bid evaluation and contract monitoring.

The need for decentralization and empowering Lebanon's local governorates and municipalities—long advocated for but with relatively limited results—may also gain extra relevance and urgency in the context of the revenues made available by petroleum production and strategies to spend them wisely. Smaller, local constituencies are more likely to demand higher standards of governance and public service delivery. For now, at a central level, local interests and agendas often translate into pressure on MPs who respond by offering their patronage in order to be re-elected.

Cash handouts

Perhaps the most radical proposal aimed at circumventing Lebanon's dismal public sector performance and widespread corruption is to use (parts of) petroleum revenues for cash transfers to all adult Lebanese citizens. Such an arrangement is carried out, in various ways, in the oil-rich US state of Alaska, in Bolivia, East Timor, and Mongolia (Gillies 2010, Ross 2012). In Lebanon, Minister of Finance Mohamad Chatah, who was assassinated in December 2013, was perhaps the most vocal proponent of cash handouts (Chatah 2012). The arguments in favor of cash handouts are manifold and include expected gains from circumventing corruption-ridden state institutions, countering citizens' dependency on politicians' patronage, and encouraging a relationship between the state, its petroleum revenues, and citizens (Devarajan 2010). From this perspective, all Lebanese will gain a direct stake in the performance of petroleum governance, and they are thereby assumed to press for greater accountability and corruption controls. Yet, at least in theory, the counter-arguments appear equally persuasive. First, it is far from certain that citizens will spend the handouts wisely, for example by saving them or by investing in education. Anecdotal evidence about how Lebanon's sizeable remittances are spent and consumed in this respect is not encouraging (*Daily Star* 2009).[69] Second, if no serious measures are taken to address the monopolistic and oligopolistic features of its economy, the opportunities of both increased consumption and investment will be merely captured by a rent-seeking business class. Third, cash handouts, if done properly, would be neutral in terms of income distribution. In some countries that may not be a problem, but given Lebanon's large disparities in income and wealth this may be viewed as an opportunity cost that is difficult to defend (Shaxson 2007, 1123–40).[70] Fourth, there are no guarantees that cash handouts will promote popular pressures for accountability and good petroleum governance; they may merely cause the public to demand higher production

---

[69] IDAL Chairman Nabil Itani claimed that only 10 percent of remittances are invested.
[70] In line with other proponents of cash handouts elsewhere, Mohamad Chatah argued in this context that, with higher incomes, the Lebanese would also pay higher income taxes. That is assuming that the Lebanese tax authorities are able to fully collect income tax, which, given large-scale tax evasion, is far from certain. Also, it raises questions about the the level of progressiveness/regressiveness of Lebanon's income tax system.

(Gillies 2010). Finally, and assuming that cash handouts will be sizeable enough to undermine politicians' patronage, there are no a priori reasons to believe that public decision makers would cooperate and this way bankroll themselves out of office.[71] Overall, and despite some of its drawbacks, the idea of cash handouts certainly deserves consideration. In this context, introducing conditional cash transfers could also be considered; for example by issuing vouchers for health and education services, either indiscriminately to all citizens or targeted at vulnerable groups (De la Brière 2006). Direct transfers, whether being monetized or in kind, will not be a panacea for solving the corruption problem once and for all. Yet, should cash transfers become part of the menu of spending items associated with a hypothetical windfall of petroleum revenues, they would perhaps be best placed within the central bank's sovereign fund where they could be kept and managed separately in a "Mohamad Chatah Account for all Lebanese Citizens".

Capitalizing a national oil company and enhancing public accountability

While there may be compelling reasons for the eventual establishment of a Lebanese NOC in terms of high-end employment generation and revenue maximization, it may also make good sense for investment policies and encouraging public accountability vis-à-vis the petroleum sector at large. There are, of course, many alternative ways to capitalize an NOC, and all need to be carefully considered from economic, financial, and commercial points of view. One option may be for the Lebanese state to direct part of its petroleum revenues, or the dividends of its sovereign fund, to capitalize an NOC that, in a lasting partnership with IOCs, will face scrutiny to operate effectively and efficiently. Next to direct majority state ownership, all Lebanese adult citizens could be made shareholders in an NOC, this way perhaps complementing or substituting for possible direct cash transfers, as discussed above. For reasons of political expediency, another part of an NOC's shares could be designated for open subscription. Accordingly, it may be reasonably expected that Lebanese citizens and the country's political class will gain not only a direct stake in the good governance of petroleum revenues but also in its production, thereby encouraging accountability and responsible expectations of sustainable petroleum production. It may be in this context that an NOC's necessary institutional insulation from Lebanon's crippling political settlement, and more conventional designs to ensure efficiency and transparency, may have a better chance to take hold and last. Certainly, any such scheme involving public distribution of shares will face challenges and obstacles that will need to be carefully addressed (Palley 2003). Yet, such efforts may be worthwhile given the accountability effects that are likely to result from the citizenry's acquired stakes in the production of petroleum that, first and foremost, belongs to them.

---

[71] Other obstacles that may trouble any Lebanese cash transfer system include (1) the issue of Lebanese nationality and/or residence in light of Lebanon's large diaspora and the already highly controversial issue of naturalization, and (2) the risk of massive fraud in the distribution of cash; not uncommon in Lebanon as illustrated by state subsidies on Internally Displaced Persons.

Conclusion and recommendations

When it comes to analyzing the risks of corruption in Lebanon's emerging petroleum sector, and indeed corruption more generally, the devil is in the details. Moreover, a sector-specific focus on the risks of corruption needs to be firmly placed and understood in Lebanon's political, social, and economic context before one can make sensible and feasible suggestions or recommendations for ways to mitigate them. The risks of corruption in Lebanon's emerging petroleum sector should not be discounted. Given the country's consistently disappointing performance in the past in terms of sound institution-building and countering corruption, it does not have a good head start for sound petroleum governance. By tracing the sector's prospective path down the value chain—from oil extraction, revenue generation, and management, up to expenditure policy options—this chapter identified various vulnerable locations or areas of concern, and it gave reasons to be wary about the risks of corruption. In doing so, this chapter is hardly comprehensive or exhaustive, but it has pointed to the daunting institutional and political challenges awaiting Lebanon when or if it becomes a significant petroleum producer. In the end, much will come down to the volume of petroleum revenues that will reach the shores of Lebanon. This, of course, depends on what petroleum reserves IOCs will eventually find. What will also matter a great deal in this context is the Lebanese government's discipline in what is now sensibly designed as a gradual and phased approach to assigning offshore blocks and opening them for production.[72] This would make sense not only in terms of countering the risk of "Dutch disease" and bureaucratic overstretch, but also in terms of mitigating the risk of widespread corruption bankrolled by large rent windfalls.

It should also be noted that Lebanon's recent legislation and establishment of new relevant institutions, such as the LPA, strongly suggest awareness of the complex issues at stake. Yet, what has thus far been put in place or foreseen in terms of maximizing transparency and accountability is far from perfect, let alone corruption-proof. Key in this context—given Lebanon's awkward political settlement—is sorting out the right politics to uphold these good intentions, and improve and strengthen the institutions and policies relevant to the sector that have already been put in place.

Regarding recommendations, there is no desire to join the chorus of "administrative reform" and "good governance" (Bukovansky 2006), which in Lebanon and elsewhere have generated a generic set of platitudes stripping institutional reform from its political underpinnings and its consequences. It also does not make sense for foreign experts to impose their recommendations for better petroleum governance onto Lebanese policy makers and the public at large; all policy options should primarily arise from a national debate that by itself would already feed a culture of greater accountability. Nevertheless, perhaps a number of suggestions can be useful for this debate to center on possible remedies.

Across the value chain of petroleum production, it will be essential that Lebanon's fractured civil society use the opportunity and momentum of building petroleum governance structures to find common ground in demanding transparency and

---

[72] Author's interview with MEW officials, Beirut, 12 June 2014.

accountability, and in jointly scrutinizing every aspect of how the sector will be managed. In this context, it should be noted that there are already various promising initiatives by civil society organizations that aim to raise public awareness and knowledge relevant to the petroleum sector and its governance, and monitor Lebanon's media coverage of the issue and enhance media capacity.[73] Lebanon seems to be on the verge of becoming a petroleum producing country. There is now momentum and an opportunity to coalesce these initiatives and expand their reach. Strikingly, and despite their differences otherwise, most Lebanese of varying sectarian and/or political backgrounds appear to be largely in agreement that strong efforts should be made to prevent the emerging petroleum sector from sinking into the all-too-familiar scenario of rampant corruption and cronyism.[74] Such efforts may perhaps be most effectively channelled into a joint and concrete initiative.

Against this background it may be worthwhile to establish a Lebanon petroleum watchdog comprising a broad coalition of Lebanese civil society organizations and activists who follow and document developments in the petroleum sector with the aim of scrutinizing petroleum-related policies and activities, increasing public awareness, and demanding full transparency and accountability.

In conjunction with this, overall petroleum governance would benefit from a proactive role of IOCs in publicizing and explaining their intentions and efforts, especially in the context of anti-corruption controls, to the Lebanese public as soon as they commence their operations. If or when Lebanon adopts EITI and enters into business with IOCs, other petroleum companies should take part in a multi-stakeholder group that could provide a platform for public outreach. Yet, given Lebanon's past of widespread corruption and opaque business practices, IOCs will need to do more. For instance, IOCs should establish a strong relationship with the Lebanon petroleum watchdog, and be highly responsive to queries on the integrity of the petroleum sector generally that will undoubtedly arise in Lebanese society as soon as production starts.

With regard to the overall governance structure put in place to regulate and manage Lebanon's petroleum sector, the following suggestions can be made:

- Grant the LPA greater institutional and full budgetary independence from the MEW
- Make the selection and appointment of all LPA staff the sole prerogative of a special committee ("the Petroleum Human Resources and Oversight Committee"), consisting of the president of the civil service board, the deputy governor of the central bank, and the minister of state for administrative reform, and supported by

---

[73] In addition to the oil and gas sector project by the Lebanese Center for Policy Studies, Lebanese civil society initiatives relevant to petroleum governance have already been launched by organizations including the Lebanese Oil and Gas Initiative, Middle East Strategic Perspectives, Publish What you Pay, Revenue Watch Institute, the Samir Kassir Foundation, Common Space Initiative, and International Alert. All of these have been producing research and encouraging debate on available governance options, raising awareness, and enhancing media capacity.

[74] A strong consensus in this respect was suggested by debates organized by International Alert in Beirut that included youth representatives of various Lebanese political parties and movements in early 2014. Author's interview with an International Alert representative, Beirut, 11 June 2014.

a review panel of internationally renowned and qualified experts and academics in the field of petroleum governance
- Clearly assign, define, and separate the MEW's prime task of formulating overall petroleum policies, subject to approval of the COM, and the LPA's role as regulator and overall policy enforcer in the petroleum sector
- Subject the MEW's prerogative to bring LPA staff before the disciplinary board to binding review by "the Petroleum Human Resources and Oversight Committee"
- Strengthen the Court of Account's capacities to audit the LPA, and ensure that all its reports and/or findings are made publicly available. To ensure full disclosure in this respect, all work carried out by the Court of Accounts will need to be saved on a protected server accessible to "the Petroleum Human Resources and Oversight Committee," which can decide to disclose these or parts of these data when it deems necessary
- Abrogate current legal stipulations that compel the LPA Board of Directors to obtain ministerial approval before making public statements.

On top of these cross-sector suggestions, a number of recommendations are more specifically relevant to locations on the petroleum value chain, following the order of contexts in which they emerged in this chapter. With regard to the pre-qualification process and tendering toward EPAs:

- Request all pre-qualified operating companies and non-operating companies, and all their participating partner companies—or all such companies that are successful in obtaining EPAs—to fully and publicly disclose their ownership and major shareholders.

Failing this:

- Present full public disclosure of ownership as a biddable item for the EPA bidding round
- Fully and publicly disclose the final EPA contracts or at least release information on the ownership of all winning companies, partner companies, and their subsidiaries, and disclose the agreements reached on all biddable items, including cost oil stipulations
- Demand that all (operating and non-operating) companies, their partners, and subsidiaries, and all subcontracting companies, be registered in jurisdictions that are fully transparent
- Place severe penalties on all companies involved in petroleum production and upstream activities that hide, conceal, or defraud provided information identifying their ownership.

With regard to plans to establish a Lebanese National Oil Company, after necessary and promising commercial opportunities have been verified, and in order to ensure that it will operate effectively and efficiently:

- Legally compel a Lebanese national oil company, even at the later stages of its development, to only engage in oil production activities in consortiums in which IOCs are a key operating partner.

With regard to upstream subcontracting:

- Adopt a robust anti-trust law and put a fully competent and independent regulator in place, and establish a unit therein specialized in petroleum-related activities
- Demand full public disclosure of all large subcontracts and the tendering process that preceded them.

Failing this:

- Oblige all consortiums to turn such a disclosure into a biddable item for their tendering and subcontracting process
- Establish an automated register that makes procurement processes fully and continuously transparent to all parties involved and to the public at large.

With regard to revenue management and efforts to enhance transparency and accountability:

- Commission the central bank to establish a unit fully integrated into its overall top management to manage the sovereign fund
- Within the sovereign fund, allocate petroleum proceeds, or fund dividends, but no more than one-third of total petroleum revenues, to pay off parts of Lebanon's public debt and refinance other parts
- Establish a new Central Procurement Agency, which takes major spending responsibilities for large projects away from line ministries, standardizes procedures, makes them fully transparent, and allows for participation of civil society organizations in both bid evaluation and contract monitoring
- Reinvigorate reforms aimed at decentralization and empowering local governance to prepare the latter for receiving earmarked expenditure from petroleum income
- Consider and weigh the arguments in favor of and against limited and/or conditional direct cash transfers via the sovereign fund's "Mohamad Chatah Account for All Lebanese Citizens"
- If or when the Lebanese NOC will be established, ensure that a majority of its shares will be held respectively by the state, in addition to a part of its shares being distributed to all Lebanese citizens, and the remainder reserved for open subscription.

References

Authored references

Abbink, K. 2000. "Fair Salaries and the Moral Costs of Corruption." Bonn Econ Discussion Paper 1, University of Bonn.

Abou Jaoude, R. 2013. "Survey Shows Lebanese Corruption at All-Time High." The *Daily Star*, 28 June.

Abu Muslih, F. 2013. "Istikhraj al-Ghaz: Yutlibahu al-Mustathmarun [Gas Extraction: What Investors Are Asking for]." *Al-Akhbar*, 6 December.

Achong, M. 2009/10. "Cost Recovery in Production-Sharing Contracts: Opportunity for Striking it Rich or Just Another Risk Not Worth Bearing?" Annual Review 14, Center for Energy, Petroleum, and Mineral Law Policy.

Al-Ayyash, G. 1997. "Azma al-Maliyya al'Ama fi Lubnan: Qissat al-Inhiyar an-Naqdi [Public Finance Crisis in Lebanon: Tale of a Decreasing Currency]." Dar an-Nahar. Christian Michelsen Institute.

Alba, E.M. 2009. "Extractive Industries Value Chain: A Comprehensive Integrated Approach to Developing Extractive Industries." Oil, Gas, and Mining Policy Division Working Paper. The World Bank.

Alieh, Y. 2017. "Oil and Gas Second Round of Prequalification Now Open." *Lebanon Opportunities*, 27 January.

Al-Kasim, F., T. Soreide, and A. Williams. 2008. "Grand Corruption in the Regulation of Oil."

Azar, G. 2017. "What to Expect from Lebanon's Parliament in 2018." *An-Nahar*, 31 December.

Balanche, F. 2012. "The Reconstruction of Lebanon or the Racketeering Rule." In *Lebanon After the Cedar Revolution*, edited by A. Knudsen and M. Kerr. C. Hurst & Co.

Barma, N.H. 2012. "Petroleum, Governance, and Fragility: The Micro-Politics of Petroleum in Postconflict States." In *Beyond the Resource Curse*, edited by B. Shaffer and T. Ziyadov. University of Pennsylvania Press.

Baumann, H. 2012. "The 'New Contractors Bourgeoisie' in Lebanese Politics: Hariri, Mikati and Fares." In *Lebanon: After the Cedar Revolution*, edited by A. Knudsen and M. Kerr. C. Hurst & Co.

Bershidsky, L. 2017. "There Is No Separating Wealth and Power in Russia." *Bloomberg*, 3 March.

Brunnschweiler, C.N. and E.H. Bulte. 2008. "The Resource Curse Revisited and Revised: A Tale of Paradoxes and Red Herrings." *Journal of Environmental Economics and Management* 55: 248–64.

Bukovansky, M. 2006. "The Hollowness of Anti-Corruption Discourse." *Review of International Political Economy* 13: 181–209.

Bulte, E. and R. Damania. 2008. "Resources for Sale: Corruption, Democracy and the Natural Resource Curse." *The B.E. Journal of Economic Analysis & Policy* 8.

Cammett, M. 2011. "Partisan activism and access to welfare in Lebanon." *Studies in Comparative International Development* 46: 70–97.

Cammett, M. and S. Issar. 2010. "Bricks and Mortar Clientelism: Sectarianism and the Logics of Welfare Allocation in Lebanon." *World Politics* 62: 381–421.

Chaaban, J. 2016. "I've Got the Power: Mapping Connections between Lebanon's Banking Sector and the Ruling Class." Working Paper 1059, Economic Research Forum, October.

Chatah, M. 2012. "Offshore Gas Belongs to the Lebanese, So Let Them See the Money." *The Daily Star*, 11 May.

Chen, B. and M. Cammett. 2012. "Informal Politics and Inequity of Access to Health Care in Lebanon." *International Journal for Equity in Health* 11: 1–8.

De la Brière, B. and L.B. Rawlings. 2006. "Examining Conditional Cash Transfer Programs: A Role for Increased Social Inclusion?" Discussion Paper 0603. The World Bank.

Devarajan, S., T. Minh Le, and G. Raballand. 2010. "Increasing Public Expenditure Efficiency in Oil-rich Economies." Policy Research Working Paper 5287. The World Bank.

Eifert, B., A. Gelb, and N.B. Tallroth. 2003. "The Political Economy of Fiscal Policy and Economic Management in Oil Exporting Countries." In *Fiscal Policy Formulation and Implementation in Oil-Producing Countries*, edited by J.M. Davis, R. Ossowski and A. Fedelino. The International Monetary Fund.

El Ghaziri, N. 2007. *Administrative Reform in Post-War Lebanon: Donor Prescriptions and Local Realities*. Shaker Publishing.

El Khazen, F. 2003. "The Postwar Political Process: Authoritarianism by Diffusion." In *Lebanon in Limbo: Postwar Society and State in an Uncertain Regional Environment*, edited by T. Hanf and N. Salam. Nomos Verlagsgesellschaft.

Engen, O.A., O. Langhelle, and R. Bratvold. 2012. "Is Norway Really Norway?" In *Beyond the Resource Curse*, edited by B. Shaffer and T. Ziyadov. University of Pennsylvania Press.

Fadlallah, A. 2012. "An-naft wa al-ghaz: min tharwa taba'iyya 'ila ra's mal intaji [Oil and Gas: From a Natural Endowment to Productive Capital]." *Al-Akhbar*, 19 May.

Frankel, J. 2012. "The Natural Resource Curse: A Survey." In *Beyond the Resource Curse*, edited by B. Shaffer and T. Ziyadov. University of Pennsylvania Press.

Gaspard, T.A. 2004. *A Political Economy of Lebanon, 1948–2002: The Limits of Laissez Faire*. Brill.

Gillies, A. 2010. "Giving Money Away? The Politics of Direct Distribution in Resource Rich States." Center for Global Development, November.

Hasbani, K. 2011. "Electricity Sector Reform in Lebanon: Political Consensus in Waiting." Center on Democracy, Development, and the Rule of Law Working Paper, Stanford University, December.

Hoteit, N. 2014. "L'enjeu du gaz est économique et industriel pour le Liban [The Gas Issue for Lebanon is Economic and Industrial]." *Le Commerce du Levant*, 29 May.

John, J. 2007. "Oil Abundance and Violent Political Conflict: A Critical Assessment." *The Journal of Development Studies* 43: 970–4.

Karl, T.L. 1997. *The Paradox of Plenty: Oil Booms and Petro-States*. University of California Press.

Kingston, P. 2013. *Reproducing Sectarianism: Advocacy Networks and the Politics of Civil Society in Postwar Lebanon*. State University of New York Press.

Kolstad, I., A. Wiig, and A. Williams. 2008. "Mission Improbable: Does Petroleum-Related Aid Address Corruption in Resource-Rich Countries?" Chr. Michelsen Institute.

Ledermann, D. and W.F. Maloney. 2007. *Natural Resources: Neither Curse nor Destiny*. Stanford University Press and The World Bank.

Leenders, R. 2012. *Spoils of Truce: Corruption and State Building in Post-War Lebanon*. Cornell University Press.

Leenders, R. 2016. "The First Time as a Tragedy, the Second as Farce? Lebanon's Nascent Petroleum Sector and the Risks of Corruption." *Mediterranean Politics* 21: 268–91.

Leite, C., and J. Weidmann. 1999. "Does Mother Nature Corrupt? Natural Resources, Corruption, and Economic Growth." Working Paper 99/85, International Monetary Fund.

Marshall, I. 2001. "A Survey of Corruption Issues in the Mining and Mineral Sector." Minerals, Mining, and Sustainable Development Project, International Institute for Environment and Development.

McPherson, C. and S. MacSearraigh. 2007. "Corruption in the Petroleum Sector." In *The Many Faces of Corruption: Tracking Vulnerabilities at the Sector Level*, edited by J. Edgardo Campos and S. Pradan. The World Bank.

Palley, T. 2003. "Combating the Natural Resource Curse with Citizen Revenue Distribution Funds: Oil and the Case of Iraq." Special Report, *Foreign Policy in Focus*: December 2003.

Papyrakis, E. and R. Gerlagh. 2004. "The Resource Curse Hypothesis and Its Transmission Channels." *Journal of Comparative Economics* 32: 181–93.

Pegg, S. 2009. "Briefing: Chronicle of a Death Foretold: The Collapse of the Chad–Cameroon Pipeline Project." *African Affairs* 108.431: 311–20.

Picard, E. 2000. "The Political Economy of Civil War in Lebanon." In *War, Institutions, and Social Change in the Middle East*, edited by S. Heydemann. University of California Press.

Redd, B. 2017. "What's in the Sovereign Wealth Fund Bill?" The *Daily Star*, 17 November.

Ross, M. 2003. "The Natural Resource Curse: How Wealth Can Make You Poor." The World Bank.

Ross, M. 2012. *The Oil Curse: How Petroleum Wealth Shapes the Development of Nations*. Princeton University Press.

Sachs, J. and A.M. Warner. 1999. "Natural Resource Intensity and Economic Growth." In *Development Policies in Natural Resource Economies*, edited by J. Mayer, B. Chambers, and A. Farooq. Edward Elgar.

Sarkis, N. 2014. "Lebanon's Faulty Oil and Gas Framework." The *Daily Star*, 23 June.

Shaxson, N. 2007. "Oil, Corruption and the Resource Curse." *International Affairs* 83: 1123–40.

Smith, B. 2007. *Hard Times in the Lands of Plenty: Oil Politics in Iran and Indonesia*. Cornell University Press.

Stel, N. and W. Naudé. 2013. "Public–Private Entanglement: Entrepreneurship in a Hybrid Political Order, the Case of Lebanon." Institute for the Study of Labour, December.

Takieddine, M. 2013. "Will Lebanon's Oil Be Christian or Muslim?" *Executive Magazine*, 21 March.

Tordo, S., M. Warner, O. Manzano, and Y. Anouti. 2013. "Local Content Policies in the Oil and Gas Sector." The World Bank.

Traboulsi, F. 2014. "Social Classes and Political Power in Lebanon." Heinrich Boll Foundation.

van den Brink, R., A. Sayed, S. Barnett, E. Aninat, E. Parrado, Z. Hasnain, and T. Khan. 2012. "South–South Cooperation: How Mongolia Learned from Chile on Managing a Mineral-Rich Economy." *Economic Premise* 90.

Zahi, J. 2013. "Al-naft al-lubani: li-man [Lebanese Oil: Who Is It for]?" *An-Nahar*, 9 December.

Non-authored references

Al-Akhbar. 2012. "Where to Find Lebanon's Worst Seafront Violations." 10 December.

As-Safir. 2012. "Diwan al-muhasaba yataraj'u dawruhu wal infaq yazid [Court of Audits' Role Diminishes While Spending Increases]." 10 July.

Crime Russia. 2017. "Head of Ministry of Natural Resources Suspected of Conflict of Interest in Distribution of Benefits for Novatek." 27 July.

Executive Magazine. 2013. "We are Being Open and Transparent." 17 October.

Extractive Industries Transparency Initiative. 2017. "Impatient to Implement the EITA Standard, Lebanon Races Ahead on Key Provisions." 18 May.

Global Witness. 2012. "A Blueprint for Reform: Lessons from Past Mismanagement and Murky Practice in Libya's Oil Sector." 13 April.

Human Rights Watch. 2004. "Some Transparency, No Accountability: The Use of Oil Revenue in Angola and Its Impact on Human Rights." 12 January.

Human Rights Watch. 2010. "Transparency and Accountability in Angola: A 2010 Update." 4 April.

International Law and Policy Institute. 2013. "Analysis of the Petroleum Sector in Lebanon." 13 March.

International Monetary Fund. 2005. "Lebanon: Report on Observance of Standards and Codes–Fiscal Transparency Module." 5 May.

Lebanon Economic Monitor. 2014. "A Sluggish Economy in a Highly Volatile Environment." The World Bank, Spring Issue.

Lebanon Oil & Gas Initiative. 2017. "Investigating Lebanon's Pre-Qualified Oil and Gas Bidders: Who Are They and How Should We Assess Them?"

Le Commerce du Levant. 2012. "Création d'un fonds réservé aux recettes du pétrole et du gaz [Creating a fund for oil and gas revenues]." 25 January.

Livemint & The Wall Street Journal. 2011. "Reliance, DGH, Oil Ministry in the Firing Line." 9 September.

Middle East Strategic Perspectives. 2017. "Can Lebanon or Israel Replicate the Success of Cyprus' Third Offshore Licensing Round?" 17 August.

Publish What You Pay. 2009. "Chain for Change Information Booklet."

Publish What You Pay. 2012. "Contracts Disclosure in the Extractive Industries Transparency Initiative." 7 December.

Revenue Watch Institute. 2014. "Natural Resource Fund Governance: The Essentials." April.

The *Daily Star.* 2009. "IDAL Urges Lebanese Expatriates to Invest Part of Their Remittances in Real Projects." 5 November.

The World Bank. 2003. "Natural Resources and Violent Conflict: Options and Actions." Report no. 28245.

World Economic Forum. 2017. "Global Competitiveness Report 2017–2018."

4

Establishing a National Oil Company in Lebanon

Valérie Marcel[1]

Introduction

Countries that are exploring for or have discovered oil and gas are keen to increase national participation in their petroleum sectors and often view a national oil company (NOC) as a corporate vehicle for the defense of national interests in the upstream. Many of these emerging producers, including Lebanon, have expressed interest in guidelines on how to time the creation of an NOC and determine an optimal role for it.

In Lebanon, there have been repeated calls by politicians and commentators for the creation of an NOC (Abi Hydar 2015, Arab American News 2005).[2] However, the 2010 Offshore Petroleum Resources Law (OPRL) clarifies a necessary threshold for creating an NOC: "When necessary and after promising commercial opportunities have been verified, the Council of Ministers (COM) may establish an NOC on the basis of a proposal by the Minister based upon the opinion of the Petroleum Administration."[3] This reasonable threshold is clearly not met in Lebanon, as the country awarded its first licenses in December 2017 and exploration is only starting. Nevertheless, political expectations are high that discoveries will be made and that the impact will be transformative for the country.

In this regard, key questions for Lebanon are: When is the right time to create an NOC? What would Lebanon want an NOC to do? What would this role cost? What corporate governance mechanisms would an NOC need in order to perform effectively and avoid major pitfalls? What governance framework would keep it in check? Ultimately, if sufficient benefit to Lebanon cannot be established, the idea of creating

---

[1] The author is very grateful to Sami Atallah and LCPS for their support, and to Patrick Heller from NRGI, Professor Paul Stevens from Chatham House, and Mona Sukkarieh from MESTRATE, whose insights and expertise greatly improved the research, although they may not agree with all of the interpretations or conclusions of this chapter.

[2] In 2013, Parliamentary Committee on Energy Chairman Mohammad Qabbani and former Minister of Energy and Water Gebran Bassil said they supported establishing an NOC, as did parliament's advisor for energy affairs, Rabih Yaghi, in 2015. Expert commentators Nicolas Sarkis and Fuad Jawad also (separately) called for an NOC in 2005.

[3] Lebanese Parliament. 2010. Offshore Petroleum Resources Law. Law 132, 24 August.

an NOC should be questioned. The experience of other emerging producers can provide Lebanon with answers to some of these questions.

Section one reviews common rationales for creating an NOC, contrasting the experience of established and emerging producers. Section two examines various types of NOCs and considers the potential benefits and risks of each model in the Lebanese context. The aim of this section is not to recommend a specific model, nor to advise for or against the creation of an NOC in Lebanon, but rather to narrow down the available options, while taking into account the national context. Section three focuses on the governance framework that would be required to establish a capable and accountable NOC. The chapter concludes with a review of the most appropriate NOC models for each stage of development of the resource base.

Why create an NOC?

This section will review various reasons why states may consider establishing an NOC, with a particular focus on historical precedents, mandates, and goals for NOCs.

Historical importance of NOCs

Emerging producers—denoting those countries in the first stages of the development of their petroleum sector—have the benefit of hindsight as they look to their more established peers for lessons. For those new producers in Africa, key lessons include how to avoid the pitfalls that marred the progress of producers like Nigeria and Angola. For emerging producers in the Middle East, the lessons are different and quite positive. Established producers from the region stand out as peers to emulate. NOCs such as Saudi Aramco and Qatar Petroleum manage their petroleum sector very capably. There is great national pride in the history of nationalization of petroleum assets and a deep emotional attachment to sovereign control over natural resources remains strong in many Middle Eastern societies (as is also the case in Latin America). For emerging producers in the region, this may translate into public expectations that foreign oil companies should not dominate their national petroleum sector and an NOC should be able to take on some responsibilities for developing resources (Middle East Strategic Perspectives 2016).

While there are lessons to be learned from the history of Middle East NOCs, they are not entirely transferable to an emerging producer context. For all their common cultural, historical, and political references, each NOC is unique. The national context in which they operate also brings with it a unique set of opportunities and challenges. For this reason, it is crucial for Lebanon to think carefully about how each type of NOC mandate would serve the interests of the country and how an NOC would interact with existing institutions and fare in the political economy of Lebanon.

Countries at the exploration phase with no proven reserve base (or only small reserves) should also be cautious about drawing lessons about how to manage the petroleum sector and how to establish an NOC from a country that has vast petroleum reserves and has managed over many years to create significant technical and managerial capacity. Emerging producers have a different national context with which to contend. They face geological uncertainty about the size of reserves, and prospectivity is not assured. They have less petroleum sector experience and commonly also low state capacity. The most obvious implications when creating an NOC are that the talent pool to draw from is limited, and the financial resources to fund the initiative will also be limited. In this respect, Lebanon is unusual in that it could draw on talented, experienced oil and gas professionals in the diaspora. However, it remains to be seen whether these expatriates can be drawn back to Lebanon.

When resources are scarce, strategic decisions must be made. This chapter will reflect on policy options available at the exploration stage, post-discovery, and in the early production phase. As we will see, options change substantially over these phases, which makes a sequenced approach, involving incremental changes as the geological situation evolves and as capacity grows, very useful. Emerging producers do not necessarily need to set a "final" institutional structure from day one. They can think a step or two ahead and anticipate future needs.[4]

It's not about profits

Inspired by the success and revenue generation of established NOCs in the Middle East, many citizens of emerging producers—and specifically in Lebanon—may assume that if their country establishes an NOC, the key questions will be "What to do with the profits?" and "Who will benefit financially?" Rather, the key concern should be how the fledgling company is financed, particularly as new NOCs are cost centers.

The capacity for NOCs to generate profits and the scale of those profits depend to a very large extent on the stage of development of the resource—in other words, whether the country has reached the production (revenue-generating) phase—and the ability of the company to retain earnings from oil or gas sales. Any company created before production will require the financial support of the state. Even after production begins (and assuming that an NOC has equity stakes in the producing fields), an NOC will likely be paying back operators of the field for its share of the costs they carried until production.

In the case of Lebanon, which is entering the exploration phase, revenues from production would likely not arrive for 10 to 15 years after the first bidding round—assuming a commercial discovery is made and the enabling legal framework and geopolitical and marketing environments are supportive. Exploration, assessment of discoveries, agreement between the host government and operators on a development plan, and the development of processing and export facilities, all take time. Tanzania, for instance, which licensed in 2007 and made several offshore gas discoveries from 2010 to 2014, is stalled in the pre-FID (final investment decision) stage because the operators are waiting for a "host government agreement" to clarify the conditions under which the project will operate. In Lebanon, which was unable to elect a president

---

[4] These are recommendations of the New Petroleum Producers Discussion Group—refer to the Chatham House Guidelines for Good Governance in Emerging Oil and Gas Producers (Marcel 2016a).

for two years and where sectarian politics amplify the risk of policy paralysis, one should expect time-to-production and to-revenues to be unusually long (perhaps even beyond 15 years). The progress of the sector toward its first licensing round has already suffered unusually long delays, with the process on hold for three years until the election of Michel Aoun as president in October 2016 resolved the deadlock.

Until production begins and revenues flow from sales of oil or gas, NOCs in emerging producer countries have relied on the following sources of revenue:

- Government budget allocations: This represents a core source of funding for NOCs in the pre-production phase. Allocations are subject to government priorities, meaning they fluctuate and are unreliable.
- Downstream sales: For NOCs with activities in refining, midstream (transport), or retail, those revenues can contribute to a significant part of their budget but will also fluctuate due to the cyclical nature of the downstream business. Some NOCs are granted the right to impose levies on the domestic sale of petroleum products so they can generate revenues outside the national budget.
- Upstream revenues from geological data sales or payments from operators: Some NOCs are granted the right to retain revenues from data sales, signature bonuses at licensing, surface rental rights, and other types of upstream revenues. These can be a significant share of an NOC's budget. They also fluctuate because they depend on exploration interest and the holding of a licensing round.

Financial constraints cause most NOCs in the pre-discovery stage to be small. Staff sizes range from 12 to 150 for NOCs without downstream operations. NOCs at the high end of that workforce range are bloated entities, with the growth in spending supported by an NOC taking some upstream revenues. These NOCs faced serious financial difficulties when the oil price fell and exploration slowed because upstream revenues dried up and they could not maintain their labor costs. NOCAL of Liberia, for instance, was forced to cut its staff by three-quarters in the summer of 2015, as it had grown beyond its means to 146 employees (Marcel 2016b).

In Lebanon, upstream revenues from operator payments (application fees for the bid round and area fees) and data sales are set to go to the treasury. Unless the government decides to allocate these revenues differently, it should be expected that an NOC would be funded primarily by a government budgetary allocation. Therefore, if an NOC is created before production starts, a key consideration will be how much the Lebanese state wants to invest in it every year. In other words, it will be necessary to determine what kind of NOC Lebanon can afford.

This question should be considered by the state in terms of risk and reward. Currently, the risk of Lebanon creating an NOC involved in the exploration phase is higher and the payoff of an investment in an NOC is highly uncertain. According to Richmond Energy Partners data,[5] industry commercial success rates for exploration from 2012 to 2016 were 31 percent overall and 7 percent for frontier provinces, such as Lebanon. Changes to upstream agreements over the last 50 years have put that exploration risk onto private companies. Indeed, given the high risk of failure during

---

[5] Refer to Westwood Global Energy Group for data: https://www.westwoodenergy.com

exploration, it is questionable whether NOCs should be responsible for exploration projects, particularly where their experience is limited. Risks should be weighed carefully, especially considering competing demands for state funds in a country with urgent development priorities. Unless the state believes an NOC would do a better job at developing the sector than the Lebanese Petroleum Administration (LPA), the risks of an early creation of an NOC outweigh the rewards. Later, should reserves be proven, the perception of risk and reward may change and justify investments in an NOC. However, even where geology is proven, investing heavily in an NOC means transferring a larger share of risk to the state, with the hope of bigger payoffs in time. It should be noted that significant risks remain during the development phase (post-discovery, during the elaboration of development plans for the project), when cost overruns and project delays can occur.

Range of state goals and the importance of a clear mandate

NOC ambitions have often led them to take on wider mandates (creeping into a state agency role or taking on non-commercial functions). They have also sought to develop technical capacity beyond the requirements of their given mandate (investing more heavily in technical upstream skills than is warranted by their role or level of activity). Sometimes this has been done with the consent of a government that was eager to see an NOC become a strong player in the upstream. Conversely, governments also have required them to hire nationals, causing them to become bloated and expensive organizations.

For these reasons, it is essential for the government to define in very clear terms the mission of an NOC and the scope and limits of its role. An NOC interacts primarily with a ministry of energy and ministry of finance and a regulatory agency where one exists (as in Lebanon). Historical and modern experience shows the prevalence of encroachment and overlap of roles between these organizations and an NOC. The asymmetric principal–agent relationship is a common problem that arises where a self-interested NOC (the agent) has more information about the sector, preventing the principal (the state) from holding it to account and ensuring that it acts in the best interest of the state. It is therefore of key importance for governments to assess what NOC role would fill a gap in the existing petroleum governance system, give careful consideration to how it would interact with other organizations with a role in the sector, and invest in building its capacity to hold an NOC to account.

At least initially, a new NOC in Lebanon would naturally play a relatively small role. The LPA is well established and assumes all responsibilities for promotion, licensing, and oversight of operations. A new NOC should respect the boundaries delineated by existing institutions.

An NOC's role should be defined by the government and guided by a clear prioritization of state objectives. Many common NOC objectives can be carried out by state agencies or even the private sector, and the state should consider whether there is a benefit in creating an NOC to do so:

- Maximizing revenue: NOCs are often created to hold minority or majority stakes in licenses on behalf of the state in order for it to capture a greater portion of rents—a share of profit oil—in addition to royalties, taxes, and dividends. But NOCs only maximize revenue transfers to the state when they are focused on cost control and make sound investment decisions. Many NOCs have failed in these aspects of their mandate.[6] NOCs in Mexico, Nigeria, Angola, and Liberia (which has not made a commercial discovery), for instance, grew into bloated entities that became vehicles for corruption and cronyism.[7]

- National control of the resource: This is a legitimate political goal, prevalent in countries with a colonial past. Oil is a politically sensitive resource in many countries. Ensuring a national company is involved in the process of transforming natural resources is a question of national pride. This objective translates into the state granting an NOC guaranteed minority stakes and sometimes in tasking an NOC to become an operator to encourage the development of upstream skills. Another vehicle for national control is an NOC with a regulatory role.

- Security of supply: This has been an important role in the pre-production phase for many companies tasked with imports of gasoline.[8] Countries in the production phase may have an NOC that is vertically integrated, refining a share of petroleum production for domestic supply.

- Providing affordable energy to domestic users: NOCs have been required to supply the domestic market with energy at cost or below cost, subsidizing domestic energy use. This is a risky course of action for an emerging producer because once subsidies for energy are in place, they are politically difficult to remove later. They lead to increasing patterns of domestic consumption, which in the Persian Gulf have proven unsustainable and costly (Lahn and Stevens 2014).

- Assisting with the implementation of economic development policies: This NOC objective is important in countries with low economic development and/or low state capacity to provide services to the population. NOCs are tasked with promoting national economic development in two ways: they make use of their role in the sector to create supply chains and foster linkages between the energy sector and the rest of the economy or they may take on activities in sectors somewhat unrelated to their core business or become sponges to absorb unemployment. Clearly the former is more beneficial to the country but needs to be strategically overseen by the government. In the absence of this oversight and accountability, these kinds of programs can be a source of patronage and corruption.

- Promoting social welfare: This was historically a central goal for NOCs tasked with funding hospitals or road construction or providing more generally for the needs of the population where the state administration was unable to do so. However, most NOCs have backed away from this role as it constitutes a drain on their resources (with the notable exception of Petróleos de Venezuela, S.A.). Government capacity also increased in most established producers, meaning they could provide services without the assistance of NOCs.

---

[6] For a discussion of the causes of poor NOC performance see Victor *et al.* 2012.

[7] For a discussion of these cases refer to Victor *et al.* 2012, Gillies *et al.* 2015, De Oliveira 2007, and Marcel 2016b.

[8] For those in the production phase, this role would entail investing in refining, midstream or retail.

The relative importance of the above objectives will vary from country to country depending on resource bases, state administrative capacity, and available petroleum sector skills. Governments must then decide how NOCs can contribute to implementing a national vision for the development of the country and what gaps it can fill. In an emerging producer context the government should expect those variables to change over time and they will need to reassess NOC objectives every three to five years, while providing a good degree of overall policy consistency.

Some changes in mission and focus of NOCs are more reactive, leading to wasted efforts and investments and erratic strategies. Even well-established NOCs have seen their missions change in response to urgent national needs or drops in the price of oil, requiring them to focus on addressing welfare needs or cost control. A similar fate befalls new NOCs. For instance, in the period 2011–14, when oil prices were high, NOC missions were ambitious across many emerging producer countries—such as the National Petroleum Corporation of Namibia (NAMCOR) and Ghana National Petroleum Corporation (GNPC), which decided to become standalone operators. Since the fall in prices, NAMCOR has abandoned its operator ambitions, while GNPC struggles to finance its growth strategy.

To avoid this, governments should assess which NOC mandate would add value (on the basis of some of the state objectives detailed above, for instance), what this would cost, how long it would take a new NOC to execute that role effectively, and what governance systems should be in place to hold an NOC to account. The success of this political process of defining a mandate and assessing performance depends on the capacity and will of the political leadership.

What NOC mandates would serve Lebanon's interests?

This section will review possible mandates for an NOC in Lebanon, questioning in each instance "What would be required to make it work?" and "Is this mandate appropriate for Lebanon today? If not, when?"

A concessionaire-type NOC

Several emerging producer countries have seen the benefits, notably through rapid capacity building in oversight, of mandating their NOC to handle some or all regulatory functions of the petroleum sector on behalf of the state (Ghana, Brazil from the 1970s to 1997, Kenya). However, in a country such as Lebanon, where a capable and independent regulatory agency already exists, giving a new NOC a regulatory function would muddle governance processes and undermine the LPA. There would likely be overlap and competition for functions between the agency and the company. Lack of clarity in roles and responsibilities is one of the greatest causes of poor governance of a national petroleum sector.

Other countries that established a regulatory agency first and a NOC second include East Timor, Uganda, and Mozambique. One of the benefits of proceeding in this sequence of institution building is that there is a greater likelihood of clear roles being delineated, with the agency able to hold its own vis-à-vis the company.

104 *The Future of Petroleum in Lebanon*

For these reasons, Lebanon should avoid giving an NOC a role that would usurp that of the LPA in licensing and regulating operators. Other governance roles that could be considered include an advisory role to the LPA and the Ministry of Energy and Water (MEW). An NOC can provide such advice if it holds the state's equity share and sits in on development committee meetings with foreign oil companies. On these committees, the company gets a closer view of operational decisions and may represent the state concerning technical and cost issues that arise. To ensure good governance, such roles should be clearly defined with clear reporting lines.

Manager of state equity shares in the upstream

An NOC that is a manager of state interests in the upstream is distinct from a commercial NOC that owns minority interests (described in the next section). The manager of state interests does not aspire to be an oil company—with functions such as participating in corporate decision making structures and investing in subsidiaries— but is a much more passive stewardship company playing an oversight role. Norway's NOC Petoro is a good example of this type of NOC. Petoro does not operate fields and does not directly own licenses. It manages the state's participatory interests in joint ventures.[9] Key elements in creating and securing value for the state are achieving optimum recovery of resources within each license and ensuring that the government obtains its rightful share of this value. Petoro does this through active participation in licenses. This aspect of its role requires a high level of technical competence. In its early years, a Petoro-styled NOC in Lebanon would not have the knowledge base to effectively ensure optimum recovery of oil and gas from each license. It would initially be learning from operators about the technical and risk management factors that shape their decision making.

Another aspect of Petoro's role is its focus on risk management and financial management for the state's direct financial interest, including preparation of budgets and keeping of accounts. This is an important aspect of its role because Norway has large holdings in oil and gas and Petoro manages the portfolio on behalf of the state. However, in Lebanon, where the reserve base will likely be on a significantly smaller scale, an NOC focused on portfolio management will not add value for the state.

This NOC mandate, as with an NOC as a commercial upstream company, rests on the idea of state participation. Many countries provide an option for a host government to "participate" in a project as a joint venture partner. Most commonly in an emerging producer country, the foreign oil company "carries" or pays the way of its NOC partner through exploration, appraisal, and possibly even development, after which an NOC must contribute its share of the costs as per its share of equity. The private investor may or may not be compensated for the funds advanced on behalf of the state (McPherson 2008). Repayment is commonly made through government revenues once oil production begins.

---

[9] It is also mandated to monitor Equinor's marketing and sale of the petroleum produced from the state's direct financial interest, but this aspect of its mandate is not relevant in Lebanon because it involves the oversight of another NOC.

In Lebanon, Article 6 of the 2010 OPRL states the following regarding state participation: "The State reserves the right to carry out or participate in Petroleum Activities pursuant to this law and its share shall be stipulated in the Petroleum License or the Exploration and Production Agreement (EPA), and shall be determined according to a COM Decree taken on the basis of a proposal by the minister based upon the opinion of the Petroleum Administration." For the first licensing round, the government decided, based on the advice of the LPA, not to adopt state participation.

Whether Lebanon decides to provide for a minority state participation in future licenses will depend on its calculations regarding risk and reward. Myers and Manley compared the state take (revenue to state) of Norway and the United Kingdom in the North Sea, finding that "Norway generated more than double the revenue the UK did from each barrel it produced" thanks to majority stakes in 11 out of 14 billion barrel fields, while the UK government "has had effectively no direct equity participation in the North Sea and has had a fully private upstream sector, with taxation as the only channel of government revenues from hydrocarbons" since 1986 (Manley and Myers 2015).[10] While it was clearly a good investment for the Norwegian state to invest funds in its equity stakes, they were risking public funds on the positive commercial outcome of petroleum projects. Emerging producers should take this investment risk seriously, especially where they have a limited understanding of how to evaluate geological and financial risk. For these reasons, it is highly unusual for the government to participate in the exploration phase. Rather, the company takes all the risk associated with exploration and the government can "back-in" to a percentage stake if there is a discovery (Kenya Civil Society Platform on Oil and Gas 2016).

Nevertheless, the rationale for state participation is not purely economic. A state stake demonstrates that a country has not licensed away its natural resources to foreign oil companies. This can be politically important for emerging producers, which commonly have a colonial legacy and must also stand to comparison with established producers that nationalized their oil sectors decades ago and now boast a degree of operational control over their upstream. Another justification for state participation is the access it gives an NOC (and other designated state agents) to decision making regarding the field. With an equity interest, the state (through its agent) participates on essentially the same terms as other private oil companies in a joint venture.

The suitability of a Petoro type company in Lebanon would also hinge on the implementation of high standards of corporate governance. The company's role is to ensure "that the state receives its rightful share and does not get charged a larger proportion of costs than is warranted."[11] To carry out this role effectively, a company should take steps to avoid regulatory capture—capture involves an NOC advancing the interests of commercial or political groups that dominate the sector it is regulating, instead of acting in the public interest. Specifically, this means an NOC would need to keep foreign oil companies at a distance in order to assess their costs with impartiality.

---

[10] Norway has generated $18.8 per barrel of oil more in revenue for the state than the United Kingdom, which has $9.1 less tax take per barrel and $9.8 per barrel in state equity cash flow and dividends (government revenues from oil and gas production in 2014 prices since 1970 on a per barrel of oil equivalent basis).

[11] Petoro website, https://www.petoro.no/about-petoro

At Petoro, "Conflicts of interest are a fixed item on the agenda at board meetings, and directors with such a conflict withdraw from the board's consideration of the relevant issue." It is also good practice for any revenue and expenses related to portfolio state equity interests to be kept apart from operational accounts of the company.

Funds for operating costs of Petoro AS and Petoro Iceland AS are provided by the government.[12] Petoro is a small organization of 70 employees. Any company established in Lebanon would require a very small staff in relation to the work to be done (likely under ten people). Such a company should be housed in an existing institution—such as the LPA, MEW, or the Ministry of Finance (MOF)—until more significant equity shares are to be managed. Even then, such a company should not become a bloated entity with a large staff.

A commercial upstream company

A commercial upstream NOC presents a slightly different mandate from the manager of upstream equity stakes in that it would own its equity shares in licenses and its mandate would be to operate commercially. Any responsibilities on behalf of the state (governance role) should normally be very limited (including at most an advisory role to the LPA or the MEW or MOF). It would be mandated to build its technical capabilities and increase its presence in the upstream sector in Lebanon, and, over time, to become a successful commercial entity. A subset of (or the ultimate evolution of companies with) this type of mandate is an operator; in other words, an upstream company that has legal authority to explore for and produce petroleum resources in a given field. This aspect of the mandate will be considered later in this section. For now, let us first consider the role of an NOC as a commercial entity holding minority equity shares on behalf of the state.

The commercial upstream NOC mandate is the archetypal mandate for an NOC in the Norwegian-inspired separation of powers model. As Lebanon is receiving Norwegian technical assistance through the Oil for Development Program, both this model NOC and the Petoro-style NOC model are relevant for Lebanon.

As Mozambique has been the largest recipient of Norwegian petroleum-related assistance, with substantial and sustained contributions since 1983 (in addition to other multilateral and bilateral aid), it is useful to examine the achievements and challenges that its NOC, Empresa Nacional de Hidrocarbonetos (ENH), faces. Foreign technical assistance allowed Mozambique to set up a well-functioning "separation of powers" model, with an independent regulatory agency (INP), an NOC (ENH), and a Ministry of Energy, each with clearly defined roles. As prescribed by the separation of powers model, ENH does not benefit from special privileges in the upstream sector in Mozambique (aside from licenses granting it minority stakes). Since ENH was established in 1998, it has worked to establish its technical capacity through its 15–25 percent equity participation in licenses. However, it has struggled financially and lacks

---

[12] Operating expenses in 2014 were NOK 301.5 million (approx $37 million) for the group. They related primarily to payroll and administration expenses and to the purchase of external services, like studies on mature fields.

the resources to invest in capacity building, and more significantly, to meet its share of costs related to its equity stakes. In contrast to many emerging NOCs whose share of costs in the license are carried through to production, ENH must finance its share of development costs. In Mozambique's Rovuma Basin offshore gas concessions, the state is entitled to 15 percent of Anadarko's Area 1, and to 10 percent of Italian gas company Eni's Area 4. Anadarko estimates that the CapEx for the first stage of the Rovuma Basin project, which consists of two LNG trains and the development of offshore gas fields, will be approximately $20 billion (Nuvunga 2015). The challenge for cash-strapped ENH is how to raise the estimated $1.5 billion to $1.7 billion to cover its share of the projects (England 2015). ENH is looking at the possibility of initially being "carried" by its partners in the projects, with foreign groups financing the Mozambican company's equity contributions.

Funding state participation can indeed be challenging. When an NOC is unable to generate enough money to meet its cash calls, project delays may ensue that are costly for state revenues. For this reason, determining the appropriate level of state participation is key. If the project is profitable, funding high levels of state participation offers a net gain for the budget. However, the timing of flows can be tricky, and the state may need to lay out funds for some time before realizing returns. In the interim, the required outlays draw resources away from other urgent budget priorities. There is also the possibility that a project will not be profitable. Project risks at the development stage can be substantial, especially in relation to the smaller size of the economy and state budget. Small levels of state participation would be more suitable in a country with immediate socio-economic budgetary priorities like Lebanon.

In Kenya, the National Oil Corporation has minority stakes that were carried to the development phase. In February 2015, it was reported that the National Oil Corporation of Kenya was seeking to raise $1.2 billion through internal sources, external debt, and other equity partners in order to finance its share of oil development costs following discoveries (Kenya Civil Society Platform on Oil and Gas 2016).

Established oil or gas producers can use sales from their production to finance the state's share of capital expenditure for new LNG projects. Emerging producers do not have this option and their NOCs struggle to finance their share of costs. One solution is to have oil companies carry an NOC financially until production, but they will expect compensation for this "carry". The companies will recover the cost of carrying an NOC once production starts, which delays revenues being delivered to the state. Another option is to wait to establish an NOC until the production phase and take an equity stake that will generate revenues (once the cost of the stake is paid for). In this case, the state's intention for an NOC to take a minority stake at the production phase should be laid out in the licensing phase. In all cases, the cost of state participation through the vehicle of an NOC should be considered carefully by governments (Table 4.1).

A related point is that the state will only benefit financially if an NOC manages its costs carefully, as well as larger costs of the project (which the NOC may not control directly). As the Kenya Civil Society Platform on Oil and Gas (2016) paper highlights, state revenues generated through state participation do not go directly to the treasury if the asset is held by an NOC—in contrast to the Petoro model. In this case, the actual revenue to government is limited to corporate income tax and dividends that an NOC

Table 4.1 State participation options

Project phases	Full Equity	Partial Carry	Full Carry
Exploration	State pays full share of costs as incurred	Company pays all costs (state may pay back)	Company pays all costs (state rarely pay back)
Development		State pays full share	Company pays all costs (state normally pay back from production)
Production		State pays full share	State pays full share
Examples	Norway, Venezuela	Kenya, Mozambique	Egypt, Ghana, Angola

Source: Kenya Civil Society Platform on Oil and Gas (2016).

pays to the treasury. It is therefore important to establish an NOC under a financial system that encourages cost reduction and profit making, so a greater share of the turnover is sent to the treasury.

If such an NOC is established in Lebanon at the exploration phase, it will be dependent on government budget allocations or upstream payments from operators (e.g. capital gains tax on transfer of rights, surface rentals, or other revenues, as determined by government) and it will need to stay lean, with a small staff (under 12 people). If an NOC is created after discoveries, during the development phase its capital expenditure will dwarf the government budget and the government will need to allow it to raise finances on capital markets and/or with equity partners. Conditions for its farm-in to existing licenses will need to have been established at the licensing stage. If an NOC is created at the production phase, those conditions will again need to be established. An NOC will need a financial structure that incentivizes cost control. Importantly, its level of activity in the upstream—presuming it takes a few minority stakes in production or development licences—will not be of sufficient scale to justify a company with a large workforce (20 to 80 people, depending on its intention to take on operator responsibilities). As a recent article on the matter pointed out, Lebanon has a strong tendency toward clientelism and the mass-staffing of public institutions. "Some of those calling for establishing an NOC at this stage have a poor record in this regard" (Middle East Strategic Perspectives 2016).

In many emerging producer countries, petroleum laws give NOCs the right to take on operator responsibilities for fields, and some specifically mandate that NOCs become operators. An NOC becomes an operator when it takes on a majority equity stake in a field. It then becomes responsible for the development of that field. This requires a high level of technical and financial expertise as well as project management capacity. An operator must be able to select the appropriate technology, propose a development plan, raise financing, manage a large project, and assess geological and financial risks. An operator manages a high level of risk, such as shouldering possible losses for dry holes in wildcat exploration that are in the range of $100 million per well. However, emerging NOCs rarely have the financial and technical capabilities to take on such responsibilities (Marcel *et al.* 2016).[13] This aspect of the mandate tends to

[13] This issue is discussed in greater detail in Marcel *et al.* (2016).

be aspirational. However, it serves neither the company nor the government to set expectations that cannot be met.

Becoming an operator takes time, between seven and 15 years, and is very costly. Without significant proven reserves, revenues from production or a history of petroleum sector experience to draw on, a new NOC in Lebanon will not be able to develop operator skills. For this reason, the recommendation of the New Petroleum Producers Discussion Group is to delay the goal of operating in the upstream until discoveries promise a reserve lifespan that is longer than the time it would take to develop these capabilities—hence waiting until the reserve base promises at least 15 years of production. Until this reserve base is established, the current government and future Lebanese governments should raise general human and state administrative capacity through training, focus on skills-building within the MOF, MEW, and LPA, and provide an NOC with only a limited budget for building operational skills (Marcel *et al.* 2016).

Lebanon should also consider that the cost of developing operator capabilities and meeting the exploration and development costs of a field are very high. There is a wide range of costs in the development of operator capabilities (depending on the type of geology, the cost of buying into assets, existing capabilities, for instance), but in all cases these costs are too high to be funded out of a state budget and a new company is not likely to obtain the capital required on financial markets. Once in production, an NOC may draw on petroleum revenues, provided its financial structure allows it to retain revenues from export sales. It is therefore a more appropriate goal for the production phase.

A commercial downstream or marketing company

A different type of NOC could be created in Lebanon in the event commercial discoveries are made and once production begins, with a mandate to market the state's share of petroleum. Its focus could be export sales or creating the infrastructure necessary to bring petroleum to shore for its productive use in Lebanon.

Cyprus's NOC provides a useful illustration of this type of company. Cyprus established the Cyprus Hydrocarbons Company (CHC) in 2014. The CHC is working with Block 12 contractors to jointly market the government's share of gas produced at the Aphrodite Field. The company will take ownership, on behalf of the country, of any major infrastructure projects that will be established in relation to the sector such as the proposed land-based LNG plant in Vasilikos or subsea pipeline (Energy Boardroom 2014). It is a lean company, due to the small scale of its activities. In 2014, the budget Law 57 (II) of 2014 granted the company a budget of 1 million euros.[14]

Another aspect of the CHC mandate is participating in management committee meetings with operators on behalf of the state. To effectively carry out this role, an NOC requires technical capacity and experience. In the case of Lebanon, the LPA is more firmly established with such capability and there would be no added value in

---

[14] Government of Cyprus, Ministry of Finance. 2015. Budget Law N.57 (II)/2014.

having an NOC duplicate skills development to carry out this role. However, as the resource base develops and the potential rewards of creating an NOC increase, the state may want to develop an expert company that increasingly builds a deep understanding of the commercial business and industry expertise over time.

This type of NOC may also have a more downstream focus, with a view to bringing (some of) the gas to shore for use in industry or the power sector. For instance, Ghana, in a drive to stop flared gas (gas associated with oil production), developed a plan for its productive use in Ghana. The country's priorities for the energy sector are power, cement, and compressed natural gas in the transport sector. The NOC, GNPC, was tasked as the National Gas Aggregator to invest in securing low-cost gas for power generation and to develop a gas market to monetize gas resources (GNPC 2015). Financing these investments is a challenge for Ghana and its NOC, especially in light of current oil market conditions and national public debt (GNPC 2016). In Lebanon, an NOC would face an additional challenge related to the higher cost of non-associated gas.

In deciding to have an NOC focused on supplying gas (or oil) to the national market, there is a risk that the company will be required to provide gas at prices below cost of supply through some form of subsidy or special transfer pricing. Such practices encourage the undervaluation of gas in society, encourage excessive consumption, and benefit the wealthy more than the poor (Marcel *et al.* 2016). Transfer pricing also tends to be opaque, which presents significant risks in terms of corruption.

A champion for maximizing in country value

Another role for an NOC could be one focused on maximizing linkages between the national economy and petroleum sector. Activities could include support of education and vocational training, and the creation of national supply chains. The Oman Oil Company (OOC) is a good illustration of this model. OOC is a commercial company wholly owned by the government of Oman. It was established in 1996 as a national flagship company with the objective of reducing national dependence on oil revenues by diversifying the economy and building human capital. Within the sultanate, it develops oil- and gas-based industries and related supply chains in partnership with international companies. A key feature of the company is that it is government owned, yet commercial, and has developed competencies in project management (Oman Oil Company Exploration & Production LLC 2014).

In Lebanon, an NOC along this model would only be justified in the production phase and if the scale of petroleum sector activities and their duration were large and long enough, respectively, to support the NOC's activities. In other words, it would be justified if there were several projects to create some demand for goods, services, and skills (Marcel *et al.* 2016).[15] In the event that discoveries promise a shorter production lifespan (e.g., 15–20 years), the focus of such a company should be on helping local businesses, universities, and vocational centers get a timely (early) understanding of

---

[15] Context appropriate decision making for local content is presented in Marcel *et al.* (2016).

the size of the demand for goods, services, and skills for the petroleum sector and of any requirements regarding the standards and certification required by the industry. In many producer countries, local companies and educational institutions do not have a clear view of the demand from petroleum sector projects, one that would enable them to build capabilities or goods to the standard required by the sector in a timely manner.

A common mistake made by emerging producers wishing to actively participate in the nascent joint sector is to train petroleum geologists and engineers, whereas the petroleum sector's likelier greater need in terms of skills will be for electricians and welders. Countries like Ghana, which invested significantly in educating young Ghanaians since discovering oil in 2007, have a growing segment of young petroleum engineering and geology graduates without jobs. In light of the energy transition, efforts to minimize dependency on the oil sector should always be made, regardless of the size of the resource base. It is particularly urgent to focus on transferrable skills and services in countries with a relatively small petroleum sector— in other words, develop a skill or service that can be used by the petroleum sector and other sectors (Marcel *et al.* 2016).

In Lebanon, the economy shows weaknesses in terms of technological readiness, as measured in the World Economic Forum's (WEF) Competitiveness Index through the availability of the latest technologies, firm-level technology absorption, university–industry collaboration in engineering and development, foreign direct investment, and technology transfer, but demonstrates high levels of business sophistication, in terms of local supplier quantity and value chain breadth and competitive advantage, in addition to quality of education and the availability of venture capital (World Economic Forum 2015). These proxy measures of the readiness of the Lebanese economy to engage with the petroleum sector are encouraging. But they also point to the value of providing Lebanese private sector companies with a forward view of the petroleum industry's expected demand (what demand, to what standard and when) and conversely for the petroleum industry to understand better what is available locally. Specifically, this could mean raising the operating standards of suppliers to meet the requirements of the industry and increasing university–industry collaboration so the right skills are developed. An NOC could take on this role, but it could also be handled (at a lesser cost) by another state institution.

In light of Lebanon's intractable problem with corruption (specifically bribes and favoritism in the decisions of government officials)—which ranks among the greatest obstacles to doing business in the country according to the WEF index—an NOC (or any other state organization) should not be responsible for determining which companies or individuals are awarded contracts to supply goods and services to petroleum projects, for instance by handling a pre-qualification process for domestic suppliers. An NOC's role could merely be to improve educational institutions' and businesses' understanding of petroleum sector needs and facilitate training and certification to bridge any gaps. In light of the size and capacity of Lebanon's local supplier base, local companies would not need preferential local content regulations. Such regulations open the door to picking winners and corruption.

Governance framework required to oversee an NOC

The following analysis of the governance framework necessary to oversee an NOC in Lebanon centers on five principles of good governance identified by a group of producer countries and Chatham House (Lahn *et al.* 2007). These principles apply to producers at any stage of development of a resource. For each principle, this section reviews governance challenges that are present in Lebanon and strategies, where available, to mitigate those risks. They are as follows:

- Clarity of goals, roles, and responsibilities
- Enablement to carry out the role assigned
- Transparency and accuracy of information
- Accountability of decision making and performance
- Sustainable development for the benefit of future generations.[16]

Clarity of goals, roles and responsibilities

Clarity of roles and responsibility is a central element of good governance in the national petroleum sector. In Lebanon, roles are broadly clear at present, with the LPA tasked with licensing and monitoring operators. The introduction of an NOC into the system would need to be carefully managed by giving the company a mandate that is clearly delineated to avoid functional overlap with the LPA and to adhere to clear oversight processes. An NOC cannot be accountable without a clear mandate and oversight structure.

Beyond the allocation of roles, there should be clear goals. From their comparative studies of 15 NOCs, Victor *et al.* (2012) concluded that the goals a government sets for its NOC (explicitly or not) are "the single most important explanatory of NOC performance". NOCs whose governments allow them to focus on their commercial oil and gas mandate perform better. The second key element in determining NOC performance is consistency in government–NOC interactions. Government should provide consistent goals and direction for an NOC. It should be able to present a unified system of control for the sector, which reduces uncertainty and gives an NOC a longer planning horizon (Victor *et al.* 2012).[17]

From 2014 to 2016, a lack of political leadership left the sector paralyzed. Government instability is ranked as the most problematic factor for doing business in Lebanon (World Economic Forum 2015). The country ranks in the seventh percentile globally for political stability (World Bank 2014). The introduction of an NOC without clear political reins and direction would certainly lead to governance failures. It may become the pet project of some powerful figures, promoting special interests rather than the public good. For this reason, it is preferable to delay the establishment of an NOC until a higher threshold of political leadership and broad-based consensus can emerge to guide and control it.

---

[16] The focus of this discussion will be on the governance risks related to the NOC's role and its interaction with other actors, rather than on policy or strategy. Therefore, this section will not review the implications for sustainable development.

[17] Victor *et al.* (2012).

Enablement to carry out the role

Enablement is a key challenge for most emerging NOCs, as they lack funds to develop their skills. They need to build capacity and technical skills in order to take on more meaningful roles in the upstream, moving from passive, financial carried, and minority equity holders to more active, commercial players with operations. Conversely, when access to funding is not sufficiently controlled, they spend too much on capacity building (Marcel 2016b).[18] It is therefore important to provide NOCs with a clear financial model that enables them to accomplish the mandate they are given and incentivizes them to control costs.

Another common problem that prevents NOCs from carrying out the role assigned to them is interference in their operations and decision making. Commercial decisions are frequently influenced by political interference.

In Lebanon, an NOC would face challenges in terms of staffing decisions, which would likely have an impact on its performance. Lebanon's confessional system is based on a formula allocating political and administrative positions to confessional communities. The Taef Accord of 1990 maintained this political sectarianism, but aimed to create a more equitable power distribution across confessions (Krayem 1997). We should therefore expect the membership of the board of directors of an NOC to be determined through drawn out haggling between political parties, with the possible nomination of members who are not sufficiently qualified or independent of political masters. Only strong political leadership, insisting on high standards of professionalism and independence at an NOC, could prevent this outcome.

The efficiency of the company's operations will also likely be affected by the practice of patronage and nepotism. There is a high risk that political expectations that an NOC could be a cash cow (though it will be a cost center for many years if created before production begins) will lead to demands on management to hire more nationals. Staffing decisions and (though it is often forgotten) salary determination should be made through a transparent meritocratic process. Professionalism, performance, and meritocracy are values that can be reinforced through corporate culture. The attitude of the state is key to enabling a strong, commercial corporate culture to take root.

Transparency and accuracy of information

Strong reporting, based on clear and independently audited accounts, is critical. In Lebanon, the capacity to keep accounts has been acquired, but the practice has been patchy. National scores on the strength of auditing and reporting standards are moderately good (in the 54th percentile globally), but transparency of government policy making scores very poorly (7th percentile) and corruption is one of the top factors inhibiting business (World Economic Forum 2015). According to the World Bank's Governance Indicators, control of corruption suffered a sharp downturn from 2005 into 2006 and has stayed stubbornly low since then.[19] Recent moves to adopt the

---

[18] NOCAL of Liberia, for instance, spent $54,794 per employee per year on training in 2014.
[19] World Bank Governance Indicators http://info.worldbank.org/governance/WGI/#home

Extractive Industries Transparency Initiative (EITI) would bring higher standards of disclosure and transparency to Lebanon. These primarily targeted foreign oil company payments to the state, but now also require disclosure of NOC transfers to either the treasury (and vice-versa) or NOC quasi-fiscal expenditures.

However, the EITI process does not shed any light on where corruption thrives: procurement. Procurement will present a greater risk for corruption once (if) Lebanon reaches the development and production stages. At those stages, an NOC's ambitions and commercial activities may grow, leading it to take on project management responsibilities as an operator of a field or a processing facility. In this role, procurement decisions would present opportunities for corruption and cronyism. Also, if exploration and production licenses are awarded to oil companies that are not listed in OECD-based stock exchanges, they will not fall under the same burden of legal responsibility regarding corrupt practices. They may be more amenable to paying bribes or to awarding procurement contracts on the basis of political connections. NOC interactions with those companies would present increased risks for corruption (similarly for the LPA).

Exposing corruption, in whichever form it presents, is risky for a whistle blower. He or she must be legally protected from punitive measures by superiors and a whistle blower law can provide such protection. This must be upheld by an independent judiciary. Lebanon ranks poorly in terms of judicial independence in the Global Competitiveness Index (ranked 117th out of 140 countries). Corporate culture in an NOC, supported by corporate messaging signalling a zero-tolerance policy regarding corruption and procedures for (anonymous) assessment and reporting, can provide some internal controls.

Plainly speaking, corruption can thrive when co-workers and clients are friends or owe each other favors. Patronage strengthens that tight-knit community in which it is difficult to challenge poor practices or crimes. Introducing processes for meritocratic hiring and promotion is recommended. But an NOC may also benefit from the introduction of outsiders. In order to benefit from an external perspective, Saudi Aramco has maintained a percentage of foreign staff in the company (14 percent). It also has foreign members on its board of directors: a former chairman of Royal Dutch Shell and Anglo American plc, a former managing director of the World Bank and Chief Executive Officer of the International Finance Corporation, and a former chairman of BG Group plc and chairman and CEO of Schlumberger Ltd. These external voices provide a degree of benchmarking for the company vis-à-vis external corporate standards. They also limit groupthink and cronyism.

Accountability of decision making and performance

Accountability processes can only be effective when roles of all organizations involved in the petroleum sector are clear and when those responsible for oversight are capable enough to detect good and poor performance. It is therefore crucial, for the sake of accountability processes, that the state is capable and interested enough to audit a company for its financial and operational performance. The bodies responsible for auditing an NOC should have the skills necessary to do so, which includes the capacity

Establishing a National Oil Company in Lebanon 115

to understand what the costs incurred by an NOC should look like. This also entails an understanding of petroleum sector activities and sufficient experience to compare NOC costs to other companies of similar size in the petroleum sector. The willingness and interest of oversight bodies to carry out their mission depends, once more, on signals given by the political leadership, but also on the professionalism of the agency. Clear performance benchmarks can support accountability processes and the company leadership should be held accountable for meeting or failing to meet those benchmarks.

Lebanon could see improved governance standards with a partial listing of an NOC. A listing on an OECD stock exchange would be more appropriate, considering the small size of the Lebanese capital market, though some shares can be reserved for Lebanese citizens. Even the listing of a minority equity stake of the company can increase transparency across the company's accounts because it will require higher, external disclosure requirements and will add a layer of accountability by bringing in private shareholders. If some of the shares are offered to Lebanese citizens, the process may increase their sense of ownership of the company, and thus encourage them to hold the company to account. A more accountable NOC is a better managed NOC.

Conclusion and recommendations

This chapter reviewed possible roles for an NOC in Lebanon and their appropriateness at various stages of development. It is useful, in conclusion, to reframe the suitability of various roles over the timeline of sector development.

It may be concluded that, at the exploration phase, the creation of an NOC is not warranted. An NOC would have little to do. Moreover, the existing legislation does not sanction its establishment, since the Offshore Petroleum Resource Law states that it could be considered "when necessary and after promising commercial opportunities have been verified."

Following commercial discoveries, an NOC could legally be established. It could be mandated to manage or to hold minority stakes on behalf of the government, provided a provision is made at licensing for back-in state participation. However, those types of NOCs are unlikely to bring substantial benefits to Lebanon, and they involve some risks. An NOC as a manager of state interests (Petoro-type NOC) would not have the technical skills to assess the operators' costs—its main function. As for the commercial upstream NOC model holding minority equity stakes, it also would not have the capabilities or influence to play a meaningful role, one where it would establish itself technically and commercially in the Lebanese upstream. The value of creating these types of companies at the development stage is that they have some years to build their skills before production starts and can learn with foreign oil company operators how to manage a complex project. The main risk of establishing a company—along the lines of any of these models—is that it would not stay lean, but would become a bloated, state owned enterprise, doing favors for the ruling elite and providing no benefit to the country. The creation of a modest NOC holding or managing minority equity stakes at the development phase should therefore only be considered if it can be designed to stay lean and focused, if financial controls are put in place to mitigate the risk of it developing into a vehicle for patronage, and if the state's back-in participation can be negotiated according to favorable terms for Lebanon.

Another option during the development phase would entail creating an NOC to take on a downstream role, in view of facilitating the creation of domestic markets and infrastructure to bring offshore gas to shore. This role could be beneficial to Lebanon, which relies heavily on energy imports to meet domestic demand,[20] but presents significant risks if an NOC is not guided by a clear government strategy for economic development and industrialization and if transfer prices are not market based (as cheap energy inputs would benefit some companies and not others and would be a disincentive for foreign oil company investors). The state should also consider that the private sector is dynamic and capable in Lebanon and investments in infrastructure to gather and process gas from offshore facilities could be made by local private companies, supported by an enabling environment for investment (e.g., fiscal incentives, clear policy and pricing signals, and early information on the petroleum project's expected supply). An NOC would also need to operate with high standards for disclosure and transparency to ensure broader accountability.

At the production phase, an NOC could be established to take on any of the above roles, as well as marketing the state's share of oil or gas and maximizing in-country value. An NOC could rely on a share of petroleum revenues for its expenditure, which means it would not have to be a burden on the state budget. However, it would be reducing the "state take" (share of revenues from production going to treasury) and the government should consider carefully what NOC role is beneficial to the country, in relation to other state goals. The ambition or scope of an NOC's mandate would also have to be guided by the size of the resource base and the capacity of the state to hold an NOC to account. In early production, some countries have let unrealistic expectations of oil revenue flows shape their decisions about NOCs' future roles. With greater revenues, NOCs grow in capacity and the state must build its own capacity to hold it to account.

For the sake of discussion, this chapter has presumed that the development of the resource would proceed in Lebanon and that discoveries will be made and produced. In reality, the political backdrops may not be favorable to the timely progress of the resource base. A lack of political leadership and policy paralysis stalled the licensing until 2017. And of course, there is never an assurance of discoveries. Exploration is a very high-risk enterprise and discoveries in the neighbor's acreage offer no guarantees in other countries.

Finally, the governance risks are real. We have reviewed processes and rules that can help mitigate some of these risks. However, as we saw, many of these processes depend on strong political leadership, and without it, it will be difficult to drive a process to a higher standard.

---

[20] In 2010, the country imported 120,000 barrels of refined oil products per day, which accounted for over 90 percent of total primary energy demand in the country.

References

Authored references

Abi Hydar, A. 2015. "Nafat lubnan fi al-baher wal-burr . . . wal-mushkilat fi makan akhar [Lebanon's Onshore and Offshore Oil . . . and Problems Elsewhere]." *Al Joumhouria*, 12 June.

England, A. 2015. "Mozambique Strives to Get Liquefied Natural Gas Projects Online." *Financial Times*, 23 November.

Gillies, A., A. Sayne, and C. Katsouris. 2015. "Inside NNPC Oil Sales: A Case for Reform in Nigeria." Natural Resource Governance Institute, 4 August.

Krayem, H. 1997. *The Lebanese Civil War and the Taif Agreement: Conflict Resolution in the Arab World: Selected Essays*. American University of Beirut.

Lahn, G., V. Marcel, J. Mitchell, K. Myers, and P. Stevens. 2007. "Good Governance of the National Petroleum Sector: The Chatham House Document." Chatham House.

Lahn, G. and P. Stevens. 2014. "Finding the 'Right' Price for Exhaustible Resources: The Case of Gas in the Gulf." Research Paper, Chatham House.

Manley, D. and K. Myers. 2015. "Did the U.K. Miss Out on £400 Billion Worth of Oil Revenue?" Natural Resource Governance Institute, 5 October.

Marcel, V. 2016a. "Guidelines for Good Governance in Emerging Oil and Gas Producers 2016." Research Paper, Chatham House.

Marcel, V. 2016b. "The Cost of an Emerging National Oil Company." Research Paper, Chatham House.

Marcel, V., R. Tissot, A. Paul, and E. Omonbude. 2016. "A Local Content Decision Tree for Emerging Producers." Research Paper, Chatham House.

McPherson, C. 2008. "State Participation in the Natural Resource Sectors: Evolution, Issues and Outlook." Paper presented at *Taxing Natural Resources: New Challenges, New Perspectives, Washington D.C., 25–27 September*. International Monetary Fund.

Nuvunga, A. 2015. "Government Negotiates Problematic Terms with Anadarko: Carry for ENH & Gas for the Domestic Market Short of Needs." Centre for Public Integrity.

De Oliveira, R.S. 2007. "Business Success, Angola-style: Postcolonial Politics and the Rise and Rise of Sonangol." *Journal of Modern African Studies* 45.

Victor, D., D. Hults, and M. Thurber. 2012. "Conclusions and Implications for the Oil Industry's Future." In *Oil and Governance: State-Owned Enterprises and the World Energy Supply*, edited by D. Victor, D. Hults, and M. Thurber. Cambridge University Press.

Non-authored references

The Arab American News. 2005. "A Practical Solution to Lebanon's Oil and Gas Dilemma." 18 February.

Energy Boardroom. 2014. "Interview with Professor Toula Onoufriou, president of the Cyprus Hydrocarbons Company." 3 October.

Ghana National Petroleum Corporation. 2015. "Adapting Expenditure Plans in Response to Falling Oil Prices." Paper presented at the *New Petroleum Producers Discussion Group, Dar Es Salaam, 29 June—1 July*.

Ghana National Petroleum Corporation. 2016. "An NOC with Operator Ambitions." Paper presented at the *New Petroleum Producers Discussion Group, Naivasha, Kenya, March*.

Kenya Civil Society Platform on Oil and Gas. 2016. "Potential Government Revenues from Turkana." Discussion paper.

Middle East Strategic Perspectives. 2016. "A National Oil Company for Lebanon? A Premature and Incomplete Debate." 11 May.

Oman Oil Company Exploration & Production LLC. 2014. "Annual Report."

World Economic Forum. 2015. "Global Competitiveness Report 2015–2016."

Management and Licensing

5

Licensing and Upstream Petroleum Fiscal Regimes: Assessing Lebanon's Choices

Carole Nakhle

Introduction

Most governments rely on private oil companies for the exploitation of their hydrocarbon resources. Wherever they are carried out, exploration and development activities present delicate legal, technical, financial, and political problems and any solution to these problems requires a balancing act between the respective interests of host governments and investors.

When countries decide to involve international oil companies (IOCs), they initially face two fundamental decisions: first, how to select the companies that should be awarded the exclusive rights to explore, develop, and produce the resource, known as the allocation strategy; second, deciding what fiscal regime—which includes not only taxes but also instruments such as royalties, bonuses, state participation, and production sharing—should be adopted. No ideal method exists for making either decision. Governments can choose a model that is most suitable for their country's opportunities and conditions from several allocation strategies. They can also select from a spectrum of fiscal instruments when deciding which combination is believed to provide their country with a fair share of hydrocarbon wealth and encourage investors to ensure optimal economic recovery of the resource.

While an allocation strategy may not be as important as fiscal terms with respect to revenue collection, it adds an important dynamic for governments competing for investors' resources (Johnston 2001). The award of licenses and contracts is not only about securing an agreement good for both sides in negotiations in the short term, but also about securing an equitable distribution of mutual benefits in the much longer term (Bunter 2002). Equally important, the process should be demonstrably free of accusations of corruption and partiality.

The design and administration of the fiscal regime will determine how any potential wealth will be shared between the state—the owner of the resource—and the investor, the provider of capital, technology, and expertise. The fiscal regime is also a critical factor in shaping perceptions of an oil and gas basin's competitiveness. Often, however, there is a misunderstanding of what the regime encompasses. Corporate income tax,

122   *The Future of Petroleum in Lebanon*

for instance, is an important component but it is only one of several fiscal and quasi-fiscal instruments that together constitute a country's petroleum fiscal regime. Potential investors evaluate the interaction of all these different instruments when assessing the attractiveness of a country. It is also the overall combination of these various instruments that will determine the government's total share of the sector.

The objective of this chapter is to assess the choices that Lebanon has opted for in terms of awarding contracts and the upstream petroleum fiscal regime, and compare them to the strategies followed in Cyprus and Israel. As of August 2018, Lebanon has not made any hydrocarbon discoveries, although offshore natural gas discoveries in the East Mediterranean indicate a positive outlook.

The chapter proceeds as follows. Section one begins with a brief review of common contract allocation methods based on international experience. The section then analyzes and compares the strategies adopted in Lebanon, Cyprus, and Israel. Section two is dedicated to the upstream petroleum fiscal regime. It first examines the main types of fiscal arrangements and the key instruments found under each system. It then studies the regime in Lebanon and compares its terms with those of Cyprus and Israel before offering recommendations and making concluding remarks.

Allocation of oil and gas rights

Enhancing oil and gas exploration and exploitation activity is a common goal for all governments. The strategies employed to achieve that goal vary significantly from country to country, starting with the awarding of oil and gas rights (Johnston 2001). Typically, awards are made for the exclusive right to explore and, if certain conditions are satisfied, exploit any commercial discovery.

In order to exploit their hydrocarbon resources efficiently, many governments rely on the involvement of IOCs, often in cooperation with a host country's national oil company (NOC). Governments, however, face a challenging task in deciding which companies should be awarded the exclusive rights to explore, develop, and produce their hydrocarbon resources, and on what conditions such rights should be awarded (Tordo 2009).

The objective of this section is to analyze different allocation strategies and block delineation methods for oil and gas, first as commonly found around the world, second, as they apply in Lebanon, Cyprus, and Israel.[1]

Options to allocate oil and gas rights

Countries can assign petroleum exploration and production rights in different ways. Irrespective of the choice, the objective in designing the award process is to find the best candidate, maximize potential revenues resulting from the award, and avoid any

---

[1]   The section focuses on countries' actual experiences and does not engage in a detailed review of the literature. For a detailed review of allocation strategies, the following references are particularly useful: Milgrom (1989), Fraser (1991), Kretzer (1993), Bunter (2002), Richardson (2004), Cramton (2006), and Tordo (2009).

Assessing Licensing Fiscal Regime Options

distortion of incentives to perform. Allocation strategies are typically grouped under two categories: open door/informal process and licensing.

The informal process is based on one-on-one negotiations and encompasses two sub-types: "first-come, first-served," and direct negotiations. Exploration and production rights are allocated as a result of negotiations between the government and interested investors through a solicited or unsolicited expression of interest.

Licensing entails administrative procedures and auctions. The former is known as a discretionary system that is based primarily on a proposed work program. Companies present plans for exploration and development according to a formal process. A government committee assesses various proposals against a defined number of criteria. The license is awarded to the plan that has the best "mix" of those criteria. Under auctions, blocks are awarded on the basis of competitive bids whereby rights go to the highest bidder.

Governments can select a combination of procedures to meet different conditions and circumstances. Auctions, however, have become the most preferred and adopted process. According to a survey of petroleum agreements made in the early 1980s by publisher Barrows, only 22 of the 103 petroleum legal systems selected used bidding to award rights for oil exploration and development. By contrast, at the beginning of the twenty-first century, the majority of countries award petroleum agreements through competitive bidding, which benefits from the competitive instinct among IOCs and has the potential to raise millions of dollars in upfront cash (Duval *et al.* 2009).

The superiority of auctions resides in the fact that, in principle, they are the most transparent way of allocating rights. A central limitation of informal processes, such as negotiation on a first-come-first-served basis, is that they lack transparency. The criteria for awarding rights are often not pre-defined and known to market participants and the government retains considerable discretionary power and flexibility in awarding exploration and production rights (Tordo 2009). As a result, informal processes are vulnerable to favoritism and corruption, which in turn undermines competition. The reduced competition inherent in an informal process reduces both the efficiency of the assignment and potential revenues (Cramton 2006). Stanley and Mikhaylova (2011) argue that direct negotiations are engaged in as a result of corrupt practices. By contrast, auctions require rules to be clearly established before the start-up process, offering transparency benefits for both bidders and auctioneers, mitigating potential corruption, and encouraging competition through a fair process (Rodriguez and Suslick 2009).

Compared to auctions, administrative procedures are also less transparent, as it may be difficult for bidders to know the reasons for government selection. In countries that lack a tradition of good governance, administrative procedures are more vulnerable to favoritism and corruption (Tordo 2009). That is why some experts often describe the procedure as a "beauty contest". The system also requires a certain level of technical capacity and resources to evaluate proposals.

One of the main features of the oil and gas industry is the presence of asymmetric information. Private investors undertaking exploration and development are likely to be better informed than host governments on technical and commercial aspects of a project (International Monetary Fund 2012). This is particularly true in the early stages of sector development when data sharing requirements have yet to be established.

124   *The Future of Petroleum in Lebanon*

Direct negotiations require detailed knowledge of the prospective profitability of a deposit, which is likely to be unavailable to governments at the time of negotiations. They also require a concentration of administrative effort, negotiating skills, and a detailed assessment of an individual investor's requirements, which in many circumstances may be difficult to achieve. Auctions, however, induce investors to reveal their own private information: how valuable the bidders believe the lease to be and which bidder values it most (Rodriguez and Suslick 2009). Competition among potential investors can help offset some of the asymmetry regarding access to information that tends to disadvantage governments in licensing. While problematic in the case of one-on-one bilateral negotiations over contract awards, this informational disadvantage is largely nullified when informed investors are made to compete against each other (Cotula 2010). This is particularly important in underexplored or frontier areas, where information is scarce and the government may not be reasonably confident of the precision of its value estimate (Tordo 2009).

Another key advantage of an auction is the tendency to assign blocks to those best able to use them. Although this does not always occur, the competitive character of auctions makes it more likely. Companies with the highest estimates of value for given blocks are likely to be willing to bid higher than others, and hence tend to win those blocks (Cramton 2006). Tordo (2009), however, clarifies that the bidder with the most optimistic—not necessarily the most accurate—view of the true value of the block will be awarded exploration rights. Even if all bidders had access to all available data, there would still be a difference in interpretation that would lead to different estimates of the true value of the same block. Each bidder has a view of the risk and expected value of the acreage on offer, and bids accordingly. The winner in an auction tends to be the bidder or consortium that might have overestimated the resource potential and paid more for the area to avoid competitors, consequently suffering the winner's curse.[2] The risk to the government with overbidding is that the winner may seek a renegotiation of terms. Tordo (2009) therefore argues that an efficient allocation system must ensure that blocks are awarded to companies that submit the most appropriate bids, not necessarily the most optimistic ones.

Overall, the popularity of competitive bidding and auctions is likely to continue, especially as many non-governmental organizations (NGOs) promote their use under the argument that they are the most transparent procedures. The success or failure of an auction, however, largely depends on its design and the government's commitment to transparency, as well as the level of competition at the time the auction is carried out.

Informal processes should not be completely dismissed. While direct negotiations may not yield the maximum achievable return to the government, especially if carried out on a "first-come, first-served" basis, some countries still engage in direct negotiations, which become inevitable for blocks that were not awarded after a competitive bid round, for instance. As put by Johnston (2001), "there is nothing worse than one failed license round for a host government." Some experts argue that a single allocation policy

---

[2] Depending on the level of overestimation, the successful bidder may later realize that the terms and conditions of award render the project not economical.

will likely not apply to all situations in a given country. That is why hydrocarbon laws can make allowances for open-door systems in particular circumstances.

Auctions tend to be the most successful approach once a proven commercial resource has been established. Prior to this, geological uncertainties can militate against large bids being offered. In fact, the strongest indicator of success of an auction program is the presence of robust competition (Cramton 2006). In any auction model, the government makes substantial gains in net expected values with more competitors, which are further incremented when bidding aggressively (Rodriguez and Suslick 2009). It is therefore always necessary to tailor a design to a particular setting.

Whatever strategy a host government decides to follow, the core requirement is that rights are allocated in a climate of transparency, openness, and the highest standard of professionalism and adherence to international practice (Bunter 2002). Even informal processes can be made transparent through the definition of clear award criteria, publication of negotiation results, and use of external oversight bodies (Tordo 2009).

It is also desirable and increasingly common practice that, to be able to apply for a license, potential investors should first meet specific minimum criteria—in other words they should pre-qualify. Pre-qualification safeguards host governments against participants not having the necessary financial and technological expertise to develop capital-intensive oil and gas projects and deal with emergencies such as spills. Non-refundable bidding fees can also be used to discourage participation from companies that are not serious market players, while guarantees may be used to discourage frivolous bids (Tordo 2009).

Since Lebanon opted for competitive bidding, the remainder of this section focuses on this type of allocation of rights.

Auction design: two key issues[3]

This section addresses two main design elements of an auction: the choice of the biddable parameters, and the block size, both of which tend to cause controversy.

Selection of biddable parameters

A key question host governments face when designing an auction is the selection of the biddable parameters. Once the credentials of potential investors have been established, international good practice favors setting a limited number of clearly specified criteria for the award of a license (a maximum of two). This is particularly recommended in countries with limited expertise in oil and gas matters and constrained administrative capacity. Even in a country like the United States, with more than one century of experience in oil and gas, the legislation forbids the use of more than one bid variable (Tordo 2009).

Typical biddable parameters include the work program and signature bonus. Other parameters can be state participation, local content, and production targets.

---

[3] For a detailed analysis of auction design see Bunter (2002), Cramton (2006), and Tordo (2009).

Experience shows that the most important biddable parameter is the investor's work commitment, which should be specified in both physical terms and financial expenditure terms.[4] By ensuring that companies commit themselves, prior to the award of a license, to a minimum work program, the government aims to guard against the possibility that companies, once awarded monopoly rights over the exploitation of the resource, might invest at a level which it considers too small.

Kretzer (1993), however, warns of the risk of overcapitalization, in that companies propose work programs that are above their optimal level of capital investment, which results in an increased per unit cost of resource extraction. Similarly, Tordo (2009) argues that allocation systems, which induce bidders to offer work programs that exceed what ordinarily would be required to efficiently explore blocks, will ultimately reduce the economic rent and may lead to future renegotiations to remove uneconomic commitments. A key prerequisite for the selection of the work program as the biddable parameter is therefore to have a highly qualified and skilled committee to evaluate the bid, to minimize the risk of overcapitalization and ensure the most efficient extraction of the resource.

The signature bonus generates up-front cash, long before any oil or gas production starts. In the US, bonus payments have been an important generator of revenues. Since the 1950s, the US government has collected $82.8 billion (nominal) in oil and gas lease bids. In real terms (2018 USD), this is over $255 billion.[5] In evaluating the potential signature bonus, the investor normally determines the expected profitability of potential developments and offers a proportion of that value as the signature bonus, which is usually much higher for a discovered oil field than for exploration, where the oil potential of the country has not been proven.

The perceived level of competition will also have an impact on the magnitude of the bonus offered. In Angola, competition for one oil block in the country's licensing round in 2005–6 was so fierce that it resulted in signature bonuses that stunned the industry and ranged from $902 million to $1.1 billion (nominal), the highest in the world for an exploration block (Brown 2009). Few countries worldwide, however, can extract such a large portion of rent through bonuses. An over-emphasis on collection of signature bonus revenues also has some limitations; money spent on bonuses is money not spent on exploration. In the long run, successful exploration and ensuing developments are likely to deliver much greater value for the state than signature bonuses.

In some countries, fiscal instruments, such as the sliding scale royalty and profit sharing, are biddable.

In this case, however, it is recommended that the government pre-set the range within which bids can be placed. Such a prudent approach has several advantages: it allows the government to achieve a greater predictability of potential rewards, which in turn will help with budget planning more generally; it minimizes discrimination among investors; and it reduces the administrative burden of managing different fiscal structures. Furthermore, there is a danger that companies will offer onerous fiscal terms to win the bid in the knowledge that the fiscal terms could be renegotiated if subsequent discoveries prove uneconomic. For instance, some companies offer a higher share to the government from profit petroleum when the R-factor—the ratio of

---

[4] Extractive Industry Source Book, http://www.eisourcebook.org
[5] Data calculated from the Bureau of Ocean Energy Management (BOEM) 2018

cumulative post-tax receipts to cumulative expenditures—exceeds a certain limit. However, cost overruns, which are very common in the oil and gas industry, would imply that the higher tier will never be triggered and in some cases may even encourage the investor to spend more than it otherwise would.

In principle, the size of the bid corresponds to the project's anticipated profitability and underlying economics, including the impact of the fiscal regime, and the level of competition. Oil projects usually attract greater bids than gas projects; given the relatively higher capital and transport costs, the profitability of a gas project tends to be lower than for an oil project of similar size should the same tax provisions apply (Le Leuch 2011). Similarly, the more onerous the fiscal terms, the lower the lease bids and vice versa.

Bids also depend on the extent to which the fiscal regime is perceived to be stable. If investors believe the fiscal terms may tighten, then they are likely to bid much less up front. There is also clear evidence that, in times of high prices, investors have been willing to contribute a significant amount in signature bonuses. They are more conservative in periods of low oil prices.

Block delineation

Countries can offer a variety of opportunities—onshore and onshore (shallow and deep water)—with varying risks. There is, however, no specific formula for dividing acreage into blocks.[6] The choice of the block size should take into consideration several factors—mainly the type of opportunity, the level of competition, the license duration, and the relinquishment provision.

For instance, a high level of competition between prospective investors, attractive geological potential such as in a proven basin, and/or a lenient relinquishment rule allow the government to offer smaller blocks. By contrast, where interest is very limited, the geological risk is high, such as in frontier areas. Additionally, the relinquishment rule is tough from an investor's perspective as larger blocks tend to be offered to mitigate business risk. Johnston (2001), however, warns against the likelihood of a greater accumulation of sunk costs prior to discovery in the case of larger blocks. These costs are typically cost recoverable and/or tax deductible and consequently, with larger accumulations of sunk costs, governments risk lower tax revenues.

It is also advisable that host governments do not award all their territory for exploration and exploitation simultaneously. Through a gradual award of blocks, the government retains the flexibility to make some changes in the terms and conditions of future awards, following newly acquired information. It is also recommended that governments award licenses to a relatively large number of companies rather than limit the exploration of a large area to a single company, to promote competition and allow different interpretations of a territory's geology.

In terms of international practice, typically an exploration license includes three phases, totaling six to nine years, and relinquishment is usually 25 percent after the first phase and 25 percent of the original area after the second phase. There is, however, a wide variation.

---

[6] Blocks are defined as rectangular blocks, as specified by a pair of longitude and latitude coordinates (Cramton 2006).

128 *The Future of Petroleum in Lebanon*

Relinquishment provisions are imposed to encourage the turnover of acreage and give the host government greater control over its assets. They are known as "use-it-or-lose-it" conditions to ensure that exploration activities are carried out by the license holders within a set time frame, or the area is released for future licensing. Relinquishment provisions are important as they avoid "warehousing," where a company sits on the acreage and delays development until the time best suits them, which is not necessarily the best time for the government (Johnston 2001). Companies can react differently to relinquishment rules; larger players clearly favor smaller relinquishment percentages. In general, a higher relinquishment rate is favored by host governments in unexplored areas to speed up exploration activity.

Comparative assessment

Licensing

Lebanon

Lebanon's offshore oil and gas sector is governed by the 2010 Offshore Petroleum Resources Law (OPRL),[7] the Petroleum Activities Regulations (PAR), and the Exploration and Production Agreement (EPA).[8] A separate law covering onshore is to apply separately.[9] In most countries, one law applies to both onshore and offshore.

The OPRL refers to awarding licenses through licensing rounds (Article 7) but does not specify the biddable terms. Moreover, Lebanon has adopted a rather prescriptive approach to awarding licenses. For instance, to qualify, applicants should satisfy a set of legal, financial, technical, quality, health, safety, and environmental (QHSE) criteria, as shown in Table 5.1. The pre-qualification criteria that the country selected clearly created

Table 5.1 Lebanon pre-qualification criteria[10]

	Legal	Financial	Technical	QHSE
Operator	Joint stock company conducting petroleum activities	Total assets of $10 billion	Operatorship of at least one petroleum development in water depths in excess of 500m	QHSE policy statement(s) Established and implemented QHSEMS
Non-operator	Joint stock company conducting petroleum activities	Total assets of $500 million	Having an established petroleum production	QHSE policy statement(s) Established and implemented QHSEMS

Source: Lebanese Petroleum Administration.

---

[7] Lebanese Parliament. 2010. Offshore Petroleum Resources Law. Law 132, 24 August.
[8] All laws and decrees are available at the LPA website: http://www.lpa.gov.lb
[9] At the time of publishing, the onshore law has not been finalized.
[10] For more details see Investigating Lebanon's pre-qualified oil and gas bidders: Who are they, and how should we assess them, 2017: http://www.lpa.gov.l b/pdf/Pre-qualification%20Application%20 Package.pdf

a bias toward large oil companies, the rationale being that Lebanon's oil and gas resources lie in deep water and the larger players have the expertise and capital to exploit them.

According to the Pre-Qualification Decree (Article 3), "the Right Holder may be either one company or a group of companies, at least one of which must prove that it is able to meet the pre-qualification eligibility criteria set forth in the present decree."[11]

The provision is in line with the OPRL's definition of a right holder, which can be "any joint stock company which is participating in Petroleum Activities pursuant to this law through an Exploration and Production Agreement or a Petroleum License that permits it to work in the petroleum sector."

However, the provision can be subject to misinterpretation and criticism, as even individual companies that do not meet the minimum criteria can still participate, indirectly, in the licensing round. One possible explanation for such a provision is that the government wants to give local, small companies with no or limited expertise in petroleum operations the chance to enter the sector.

According to the OPRL (Article 1), the EPA is concluded between the state and "no less than three Right Holders," one of which is the operator. Lebanon also requires that the operator hold a minimum participating interest of 35 percent while each non-operator holds a minimum of 10 percent. Companies pay a license application fee of $50,000 (PAR, Article 26).

The rationale for the Lebanese government to fix the minimum number of right holders might be to establish a competitive landscape with a variety of players, to control costs and share risks and capital. From a company's perspective, the unincorporated joint venture facilitates risk and capital sharing. From a government's perspective, the structure sets up conflicting interests from which tax authorities can benefit in controlling costs (IMF 2012).

Some would argue that such a provision is not necessary, since, in practice, unincorporated joint ventures are a well-established feature of the oil and gas industry structure, particularly in the upstream sector.[12] Most exploration and production licenses are issued to multiple parties, with a single business designated as the "operator".

According to the EPA decree of 19 January 2017, the following parameters are biddable: the work program, cost recovery ceiling, and profit sharing—the latter being on a sliding scale related to profitability (R-factor). The main concerns about having two key fiscal parameters biddable are explained in section 1 and are further elaborated on in section 2.

Cyprus

In Cyprus, oil and gas activities are governed by the Hydrocarbons (Prospection, Exploration, and Exploitation) Law of 2007 and the Hydrocarbons (Prospection, Exploration, and Exploitation) Regulations of 2007 and 2009.[13]

---

[11] Lebanese Petroleum Administration. Lebanon Pre-qualification Decree. http://www.lpa.gov.lb/pdf/Prequalification%20Application%20P ackage.pdf

[12] See Ernst and Young (2011).

[13] For various documentation refer to: http://www.mcit.gov.cy/mcit/mcit.nsf/dmlhcarbon_en/dmlhcarbon_en?OpenDocument

Like Lebanon, Cyprus awards licenses through competitive bidding. The island held its first licensing round in 2007 but attracted limited interest. Only three applications for three blocks out of 11 were made, by two parties: one the US-based Noble Energy and the other a consortium of Norwegian, United Kingdom, and United Arab Emirates companies. Originally, a range of international energy companies including Russian, Chinese, United States, Indian, German, French, and Norwegian firms were thought to be considering submitting an offer. Noble Energy, which already had a strong interest in the region, namely Israel, was granted the license in 2008 for exploration of Block 12, where Cyprus's first offshore gas discovery, Aphrodite, was later made in 2010. Following appraisal, the field's size had a mean of 5 trillion cubic feet (Tcf) of gas.

The discovery of the Aphrodite field reversed the tide in favor of the government. A second round was launched in 2012 for 12 offshore blocks. Ten consortia (25 companies) and five companies expressed interest. The strong presence of Israeli companies was notable. At the end, five contracts were signed: with Italian company Eni and South Korea's Kogas for Blocks 2, 3, and 9, and with France's Total S.A. for Blocks 10 and 11 (BankMed 2014).

Unlike Lebanon, there is no restriction on the minimum number of right holders. In the second round, applications were made by single companies as well as by consortia varying between two and five companies, large and small alike.

Cyprus also offers more relaxed rules in terms of pre-qualification requirements. According to the island's oil and gas regulations, in addition to national security considerations, applicants are selected based on:

- Their technical and financial ability
- The ways in which they intend to carry out the activities that are specified in the license
- The financial consideration that they are offering in order to obtain the license
- Any lack of efficiency and responsibility that they have shown under any previous license or authorization of any form in any country.

The regulations further add that if,

following evaluation under the above criteria, two or more applications have equal merit, the proposals of the applicants regarding the protection of public safety, public health, security of transport, protection of the environment, protection of biological resources and of national treasures possessing artistic, historic, or archaeological value, safety of installations and workers and planned management of hydrocarbon resources, shall be taken into account.

One application is made per block and separate applications can be made by the same applicant for more than one block. Under the latter condition, applicants "may mention the priority order they assign to each Block."

With respect to the biddable parameters, Cyprus is perhaps an extreme example, as almost all fiscal and non-fiscal terms are biddable or negotiable. These include the work program, signature and production bonuses, cost recovery ceiling, profit

Assessing Licensing Fiscal Regime Options 131

petroleum, and training fees (as per the Model PSC 2007 and 2012). Such a system makes it difficult to compare the terms of various contracts, discriminates among investors by creating different fiscal structures, and imposes a significant administrative burden on the government.

Israel

Compared to Cyprus and Lebanon, Israel is well ahead in terms of exploiting its oil and gas potential. In 1999, Israel made its first offshore natural gas discovery—the Noa field. Subsequent discoveries (Mari-B field in 2000, Dalit and Tamar in 2009, Leviathan in 2010, and Tanin in 2011) confirmed the presence of significant quantities of natural gas in the Levant Basin (Energy Information Administration 2013) (Table 5.2). The Tamar discovery in 2009 was the largest conventional gas discovery in the world.[14] Production at the field commenced in March 2013. Leviathan, with nearly 22 Tcf of contingent natural gas resources, represented the largest deepwater natural gas discovery in the world over the past decade.[15]

Israel's oil and gas sector is governed by the Petroleum Law (57121952),[16] applying to both onshore and offshore activities, and the Petroleum Regulations (Principles for Offshore Petroleum Exploration and Production, 5766-2006), in addition to the Natural Gas Sector Law, 5762-2002 (the "Gas Law"), which establishes conditions for

Table 5.2 Main natural gas discoveries in the Eastern Mediterranean region (1999–2017)

Country	Discovery Year	Name	Size (Tcf)
Cyprus	2011	Aphrodite	5.00
Israel	1999	Noa	0.04
	2000	Mari-B	1.50
	2009	Dalit	0.70
	2009	Tamar	10.00
	2010	Leviathan	19.00
	2011	Dolphin	0.08
	2012	Simson	0.55
	2012	Tanin	1.20
	2013	Karish	1.80
	2014	Royee	3.20
	2016	Daniel	8.9
Palestinian Territories	2000	Gaza Marine	1.00

Sources: Compiled by Author using information from Delek Energy (Tamar 2014), the United States Energy Information Administration (2013), Noble Energy, and Israel Opportunity Energy Resources (2015).

---

[14] Information on Tamar: http://www.delekenergy.co.il/?CategoryID=171&ArticleID=84
[15] "Classification of the contingent resources in the Leviathan Reservoir as reserves is contingent, inter alia, on approval of a plan for the development and commercialization of the natural gas and the condensate from the reservoir and a reasonable forecast for natural gas and/or condensate sales ... There is a reasonable chance that the contingent resources in the best estimate category will be economic" (Delek Energy 2014, "Re: Updated Resource Appraisal for the Leviathan Reservoir," http://www.delekenergy.co.il/?CategoryID=194&ArticleID=273)
[16] Amended in 1965.

132   *The Future of Petroleum in Lebanon*

the development of natural gas, regulates investment in the sector, and ensures the safety of operations.[17]

Petroleum Rights are granted in response to applications submitted from time to time.[18] The petroleum law also enables the granting of licenses for exploration and leases for production by way of competitive bidding. Israel's first offshore licensing round was announced in 2016, with the two main bidding parameters being the work program and signature bonus of not less than $100,000.

There are several explanations for the relatively late adoption of the licensing round. First, according to Israel's Ministry of National Infrastructures, Energy, and Water Resources, in 2012, authorities stopped granting new offshore exploration licenses to allow the ministry to assess new gas discoveries, update its gas policy, and improve its regulatory system and technical capabilities. However, the review of various terms and policies related to oil and gas has been more frequent since major gas discoveries were made in the Eastern Mediterranean and has contributed to limiting the level of activity in offshore Palestine to a few companies, primarily Noble Energy and Delek. In 2015, the Israeli antitrust authority voiced concerns over a lack of competition and called the consortium of Noble Energy and Delek, which controls the Tamar and Leviathan fields, a monopoly, leading to halting the development of Israel's largest gas fields and then requiring the partners to sell off some smaller assets. The need to encourage more competition could have enticed Israeli authorities to announce the first offshore licensing round in 2016. In fact, companies with significant holdings in active offshore leases with estimated reserves of more than 200 billion cubic meters will not be allowed to bid.[19]

Second, the licensing round's late adoption is partly explained by relatively limited international interest. On the one hand, the geological risk was high. On the other hand, the IOCs appeared to be hesitant about investing in Israel because they feared endangering their more lucrative investments in Arab countries. The political risk in Israel is seen as significant. A study done by IHS CERA (2011) carried out a comparison of the political risk in terms of political, socioeconomic, and commercial attributes, across several countries. Israel was ranked poorly at 113 alongside countries including Sudan, Bolivia, Myanmar, and Sierra Leone. As summarized by IHS CERA (2011),

> three factors serve as significant external constraints on foreign investment. First, the announcement from Israel's National Infrastructure Ministry in July 2000 that it was suspending new licenses and permits to consider what would be tougher terms has had a chilling effect on investors, who were quick to announce they would reconsider further investment in Israel if royalty rates were significantly

---

[17] Various documentation can be found on the website of Israel Ministry of National Infrastructure, Energy, and Water Resources.

[18] The Petroleum Law defines three types of rights for the different stages of exploration and production of petroleum: the Preliminary Permit enables its holder to conduct preliminary investigations; the Petroleum License confers on its holder the exclusive right to explore for petroleum in the licensed area; and the Petroleum Lease is granted to a holder of a petroleum license that made a discovery of Petroleum in commercial quantities—it confers on its holder the exclusive right to explore for and produce petroleum in the area covered by the Petroleum Lease.

[19] For further details: http://www.energy-sea.gov.il/English-Site/Pages/Regulation/Call%20for%20 Bids_Israel%201st%20Offshore%20Bid%20Round.pdf

altered [and] that threat has been reiterated as legislation slowly makes its way through government. Second, the threat of a Middle East war involving Israel is omnipresent and companies cannot help but account for this in their investment plans. Third, the omnipresent threat of internal violence is one that cannot be ignored, even during times of relative peace in the nation.

Furthermore, following the Tzemach committee recommendations in September 2012, the Israeli cabinet decided to cap gas exports at just 40 percent of potential reserves to guarantee domestic supply for the next 25 years. There have also been calls to impose additional taxes on future gas exports. Strong public feeling against exporting gas can act as a disincentive for companies aiming for the most economically efficient solution to exploit gas resources.[20]

From 2000 to 2013, Israel's regulatory and fiscal framework for upstream oil and gas has been revised on several occasions, negatively affecting investors' confidence. According to Dor and Danishefsky (2011), in 2000 the then Israeli Ministry of National Infrastructure (which later became the Ministry of Energy and Water Resources) froze all offshore activities to allow the government to consider amending regulations and the fiscal regime. More than six years later, the sector was opened to new exploration. Following the discoveries of Tamar and Leviathan, the Israeli government further introduced restrictive regulations and tightened its fiscal terms.

Like Cyprus, there are no requirements on the number of applicants per petroleum right, which can be granted to one or more parties. But in a sharp contrast to Cyprus, Israel petroleum regulations are highly prescriptive. For instance, the regulations demand certain minimum experience requirements in offshore exploration and production activities, as a pre-condition to granting petroleum rights covering offshore areas of various water depths:

- For a license in which the water depth does not exceed 100 meters, experience of drilling at least one offshore well
- For a license in an area in which water depth does exceed 100 meters, experience of drilling at least one well at a depth exceeding 100 meters.

The regulatory changes made in 2010 imposed for the first time the need to appoint an operator with experience in managing and performing at least one offshore project of $100 million, within the last five years.[21] They also set the criteria for determining the minimum financial ability of an applicant who must be able to fund at least half of the approved project's expected cost, estimated to be $100 million.

The new set of guidelines that were added in 2011 introduced additional experience requirements for drilling in water depths up to 500 meters, up to 1,000 meters, and above 1,000 meters (as opposed to the single 100-meter threshold under the 2006 regulations). An operator must be a partner in the oil and gas right and hold at least a 5 percent interest in the license, while foreign operators are required to submit a questionnaire on their foreign trade and relations (Dor and Danishefsky 2011).

---

[20] An inter-ministerial committee charged with recommending a national gas policy.
[21] As later specified in the 2011 regulatory changes.

134   *The Future of Petroleum in Lebanon*

To pre-qualify for the first licensing round, an operator must meet minimum technical and financial requirements, including having experience of at least five years in performing the roles of an operator during the ten years preceding the submission of the bid and total assets in the operator's balance sheet of at least $200 million and total equity of at least $50 million.

The regulations limit the maximum size of an offshore right to 400 square kilometers (400,000 Dunams) and no person shall hold more than 12 licenses or hold licenses for an aggregate exceeding area of 4,000 (4 million Dunams).[22] For instance, the Pelagic Licenses awarded to Israel Opportunity Energy Resources LP covers five blocks of 400 km^2 each, resulting in a total area of 2,000 km^2. According to the call for bids for Israel's first offshore licensing round, "bidders, either alone or in consortia, may bid for any amount of blocks, up to the twenty-four blocks," but "the total amount of licenses that can be granted to a single corporation will not exceed eight licenses, alone or together, if applicable, with a consortium where the corporation's interest is more than 25%," whereby the total acreage of each block does not exceed 400 km^2.

Licensees must pay a fee set by the minister of energy and water based on various factors, such as the length of the license, size of the covered area, and other relevant factors (Hayes 2011).[23] The petroleum license includes a work program slated to be carried out during the term of the license—typically at least one exploration well for a predefined minimum depth (Hacohen 2014). The merit of each application is assessed per various criteria, mainly experience and financial capacity.

License duration and acreage

There are significant variations between license durations and extensions as well as relinquishment rules between the countries assessed.

In the case of Lebanon, the issues of exploration license duration and extension would have benefitted from further clarification, as the existing provisions in the OPRL and Model EPA can lead to different interpretations, especially with respect to the exploration phase and period.

According to the OPRL (Article 21), "if the Exploration phase, provided by the Exploration and Production Agreement is shorter than ten years, the Council of Ministers may, upon an application submitted to the Minister, and on the basis of a proposal by the Minister based upon the opinion of the Petroleum Authority, extend the Exploration phase within the ten year time limit." As such, one concludes that the exploration phase is of a maximum of ten years including any potential extension.

The OPRL does not refer to the division of the exploration phase into several periods. The PAR, however, in Article 30, states that the phase "may be divided into periods of time related to the work plans submitted by the Right Holder in the Exploration and Production Agreement." Following direct input from the LPA and according to the Model EPA, the exploration phase is divided into two periods: period

---

[22] Deloitte. 2014. "Licensing rounds": http://www.psg.deloitte.co.uk/NewsLicensingRounds.asp
[23] Licenses under the 1950s regime were allocated free of charge.

1 (three years) and period 2 (two years). Only period 2 can be extended by one year for appraisal, thus the total exploration phase period could be six years. At the end of period 1, the right holders relinquish 25 percent of the block.

The exploration phase can be extended "for justified operational reasons or Event of Force Majeure, subject to Council of Ministers approval," as long as the total phase does not exceed ten years. On each extension, a relinquishment rule of 50 percent would apply. This is the only rate specified in the OPRL.

As shown in Table 5.3, compared to Cyprus and Israel, Lebanon offers the shortest duration of the exploration phase (five years compared to seven in Cyprus and Israel, excluding the possible extension for appraisal). However, when including the possible extension of the exploration phase, Lebanon offers the longest duration. With respect to the relinquishment rule, the provision in Lebanon falls at the lower end, except when the extension of the exploration phase is provided, when the relinquishment rule falls at the other end.

The treatment of the appraisal time varies between the three countries. In Lebanon, in principle the extension is for one year; in Israel it is for two years. According to the 2012 Model Production Sharing Contract (PSC), Cyprus offers six months for the appraisal of an oil discovery and up to two years for a gas discovery. Investors typically need a longer appraisal period for natural gas before declaring a discovery commercial—the latter depends on the availability of sufficient gas reserves and on guaranteeing commercial markets.

Table 5.3 Duration of petroleum rights in Cyprus, Israel, and Lebanon

	Lebanon	Israel*	Cyprus
Exploration			
Initial period	3	3	3
2nd Period	2	–	–
1st Renewal Period		Up to 4	2
2nd Renewal Period			2
Total Excluding Appraisal	5	Up to 7	Up to 7
Extension for Appraisal	5	Up to 2	0.5–2
Total	Up to 6	Up to 9	7.5–9
Exploration Phase Extension	Total phase 10		
Relinquishment Rule	25%–50%**	Up to 40%	At least 25%
Production			
Phase I: Initial period	25	30	25
Phase II: Extensions	5	20	10
Total	Up to 30	Up to 50	Up to 35

* In the 2016 call for bids, the exploration petroleum license will have a duration of 3 + 3 = 6 years. If no well is drilled in the first three-year period, the extension of the license to the second three-year period will be subject to the license holder's committing to drill an exploration well (the drill or drop point) during that second period, and to the relevant conditions of the law and the regulations promulgated thereunder.

** 25% of Area must be relinquished at the beginning of Second Exploration Period; 50% of Area (cumulative) must be relinquished in case of extension of Exploration Phase.

Sources: 2010 Offshore Petroleum Resources Law; Israeli Petroleum Law No 5712-1952; Cyprus Hydrocarbons, Prospection, Exploration and Exploitation Regulations. 2007 and 2009 and 2012 Model Production Sharing Contract.

136 · The Future of Petroleum in Lebanon

Table 5.4 Size of block areas in km^2

	Lebanon	Israel	Cyprus
Minimum	1,259	128	1,440
Maximum	2,374	400	5,741
Average	1,790	369	3,920

Sources: Deloitte, Israel Opportunity Energy Recourses LP, Adira Energy, Zion Oil and Gas.

There also seems to be wide variation between block sizes across the three selected case studies as well as within the same country (for instance, Cyprus).[24] As shown in Table 5.4, Cyprus offers the largest blocks on average, while Israel offers the smallest.

Lebanon has divided its offshore area into ten blocks, covering what Israel claims to be a disputed area of 854 km^2. The size of the blocks, however, has been criticized as too large. In practice, and as discussed earlier in this chapter, there is no ideal block size: the geological risk, the type of opportunity, and the relinquishment rules should all be taken into consideration.

Petroleum fiscal regime

The central objective of the upstream petroleum fiscal regime is to acquire for the state in whose legal territory the resources in question lie a fair share of the wealth accruing from the extraction of that resource, while encouraging investors to ensure optimal economic recovery of the hydrocarbon resources. How to achieve this balance is a subject of enduring controversy.

While the taxation of corporations from any sector is of interest, the taxation of oil and gas merits special attention simply due to the scale of the numbers involved. For prolific oil and gas provinces, annual taxes collected run into billions of US dollars, and globally in the trillions per annum. No other commodity, manufacturing industry, or service sector can offer sustained tax revenues on this scale. In the Organisation for Economic Co-operation and Development (OECD) countries, for instance, all sectors in the economy, except the petroleum sector, are subject to an average income tax of 23 percent, down from 30 percent in 2000 (Organisation for Economic Co-operation and Development 2014). In the oil and gas sector, however, the average government take— that is, the total share of government revenues from a project's net cash flows—varies from 65 percent to 85 percent (International Monetary Fund 2012). The underlying reason resides in the special features of the petroleum industry, in particular the fact that these resources are non-renewable and state-owned, with significant potential for economic rent.

The industry also has additional attributes that need to be taken into consideration when designing a fiscal regime. Substantial uncertainties exist across the supply chain.

---

[24] Turkey disputes the blocks delineation made by Cyprus. The analysis of this dispute is for the legal community and goes beyond the purpose of this chapter.

Of relevance are those associated with petroleum geology, the specific characteristics of individual fields, and investment returns. The costs of petroleum projects tend to be incurred up-front and the time lags are considerable, often of many years and even decades, from the initial discovery of oil or gas to the time of first production, which can then last for more than 30 years. That is why it is not just the tax rates that are important; the timing of when various fiscal instruments hit investors is equally relevant.

A common trap that non-fiscal experts often fall into is commenting on a petroleum fiscal regime by looking only at its type, the headline tax rates, or a specific instrument. This is simplistic and inaccurate to say the least, as the type of fiscal regime does not affect the sharing of potential wealth; it is the combination and interaction of all various instruments that determine the final outcome.

Practitioners in the field of upstream taxation are more familiar with the typical fiscal ingredients that make up the structure of most of the world's tax regimes, which include royalties, resource rent tax, corporate tax, profit oil/gas, and cost oil/gas. What is less familiar, however, is a wide range of commercial and regulatory obligations placed on investors, which, although in most circumstances are not labelled as taxes, are in effect just that in terms of their economic consequences. These obligations confer additional benefits to the state. They include: state participation, bonus, ring fencing, depreciation, Domestic Market Obligations (DMO), and capital gains tax—all of which affect a project's profitability directly.

The objective of this section is first to describe the main types of fiscal arrangements and their key instruments, and second to conduct an analysis of Lebanon's petroleum fiscal regime and compare it with the regimes of Cyprus and Israel.

Types of fiscal regime[25]

Two types of fiscal regime prevail in oil and gas exploration and production activities: concessionary systems and contractual systems. The concessionary system originated at the very beginning of the petroleum industry (mid-1800s) and still predominates in OECD countries. The contractual regime emerged one century later (mid-1950s), and has been typically favored by developing countries. Australia, Canada, Norway, and the UK, for example, operate a concessionary regime, with companies being entitled to the ownership of the petroleum extracted. By contrast, countries like Angola, Azerbaijan, Iraq, and Nigeria apply a contractual regime, whereby the government retains ownership of the production. Contractual regimes are widely spread among developing countries. Lebanon opted for the contractual arrangement, which is also popular in the region.

Modern concessionary regimes include various combinations of a royalty, an income tax, and a resource rent tax, falling under the category of Royalty and Tax Systems (R&T). The basic features of oil and gas concessionary regimes are similar, but the fiscal terms or ingredients vary considerably and are likely to evolve over time as a basin matures.

---

[25] Based on Nakhle (2008a and b).

It is tempting to pass judgment on a fiscal regime based solely on its type—concessionary or contractual. Reference is sometimes made to the early "generous" concessions as an illustration of the unsuitability of the concessionary system from a government's perspective. The establishment of particular fiscal regimes, however, should be considered within the broader conditions that prevailed in the oil industry at a certain period of time. For instance, in the early stages of the industry, exploration was a very risky business (for example, it took 25 years to strike oil in Oman), sizeable reserves had not yet been established, the usefulness of petroleum was only beginning to be recognized, and the oil market was relatively small in scale. Competition was limited and a small number of global players dominated the oil industry. Furthermore, early concessions were granted by governments lacking specialized knowledge of petroleum economics, often under foreign political influence and not possessing a cadre of professional staff capable of constructing and implementing a legal and regulatory framework to guide petroleum operations.

Following a series of changes of a political, economic, social, and legal nature, including the nationalizations of the 1960s and 1970s, the emergence of the Organization of the Petroleum Exporting Countries, accelerating oil demand, the opening of new oil provinces, advances in technology, and increased competition, to name but a few, it was inevitable that new agreements would emerge and existing concessions would be revised.

Today there are more fiscal regimes than there are countries and many countries use more than one fiscal structure and regime. Fiscal regimes can be made equivalent in terms of both control and overall economic impact. Variations in tax rates as well as the interaction of different fiscal and non-fiscal instruments play a role—in other words, the way a fiscal regime is designed determines the differences in a project's post-tax economics and risk-reward balance across countries.

Concessionary regimes

The basic features of concessionary regimes are similar, but the fiscal terms or ingredients vary considerably and are likely to evolve over time as fields and basins mature. The main instruments in such arrangements include:

- Royalty: This is typically imposed on a specified level of production or on the value of the output or gross revenues. From a government's perspective, a royalty is relatively simple to administer, difficult to avoid, predictable, and provides revenue as soon as production starts. From a company's perspective, a royalty may deter marginal projects, since it is not profit related and is therefore a regressive instrument, whereby the lower a project's profitability, the higher royalty payments are relative to profits. Some governments apply a sliding scale royalty to make it more progressive, by linking the rates to production level, oil prices, or project economic milestones such as payback or rate-of-return triggers. These features not only complicate the regime but also fail to address the fundamental drawback, namely that a royalty is still imposed irrespective of cost or underlying project profitability. An additional problem with a sliding scale royalty is that there is no objective yardstick for the scale.

- Corporate Income Tax (CIT): This usually consists of a single-rate structure, levied at a corporate or legal entity basis rather than at the field level. Some countries include the oil industry within the standard CIT regime for all industries, although they may use a higher rate to capture more rent or incorporate additional tax incentives to adapt the system to the specific nature and needs of petroleum operations. In addition to cost deductions, interest expenses and losses carried forward and/or back are commonly allowed in the computation of the tax base. Most countries provide an incentive for exploration and development by allowing exploration costs to be recovered immediately and allowing accelerated recovery of development costs. Accelerated depreciation brings forward the payback date for the investor.
- Resource Rent Tax (RRT): This tax is levied on a project's or field's cash flows and aims to capture a larger share of the economic rent. It is considered to be neutral because it is not paid before a project reaches payback and achieves a certain rate of return. The RRT can take many forms. A common method is based on an R-Factor, which is linked to payback. The RRT applies only when a project reaches a specific ratio. The other method is the use of the Rate of Return (ROR), or the internal rate of return (IRR), as a threshold. The RRT is imposed only when cumulative net cash flows (NCF) turn positive. Negative cumulative NCF are normally uplifted by a specific rate, carried forward in one year and added to the next year's NCF. The accumulation process continues until the cumulative NCF turns positive and at this point the RRT applies. In both methods, if costs rise or prices fall, taxable profits change in sympathy, as does the RRT burden. Some countries opt for multi-tiered RRT rates to capture higher rents. The main disadvantages of this method include: how to determine the tiers, additional complexity, and the perceived risk of "gold plating" (interventions to manage the trigger points), where an acceleration of investment, for instance, can delay the trigger point to a higher RRT.

Contractual arrangements

Under typical contractual systems, an oil company is appointed by the government as a contractor for operations in a certain license area. A company operates at its own risk and expense, providing all the financing and technology required for operations, in return for remuneration if production is successful. It has no right to be paid in the event that discovery and therefore development do not occur.

If a company receives a share of production (after deduction of the government's share), the system is known as a Production Sharing Contract (PSC)—also called a production sharing agreement (PSA)—which is a binding commercial contract between an investor and a state (or its NOC). Since a company is rewarded in physical barrels, it takes title to that share of petroleum extracted at the delivery point (export point from the contract area). If the reward is a cash fee, the system is called a service agreement, where, in the case of commercial production, a company is paid a fee (often subject to taxes) for its services without taking title to any petroleum extracted. The

140   *The Future of Petroleum in Lebanon*

service agreement is the least popular; it is found in less than ten countries around the world.

Just like concessionary regimes, contractual regimes can be designed in many different ways, with terms varying both within and across basins. In their most basic form, they include: cost recovery, profit sharing, service fees, and income tax. It is also increasingly common to include royalties.

- Cost recovery: In the case of a commercial discovery that moves forward to development, a company can recover the costs it has incurred. The mechanism is called cost recovery or cost oil/gas (cost petroleum), which is similar in concept to deductible expenses for tax purposes under the concessionary system. In any one year there is a fixed proportion of total production that investors can use to recover their costs. If costs exceed the cost recovery limit, the difference is carried forward for recovery in subsequent periods. The ceiling on cost petroleum secures up-front revenues for the government as soon as production commences. In this sense the ceiling achieves a similar outcome to a royalty. Cost recovery limits can be set at a specific rate or variable. The more generous the limit is, the longer it takes for the government to realize its take, while low ceilings can negatively affect the development of marginal fields. Any cost petroleum that is available but not used for cost recovery (i.e. excess cost petroleum) is usually added to the profit sharing pool.
- Profit Sharing: Under a PSC, the value of the oil or gas that remains after a company has taken its cost oil/gas is usually termed profit oil/gas. The cost recovery ceiling ensures there is always a minimum quantity of profit oil/gas, which is divided between a host government and a company according to a predetermined percentage agreed to in the contract. The split can be constant, or on a scale linked to cumulative or daily production rates, or to levels of project profitability (ROR, or R-factors). Under a service contract, since the contractor does not receive a share of production, terms such as profit petroleum are not appropriate, even though the arithmetic will often carve out a share of revenue in the same fashion that a PSC shares production does.
- CIT: Both profit oil/gas and the service fee can be subject to the CIT. In some countries such as Cyprus, the government pays the contracting company's income tax from its share of profit oil; these are called "pay on behalf" PSCs. Non-tax specialists tend to confuse this aspect with a zero corporate tax rate. Table 5.5 summarizes the key features of the concessionary and contractual regimes.

Investors typically prefer regimes that impose less up-front burden and are more profit-linked, in other words "progressive." Instruments such as a royalty, bonus, carried state participation, and low cost recovery ceiling, tend to lengthen payback and make the regime more regressive—as overall profitability goes up the government's share of profits goes down and vice versa. However, the latter instruments allow the government to generate revenues as soon as production starts, unlike profit-related taxes. To maintain the balance between host governments and investors' interests, a combination of several instruments is often employed to form a country's petroleum fiscal regime.

Assessing Licensing Fiscal Regime Options 141

Table 5.5 Key features of concessionary and contractual arrangements

Concessionary	Contractual: PSC	Contractual: Service Contracts
State owns resource; IOC owns production	State owns resource and production; contractor's remuneration is a share of production	State owns resource and production; contractor's remuneration is a fixed fee
IOC bears all risks and gets all rewards; pays taxes accordingly	Contractor bears all exploration and development risks; shares commercial (oil price) risks	Contractor bears all exploration and development risks; government takes commercial (oil price) risk
IOC entitlement: gross production less royalty, taxes, bonus	Contractor's entitlement: cost oil plus profit oil, less income tax	Contractor's entitlement: cost oil plus remuneration fee, less income tax
IOC owns facilities	State owns facilities	State owns facilities

Source: Compiled by author.

Lebanon's petroleum fiscal regime

Lebanon's OPRL provides for a PSC as the fiscal framework for oil and gas, although the regime is described by some Lebanese officials as hybrid, mainly because it combines a royalty with profit sharing. In reality, petroleum fiscal regimes have become very elaborate and continue to evolve. Many can be described as hybrids, borrowing features from each other up to the point where the classification of a fiscal regime under a specific terminology has become more difficult, at least from an economic perspective. For example, a royalty is common in concessionary regimes, as it is imposed as compensation for the transfer of ownership of the oil produced—at least that is the theory. In practice, however, a royalty is used to provide an early and relatively predictable flow of tax revenues. As a result, many PSCs around the world have a strong royalty component, even though it is not consistent with the legal nature of such arrangements, since governments retain full production ownership rights. Furthermore, many concessionary regimes today do not have a royalty (e.g. Norway and the UK).

The OPRL does not include the details of fiscal terms, which are given in the EPA instead. There is a debate concerning this practice. International organizations such as the IMF favor the inclusion of the fiscal terms in the hydrocarbon legislation as this reduces administrative costs, political difficulties, and investors' perceived risk, and increases transparency. According to the IMF (2012), "The alternative of setting the fiscal terms out in a model agreement can make them little more than a basis for negotiation."

Lebanon's fiscal regime includes: a royalty, cost recovery, profit sharing between the government and the company extracting the resource, income tax on the company's share, and state participation.

The royalty on oil (and natural gas liquids [NGL], if any) is imposed on a sliding scale varying with incremental daily production, as shown in Table 5.6. The royalty rate for gas is flat at 4 percent. The limitations of a royalty were discussed earlier in this chapter. A royalty is a regressive instrument as it is imposed irrespective of cost. Linking the royalty rate to production does not overcome this problem since a field's size is a poor proxy for profitability. Furthermore, it is unclear on what basis the scale was set.

Some non-fiscal experts have limited their assessment of the fiscal regime in Lebanon to the royalty and condemned its low rates by international standards. As highlighted earlier in this chapter, all the fiscal instruments—their rates and design, as well as the way they interact with other instruments—should be taken into consideration when assessing the petroleum fiscal regime. In Lebanon's case, special attention should be paid to the net impact of the combination of a royalty with a cost recovery ceiling. · Furthermore, it is unusual to find high royalty rates imposed on natural gas, as the economics of gas projects are more challenging than those of oil. Lebanon can consider keeping the differentiated rates between oil and gas but it should set a reasonable flat rate for oil instead of a sliding scale.

The cost recovery ceiling is meant to achieve the same objective as the royalty—that is, to generate revenues for the government as soon as production starts. The application of a royalty, however, will delay the cost recovery for investors and further extends the payback period. Disposable petroleum (the net revenues available for cost recovery after the royalty payment) will be partly used by a contractor for cost recovery, depending on the level of the ceiling. Therefore, when a royalty applies, it reduces the amount of petroleum available for cost recovery, which in turn lengthens the cost recovery period.

According to the model EPA of 2017, the cost recovery ceiling is one of the biddable parameters, along with profit sharing, which is on a sliding scale related to profitability (R-factor) (Table 5.7), although the maximum cost recovery ceiling is fixed at 65 percent and the minimum profit sharing to 30 percent (government share). Having such key fiscal parameters biddable is one concerning feature of the regime as it can

Table 5.6 Sliding scale royalty on oil

Daily Oil Production in Barrels Per Day (b/d)	Royalty Rate (%)
<15,000	5
15,001–25,000	6
25,001–50,000	7
50,001–75,000	8
75,001–100,000	10
>100,000	12

Source: Compiled by author.

Table 5.7 R-Factor and profit sharing rates

R-factor	State's Portion	Right Holder's Aggregate Portion
$R \leq 1$	A% ($\geq$30%)	100%-A%
$1 < R < RB$	Formula below	100%-percentage determined below
$R \geq RB$	B%	100%-B%

Source: Compiled by author.

lead to a wide range of government takes, varying between contracts and consequently increasing the administrative burden and complicating revenue forecasting.

The R-factor is calculated on a quarterly basis as the ratio between cumulative cash inflow and cumulative capital expenditures (CAPEX), whereby cumulative cash inflow equals profit petroleum plus cost petroleum minus operating expenditures (OPEX), from the beginning of the production phase through to the end of the quarter. The profit sharing mechanism should make the regime more progressive, although the final outcome will depend on the rates and interaction of different instruments.

Some countries adopt a single rate for profit sharing since the mechanism is based on profits, not revenues, meaning a single rate will still safeguard the progressivity of the system and an application of several bands is therefore deemed unnecessary. The inclusion of tiers became more fashionable as a single rate was found hard to determine. If countries use different bands for profit sharing and make them biddable, international good practice recommends fixing the minimum band and allowing companies to bid on the higher tiers. The latter approach, however, does not solve the issue of multi-fiscal structures, especially when combined with a biddable cost recovery ceiling, as is the case in Lebanon.

According to the Model EPA, when the R-factor is between 1 and RB, the state share of profit petroleum will be determined according to the following formula: $A + [(B - A) \times (R - 1)/(RB - 1)]$; where A and B are the minimum (30 percent) and maximum state shares of profit petroleum.

Originally, there was some ambiguity with respect to the CIT rate, with some parties calling for using the general income tax rate of 15 percent on the contractor's total share of profit petroleum as a starting point for the draft taxation law to be finalized by the Ministry of Finance. Others argued in favor of increasing the income tax rate on petroleum activities to 25 percent. On 5 October 2017, the parliament passed the Lebanese Petroleum Activities' Tax Law, which fixed the CIT rate at 20 percent.

While it is important not to look at each tax in isolation but rather to consider the total impact of the fiscal regime, fiscal experts typically recommend the imposition of the general CIT rate on the oil industry, instead of treating it differently and complicating the regime.

Consistency should also be maintained between the income tax law and the EPA, especially with respect to cost recovery and deductions of expenses. For instance, while finance costs are tax deductible, they are not cost recoverable.

Contractors pay a fee for the training of public sector personnel with functions relating to the oil and gas sector, in an amount up to $300,000 per year (increased by 5 percent each year) until the beginning of the production phase, and thereafter $500,000 per year (increased by 5 percent each year). These costs are recoverable.

Some concerns have been expressed about the local employment requirement where, according to the Model EPA (Article 20), "as of the beginning of the Production Phase, no less than 80 percent of the aggregate number of employees of the Right Holders (including the operator) shall be Lebanese nationals." Some companies fear that this threshold may not be easy to reach given limited oil and gas expertise in the country. Additionally, it is unclear how this threshold was imposed in the absence of a modern petroleum policy and a broader employment strategy.

144   *The Future of Petroleum in Lebanon*

The OPRL refers to state participation (Article 6) as a "back-in right" option where the state maintains the right to acquire a given interest following the declaration of a commercial discovery. This is the typical form for state participation, although there are examples where the state pays its way. Under the former option, the state does not contribute its share of costs and is carried by the IOC during the exploration period, until a commercial discovery is declared, or until first revenues flow at first production. The risk is that no commercial discoveries are made, in which case the carried costs are never recovered. State-carried interests can be very expensive for IOCs, particularly in high-cost areas, such as deep water. Furthermore, carried state participation extends the cost recovery period as the carried costs are recovered from the state's/NOC's equity share of production until the carry is repaid. Generally, IOCs do not favor such arrangements since they materially increase the exploration risk (cost of failure) and reduce the project's economics, especially when combined with tough fiscal terms.

In Lebanon, the state participation provision was not enacted in the first licensing round. For future rounds, its rate and form are still to be determined. If enacted, and depending on its form, state participation can increase the overall government take in the venture.

Two important aspects should be taken into consideration when fully assessing Lebanon's upstream petroleum fiscal regime. First, whatever combination of rates Lebanon selects, the fiscal regime should be internationally competitive and the total government take should be in line with the global average of 65–85 percent. As put by the IMF (2012), "fiscal regimes that raise less than these benchmark averages may be cause for concern, or—where agreements cannot reasonably be changed—regret." Higher rates are also not recommended as they can deter the attractiveness of the country to IOCs. Second, investors are not only concerned by the level of government take; they put perhaps equal emphasis on the extent to which the regime imposes upfront burdens on their projects. That said, the value of the government take should be treated with caution, as it has several variables and does not reveal the important features of the fiscal regime including the timing of revenues and risk sharing. In Norway, for instance, the government take is 78 percent. Though this is at the "higher" end, the Norwegian fiscal regime has several important features that make it attractive to investors, namely, that it is one of the most stable regimes in the world and the tax value of exploration costs for each tax year loss is refunded in the following tax year for those companies that are not in a tax-paying position.

Comparison of regional fiscal terms

This section analyzes the petroleum fiscal terms in Cyprus and Israel and compares them to Lebanon.

Cyprus's petroleum fiscal regime

Like Lebanon, Cyprus adopted a PSC. It is also difficult to conduct a detailed analysis of the Cyprus petroleum fiscal regime as all fiscal terms are biddable or negotiable and none of the signed contracts have been made public.

Cyprus does not have a royalty but imposes signature and production bonuses. This can be partly explained by Cyprus's urgent need for cash given its economic circumstances. The government imposes a ceiling on its cost recovery and profit sharing based on the R-factor. The general CIT rate is imposed on the contractor's share of profit petroleum but it is paid on its behalf.

The following terms have been referred to in the 2012 Model Production Sharing Contract issued in connection with the second licensing round:

- Signature and production bonus: The former is paid within thirty days after the date of execution of the contract while the latter within thirty days after average daily production from the contract area measured over sixty consecutive days meets biddable production thresholds. The cost recovery ceiling is biddable. Unrecovered costs may be carried forward indefinitely until fully recovered but not beyond the duration of the contract.
- Profit sharing is imposed on a biddable, incremental sliding scale linked to the R-factor, which is calculated quarterly as follows:

R-factor = Cumulative Net Revenue/Cumulative Capital Costs where:

- Cumulative Net Revenue is the contractor's Cost Recovery plus Profit Share minus Operating Costs incurred from the start of the project until the end of the preceding quarter.
- Cumulative Capital Costs are the contractor's exploration and development capital costs incurred from the start of the project until the end of the preceding quarter.

  Under the 2007 Model Agreement used for the First Licensing Round, profit sharing was based on an incremental sliding scale linked to average daily production rates and the price of oil.
- CIT: There is no specific regime within the Cypriot income tax law concerning the oil and gas sector. CIT is paid by the state from its share of production (it is the normal CIT rate of 10 percent). Confusion arose in the second licensing round when the model PSC was released without a tax clause following continued statements by the Ministry of Commerce that "no tax is payable" on oil and gas production profits. By contrast, the 2007 Model PSC includes a tax clause providing that "applicable corporate tax shall be deemed to be included in the Republic of Cyprus's share of Profit Oil" and "the portion of Available Oil which the contractor is entitled to ... shall be net of corporate tax" (Mallis 2012). The ministry then posted a clarification that each second-round PSC would include a similar clause, although "a statement showing the amount of corporate tax paid for each specific calendar or tax year cannot be prepared or obtained." The latter has important implications for international investors. When "pay on behalf" is used, the precise legal provisions are important in the context of assessing the foreign tax credit position of IOCs, which may give rise to additional tax liability in their home country if poorly constructed.
- Training Fee: The contractor is required to contribute negotiable/biddable amounts toward the training of Cypriot civil servants. The amounts may be

146   *The Future of Petroleum in Lebanon*

different in the periods before and after the declaration of commerciality. Training fees are cost recoverable.

Israel's petroleum fiscal regime

Israel illustrates a typical example of the fiscal cycle. In untested offshore environments in particular, governments are likely to adopt a cautious attitude and offer attractive fiscal terms to arouse sufficient interest from IOCs and as a spur to kick-start activity. Once discoveries are made, host governments feel empowered as it becomes clear that a hydrocarbon basin exists. Often, such an outcome leads to tightening regulations and fiscal terms.

Israel applies a concessionary regime, formulated in 1952 and largely left unchanged for decades until 2011. The original fiscal regime was very generous from an investor's perspective, whereby the government's take at only about 30 percent was one of the lowest in the world. That level was deemed inappropriate and the regime obsolete following a series of gas discoveries. The original system included: fees, a royalty, CIT, and special deductions for depletion. Such a combination made the regime regressive.

In 2010, the minister of finance appointed the Sheshinski committee to examine the country's petroleum fiscal regime. The committee found that "the current system does not properly reflect the public's ownership of its natural resources" (Ratner 2011). The committee's draft conclusions recommended two major changes to Israel's tax treatment of the oil and gas industry:

- First, eliminating the existing depletion deduction, which the committee describes as an anomaly in the legislation and lacks any economic justification. The depletion allows taxpayers to deduct from their taxable income (gross revenues less royalty) about 27.5 percent for a reduction in a product's reserves, thereby cutting their tax liability.
- Second, introducing a progressive special profit tax (or windfall tax), based on an R-factor of a minimum of 1.5 and a maximum of 2.3. The tax rate would begin at 20 percent when cumulative net income is equal to 150 percent of its exploration and development costs. It then increases linearly up to a maximum of 50 percent (imposed when the R-factor reaches 2.3), as shown in Figure 5.1.

The committee also recommended keeping the royalty rate at 12.5 percent (deductible from the income tax base). Additionally, the regular CIT rate applies to oil and gas corporations (whether registered as an Israeli company or as a foreign company operating in Israel) and pertains to all sectors in Israel. The rate applies at 25 percent, effective from January 2016. In terms of structure, the existing Israeli fiscal regime bears similarities to the fiscal regimes of Norway and the UK as they applied in the early life of the North Sea province.

Following the above changes, the government fiscal take would vary from 52 percent to 62 percent, which is still below the world average. Johnston (2010) describes Israel's new fiscal regime as "state-of-the-art in fiscal design" and "one of the more progressive systems in the world."

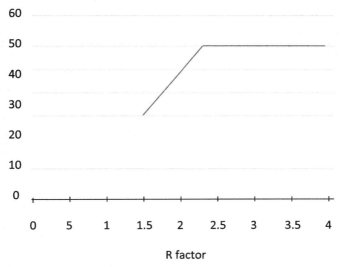

Figure 5.1 R-Factor and windfall tax rate.
Source: Produced by author.

Table 5.8 summarizes the key features of the petroleum fiscal regimes in Lebanon, Cyprus, and Israel.

Additional features

The design of a fiscal regime should take into consideration the conditions of the oil and gas region. A high level of government take may not be justified in cases of high-risk exploration and high-cost development, or for those areas with remaining modest petroleum potential. From an investor's perspective, a combination of commercial and non-commercial factors comes into play when assessing the competitiveness and attractiveness of an oil and gas province. Investors seek to achieve reasonable returns at an acceptable level of risk. They compare future expenditures with potential rewards. The evaluation looks at factors such as geological potential, commercial prospectivity, political risks, and, of course, fiscal terms. The end result of this process permits opportunities to be ranked across the global portfolio. Experience also shows that low levels of government take are rarely stable.

Other important features of a fiscal regime include its simplicity and stability. Simple regimes reduce the administrative burden. A tax regime that is simple to understand, implement, and administer is levied on a well-defined tax base. It increases transparency and reduces the administrative burden, for both administrations and taxpaying businesses. The more transparent the means by which the government obtains revenues, the better informed investors are and the less the scope for maladministration or administrative discretion.

Unstable fiscal regimes negatively affect the confidence of investors in government policy. Of course, fiscal regimes cannot be expected to be set in stone. Circumstances

148   *The Future of Petroleum in Lebanon*

Table 5.8 Summary of economic terms

	Lebanon	Cyprus	Israel
Type	PSC	PSC	Concessionary
Royalty	4% gas 5–12% sliding scale with production	None	12.5%
Signature Bonus	None	Biddable	Biddable
Production Bonus	None	Biddable	None
State Participation	Applicable but not in 1st round	None	None
Windfall Tax	None	None	20–50% R factor based
Cost Recovery Ceiling	Biddable	Biddable	None
Profit Sharing	Biddable	Biddable 1st Round: based on production and price for oil; based on production tiers for gas 2nd Round: based on R factor	None
CIT	20%	10% paid on behalf	25%
Training Fee	Up to $300,000/ year (increasing by 5% annually) until beginning of Production; thereafter $500,000/year (increasing by 5% annually)	Biddable	None

Source: Compiled by author.

are constantly changing in any basin. A certain degree of flexibility needs to be allowed in any tax system if it is to respond to differing conditions, such as maturity, and to evolve as a result of major changes in the external environment. However, if a tax system changes frequently and unpredictably, it may seriously affect future development projects since it increases political risk and reduces the value placed by investors on future income streams. It is recommended that the variation of taxes over the life of a project can be minimized and as such it is imperative to get things right from the beginning.

The design of a progressive regime allows the system to respond automatically to changes in conditions, giving investors greater predictability. Emphasis on stability is equally important to governments. A tax system that has some level of predictability and reliability enables governments to know how much revenue will be collected and when, clearly assisting with reliable expenditure forecasting and budgeting.

The adoption of profit sharing linked to the R-factor makes the Lebanese fiscal regime more progressive. However, this progressivity should be weighed against the other regressive instruments in the regime, namely the royalty and cost recovery ceiling.

Conclusion and recommendations

The chapter analyzes the choices that Lebanon has made in terms of awarding oil and gas contracts and the upstream fiscal regime and compares them to policies adopted in Cyprus and Israel.

In terms of the allocation strategy, Lebanon selected competitive bidding, which is increasingly popular as it allows host governments to benefit from the competitive instinct of IOCs. The popularity of auctions is likely to continue, especially as many NGOs promote their use under the argument that they are the most transparent procedures. However, the success or failure of an auction largely depends on its design and a government's commitment to transparency. Countries can adopt a range of allocation policies because a single strategy may not be suitable for all circumstances and opportunities, as the case of Israel shows.

An important aspect of competitive bidding is the choice of biddable parameters, where the use of fiscal parameters is not recommended. Lebanon has included two key fiscal elements—cost recovery ceiling and profit sharing—as biddable. Although the LPA has fixed the maximum ceiling and minimum profit sharing, such a step does not eliminate the likely outcome of different fiscal structures varying per contract, thereby rendering the management of the regime more burdensome and less transparent. Cyprus is an extreme case where all economic parameters are biddable. Israel has adopted a more sober approach, limiting the biddable terms to two—the work program and signature bonus—thereby excluding key fiscal terms which have been pre-fixed.

In terms of block delineation, Lebanon offshore block sizes do not fall outside the reasonable range, especially when the exploration risk and the relinquishment rule are taken into consideration.

With respect to petroleum regulations, Lebanon seems to offer a middle ground between Cyprus and Israel—the former being more lenient, while the latter is more prescriptive, especially after the 2010 and 2011 changes.

Some question whether the choice of regime Lebanon made is the right one. In reality, the type of the regime is less relevant. Fiscal regimes can be made equivalent in terms of both control and overall economic impact for given oil and gas prices. The design of the regime, the interactions of different fiscal and quasi-fiscal instruments, and the details related to the imposition of different instruments, among others, are far more important. Limiting the assessment of the effectiveness or strengths of the fiscal regime to the choice and rate of the major headline taxes is restrictive. Several factors, such as the fiscal reliefs and the process of calculating the tax base, can lead to significant differences among fiscal packages, while different structures and regimes can produce the same results in terms of revenue and tax take.

After more than sixty years, Israel introduced new fiscal changes in 2012. These made the regime more progressive and competitive by international standards. Apart from the signature bonus that is typically used as a biddable parameter, all the fiscal terms are fixed. Cyprus does not impose a royalty, but uses signature and production bonuses along a biddable cost recovery ceiling. The island changed its fiscal terms in the second licensing round, especially with respect to the profit sharing basis.

150   *The Future of Petroleum in Lebanon*

While the overall government take is important, the timing of when tax instruments hit investors, and therefore affect their payback, is equally relevant. The best investor incentive is probably the chance of rapid payback of capital. In Lebanon, the combination of royalty and cost recovery ceiling, with the possibility of state participation, can result in lengthening the payback period and make the regime more regressive.

No single, ideal solution exists for all countries. The perfect fiscal regime has yet to be invented. What matters is what governments want to achieve. Since there is no objective yardstick for sharing economic wealth between the various interests involved in petroleum activity, controversy and tensions will always prevail between investors and the host government. It is important, however, to maintain the delicate balance between ensuring an adequate share of revenues for tax-levying authority while simultaneously providing sufficient incentives to encourage investment. These issues arise in almost all taxation policy activities, but in the case of oil and gas they assume a special character and complexity.

This chapter's recommendations for improving the existing system in Lebanon focus on three specific areas:

Law

- The government should consider adopting one law that governs both offshore and onshore operations, in line with international practice.

Licensing

- The government needs to ensure that licenses are allocated in a climate of transparency and openness and meet the highest standard of professionalism and adherence to international practice.
- Blocks should be awarded to companies that submit the most appropriate bids, not necessarily the most optimistic ones. To minimize the risk of overcapitalization, which could result from a biddable work program, Lebanon should have a highly qualified and skilled committee evaluate various offers.
- The block sizes do not fall outside the norm, especially when taking the geological risk into consideration. There is no ideal block size: the geological risk, the type of opportunity, and the relinquishment rules should also be taken into consideration.

Fiscal Regime

- Lebanon should consider including the details of the fiscal terms in the hydrocarbons legislation, not just in the agreements.
- The main weakness of the fiscal regime is the fact that two important parameters—the cost recovery ceiling and profit sharing—are biddable. While the maximum recovery ceiling and minimum profit sharing have been fixed, the fact that such key elements of the fiscal regime are biddable will create different fiscal structures for each contract area and complicate the regime.
- The value of the government take should be treated with caution as it does not reveal important features about the fiscal regime, including its progressivity and the timing of revenues.

- Some non-fiscal experts have limited their assessment of the fiscal regime in Lebanon to one instrument (royalty or CIT). In reality, all fiscal instruments—their rates and design, as well as the way they interact with other instruments—should be taken into consideration when assessing the regime. Special attention should be given to the net impact of the combination of a royalty with a cost recovery ceiling.
- The government can impose a single royalty rate for oil, while maintaining differentiated rates between oil and gas. It is the R-factor that will provide flexibility to the system, in line with changing costs and profitability.
- R-factor-based profit sharing should make the regime more progressive, although the final outcome will depend on the rates and interaction of different instruments.
- International practice tends to support the imposition of the general CIT rate on the oil industry, instead of creating a separate regime as Lebanon did.
- Consistency should be ensured between the OPRL, Petroleum Taxation Law, and the EPA.

References

Authored references

Blinn, K., D. Claude, L. Honoré, and P. Andre. 1986. *International Petroleum Exploration & Exploitation Agreements—Legal, Economic and Policy Aspects*. Barrows Company Inc.

Brown, C. 2009. "A Golden Decade for Angola's Deepwater." *Offshore Magazine*, 1 December.

Bunter, M. 2002. *The Promotion and Licensing of Petroleum Prospective Acreage*. Kluwer Law International.

Cotula, L. 2010. *Investment Contracts and Sustainable Development: How to Make Contracts for Fairer and More Sustainable Natural Resource Investments*. The International Institute for Environment and Development.

Cramton, P. 2006. "How Best to Auction Oil Rights." Working Paper Series, Initiative for Policy Dialogue.

Dor, N. and M. Danishefsky. 2011. "A Legal Vacuum Filling Up with Gas: Israel's New Regulatory Environment." *Offshore Magazine*, March.

Duval, C., L. Honoré, P. Andre, and L. Jacqueline. 2009. *International Petroleum Exploration and Exploitation Agreements: Legal, Economic and Policy Aspects, 2nd Edition*. Barrows Company Inc.

Fraser, R. 1991. "Licensing resource tracts." *Resources Policy* 17: 271–83.

Hacohen, D. 2014. "Israel's Gas Development: Overview of the Israeli Oil and Gas Legal and Regulatory Framework. An Israeli Counsel Perspective." International Comparative Legal Guides.

Hayes, E. 2011. "Legal Aspects of Natural Gas Exploration, Production and Distribution in Israel." Petroleum Law White Paper. Leake & Andresson Associates.

Johnston, D. 2001. "International Petroleum Fiscal Systems." Discussion Paper No. 6, United Nations Development Programme.

Johnston, D. 2010. "Israel Hydrocarbon Fiscal Analysis and Commentary." Daniel Johnston & Co.

Kretzer, U. 1993. "Allocating Oil Leases: Overcapitalization in Licensing Systems Based on Size of Work Programme." *Resources Policy* 19: 299–311.

Le Leuch, H. 2011. "Good Practice Note on (Upstream) Natural Gas, a Guidance Note to Complement the EI Source Book." University of Dundee.

Mallis, P. 2012. "Cyprus: Industry & Tax Update." Deloitte Oil & Gas Tax Newsletter, October.

Milgrom, P. 1989. "Auctions and Bidding: A Primer." *Journal of Economic Perspectives* 3: 3–22.

Nakhle, C. 2008a. *Petroleum Taxation: Sharing the Oil Wealth—A Study of Taxation Yesterday, Today and Tomorrow.* Routledge.

Nakhle, C. 2008b. "Iraq's Oil Future: Finding the Right Framework." Surrey Energy Economics Centre/International Tax and Investment Centre.

Ratner, M. 2011. "Israel's Offshore Natural Gas Discoveries Enhance Its Economic and Energy Outlook." Congressional Research Service.

Rodriguez, M. and S. Saul. 2009. "An Overview of Brazilian Petroleum Exploration Lease Auctions." *Terrae* 6.

Richardson, C. 2004. "The Influence of Offshore Leasing Regimes on Commercial Oil Activity: An Empirical Analysis of Property Rights in the Gulf of Mexico and the North Sea." *Georgetown International Environmental Law Review* 17: 97.

Stanley, M. and E. Mikhaylova. 2011. "Mineral Resource Tenders and Mining Infrastructure Projects Guiding Principles." Extractive Industries for Development Series 22, The World Bank.

Tordo, S. 2009. "Countries' Experience with the Allocation of Petroleum Exploration and Production Rights: Strategies and Design Issues." The World Bank.

Non-authored references

BankMed. 2014. "Oil and Gas in Lebanon." Market and Economic Research Division.

Bureau of Ocean Management. 2018.

British Petroleum. 2014. "Statistical Review of World Energy 2014."

Energy Information Administration. 2013. "Overview of Oil and Natural Gas in the Eastern Mediterranean Region."

Ernst & Young. 2014. "Global Oil and Gas Tax Guide 2014."

IHS Cambridge Energy Research Consultants. 2011. "Comparative Assessment of the Federal Oil and Gas Fiscal System." Bureau of Ocean Energy Management.

The International Monetary Fund. 2012. "Fiscal Regimes for Extractive Industries: Design and Implementation."

Israel Ministry of National Infrastructures, Energy and Water Resources. 2014. "Conclusions by the Committee to Examine the Fiscal Policy on Oil and Gas Resources in Israel, Headed by Prof. Eytan Sheshinski."

Israel Ministry of National Infrastructures, Energy and Water Resources. 2014. "Oil and Gas Exploration."

Israel Opportunity Energy Resources LP. 2015. "Discoveries in Israel."

Israel Opportunity Energy Resources LP. 2017. "Ishai Lease (Pelagic)." http://oilandgas. co.il/englishsite/assetsmap/pelagic-licenses.aspx

Organisation for Economic Co-operation and Development. 2014. "Corporate and Capital Income Taxes."

Republic of Cyprus Ministry of Energy, Commerce, Industry and Tourism. 2012. 2nd Licensing Round Offshore Cyprus: Submission of Applications Guidance Note.

Republic of Cyprus Ministry of Energy, Commerce, Industry and Tourism. 2012. "Notice from the Government of the Republic of Cyprus Concerning Directive 94/22/EC of the European Parliament and of the Council on the Conditions for Granting and Using Authorisations for the Prospection, Exploration and Production of Hydrocarbons." (2012/C 38/10). Official Journal of the European Union.

Republic of Cyprus Ministry of Energy, Commerce, Industry and Tourism. 2014. The Hydrocarbons (Prospection, Exploration and Exploitation) Regulations, 2007 and 2009.

6

Lebanon's Gas Trading Options

Bassam Fattouh and Laura El-Katiri[1]

Introduction

Lebanon's exclusive economic zone (EEZ) forms part of the Levantine Basin,[2] which has been estimated to hold up to 122 trillion cubic feet (Tcf) (3.45 trillion cubic meters [tcm]) of recoverable natural gas, in addition to some 1.7 billion barrels of recoverable oil (United States Geological Survey 2010). Lebanon's seabed could contain significant hydrocarbon potential; an initial estimate indicates up to 30 Tcf of natural gas (about 850 billion cubic meters [bcm]) and 660 million barrels of oil. Then Minister of Energy and Water, Gebran Bassil, raised these estimates to 95.5 Tcf of natural gas and up to 865 million barrels of oil, in October 2013, although no exploratory drilling had been conducted (Reuters 2013b). Spectrum—a Norwegian company that carried out Lebanon's first 3D seismic survey in August 2012—has estimated the country's recoverable offshore gas reserves at 25.4 Tcf (Wood 2013). Clearly these varying estimates are representative of considerable uncertainty.[3]

A long-term importer of energy, Lebanon could benefit tremendously from developing its prospective gas reserves by generating a new and potentially important stream of revenue, enhancing its energy security, and reducing air pollution by replacing fuel oil in power generation. But a long history of paralysis in the decision making process due to the sectarian nature of the political system and long delays in the implementation of a suitable legal and regulatory framework constrains Lebanon's prospects for development of gas reserves,[4] taking the time period for possible Lebanese gas developments further into the mid-2020s. Therefore, in the short term, it

---

[1] The authors thank Howard Rogers and Waleed Khadduri for their helpful comments on an earlier draft of this chapter. All remaining errors remain those of the authors alone.

[2] The Levantine Basin is bordered by Turkey, Syria, Lebanon, Israel, the Gaza Strip, Egypt, and Libya.

[3] A number of companies have been acquiring data on offshore Lebanon. In 1993, 2D seismic surveys covering 508 linear km off Tripoli were acquired by Geco Prakla. A data set from Spectrum (a Norwegian company that provides seismic surveys) includes 3D seismic surveys covering 5,360 km^2 (2012–13) and 5,172 linear km of 2D (2000–2). Petroleum GeoServices (also a Norwegian company) data sets include 3D seismic surveys covering 9,700 km^2 (2008–11) and 9,700 linear km of 2D seismic data. For more information, see Lebanese Petroleum Administration, www.lpa.gov.lb

[4] Total, Eni, and Novatek have submitted bids to the LPA in October 2017 for Blocks 4 and 9. In December 2017, the government approved the blocks' awards.

is expected that Lebanon may decide to import natural gas to help it gradually replace oil in power generation, and prepare the domestic market for what may yet lead to a fundamental turn of fortunes. The successful development of Lebanon's offshore gas resources could indeed transform the country into a self-sufficient producer and a potential exporter of natural gas.

Central to the government's objectives of maximizing economic gain from the development of Lebanon's offshore gas reserves and providing the right incentive structure for international oil and gas companies to develop these resources will be decisions on whether to export part of Lebanon's hydrocarbon wealth, what share of reserves should be earmarked for export, and how to identify and secure export markets for natural gas. This chapter provides an introduction to Lebanon's available options for the monetization of its expected offshore gas resources. While decisions concerning the destination of Lebanon's eventual hydrocarbon wealth—if and when this materializes during the 2020s—are key to putting the right policy framework in place, Lebanon will also need to consider interim solutions in order to secure gas for its domestic energy market until the country's own offshore gas production is able to supply the domestic market. Lebanon's economy could significantly benefit from interim imports of natural gas; flexible liquified natural gas (LNG) imports would be the most practical option given the current lack of regionally available pipeline gas supply options.

Lebanon's latecomer status within the East Mediterranean, both as a natural gas importer and as a potential gas producer and exporter, is likely to constrain its future policy choices. It is important to stress that the constraints affecting Lebanon in this sense are mainly driven by internal factors, due to the political polarization and fragile political consensus that have crippled key institutions for many years, in addition to delays and inefficiencies in the decision making process that have already resulted in many lost opportunities. All the more important to an assessment of the different import and export options for Lebanon will be the eventual timing of gas exports. In addition to these internal dynamics, the complex geopolitical landscape and long-term conflicts across the region will have an impact on Lebanon's choices over possible monetization options.

The chapter proceeds as follows. Section one offers an overview of Lebanon's import options, with a focus on the high degree of uncertainty concerning prospective decisions and the advantages of flexible LNG. Section two examines Lebanon's various export options; these remain highly time sensitive, and are hence indicative only. The chapter then concludes with recommendations.

Short-term natural gas imports for Lebanon

Natural gas has played a very limited role in Lebanon's energy mix. The main constraint to the penetration of natural gas in its energy mix has been a lack of access to gas supplies. Lebanon has no proven natural gas reserves and its options to import gas from neighboring countries have been limited. Furthermore, relatively low world market prices for oil during the 1980s and 1990s reduced the incentive to switch from the use of fuel oil in the power sector.

Rapidly growing electricity demand and higher prices for crude oil and petroleum products in international markets from the mid-2000s, however, contributed to a reconsideration of Lebanon's energy supply options throughout the last decade. As end-user electricity prices are essentially determined by the government (at levels significantly below the full cost of generation), the budget for the state-owed power generating sector could be significantly reduced by switching from oil to gas. The Ministry of Energy and Water (MEW) estimates that, at the price of $90 per barrel, Lebanon can save $1.9 billion on its annual fuel bill if it switches its power generation to gas (Middle East Economic Survey 2013a). Figure 6.1 illustrates the size of the deficit associated with the level of fuel prices incurred by the public electricity company Electricité du Liban (EdL), using the example of $40 and $90 per barrel fuel costs for imported petroleum under a business-as-usual scenario.

The prospects of Lebanon establishing its own offshore gas reserves and lower oil prices have not fundamentally changed this rationale. However significant Lebanon's eventual hydrocarbon reserves may ultimately be, their development and production is many years away, leaving a domestic gas supply gap over the short and probably the medium term that may turn Lebanon into a net importer of natural gas well into the mid-2020s. By this time, Lebanon would likely benefit from having begun to address some of its structural problems in the power sector. This would entail addressing the urgent need to reform the power sector, a crackdown on illegal electricity connections, and an overhaul of social services that provide the neediest elements of society with stable, secure electricity access, including those living in shanty towns and informal living spaces.

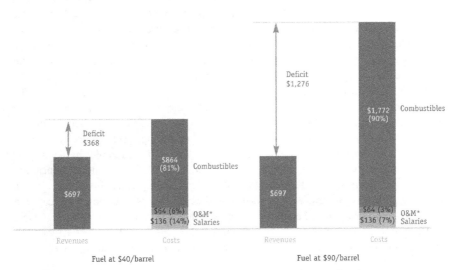

Figure 6.1 EdL deficit increases relative to rising fuel costs (in $ million).

*O&M: Operations and Management.

Source: Report published by former Lebanese Minister of Energy and Water, Alain Tabourian.

158   *The Future of Petroleum in Lebanon*

The importation of natural gas, until Lebanon's own potential gas reserves are developed, could prove advantageous in light of its envisaged and hoped for self-sufficiency by the mid-2020s. While there is certainly potential for Lebanon's natural gas deposits to contribute to a more diversified energy mix and reduce import costs, the country will need to be prepared—with infrastructure in place and end-user market sectors established—to absorb its own natural gas production when that time comes. Steps toward creating this state of readiness would include: building new pipelines, converting some existing power plants to use natural gas, investing in new gas-fired power plants, and, potentially, investing in other gas-based sectors. Importing natural gas during the next few years could facilitate the shift toward natural gas, allowing a gradual switch from oil-fired to gas-fired power generation, as well as opportunities for research and development in areas such as the application of natural gas in the transport sector.

Lebanon's gas import requirements could be large

Despite the potential penetration of gas in other sectors of the economy, the future evolution of natural gas demand will be strongly interlinked with that of electricity demand. From 2000 to 2009, electricity demand in Lebanon increased at an annual average rate of 5.3 percent, slightly higher than the average real GDP growth rate during this period. This average number, however, masks some important trends, as most of the growth in electricity consumption occurred in the earlier years of the period. For instance, from 2004 to 2009, net electricity consumption grew on average by 2.15 percent per annum while real GDP expanded at an annual average rate of 5.7 percent. This is atypical of a developing country such as Lebanon where electricity demand can generally be expected to grow faster than GDP. In fact, publicly available data on electricity consumption does not give an accurate reflection of the actual growth in electricity demand, due to the fact that a significant portion of demand is met by self-generation (mainly diesel powered), while a large portion of electricity demand remains unsatisfied due to a lack of capacity in power generation (World Bank 2008).

In Lebanon, installed power generation capacity effectively stagnated during the 2000s, increasing only marginally from about 2,292 megawatts (MW) in 2000 to 2,314 MW in 2009, equivalent to an average annual growth rate of only 0.25 percent during this period. EdL suffers from huge financial and operating losses, which have to be covered by direct transfers from the government. In 2008 and 2009, these transfers constituted 25 percent and 20 percent, respectively, of the government's primary expenditure (*Daily Star* 2013).[5] EdL also suffers from chronic under-investment, which has prevented it from modernizing its grid and expanding power generation capacity up to now. The slow pace of expansion in new generation capacity in the face of rapid electricity demand growth has had a large impact on the quality of electricity supply in Lebanon; estimates suggest that residential consumers suffer up to 220 days of

---

[5] The *Daily Star* report suggests that, out of the $2 billion annual losses incurred by EdL, nearly 15 percent is due to theft and technical losses and the remainder is due to the high cost of fuel.

interruption per year—the worst record in the MENA region. A similar situation prevails in the industrial sector which, despite heavy investment in private power plants for backup supplies, still suffers huge financial losses from power supply interruptions, with the average firm losing up to 7 percent of its sales value (World Bank 2008). Public investment in new generating capacity needed to meet this increase in electricity demand is unlikely to be forthcoming anytime soon; this suggests that even if (or when) its own natural gas supplies become available, Lebanon's electricity supply problem will be far from resolved.[6]

The Lebanese government has very ambitious plans to increase the share of gas in the power generation mix. A 2010 policy paper for the electricity sector prepared by the MEW proposes a diversified fuel supply, with an ambitious plan to increase the share of natural gas from its current level of zero to two-thirds of the fuel mix by 2030 (Bassil 2010).[7] This, however, requires major investment, not only in the construction of new gas-fired plants, but also in changing the configuration of existing power plants. Lebanon has combined cycle gas turbine plants (Beddawi/Deir Ammar and Zahrani) with an installed net capacity of 435 MW each, constituting about 50 percent of Lebanon's generation capacity. These plants can run on gas feedstock but have not been operating optimally due to a shortage of gas; in 2011, following the cessation of Egyptian gas imports, the share of gas in the fuel mix of the power sector declined to zero (Darbouche, El-Katiri, and Fattouh 2012). Furthermore, Deir Ammar is currently Lebanon's only power plant that can burn gas without reconfiguration, making technical upgrades for Lebanon's three other power plants (Zahrani, Zouk, and Jiyyeh) necessary, in order for gas entering Lebanon's energy mix to be used efficiently (Middle East Economic Survey 2013a, Middle East Economic Survey 2014).

A 2010 Energy Sector Management Assistance Program study estimates that Lebanon's gas demand will reach 2.6 bcm in 2020 and increase almost 4 bcm/year by 2030 (The Energy Sector Management Assistance Program 2010). The MEW puts the figure at the higher level of 5.8 bcm/year by 2030 (Sleiman 2012) and more recently at 7 bcm/year by 2030. Although the MEW also has ambitious plans to extend the use of natural gas to the industrial, commercial, and residential sectors, and to convert the nation's ground transport fleets to compressed natural gas (CNG), in the timeframe of this study, it is unlikely that an appropriate distribution system will be in place. It is therefore safe to assume that the power sector will remain the main source of gas demand. Regardless of estimates of Lebanon's potential gas demand, a key issue remains: how Lebanon can secure gas supplies to meet the expected increase in gas demand over the next decade.

Regional pipeline imports

The main historical barrier to raising the share of gas in Lebanon's energy mix has been access to gas supplies. Natural gas entered the energy mix for the first time in 2009 when the Arab Gas Pipeline (AGP), which also supplied Jordan, started supplying

---

[6] The latest plans to build a 450 MW combined-cycle gas turbine and a 180 MW reciprocating engine unit have been postponed over allegations of corruption and the lack of a clear energy policy.

[7] The latest National Energy Strategy for Lebanon (2017) reconfirms this target.

some 200 million cubic meters (mcm) of Egyptian gas to the Beddawi power plant.[8] However, the entry of natural gas was very brief. Since 2009, the flow of Egyptian gas has been subject to frequent disruptions due to delays in payments and, more recently, to a series of explosions targeting the AGP. The last delivery of Egyptian gas to Lebanon was made in November 2010, while Jordan has since been subject to frequent delivery cuts, reductions in contract volumes, and parallel price rises (Middle East Economic Survey 2012a). Egypt's unstable political situation and its growing domestic demand for natural gas have since cast severe doubt over its capability, or indeed willingness, to continue supplying regional partners with low-cost pipeline gas over the short and medium term; Israel has already experienced this, having seen its separate gas supply contract cancelled in April 2012 (Darbouche and Fattouh 2011, *Platts* 2012).

Other neighboring countries seem increasingly short of gas themselves. In 2003, Lebanon signed a 25-year contract with Syria to import about 1.5 bcm/year of natural gas (World Bank 2004). The Gasyle pipeline, a 32-km pipeline with capacity for 3 mcm/day, stretching from the Syrian border to the Beddawi power plant, was completed in 2005. However, Syria has not been able to supply Lebanon with gas, as its production has not been sufficient to meet domestic consumption, and the country's ongoing civil conflict at the time of writing casts substantial doubt over Syria's ability to significantly change its natural gas supply picture within the next decade.

Iran has been discussed as a potential gas supplier to Lebanon (Middle East Economic Survey 2012b). A pipeline project carrying up to 25 bcm of Iranian gas to neighboring Iraq and Syria (the "Islamic pipeline") could have turned into a lifeline for Lebanon. However, since its announced construction launch in November 2012, the project has suffered from a series of funding issues and from practical above-ground issues related to the complicated security situation in Iraq and, since 2011, the deteriorating political and security situation in Syria (Middle East Economic Survey 2012d).

Similar considerations could be applied to eventual gas imports via Turkey, possibly with gas supplied by Russia, Azerbaijan, or Iraq. Plans for the connection of the existing AGP to Turkey have been discussed for many years and would, in practice, be straightforward and cost-effective, particularly when compared to more capital- and infrastructure-intensive LNG imports (Middle East Economic Survey 2012b). However, the Iraqi central government's plans to produce enough natural gas for export have slipped. Once again, political turmoil in Syria and Iraq renders any prospects for a near-term progression of gas imports via Turkey from any supplier country more remote and at best years away, past the point at which Lebanon would aim to be importing natural gas.

Flexible LNG imports

Given Lebanon's limited opportunities for securing pipeline gas imports from neighboring countries, LNG remains the country's only realistic option. Lebanon initially announced plans to import flexible LNG as of 2015, expecting 12 years of imports until its own domestic production (currently earmarked for beyond the

---

[8] In reality, Syria supplied the gas via a gas swap agreement between Egypt and Syria at the time.

mid-2020s) can replace imported LNG (Middle East Economic Survey 2012c, Middle East Economic Survey 2013b, 2013c). Such plans are not new; LNG has been considered an option since the 1990s, but the initially high construction costs for an onshore regasification terminal turned policy efforts toward securing lower-cost regional pipeline gas imports (LNG Intelligence 2013).

The MEW has meanwhile proposed the construction of a floating storage and regasification unit (FSRU) in offshore Lebanon's coastal areas (Middle East Economic Survey 2012c). Designed as a stop-gap measure, the FSRU offers relatively shorter construction times than those otherwise associated with a permanent, onshore regasification facility, with some potential for additional, moderate, cost savings. In 2013, Lebanon closed bids for two LNG tenders: one to install a build-operate-transfer (BOT) FSRU and the other for an LNG import contract. A shortlist of three possible FSRU candidates was reportedly prepared for submission by the MEW to the Council of Ministers (COM) in April 2014, with similar steps about to be taken for the LNG supply contract. However, endemic delays in decision making tied to Lebanon's political deadlock (also affecting the onshore pipeline system intended to link Beddawi, as the entry point for imported gas, to Lebanon's three other power plants) delayed these plans. The MEW is now planning to implement up to three FSRU projects (Tripoli, Zahrani, and Selaata), and four natural gas pipelines (Deir Ammar–Selaata, Selaata–Zouk, Jiyyeh–Zahrani, Zahrani–Sour) and an LNG tender, but the current status is not yet clear.

Monetizing Lebanese gas: export options for the medium term

Assuming that Lebanon does eventually develop its natural gas reserves, the country will face an array of choices concerning how to monetize its hydrocarbon riches via gas exports. Lebanon's location in the Eastern Mediterranean, with good coastal and land access, provides it with a natural advantage for gas exports. Lebanon has a number of regional trading options (Darbouche, El-Katiri, and Fattouh 2012, Fattouh and El-Katiri 2015). Export potential will be critical for securing the initial interest of foreign investors. Lebanon's eventual export strategies will, to a large extent, depend on:

- The potential size of recoverable gas reserves
- The price range it is able to secure (this will be determined by the eventual size of its reserves, its production targets, the cost of its gas production and potential competing gas exports within the East Mediterranean region and beyond)
- Timely development of gas supply and export infrastructure
- The timing of its first gas exports, in view of rapidly changing regional and global gas market dynamics.

Lebanon's likely option of cooperating with neighboring Cyprus over shared LNG facilities may also impact Lebanon's export choices, provided these choices are available by the time Lebanese gas production is set to commence.[9] While many foreign investors

---

[9] This has become a less realistic option. Cyprus is already considering exporting its gas from the Aphrodite field (when the field is developed) through Egypt's LNG facilities.

162 *The Future of Petroleum in Lebanon*

may indeed pressure Lebanon to consider LNG exports as a first priority, Lebanon will be well advised to consider carefully all available export options, including regional pipeline exports to the Middle East, as well as to Turkey (and possibly onward to Europe). The latter options may prove of particular value if Lebanon's eventual reserves prove to be significantly below current government estimates, thereby placing limits on the commerciality of LNG exports under long-term contracts.

Indeed, the degree to which all of these options will apply likely depends to a large extent on the timing of Lebanese gas exports and the country's ability to use the right time windows to enter into its preferred markets. By that time, Lebanon will likely find itself in a fundamentally different market than it is today—it will be one of the last countries in the region to choose how and where to market its natural gas, and it could therefore be forced to target more distant markets, which would be much harder to access.

Pipeline options (i): The Middle East

Traditionally, the first option considered for exporting natural gas has been via regional pipeline exports to neighboring countries in the vicinity of natural gas producers. While the natural gas trade has gradually been moving toward more flexible exports via LNG, there are good reasons to consider the pipeline option before all others, including:

- The general shortage of natural gas throughout the Levant region (hence, there are potentially receptive markets)
- Regional pipeline exports typically entail the lowest infrastructure costs, especially where exports are over land (rather than via sub-sea pipelines which tend to be more expensive),[10] thereby promising (at well-negotiated contract prices) a high proportion of export rents to initial capital expenditure
- Lebanon's fairly good relations with neighboring countries (such as Turkey, Syria, and Iraq) strengthen its case as a logical gas trade partner with these countries which are, and will likely remain, important growth markets for at least another few decades
- Low infrastructure costs make the pipeline option affordable even to countries with limited public finances (with the additional benefit of reducing the reliance of newly producing countries on foreign partners). This also makes regional pipeline exports the most feasible export option for Lebanon in the event that reserves turn out to be smaller than expected and are not sufficient to allow for LNG exports. Pipeline exports therefore remain the most realistic fallback option in the event that Lebanon's natural gas reserves prove to be significantly smaller than current government estimates.

Lebanon is not short of gas-hungry neighbors, and given the MENA region's expected growth in natural gas demand over the coming decade (Figures 6.2 and 6.3), it may indeed find itself in the fortuitous position of being able to negotiate with several countries over pipeline gas exports once Lebanese gas comes on stream. This is likely to be the case even if gas exports commence in the mid-2020s, as the expected surge in

---

[10] Cross-border pipelines through the East Mediterranean region could be quite costly on account of the difficult seabed conditions of the area.

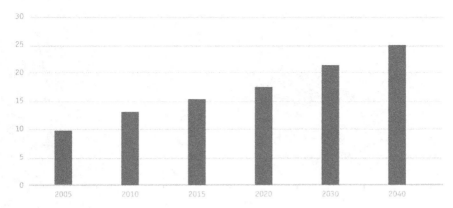

Figure 6.2 Projected natural gas demand in the Middle East* (bcf), 2010–40.

*The Middle East includes Bahrain, Iran, Iraq, Jordan, Kuwait, Lebanon, Oman, Qatar, Saudi Arabia, Syria, the United Arab Emirates, and Yemen.

Source: Environmental Impact Assessment (2014).

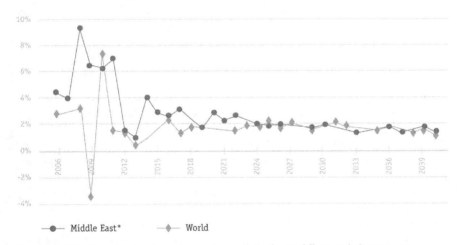

Figure 6.3 Projected natural gas demand growth in the Middle East (%), 2010–40.

*The Middle East includes Bahrain, Iran, Iraq, Jordan, Kuwait, Lebanon, Oman, Qatar, Saudi Arabia, Syria, the United Arab Emirates, and Yemen.

Source: Environmental Impact Assessment (2014).

natural gas demand across the Middle East—a result of switches from higher-cost oil and oil products toward natural gas, and the expected rapid growth in electricity demand—is likely to continue throughout the 2020s and well into the 2030s (International Energy Agency 2013).[11]

---

[11] IEA estimates indeed suggest that gross Middle Eastern demand for natural gas—including Lebanon's immediate neighborhood in the Mashreq, together with Iraq, Iran, and countries in the Arabian Peninsula—may overtake United States demand for gas by 2030.

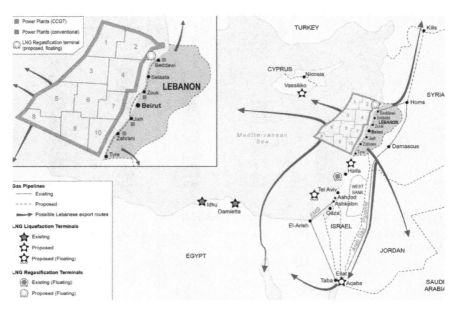

Figure 6.4 Lebanese natural gas trading option.
Source: Oxford Institute for Energy Studies.

While the markets of Jordan and Egypt, Lebanon's southern neighbors, could be particularly favorable in terms of low initial infrastructure costs, as they are already connected to Lebanon via the AGP (Figure 6.4), the start of the 850 bcm Zohr field in December 2017 and BP's West Nile Delta project during the first quarter of 2017 would limit Egypt's potential gas imports in the medium term. Jordan also started importing LNG in 2017 through an FSRU permanently moored in Aqaba, which can take up to 160,000 cubic meters of LNG. But even if these supplies are not enough to meet booming domestic demand, Lebanon will face tough competition from Israel which has been keen to export gas to Egypt and Jordan—a development which, if it materializes, may yet render all talk about Lebanese gas exports to these countries redundant, as Israel will have captured these markets by the time Lebanon could be in a position to export.

Its relatively uncomplicated relations with various neighboring Arab countries also predestine Lebanon—unlike Israel, its only other current competitor on land in the East Mediterranean—to consider gas exports to other neighbors in the Middle East, particularly Syria and Iraq. While both countries may yet develop their own natural gas reserves over the medium and longer term, to become self-sufficient producers of gas they both face medium-term supply gaps, creating opportunities for Lebanese gas throughout the 2020s (Alsumaria 2013, United States Energy Information Administration 2013a, 2013b). Furthermore, since neither country has diplomatic relations with Israel at the time of writing, Lebanon could fill an important role as a geographically close supplier of natural gas, maximizing the value of its exports through low transport costs via regional pipelines, while offering prices which are competitive with both pipeline gas transported over longer distances from Inner Asia and high-cost contracted LNG imports. Both Iraq and Syria, at the time of writing, continue to be entangled in severe domestic instability.

While the above export options may be short in term, they also promise regional low-cost possibilities. They are particularly attractive if smaller than expected natural gas reserves in offshore Lebanon do not favor high volume, long-term contract options.

Some of the biggest challenges that could prevent Lebanon from realizing the commercial advantages of these regional export options will lie within the country itself. The primary challenge will be in Lebanon's ability to provide a domestic contracting framework to foreign investors—one that is sufficiently competitive and stable to allow for the development of gas resources tied to pipeline export options that involve some political and commercial uncertainty. A further challenge is presented by the need to stabilize the country's domestic political situation and its future gas contracting frameworks—rendering Lebanon a desirable, reliable, and stable gas exporter to potential regional clients. Political instability in Lebanon, in the form of contracting indecision, can in this context be as harmful as the threat of sabotage to infrastructure. Lebanon's regional gas exports will also depend strongly on whether potential regional export partners find and contract alternative gas sources by the time Lebanon decides to negotiate over regional gas exports. The ability of negotiating parties on both sides to agree on gas prices, a contentious issue that has previously prevented other regional neighbors—such as the GCC economies—from agreeing on mutually beneficial regional gas pipeline trade (Fattouh and El-Katiri 2015) will also be of great importance.

Pipeline options (ii)

Lebanon's pipeline export options are not limited to the Middle East alone. Its proximity to Turkey, and thereby to European markets, also offers the potential for Lebanese gas exports northward, supplying the Turkish market and/or feeding into regionally sourced pipeline options toward Europe.[12] The potential benefits could be multiple:

- Turkey's explicit interest in becoming an energy hub for pipeline gas toward Europe renders it a potential key transit market for European pipeline gas from the East Mediterranean as well as the Caspian Sea, thus presenting an ample opportunity for Lebanese gas to feed into the European market
- Pipeline gas to Turkey promises significantly lower initial infrastructure costs than an LNG plant (as seen above in the discussion of pipeline export options to the Middle East), especially as part of the pipeline infrastructure (up to the Syrian border) is already in place; it would also be a viable commercial option even in the face of lower than expected natural gas reserves
- Pipeline options could also complement Lebanese LNG, particularly where ample reserves offer potential for parallel export options, as is currently being considered in Israel.

---

[12] Existing pipelines in Turkey need to be upgraded or new pipelines should be built to allow for gas transit to Europe.

166 *The Future of Petroleum in Lebanon*

Both Israel and Cyprus have already been exploring the option of northward pipeline gas exports and, while the political complications concerning Turkey–Cyprus relations may yet preclude Cypriot gas from entering the European market via the Turkish route, Israel and Turkey are understood to have very serious interest in the exploration of mutual gas trading advantages (Gloystein 2012, Linke and Vietor 2010). Lebanese gas may eventually benefit from preferential economics given the availability of a land route via Syria, rather than a sea route, an option that Israel does not have. Turkey also offers an attractive market option in its own right, given its healthy historical growth rates, and a local gas price range superior to anything offered by alternative Middle Eastern markets at present (Republic of Turkey Ministry of Foreign Affairs 2013).[13]

The Turkish option with its European link may also prove highly attractive from a geopolitical point of view. Lebanese gas exports to Europe offer Lebanon the profile of being a European energy supplier irrespective of export volumes. Similarly, gas trade links with Turkey may provide Lebanon with a valuable regional ally and contribute toward constructive regional integration. Unlike the case of exports to the European market, the Turkish market looks commercially realistic irrespective of other supply sources.

However, several issues will determine the viability of this option by the time Lebanese gas production comes on stream. European and Turkish gas demand constitute a significant source of uncertainty given the range of other supplies—pipeline and LNG options—that will appear on the horizon during the early 2020s (Darbouche, El-Katiri, and Fattouh 2012, Honoré 2010). Not only did European gas demand slump in the early 2000s, but a number of planned pipeline projects are competing over the European market share. This renders the Southern Corridor (into which Lebanese gas would feed) far from a "done deal" (Linke and Vietor 2010, Ratner *et al.* 2013, Giamouridis and Paleoyannis 2010, PÖYRY Energy Consulting 2010).[14] Turkish market demand may similarly decelerate, or the country may secure ample gas supplies from alternative suppliers by the early 2020s; such supplies could range from LNG, to Israeli (and perhaps Cypriot) gas, to new gas supplies from Iraq.

Pricing mechanisms, including Europe's accelerated moves toward gas-to-gas pricing under long-term contracts and the preference for shorter and flexible contracts, may eventually offer small gas exporters more variable and possibly lower returns. This issue is particularly acute for Lebanon, whose offshore gas reserves may yet prove to be higher in cost than those of alternative European gas providers such as Russia (Stern and Rogers 2011, 2012; Stern 2009). All these uncertainties raise the essential question of whether the Turkish or European gas markets will eventually offer Lebanon the type of returns it desires for its gas exports, drawing attention to the LNG option.

---

[13] The Turkish government estimates that Turkey's total energy demand (as well as its demand for natural gas) will more than double from its 2011 levels by 2020, to some 59 bcm of natural gas, through a dedicated policy of diversifying suppliers and supply routes (http://www.mfa.gov.tr/turkeys-energy-strategy.en.mfa).

[14] The Southern Corridor is a European initiative aimed at diversifying the European Union's gas mix by transporting gas to Europe from the Caspian Sea region and the Middle East. It is not clear precisely which countries will be linked to the initiative as the corridor remains in the very early stages of planning.

The LNG option

Both for the government and for international investors, LNG is probably the most attractive option for exporting Lebanese gas, for several reasons:

- LNG offers Lebanon the most flexible option for exports of its natural gas, allowing access to extra-regional markets such as Europe and East Asia
- LNG can be supplied both via long-term contracts and, additionally, on a spot market or short-term basis, promising additional returns for producers with some flexible production capacity or seasonal surpluses
- LNG is also an attractive option politically, for it would place Lebanon on the map of global gas market suppliers, a geo-strategically desirable position irrespective of the volume of Lebanese LNG exports.

The LNG export option, however, remains subject to many uncertainties. One of the key uncertainties relates to the actual size of Lebanon's gas reserves, together with its potential production rate, the size of domestic demand, and hence the actual volume of gas that would be available for export under a typical long-term contract. The production of Lebanese LNG will require sufficient reserves, production, and allocations of its natural gas production to export markets—locking in Lebanese gas under long-term export contracts for about 15 to 20 years. Assuming Lebanon could prove up a resource base comparable to that of Cyprus and Israel—in the range of 5–30 Tcf proven recoverable reserves (Darbouche, El-Katiri, and Fattouh 2012)[15]—Lebanon's initial LNG potential could amount to 5–10 mtpa (6.8–15.5 bcm), a small volume but large enough to render one or two LNG trains commercially viable.[16]

By the time Lebanese LNG might be ready for export—currently the mid-2020s— the country will also be competing with a number of new market entrants, many of them with considerably more weight over key markets in Asia/Pacific and Europe, including Australia, East Africa, and North America.

Existing contracting for Australian and East African LNG means that a significant share of the market by the early 2020s will already be locked into long-term supply contracts by the time Lebanon could be in a position to begin serious consideration of LNG exports. This means that Lebanon's ability to capture premium markets through LNG might not materialize within the given time frame. Nor may Lebanon, by then, be in a position to capture the sort of price ranges it would likely be looking for—a problem Cyprus has found to be an increasing obstacle to its own, delayed and currently uncertain LNG plans (Stern 2014).

Alternative markets, of course, exist. Europe may turn out to be Lebanon's best option as a destination for gas exports. However, the basis of pricing for European

---

[15] Cyprus's resource estimates for block 12 (following appraisal drilling in October 2013) confirmed a resource range of 5–8 Tcf, although analysts have suggested that the six offshore blocks tendered out so far by Cyprus could hold as much as 40 Tcf of overall gas resources, based on initial seismic findings. Total Israeli gas discoveries so far amount to about 30 Tcf, including the 19 Tcf Leviathan field and the 9.7 Tcf Tamar field.

[16] This is comparable to Cyprus's potential LNG output by the early to mid-2020s, based on one to two producing blocks.

LNG differs from that of East Asia, possibly resulting in considerably lower price ranges than those realized in Asian premium markets, at least while current pricing mechanisms and linked oil price levels persist. It is in this context that Lebanese policy makers will need to consider carefully, when the time is right, whether LNG really does offer Lebanon the best commercial deal for its natural gas, or whether regional pipeline options may indeed provide better value for money.

Lebanon may also consider other options for exporting LNG—not from its own coastal liquefaction facility, but by making use of existing, or likely upcoming, regional export hubs. The first option worth considering is, without a doubt, the export of LNG via shared facilities with Cyprus (though this is becoming a less realistic option as Cyprus is seeking LNG exports through Egypt's facilities). Sharing LNG export facilities with Cyprus could offer significant cost savings if technical, commercial, and political obstacles can be overcome. Joint monetization between Lebanon and Cyprus, with a view to LNG production, might become viable at a much later stage, depending on the size and location of any new discoveries in offshore Lebanon and Cyprus (Giamouridis 2013).

Cyprus and Israel have been engaging in high-level discussions over the possibility of sharing, and thereby pooling, regional LNG exports via Cyprus (an option that has also gained political support from external partners such as the European Union, though it no longer seems an active option). The combined LNG potential of an Israel–Cyprus hub could, by the mid-2020s, reach between 10 and 25 mtpa (up to 35 bcm), thereby creating a larger regional export hub. Such a hub would be able to secure market share on a basis that separate Cypriot, Israeli, and Lebanese LNG exports might be unable to match. Lebanese gas, too, could form part of such a regional LNG option, offering Lebanon significant infrastructure-related cost savings, with existing contract structures and export experience locally present by the time Lebanese gas would likely join in. As desirable as this option would be commercially, political hurdles would limit its likelihood.

Another option could see Lebanese gas being directed to two Arab neighbors and their export facilities: Egypt or Jordan. Egypt already has two LNG export terminals. These are currently underused, owing to Egypt's own domestic gas needs. While Lebanon's delayed natural gas development will likely deprive it of the more immediate, and lucrative, option of exporting gas to Egypt to help the country fulfil its existing LNG export contracts, the option to use Egyptian LNG export facilities in the event that Egyptian production does not use up their full potential still exists over the long run (Reed 2014). Similarly, Jordan is likely to be receptive to an LNG export facility at its Aqaba port, offering a favorable LNG export location with easier geographical access to Asia (though this a very challenging option to implement). Both options entail that a sub-set of questions be resolved. These include transit and export fees for the country providing export facilities and, in Egypt's case, the security of gas pipelines (in view of the frequency of pipeline attacks on the Sinai Peninsula over the past few years). Again, Lebanon may face a reduced option set due to its latecomer status, particularly as Israel has been exploring the same options and is likely to reach an agreement before Lebanon is in a position to negotiate how to market its natural gas.

Conclusion and recommendations

The road to Lebanon becoming a gas producer is a long one, fraught with many uncertainties. In the next few years, its government will be confronted by many complex decisions. One of these relates to the monetization of its gas reserves, assuming a successful outcome of future exploration if and when this materializes. The size of the reserves, the timing of their development, and the balance between the use of gas to meet domestic demand and for export purposes, will ultimately determine whether Lebanon will be able to consider gas exports. The discovery of small commercial gas resources could provide Lebanon with an opportunity to feed primarily into its domestic market and develop small-scale exports into neighboring countries such as Turkey, Syria, Egypt, and Jordan. In a more favorable scenario—in which discovered resources correspond more closely to initial government estimates—Lebanon could eventually consider an LNG export strategy, bearing in mind the various opportunities and constraints that LNG may face by the time Lebanon enters the market.

By the time Lebanon may be in a position to start production (by the mid-2020s), the country will face very different regional and global gas market dynamics from those seen today. This makes our discussion above indicative of the opportunities currently available and, if there are further delays to Lebanon's upstream development, of opportunities lost.

References

Authored references

Aissaoui, A. 2013. "Between a Rock and a Hard Place: Egypt's New Natural Gas Supply Policy." *Middle East Economic Survey* 56: 11–15.

Bassil, G. 2010. "Policy Paper for the Electricity Sector, Ministry of Energy and Water." Lebanese Ministry of Energy and Water.

Darbouche H. and B. Fattouh. 2011. "The Implications of the Arab Uprisings for Oil and Gas Markets." Working Paper, Oxford Institute for Energy Studies, September.

Darbouche, H., L. El-Katiri, and B. Fattouh. 2012. "East Mediterranean Gas: What Kind of Game Changer?" Research Paper, Oxford Institute for Energy Studies, December.

El-Katiri, L. 2013. "Egypt's Energy Trap." Egypt Oil and Gas Newspaper, August.

Fattouh, B. and L. El-Katiri. 2012. "Energy and Arab Economic Development." Research Paper, United Nations Development Programme.

Fattouh, B. and L. El-Katiri. 2015. "Lebanon: The Next Eastern Mediterranean Gas Producer?" Policy Paper, Oxford Institute for Energy Studies, February.

Giamouridis, A. 2013. "Natural Gas in Cyprus: Choosing the Right Option." Mediterranean Paper Series. German Marshall Fund of the United States, September.

Giamouridis, A. and S. Paleoyannis. 2010. "Security of Gas Supply in South Eastern Europe: Potential Contribution of Planned Pipelines, LNG and Storage." Oxford Institute for Energy Studies.

Gloystein, H. 2012. "Cyprus, Israel Mull Gas Options." World Gas Intelligence, 4 July.

Henderson, J. 2012. "The Impact of North American LNG Exports." Research Paper, Oxford Institute for Energy Studies.

Henderson, J. and D. Ledesma. 2014. "The Future of LNG from Australia." Research Paper, Oxford Institute for Energy Studies.

Honoré, A. 2010. *European Natural Gas Demand, Supply & Pricing, Cycles, Seasons and the Impact of LNG Price Arbitrage.* Oxford University Press.

Ledesma, D. 2013. "East Africa Gas—The Potential for Export." Research Paper, Oxford Institute for Energy Studies.

Linke, K. and M. Vietor. 2010. "Beyond Turkey: The EU's Energy Policy and the Southern Corridor." International Policy Analysis, Friedrich Ebert Stiftung.

Ratner, M., P. Belkin, J. Nichol, and S. Woehrel. 2013. "Europe's Energy Security: Options and Challenges to Natural Gas Supply Diversification." CSR Report for Congress, Congressional Research Service.

Reed, J. 2014. "Israel gas supply deals to Egypt and Jordan draw closer." *Financial Times,* 21 May.

Sleiman, Z. 2012. "Lebanese Current and Future Gas Market." Paper presented at Lebanon International Petroleum Exploration Forum and Exhibition, Beirut, 27–29 May 2014.

Stern, J. 2009. "Continental European Long-Term Gas Contracts: is a transition away from oil product-linked pricing inevitable and imminent?" Working Paper NG34, Oxford Institute for Energy Studies.

Stern, J., ed. 2014. "Reducing European Dependence on Russian Gas: Distinguishing Natural Gas Security from Geopolitics." Paper, Oxford Institute for Energy Studies.

Stern, J. and H. Rogers. 2012. "The Transition to Hub-Based Gas Pricing in Continental Europe." In *The Pricing of Internationally Traded Gas,* edited by J. Stern. Oxford University Press.

Vakhshouri, S. 2012. "Sanctions Raise Questions About Iran's Export Capacity." *Middle East Economic Survey* 55: 46.

Wood, J. 2013. "Lebanon Pins Economic Hopes on Oil and Gas." The *New York Times,* 17 April.

Non-authored references

Alsumaria. 2013. "Al-Iraq jatlubu min Iran ziadat hajm waridat al-ghaz al-tabi'aiy ilayhi [Iraq Requests that Iran Increase Natural Gas Imports]." 5 November.

The *Daily Star.* 2013. "EDL tests smart meters to prevent electricity theft." 17 September.

The Energy Sector Management Assistance Program. 2010. "Potential of Energy Integration in Mashreq and Neighboring Countries." Report No. 54455-MNA.

Globes. 2013. "Noble Energy Prefers Selling Leviathan Gas Regionally." 24 November.

International Energy Agency. 2013. "World Energy Outlook."

LNG Intelligence. 2013. "Lebanon Revisits LNG Import Plan." 1 April.

Middle East Economic Digest. 2012. "Lebanon to Import 2.5Mn T/Y of LNG, Convert Transport to CNG."

Middle East Economic Digest. 2013. "Egypt Struggles with Gas Supply Challenge."

Middle East Economic Survey. 2012a. "Beirut Eyes LNG Import Decision, Touts Reserves."

Middle East Economic Survey. 2012b. "Lebanon Approves Plans for North-South Gas Pipeline."

Middle East Economic Survey. 2012c. "Lebanon LNG Imports a Distant Prospect Amid Bidding Confusion."

Middle East Economic Survey. 2012d. "Lebanon's Economy Hit by Power Crisis and Syrian Turmoil." 55: 33.

Middle East Economic Survey. 2013a. "Lebanon Faces Obstacles to LNG Imports."

Middle East Economic Survey. 2013b. "Lebanon LNG Tender."

Middle East Economic Survey 2014. "Lebanon's LNG Import Plans Inch Forward."

Platts. 2012. "Egypt's EGPC Confirms It Has Scrapped Israel Gas Contract." 23 April.

Pöyry Energy Consulting. 2010. "Security of Gas Supply: European Scenarios, Policy Drivers and Impact on GB: A Report to Department of Energy and Climate Change."

Reuters. 2013a. "Cyprus Looks to Israel to Back East Med LNG Terminal Plan." 19 June.

Reuters. 2013b. "Lebanon Says Gas, Oil Reserves May be Higher Than Thought." 27 October.

United States Energy Information Administration. 2013a. "Iraq Country Analysis Brief." http://www.eia. gov/countries/cab.cfm?fips=IZ

United States Energy Information Administration. 2013b. "Syria Country Analysis Brief." http://www.eia. gov/countries/cab.cfm?fips=SY

World Bank. 2004. "Republic of Lebanon Hydrocarbon Strategy Study." Report No. 29579-LE, Finance, Private Sector Development and Infrastructure Group Middle East and North Africa Region.

World Bank. 2008. "Republic of Lebanon Electricity Sector Public Expenditure Review." Report No. 41421-LB, Sustainable Development Department Middle East and North Africa Region.

Zawya. 2012b. "Iran Starts Construction of Iran-Iraq-Syria Gas Pipeline." 20 November.

Zawya. 2012a. "New Blast Hits Egypt's Gas Pipeline to Israel." 4 February.

7

Managing Oil and Gas Revenues in Lebanon

Bassam Fattouh and Lavan Mahadeva

Introduction

Lebanon is the Levant's most recent candidate to have the potential to join the ranks of East Mediterranean gas producers. The country's waters are believed to hold large hydrocarbon reserves, making offshore Lebanon an attractive location for oil and gas companies. While developing and monetizing these reserves will entail many geological and technical challenges, a key policy challenge that Lebanon will have to face is how to manage its oil and gas revenues in order to maximize the economic benefits for Lebanese citizens. This challenge is pronounced, given the country's weak institutional framework and poor governance structure, perceptions of widespread public sector corruption,[1] political polarization, and rising sectarian tensions.

The prospect of natural resource discoveries has already generated a lot of "hype" in Lebanon. Across the country, billboards sponsored by the Ministry of Energy and Water (MEW) have been erected along highways announcing a number of promises— better transportation networks, a better healthcare system, more jobs, and a better equipped army—all to be funded by revenues from potential hydrocarbon wealth. Lebanon also has plans to establish a savings fund for future generations; the Offshore Petroleum Law requires that part of the revenues from hydrocarbon wealth should be placed in a savings fund. Specifically, Article 3 of the law stipulates that "the statute regulating the fund, the rules for its specific management, the principles of investment, and use of proceeds shall be regulated by a specific law, based on clear and transparent principles for investment and use of proceeds that shall keep the capital and part of the proceeds in an investment fund for future generations, leaving the other part to be spent according to standards that will guarantee the rights of the state and avoid serious, short-, or long-term negative economic consequences."[2]

While it may be many years before Lebanon can find, develop, and monetize its hydrocarbon reserves, it is important for the government to initiate a debate on how best to manage revenues from its potential oil and gas wealth. Lebanon should be wary of importing other countries' strategies, as optimal choices depend on economic and

---

[1] See, for instance, Leenders (Chapter 3 in this volume).
[2] All laws and decrees are available on the LPA website.

institutional contexts. For instance, a savings fund that could suit a country like Norway (with a high level of per capita income and strong institutional frameworks) might not be appropriate for Lebanon. Similarly, it could make sense for big oil exporters (such as Saudi Arabia, the United Arab Emirates, and Kuwait) to have a sizeable liquidity fund to cope with oil price volatility, but that may be much less important for Lebanon, whose hydrocarbon reserves could turn out to be relatively modest in size. In short, there is no one-size-fits-all rule, and any future strategy should take into account Lebanon's key economic, political, and institutional features.

This chapter highlights some of the key features that may have direct implications for the Lebanese government's choices on how best to manage oil and gas revenues. Specifically, we identify the following features:

- A high level of sovereign debt and large interest payments that crowd out priority spending and capital expenditure
- A banking system whose stability hinges on the government's ability to service its debt
- A persistent current account deficit whose financing relies on the continued flows of bank deposits and remittances from its extensive diaspora
- An over-valued exchange rate
- Poor infrastructure
- A weak governance structure and public investment system, both of which are in need of serious reform.

Given these macroeconomic and institutional features, we argue that, rather than aiming to establish a large savings and/or liquidity fund, it is more appropriate for Lebanon, at least initially, to use any potential revenues to pay off the country's large public debt, beginning with the riskiest liabilities, namely foreign currency external debt. Debt repayment should be carried out with maximum transparency and accountability, with an emphasis on demonstrating the consequences of debt repayment. In the very optimistic scenario that debt is significantly reduced and there are ample natural resource revenues left over, it is then worth considering direct cash transfers given the lack of an efficient public investment system, the widespread perception of public corruption among citizens, and the dynamism of the private sector. However, given the poor state of current infrastructure and some of the shortcomings associated with cash transfers, there is also a strong case for public investment in infrastructure if an efficient public investment system is put in place.

This chapter analyzes and evaluates possible policy responses to Lebanon's potential gas discovery in the Levantine basin. Section one discusses the perils which can befall countries enjoying an abundance of natural resources: the so-called "resource curse" and "Dutch disease." Our strategy is first to survey the general lessons from the literature, and then to outline the current economic vulnerabilities and resiliencies of Lebanon. Section two examines issues relating to the management of resource revenues. Section three then focuses on the macroeconomic and institutional issues facing Lebanon, before combining the insights of the previous sections and making policy recommendations.

It remains unclear how large or small Lebanon's gas discovery will be and how much rent will be earned; it is therefore not possible at this stage to calculate the size of

Managing Oil and Gas Revenues in Lebanon 175

the windfall or its significance relative to the country's GDP. Therefore, this chapter will approach the issue of how best to manage oil and gas revenues from a purely qualitative perspective.

The resource curse and Dutch disease

Revenues derived from the sale of exhaustible resources such as oil and natural gas have three special features. First, exhaustible resources are depletable by definition—hence, streams of revenue derived from these resources are only temporary in nature. Second, given the high volatility in oil and natural gas prices, revenues streams are also highly volatile. Third, rents from oil and gas are often large, typically larger than those for other commodities, and are often received by a local monopolist producer (Ross 2012). These special features present governments with challenges and difficult policy choices (Collier *et al.* 2010).

Since revenues are temporary in nature, decisions on how much to save and in what assets to invest to secure a sustainable consumption path are of paramount importance, with far reaching consequences for the domestic economy. Saving is key to transforming exhaustible subterranean reserves into a portfolio of assets that yield a regular flow of income to a country's citizens (Collier and Venables 2011), although saving all the revenues from a resource boom is economically undesirable. However, using all the revenues from a resource boom to boost private and public consumption is unsustainable in the long term. Once the resource boom is over, consumption must fall. Given consumption habits and most governments' commitment to higher consumption levels, this strategy is highly undesirable both economically and politically (Collier *et al.* 2010). Governments can use these revenues to kick-start their economies through investment in public infrastructure and human capital, to tackle poverty and inequality, and/or to reduce the vulnerability of their economies—for instance by reducing the size of external debt. Second, since revenues are volatile by nature, a government must design appropriate tools to smooth the impact on the economy and protect the country from some of the resource curse and Dutch disease effects. Third, as revenues accrue (in the form of a large rent to the government) it is necessary to complement these tools with the construction of effective institutions that promote good governance, fiscal accountability, and transparency in order to assure citizens that the rents are being converted into national productive assets.

There is a large body of literature that links dependence on natural resources to poor economic performance (the so-called "resource curse").[3] An established conclusion from the literature on the resource curse is that higher price volatility exerts a negative impact on economic growth, acting through a lower accumulation of physical and human capital. Collier and Goderis's (2008) dynamic panel estimates provide strong evidence that high rent non-agricultural commodity booms have only

---

[3] See, for instance, Gelb (1988), Sachs and Warner (2001), Bulte and Wick (2009), Frankel (2010), van der Ploeg (2011), and Ross (2012).

176   *The Future of Petroleum in Lebanon*

short-lived favorable effects on output and that the lower average growth rate of commodity-exporting economies is almost entirely due to a higher incidence of sharp slowdowns. However, "the resource curse is not cast in stone" (Collier *et al.* 2010, Collier and Venables 2011). While some countries have been able to harness resource revenues for sustained growth, others have not, with governance and the quality of institutions playing a key role (Mehlum *et al.* 2006, Acemoglu *et al.* 2001). If the size of the hydrocarbon find in Lebanon proves to be large and no measures are put in place to strengthen institutions and governance structures, a prudent view is that "resource curse" and corruption considerations are likely to apply in full force in the case of Lebanon.[4]

Another related concern is Dutch disease.[5] Strong capital inflows can cause real exchange rate appreciation and can trigger a boom in the non-tradable sector—mainly in construction and banking—by lowering import prices or stimulating external credit (Collier *et al.* 2010, Hausmann and Rigobon 2003). While other export-oriented sectors can lose out, total GDP is buoyed by the oil and gas sector and by the non-tradable sector. However, a boom in the non-tradable sector undermines financial resilience and exposes an economy to high risks when world oil and gas prices and revenues fall. Furthermore, exchange rate appreciation affects the entry of firms into the tradable sector, limiting diversity in production and hindering firms from developing their export capability. Using data on 41 resource exporters for the period 1970–2006, Harding and Venables (2013) find that the impact of the export of natural resources falls most heavily on non-resource exports; with every dollar increase in resource exports being associated with a $0.74 contraction in non-resource exports and a $0.23 rise in imports. The recent experience of Lebanon shows that, while its banking sector has shown resilience in the face of many political and financial crises, its economy is still prone to volatility and instability caused by real estate expansions and contractions—a relatively weak tradable sector—and persistent current account and budget deficits. Therefore, in the absence of countervailing measures, Lebanon could be affected by Dutch disease, particularly as its currency is already showing signs of over-valuation (International Monetary Fund 2012a).[6] A specific concern is that a sharp real appreciation of the currency could undermine the competitiveness of the tourism sector, resulting in employment losses.

Managing resource revenues: three key questions

Policy makers expecting an influx of revenues due to a resource boom face three interrelated policy decisions. The first is how much to save from resource rents. The

---

[4] In the context of Lebanon, see Leenders (Chapter 3 in this volume).
[5] For early contributions, see Corden (1984), Corden and Neary (1982), and Van Wijnbergen (1984). For more recent contributions, see Rajan and Subramanian (2005) and Ismail (2010).
[6] While there is strong evidence that resource booms are associated with some Dutch disease effects (such as appreciation of the real exchange rate, factor reallocation, and the reduction of manufacturing output and net exports), any evidence that Dutch disease reduces economic growth is not conclusive. See, for instance, Magud and Sosa (2010).

second is how to protect the economy from volatility in revenues. The final one is how to select the type of financial assets the country should invest in (in other words, the form of saving) (Collier *et al.* 2010). There are no clear-cut answers to any of these questions and the optimal choice depends on the country's specific conditions, such as: the level of economic development, quality of institutions and governance structures, efficiency of the public investment system, and sources of macroeconomic vulnerabilities.

How much to save from resource rents?

One of the key choices facing policy makers is how much to save from a resource boom. Sustainable development depends on the ability of a government to transform rents from hydrocarbon resources into a sustainable source of income, through saving and investing part of the revenues in a portfolio of assets (Collier and Venables 2011). According to the permanent income hypothesis (PIH), consumption of temporary income should be kept to a minimum and should have the following profile: at the time of the natural resource discovery, when permanent income is above actual income, the government should borrow and accumulate debt; when actual income is above permanent income, the government should save and accumulate assets and/or pay off its debt; at the point when the resource is exhausted, the size of the fund and the level of consumption should be such that the interest received from the fund equals increased consumption (Collier *et al.* 2010). In other words, given the temporary nature of the windfall, the recommendation is to build up sufficient foreign assets that generate income such that a permanent increase in consumption is sustained after the exhaustion of a natural resource. The Bird in Hand theory is even more conservative, suggesting that governments should consume only the interest earned on financial assets accumulated from the natural resource windfall. Based on the experience of Norway, many have recommended that revenues from exhaustible resources should be saved in the form of foreign financial assets under the auspices of a sovereign wealth fund.[7]

One implication of both PIH and Bird in Hand theories is that consumption should grow slowly and reach its maximum level only after the resource has been exhausted. They also tend to place much more weight on the welfare of future generations vis-à-vis the current one and hence provide a sense of inter-generational equity.

The PIH has been criticized for not taking into account the possibility that some economies may suffer from shortages of capital and/or face tight constraints on public spending and external borrowing (Takizawa *et al.* 2004, Collier *et al.* 2010, Araujo *et al.* 2012, Baunsgaard *et al.* 2012). Many have argued that if the economy is capital-scarce, then devoting part of the revenues to scaling-up investment and consumption can have positive effects on the domestic economy (Wakeman-Linn *et al.* 2004). In other words, it is not always the case that saving in the form of foreign assets is superior to investment in domestic assets. If the return on domestic public and private investment is higher in capital-scarce economies than the alternative return on foreign assets and/

---

[7] See, for instance, Davis *et al.* (2001) and Barnett and Ossowski (2003).

or if relaxing the constraint on public investment can induce a shift in economic growth to a higher path and/or help the country escape poverty traps (Baunsgaard et al. 2012), then the strategy of building a sovereign wealth fund can be associated with a high opportunity cost in terms of foregone growth and higher and better quality capital and human stock. It is important to note that in the case of capital scarcity, the implications in terms of consumption and saving are different from those of the PIH. First, the increase in consumption is largest for the current generation. This may not necessarily imply inequitable inter-generational distribution, as future generations are likely to be wealthier than the present one. Second, when capital is scarce, not all of the windfall should be invested in foreign assets, part of it should be allocated to building domestic capital stock. The optimal balance will depend on many factors including the level of a country's development, the efficiency of public investment, and the quality of institutions (Collier *et al.* 2010).

While there is a strong case for investing part of the resource rents in a capital-scarce economy, other considerations should be taken into account. If capital accumulation occurs too fast, the efficiency of capital formation may fall and the price of purchased investment goods and raw materials can rise. Furthermore, rapid increases in public spending can lead to lower scrutiny and hence, low quality spending (Collier and Venables 2011). Thus, in addition to the volume of investment, the quality of investment also matters. If public investment is directed toward poor quality projects or is plagued with corruption,[8] then the chances of placing the economy on a higher growth trajectory are slim and future generations may be worse off. Furthermore, the economy may suffer from the "absorptive capacity" problem due to bottlenecks, especially in the non-tradable sector (Buffie *et al.* 2012). This could result in exchange rate appreciation, exacerbating the Dutch disease problem (Collier and Venables 2011).

One of the implications of the absorption constraint problem is that there are limits on the extent to which governments can increase their investment in the domestic economy. Consequently, the level of spending should be set in such a way that it is consistent with prudent macroeconomic management, the ability of governments to implement efficient spending choices, and efforts to minimize some Dutch disease effects. The revenues not spent domestically should be invested in foreign financial assets. Thus, in addition to inter-generational equity and consumption smoothing considerations, investing in foreign assets can be used for "parking" purposes, until the absorption constraints facing the domestic economy are diminished (van der Ploeg and Venables 2012).

How to cope with revenue volatility

The decision on how much to save should not be separated from another related key decision: how to cope with volatility in oil and gas revenues. Manzano and Rigobon (2001) show that the natural resource curse is not caused by excessive dependence on natural resources, but by credit market imperfections, which amplify the debt cycle in many resource-rich countries. Specifically, an increase in the price of natural resources

---

[8] For instance, Collier and Venables (2011) offer examples of rampant corruption in construction projects and ghost construction firms.

relaxes the credit constraint, allowing governments to increase their foreign debts. When prices then fall, countries are not able to access credit markets, forcing them to repay part of their debts. Devaluations and other contractionary measures that follow debt restructuring take their toll on growth. Van der Ploeg and Poelhekke (2009) allow for both a direct effect of natural resource dependence on growth and an indirect effect of natural resources on growth performance via volatility. Using cross-sectional analysis, they find that the direct positive effect of resources on growth is overshadowed by the indirect negative effect through volatility. In a similar vein, Cavalcanti *et al.* (2011) find that volatility rather than resource abundance per se drives the resource curse paradox.

In theory, in the presence of perfect insurance markets, there is no reason why governments should establish stabilization funds to cope with revenue volatility (Daniel 2001). Governments can hedge against revenue volatility through the use of financial instruments such as futures, options, commodity swaps, and other bespoke instruments. In practice, however, very few governments have resorted to these instruments. This indicates the difficulties involved in hedging commodity prices through the use of derivatives markets. These difficulties include the short-term maturity of some of these financial instruments, the lack of expertise in hedging, limited access to futures markets, the cost of hedging, and the fear of political backlash if the options are not exercised. Thus, rather than reliance on insurance markets, evidence suggests an ever-increasing reliance of oil and gas producers on liquidity funds to stabilize oil and gas revenues.

In the absence of opportunities to hedge, the first and most straightforward option is to allow foreign assets and liabilities to fluctuate in response to volatile oil and gas revenues. In other words, the government can establish a sovereign liquidity fund or stabilization funds to invest in foreign assets when prices are high and draw on these assets when prices are low. This will help shield the economy against fluctuations in domestic consumption and investment. To retain flexibility, stabilization funds largely invest in highly liquid assets (Al Hassan *et al.* 2013), often yielding a low rate of return.

Although the general principles and rules for establishing a liquidity fund are straightforward, their implementation in practice is quite complex. One key issue is how big the stabilization fund should be. There are many factors that enter into this decision, including the prudence of policy makers, the extent of volatility of the revenue flow, and intergenerational inequality aversion (van der Ploeg 2010, van den Bremer and van der Ploeg 2012).[9] Van den Bremer and van der Ploeg (2012) show that the optimal savings rule requires the balancing of investment needs against liquidity needs and, as such, the size of optimal buffers varies tremendously across countries. Some studies have found that to smooth revenues effectively, a large fraction of the resource boom should be saved.[10]

---

[9] Van der Ploeg (2010) shows that factors such as rising scarcity rents, temporary oil price spikes, declining paths of oil revenues caused by temporary booms in oil demand, and more aggressive oil depletion policies undertaken by prudent policy makers will increase precautionary savings.

[10] For instance, Cherif and Hasanov (2012) show that precautionary savings should be sizable, about 30 percent of initial income. This, however, is affected significantly by the productivity of investment in the tradable sector. If productivity is sufficiently high, the investment rate increases substantially (from about 15–20 percent to about 50 percent of initial income), reducing the need for large buffer stock savings.

180   *The Future of Petroleum in Lebanon*

Daude and Roitman (2011) show that misperceptions about the underlying process driving commodity prices can lead to substantial over or under saving, with important associated costs. Furthermore, the effectiveness of stabilization funds is also an issue. Davis *et al.* (2001) show that, in countries with stabilization funds, the establishment of the fund did not have an identifiable impact on government spending. This may, however, suggest that it is only those countries with more prudent expenditure policies that tend to establish a fund, rather than the assumption that the fund itself leads to increased restraint on expenditure.

How to allocate revenues

Governments face different options regarding the allocation of hydrocarbon revenues (Collier *et al.* 2010). These can be broadly divided into five different channels:

- Distribute revenues directly to citizens through cash transfer schemes, by introducing subsidies and other social protection schemes, and/or by lowering taxes
- Increase public spending that could either be directed toward public consumption (for instance wages) or investment in public assets (such as schools, roads, water, and electricity)
- Increase public lending to the private sector, for example by establishing development banks
- Reduce the size of the domestic and foreign sovereign debt by using revenues to pay off existing debt
- Accumulate foreign financial assets through sovereign wealth funds (SWFs) and/ or by building foreign reserves at the central bank.

Each of these options to allocate revenue differ fundamentally in various aspects, most importantly in whether the decision to save and invest is left to the government or to the private sector.

Cash transfers, subsidies and tax adjustments

Recent literature on natural resources has shown great interest in cash transfers.[11] The idea is for the state to simply transfer resource revenues, as they are earned, to resident citizens at a fixed amount per head. These transfers can be universal or targeted toward certain segments of society. It is often argued that there are important benefits to cash transfer schemes (Birdsall and Subramanian 2004, Gillies 2010). In essence, they avoid the risk of triggering a voracity effect or appropriation by the rent-seeking elite. In a similar vein, some have argued that cash transfers have the advantage of keeping funds out of a government's hands, especially if that government is perceived to be corrupt. Another advantage is that cash transfers place the decision to invest in the hands of individuals in the private sector who are in a better position than those in the public

---

[11] See, for instance, Sala-i-Martin and Subramanian (2003), Birdsall and Subramanian (2004), Gelb and Majerowicz (2011), and Moss (2011).

sector to identify productive projects. Furthermore, cash transfers, if large enough, can help relieve some of the credit constraints facing individuals, enabling better access to credit markets (Collier *et al.* 2010).

However, cash transfers have their own problems. Given that financial markets are imperfect, the cash may be spent or saved by individuals in ways that are not socially optimal. For instance, individuals may attach little weight to the welfare of future generations and decide to invest little of the cash transfer—using the transfer instead to increase consumption. Furthermore, the financial system may not provide individuals with the appropriate financial assets to enable them to make optimal decisions, in which case a large-scale cash transfer policy would have to be backed by both increasing the efficiency of and developing the financial system (Collier *et al.* 2010). In addition, implementation of cash transfer schemes, especially schemes targeted toward the poor,[12] involves many institutional, infrastructural, and technical challenges which should not be underestimated.

Rather than distributing revenues through pure cash transfer schemes, the government can provide natural gas, petroleum products, or electricity at subsidized prices. Subsidies are highly popular among citizens and, if universally applied, are one of the ways of distributing revenues without necessarily building institutional capacity. However, energy subsidies often come at a huge cost (Fattouh and El-Katiri 2013, Al Hassan *et al.* 2013). Energy subsidies distort pricing signals and result in a misallocation of resources, preventing the country from optimizing the use of its resources and potentially leading to underinvestment in the energy sector (Fattouh and Mahadeva 2014), causing fuel shortages. Although energy subsidies constitute an important social safety net for the poor, they are regressive in nature because in many instances wealthier households tend to capture the bulk of subsidies. Energy subsidies also have negative environmental impacts as they encourage wasteful consumption of fossil fuels. Finally, energy subsidies once introduced are very difficult to reverse, reducing flexibility in designing macroeconomic policy.

Rather than cash transfers and subsidies, the government has the option of reducing taxes on individuals and/or the private sector. If these taxes are distortionary, the overall impact on the economy can be positive. However, in countries where tax rates and tax collection efforts are low, governments should be wary about reducing taxes. Recent studies suggest that taxation is key for "state-building" and any reversal in the government's effort to build its tax base could have serious drawbacks.[13]

Increasing public spending

Rather than leaving investment decisions to the private sector, the government can use resource revenues to increase its spending. While current government expenditures

---

[12] Targeted transfers can suffer from systematic shortcomings such as administrative and private costs and problems in assessing income levels and in identifying beneficiaries; this can lead to incomplete coverage, as well as social stigma. Unsuccessful targeted programs can bring about loss of political support for the scheme, hence reducing the allocation of resources devoted to it. See Van de Walle (1998).

[13] See, for instance, Bird *et al.* (2006), Brautigam *et al.* (2008), and Everest-Phillips (2008).

(such as wages for public sector employees) are normally classified as consumption, public investment in infrastructure projects and/or spending on health and education can be considered a form of saving, but only to the extent that a capital stock that provides a permanent flow of productive services is created. Furthermore, rather than crowding out private investment, recent evidence suggests that public spending complements investment by the private sector. Erden and Holcombe (2005) apply several pooled specifications of a standard investment model to a panel of developing economies for the period 1980 to 1997; they find that public investment complements private investment, and that, on average, a 10 percent increase in public investment is associated with a 2 percent increase in private investment. Therefore, if part of the revenue is not used to release the public finance constraint, there could be a high opportunity cost in terms of foregone higher capital stock.

One key issue concerning public investment is its quality and efficiency. Evidence shows that in many countries the efficiency of public investment is generally quite low due to the lack of a well-trained civil service, poor project selection, investment in white elephant projects that are politically attractive but have a low rate of return, delays in design and completion of projects, inadequate checks and balances in the political and budgetary process, corrupt procurement processes, cost over-runs, incomplete projects, and failure to operate and maintain assets effectively, resulting in benefits being lower than projected (Chu *et al.* 1995). Thus, while in principle the use of resource revenues to scale up public spending yields higher returns when compared to parking funds abroad, the government must ensure that it puts in place a well-functioning public investment system, which is a very challenging task (Collier and Venables 2011).

Public lending to the private sector

Another route would entail the government using revenues to increase public lending to the private sector, for instance through the establishment of development banks (Collier *et al.* 2010). This has the effect of transferring the decision to invest to the private sector, while enabling the government to retain control of macro-aggregates through controlling the volume of public lending. Experience with development banks, however, has been poor. Development banks can develop discretionary powers to "pick winners" and can create an environment conducive to cronyism as they can be open to political interference, poor governance, and outright corruption (Gutierrez *et al.* 2011).

Debt repayment

An alternative is for the government to repay—partly or fully—its domestic and foreign debt. Van der Ploeg and Venables (2012) find that, if a country faces debt-elastic foreign interest, then it is optimal for the government to use part of the revenues to pay off its debt, especially foreign debt. They find that there is a positive relationship between the stock of foreign debt and credit spreads and that the reduction in spreads due to lower debt stock has a positive impact on investment and growth. Another effect of reducing the size of government debt is to induce banks to hold assets other than government assets (such as bonds) and make credit more available to the private sector. However, this is not automatic and depends on the availability of investment opportunities, the ability of banks to assess risk, and their willingness to increase lending to the private sector, especially in an environment where data about borrowers is of poor quality and contract enforcement is weak. In fact, empirical evidence suggests that a reduction in domestic debt is associated with a small increase in bank lending to the private sector (Collier *et al.* 2010).

Accumulation of foreign assets

The government can use resource revenues to accumulate foreign assets through the central bank or SWFs. The motives behind establishing SWFs are various and include: fiscal and macroeconomic stabilization, setting aside funds for future generations, and establishing development funds and pension reserve funds (Das *et al.* 2010, International Working Group on Sovereign Wealth Funds 2008). Given the multiple objectives, there is no straightforward manner by which to assess the effectiveness of SWFs. For instance, evidence suggests that SWFs have not always been effective in smoothing out government spending over the price cycle (Davis *et al.* 2001). Furthermore, if SWFs are not properly designed (for instance by not integrating them into the budget system, or by not instituting flexible operational rules, and/or by failing to promote transparency and accountability), they can have undesirable effects on the economy. Also, as argued above, establishing an SWF can entail a large opportunity cost if funds could otherwise be used in the domestic economy to build capital stock, improve infrastructure, and/or reduce the size of public debt.

While the literature is quite extensive and diverse, it is possible to draw the following broad conclusions:

- There is no one-size-fits-all rule for the form of saving, nor is there for the amount saved. Therefore, before drawing any policy recommendations, it is important to understand the macroeconomic context in which policy decisions are being made, analyze some of the salient economic and institutional features of the country in question, and try to identify key sources of economic vulnerability
- Establishing savings or SWFs by accumulating foreign assets is only one of the many options available and, while it helps to achieve intergenerational equity and protect the economy from Dutch disease effects, this policy is perhaps not the most suitable in countries with scarce capital, poor infrastructure, and high levels of debt
- In countries that suffer from absorption constraints and institutional deficiencies, scaling up public investment should take place gradually. Hence, there is a precedent for parking funds until the right institutional framework is put in place or constraints are alleviated
- To cope with volatility in oil and gas revenues, governments need to establish liquidity funds, though the size of such a fund depends on a wide range of factors, with some countries requiring much larger liquidity funds than others.

Macroeconomic and institutional context

On the basis of its GDP value added per capita, Lebanon is categorized as an upper-middle income country. The country's private formal value added income has been generated mainly from its service sectors: retail trade, commercial and financial services, tourism, and construction (Nakhle 2011). Agriculture and manufacturing are less important for formal GDP, but, along with tourism, these dominate export receipts. Nevertheless, imports have outstripped exports, and Lebanon has persistently had a trade and current account deficit.

The trade deficit is only partially offset by another crucial feature of Lebanon's economy: the size of remittances from its extensive diaspora. Remittances are so large that they can be considered another productive sector. Lebanon received remittances that peaked at 23.9 percent of GDP in 2008, and were 16.1 percent in the latest data for 2012.[14] As far as can be gathered from survey data, and extrapolating from other countries' experiences, these remittances are spent on consumption (including imports) and residential construction. This, in part, explains the strong growth in household-oriented sectors in Lebanon. However, there is also evidence that remittances finance education, which is important given that Lebanon's education system is predominantly private (Chaaban and Mansour 2012).

Gross capital formation as a ratio of GDP is relatively high for the non-government sector and stood at about 27 percent in 2010. This contrasts with the low level of gross capital formation by the government of less than 1.5 percent of GDP in the same year (Table 7.1). Lebanon also receives strong inflows of foreign direct investment (FDI); according to United Nations Conference on Trade and Development (UNCTAD) in 2012, its net FDI stock was 128 percent of GDP. Prima facie, this indicates that the Lebanese private sector is adding to its productive stock and supporting future growth in domestically generated GDP per capita. However, a more accurate picture would be obtained by adjusting these gross investment rates for locally measured rates of depreciation and also for riskiness, in order to calculate the true addition to productive capital. Indeed, most FDI inflows tend to go into real estate and retail commercial property (Credit Libanais 2012).

Lebanon's educational output is of a very good standard. The World Economic Forum (2013) ranks the country's education sector highly in terms of access, quality of provision, and attainment; in 2013 it placed Lebanon at 32 out of 122 countries (sandwiched in between Spain and Hungary), scoring much better than the average upper-middle income or Middle Eastern country. The health and wellness of the nation's workforce is similar to the average of the region. The population is young, with favorable demographics, without the looming pension or age-related health sector liabilities of other countries. However, this favorable picture disguises the difficulties faced in translating higher educational attainment into improved productivity in the resident workforce. Lebanon's workforce and employment prospects are relatively weak according to the World Economic Forum (2013), which ranked the country at a

---

[14] The World Bank. 2014. Data Indicators. https://data.worldbank.org/indicator

Managing Oil and Gas Revenues in Lebanon

Table 7.1 Selected macroeconomic indicators for Lebanon

	2009	2010	2011	2012	2013	2014
Gross capital formation (government, % of GDP)	1.4	1.4	1.8	3.3	2.9	2.9
Gross capital formation (non-government, % of GDP)	32.2	26.7	19.6	20.7	23	23
Gross national saving (government, % of GDP)	−6.8	−6.0	−6.6	−5.0	−5.2	−5.2
Gross national saving (non-government, % of GDP)	30.7	23.6	13.8	15.2	18.1	19.1
Overall balance (% of GDP)	−8.2	−7.5	−8.3	−8.3	−8.1	−8.0
Total government debt (% of GDP)	146	137	134	132	130	130
Current account (% of GDP)	−9.7	−10.6	−14.1	−13.9	−13.0	−12.0
Gross reserves (Billions of United States dollars)	27.4	30.2	30.6	34.4	37.6	41.6
Gross reserves (% of short-term external debt)	52.6	56.4	55.4	56.9	55.4	54.8

Notes: Actual figures for 2009; Preliminary figures for 2010; Projected figures for 2011–14.

Source: International Monetary Fund (2012a).

low 96 out of 122 countries in terms of its workplace human capital. Labor participation rates are low and the country is estimated to have a poor capacity to attract high-level talent and train staff. Furthermore, the high average levels of education mask deep differences: Lebanon has a relatively large poor population, and according to Laithy, Abu Ismail, and Hamdan (2008) nearly 20 percent of its population was living on less than \$4 a day in 2008. Unemployment is high (youth unemployment is particularly high at 34 percent) and there is a large informal sector (World Bank 2012). The average labor share of income for Lebanon is relatively low for an upper middle-income country, with a higher share going as profits (Guerriero and Sen 2012). The dual nature of Lebanon's labor market can be explained by the high levels of immigration of less qualified workers from neighboring countries, notably Palestine and more recently Syria, such that the number of people residing in Lebanon, but born elsewhere, represented 17.5 percent of the population in 2010.[15]

The Lebanese banking sector became a special case internationally when it expanded strongly in the aftermath of the 2008 global financial crisis. Its resilience comes from the fact that it holds many foreign deposits and a large part of the remittances are intermediated through the banking system, while the external crisis encouraged additional inflows. Foreign residents' deposits were 19.35 percent of all deposits in 2013 and were mostly in foreign currency (Kanj and El Khoury 2013). In general, Lebanese banks are heavily deposit-funded rather than debt-funded and these deposits have proven to be resilient even in the face of Lebanon's political and conflict

[15] Ibid.

risks. On the asset side, banks hold relatively large amounts of government debt. However, in recent years, banks have expanded their private sector lending share, though much of this remains concentrated in real estate and in trade-related and consumption-oriented sectors.

The Lebanese central bank holds large foreign and gold exchange reserves, of about the same size as the country's GDP, and has maintained a fixed exchange rate with capital mobility, by a policy of sterilized interventions and keeping domestic interest rates high. The International Monetary Fund (IMF) (2012a) estimates that the country's currency is overvalued in the range of 3 percent to 17 percent, depending on the method used. Gross official reserves (excluding gold) stood at $30.2 billion in 2010, accounting for almost 56 percent of short-term debt. These reserve levels place Lebanon typically in the top five across countries when measured as a ratio of GDP. Yet, given the risks concerning Lebanon's capital flows, its large sovereign debt, and import dependence, they are arguably at the appropriate level.

Lebanon's other outstanding economic characteristic is its very high level of sovereign debt. Total gross sovereign debt was close to 146 percent of GDP in 2009 and declined to 127 percent of GDP in 2010 (Table 7.2). Despite a fiscal adjustment program by the government, it is projected to remain above 130 percent of GDP for the rest of the decade. To some extent, the high level of debt is a legacy of reconstruction following the civil war. However, government spending continues to be high; in 2010 the overall deficit was over 8 percent and this is expected to persist until the end of the decade. A major factor is the high level of transfers from the state in support of lower-than-market prices for electricity (International Monetary Fund 2012b). State support for Electricité du Liban, the state-owned electricity company, reached 4.61 percent of GDP in 2011—the sixth-highest among 75 countries worldwide that provide electricity subsidies and the highest among 17 countries in the MENA region (Byblos Bank 2013). By contrast, the cost of the state social safety net through official channels is small, estimated at about 1 percent of GDP in 2010, which is low by international standards (International Monetary Fund 2012b).

Table 7.2 Lebanon government debt, 2009–14 ($ millions unless otherwise indicated)

	2009	2010	2011	2012	2013	2014
Gross debt	51,152	52,602	54,372	58,022	61,860	65,926
Banking system	37,558	38,318	40,541	42,767	45,370	48,146
Non-banks	13,594	14,284	13,831	15,254	16,490	17,780
Euro-bonds	5,402	5,349	5,236	6,022	6,955	7,986
Concessional loans	3,018	2,807	2,621	3,199	6,955	7,986
Foreign currency T-bonds	297	49	53	53	53	35
Gross debt (% of GDP)	146	127	129	127	126	126
Net foreign currency debt (% of gross debt)	42	39	38	42	45	48

Notes: Actual figures for 2009 and 2010; Projected figures for 2011–14.

Source: International Monetary Fund (2012a).

About half of Lebanon's debt is held domestically, mainly by its commercial banks (Table 7.2). Interest rates payments on debt are high at 7 percent of domestic currency debt, 4 percent on foreign currency debt, and hence 11 percent in total as a percentage of GDP in 2009 (falling slightly to 10.2 percent in 2010 [Table 7.3]). Payments would be even higher if Lebanon did not maintain a reputation for meeting payment and without the perceived high levels of official support from other countries. Payments would also be higher if remittance flows shrank further, given the extraordinary dependence of the economy on this sector.

Lebanon also suffers from very poor infrastructure (International Monetary Fund 2012b). In its latest Global Competitiveness Report, the World Economic Forum ranks Lebanon at 140 out of 144 countries in terms of the quality of overall infrastructure (Table 7.4). One particular indicator on which Lebanon performs quite poorly is the quality of electricity supply, where the country ranks at the bottom of the competitiveness table. One of the reasons for the country's poor infrastructure is low investment by the government—whose capital spending accounted for only 1.4 percent of GDP and less than 5 percent of total expenditure in 2010. In fact, in that year, interest payments

Table 7.3 Central government overall deficit and financing, 2009–14 (percent of GDP, unless otherwise specified)

	2009	2010	2011	2012	2013	2014
Revenues	24	21.9	22.2	24.2	24	23.9
Tax revenue	17	17.2	15.7	17.7	17.6	17.5
Non-tax revenue	5.8	3.5	5.4	5.4	5.4	5.4
Other treasury revenue	1.1	1.1	1.2	1.1	1.1	1.1
Expenditures	32.5	29.2	30.7	32.6	32.1	32
Current primary expenditure	20	17.6	19.6	20.7	20.6	20.5
Interest payments	11	10.2	9.3	8.6	8.7	8.6
Capital expenditure	1.4	1.4	1.8	3.3	2.9	2.9
Overall balance (% of GDP)	−8.2	−7.5	−8.3	−8.3	−8.1	−8.0

Notes: Actual figures for 2009 and 2010; Projected figures for 2011–14.

Source: International Monetary Fund (2012a).

Table 7.4 Quality of Lebanon's infrastructure (rank out of 144 countries)

Indicator	Rank
Quality of overall infrastructure	140
Quality of roads	120
Quality of port infrastructure	73
Quality of air transport infrastructure	65
Quality of electricity supply	143

Source: World Economic Forum (2014).

accounted for more than one-third of total expenditure, crowding out any expenditure on infrastructure projects or social safety nets. Another factor explaining Lebanon's poor infrastructure is its market structure, under which key services such as electricity and water are dominated by state-owned monopolies, with no competition and very limited or no participation from the private sector. A direct implication of poor infrastructure (and of a poor enabling environment for human capital) is that the relatively high education level of the average Lebanese resident fails to translate into better income streams.

The World Bank (2012) estimates that a budget-neutral increase of 0.05 percentage points in the share of public spending allocated to investment in infrastructure would increase the country's growth rate by about 0.5 percentage points. Higher investment increases the public–private capital ratio, which in turn promotes the production of final goods, the accumulation of human capital, and research and adaptation activities (R&A). There are also further indirect effects, as the increase in human capital helps promote activity in both the final goods and R&A sectors.

In this context, it is important to highlight another key feature of Lebanon: the low rate of return on economic activity due to its low appropriability, as producers are unable to capture a significant part of the wealth they create due to various distortions. The IMF (2012b) identifies institutional failures—in particular a poor business and governance environment and the high level of corruption—as major constraints on growth. These institutional features have direct implications on both government effectiveness and the efficiency of public investment, which are low in Lebanon.[16] Public investment inefficiency in Lebanon is reflected in different stages, including: strategic guidance and project appraisal, project selection and budgeting, project implementation, and project evaluation and audit. The World Bank (2012) estimates that improvements in the efficiency of government spending would increase Lebanon's long-run GDP growth outlook by 0.3 to 0.5 percentage points. Thus, while there is a case for Lebanon to use part of its resources to invest in public infrastructure projects, it is key for the country to improve its approach to public finance management.

In summary, over the past few years, Lebanon has managed to navigate through various shocks and safeguard its economic stability. However, many sources of macroeconomic and institutional vulnerability remain. A key role in the decision of how best to manage oil and gas revenues will be played by factors relating to these vulnerabilities:

- An extraordinarily high level of sovereign (both foreign and domestic) debt that requires constant rollover
- A high level of debt that entails large interest payments which crowd out priority spending and capital expenditure
- A banking system whose stability hinges on the government's ability to service its debt

---

[16] For instance, out of 144 countries, Lebanon scored 144 in terms of public trust in politicians, 143 in wastefulness of government spending, 142 in irregular payments and bribes, and 137 in diversion of public funds (World Economic Forum 2014).

- A persistent current account deficit whose financing relies on continued flows of deposits and remittances
- A persistent government deficit, the financing of which will keep the country's debt-to-GDP ratio at high levels for the foreseeable future
- An overvalued exchange rate underpinned by a strong commitment to peg the Lebanese pound to the United States dollar, which is considered to be the linchpin of financial stability
- Poor infrastructure and a weak business and regulatory environment that hinder human capital accumulation and sustainable and inclusive growth
- A weak governance structure and public investment system which are in need of serious reform.

Conclusion and recommendations

Having summarized Lebanon's main economic features and some potential sources of vulnerability, and described the relevant literature, it is now possible to combine insights from the previous sections to make a set of suggestions for Lebanon.

However large or small its resource earnings turn out to be, the clear policy prescription for Lebanon is to use these revenues initially to pay off its large public debt, beginning with the riskiest liabilities, namely foreign currency external debt (which is sizeable in Lebanon). In particular, the short-term component of the country's external foreign currency debt should be reduced to a small share of GDP, given that a well-established conclusion of the literature is that large short-term foreign exchange external liabilities expose the domestic economy to external market shocks (Bordo *et al.* 2010).

The discovery and exploitation of a large gas reserve will further increase the country's exposure to world market volatility, so other sources of risk should be reduced in order to limit overall exposure. The World Bank (2014) emphasizes the benefits of a drop in the country's debt levels, such as lowering the sovereign risk premium and reducing the total cost of its public debt.[17] Lebanon's improved sovereign rating could also lower the interest rates at which the private sector can borrow, improving the competitiveness of the economy and boosting growth. Furthermore, the repayment of public debt should encourage banks to lend to the private sector and thus help support the private sector and boost economic growth. One sector that might benefit is infrastructure, which could be built using a combination of private and public funds. While the benefits of debt reduction are obvious, many risks are associated with this strategy.

If natural resource revenues are absorbed into the political process, with a lack of transparency about how they are being spent, there is a significant risk of triggering

---

[17] The World Bank (2014) calculates that a reduction in Lebanon's debt-to-GDP ratio—to 100 percent for example—would reduce the interest cost of the entire 100 percent of GDP. If as a result of the repayment of some of Lebanon's public debt, the risk premium on Lebanon's debt were reduced by 100 basis points, this would save the annual budget 1 percent of GDP (or $4.4 billion every year based on 2014 GDP).

voracity effects and rent-seeking behavior (Tornell and Lane 1999). Furthermore, reducing public debt may not be politically feasible and may indeed provoke public resistance, especially when expectations are raised in a range of constituencies that then press for more public expenditure, as impressions will have been created of ample availability of financial resources. Also, there is a risk that reducing the size of public debt will improve Lebanon's credit rating, resulting in lower interest rates, which in turn will provide an incentive and irresistible opportunity to borrow more, inducing Lebanon into a cycle of re-borrowing.

Despite the government's desire to establish a savings fund for future generations, there is no imperative to create a sovereign wealth fund in Lebanon. Although this has been a viable and successful strategy for some countries—such as Norway, which already has high levels of income per capita—such a fund may not be appropriate for Lebanon. For countries such as Lebanon (with high levels of debt, potential sources of vulnerabilities, and poor infrastructure) the opportunity cost of establishing a large SWF is quite high in terms of the foregone opportunities to reduce macroeconomic vulnerability and to free government finances for investment in infrastructure projects. There also seems to be little need for Lebanon to create a liquidity fund given the large size of its foreign exchange reserves and the short-run stability of its bank liabilities and remittance inflows. In fact, the best way to protect Lebanon against fluctuations in public investment is to reduce the size of its debt, thus reducing interest payments and freeing up more resources to be used elsewhere.

In the very optimistic scenario that debt is reduced (for example, to less than 100 percent of GDP) and there are ample natural resource revenues left over, it is worth considering direct cash transfers, given the lack of an efficient public investment system, the high perception of public corruption among citizens, and the dynamism of the private sector. One drawback is that capital markets in Lebanon are underdeveloped and may not provide individuals with the appropriate financial assets to enable them to make optimal decisions (World Bank 2013).

Also, as noted by Leenders (Chapter 3 in this volume), citizens may not spend handouts wisely (for instance, on education). Leenders writes: "if no serious measures are taken to address the monopolistic and oligopolistic features of its economy, the opportunities of both increased consumption and investment will be merely captured by a rent-seeking business class." There are also some political barriers preventing the implementation of such a scheme. If the cash handouts are sufficiently sizeable to undermine politicians' patronage, Leenders writes, "there are no a priori reasons to believe that public decision makers would cooperate and this way bankroll themselves out of office." Therefore, while a cash transfer scheme offers some advantages in the case of Lebanon, the design of such a scheme is fraught with challenges and may not achieve the desired objectives.

Lebanon should avoid wealth transfers through energy subsidies, as these distort pricing signals and result in a misalloc ation of resources. Although energy subsidies constitute an important social safety net for the poor, they are regressive in nature because in many instances wealthier households tend to capture the bulk of subsidies. Energy subsidies also have negative environmental impacts by encouraging wasteful consumption of fossil fuels, in addition to the fact that once they are

Managing Oil and Gas Revenues in Lebanon 191

introduced, fuel subsidies are very difficult to reverse, reducing macroeconomic policy flexibility.

An alternative is for Lebanon to reduce taxes on its citizens. However, the Lebanese government is currently trying to improve its tax gathering efficiency and, given the link between taxation and scrutiny of public institutions, it is important not to interrupt this process.

There is scope for increasing public spending, especially on infrastructure projects such as electricity and transportation. Infrastructure constraints pose a serious barrier to the enhancement of Lebanon's competitiveness. But as argued above, the quality of spending is key. Some issues—such as limited administrative and technical capacity and restricted access to information, which prevent the scaling up of investment at a rapid pace, together with misaligned incentives, which could result in sub-optimal investment (with corruption and unproductive rent-seeking constituting some extreme forms of this misalignment)—can limit efforts to increase public spending in Lebanon. While it seems true that Lebanon is short of infrastructure in transport and electricity, it is worth being wary of increasing infrastructure spending while still leaving subsidies in place. The experience of other countries suggests that, without price reform, large-scale infrastructure spending could be overtaken by demand (Fattouh and Mahadeva 2014). Hence, the priority should be to remove subsidies, perhaps replace them with cash transfers, and then expand infrastructure with private participation.

If natural resource revenues are large enough to dominate exports and act as a source of capital inflows, it is clear that a countercyclical macro-prudential policy will be needed in Lebanon. Unlike a standard macro-prudential policy that acts uniformly across all borrowers, it would be better to focus on controlling non-tradable sector liabilities. Argüello *et al.* (2013) demonstrate the need for such a sectorally skewed scheme in an energy exporting country. They show that blanket countercyclical macro-prudential policies in times of buoyant resource revenues will tend to hurt the non-gas tradable sector most, and have less impact on the booming non-tradable sector where most of the financial instability risks actually lie. A good example of such a targeted policy would be to raise sectoral risk weights on real estate borrowing in banks' regulatory capital ratios when gas revenues are buoyant.

In summary, although the literature on the macroeconomics of natural resources seems complex, the messages for Lebanon are straightforward. The first priority should be to pay off part of the country's debt, although there is a strong case for investment in infrastructure if the public investment system can be revamped. In either case, macro-prudential controls on the non-tradable sector should be tightened.

References

Authored references

Acemoglu, D., S. Johnson, and J. A. Robinson. 2001. "An African Success Story: Botswana." Working Paper, Massachusetts Institute of Technology.

Al Hassan, A., M.G. Papaioannou, M. Skancke, and C.C. Sung. 2013. "Sovereign Wealth Funds: Aspects of Governance Structures and Investment Management." Working Paper, International Monetary Fund.

Araujo, J., B. Grace Li, M. Poplawski-Ribeiro, and L. Zanna. 2012. "Current Account Norms in Natural Resource Rich and Capital Scarce Economies." International Monetary Fund.

Argüello, R., J.J. Echavarría Soto, A. Gonzaléz, and L. Mahadeva. 2013. "The Sectoral Effects of Exchange Rate Fluctuations: A Case Study of Colombia." Oxford Institute for Energy Studies.

Barnett, S. and R. Ossowski. 2003. "Operational Aspects of Fiscal Policy in Oil-Producing Countries." In *Fiscal Policy Formulation and Implementation in Oil-Producing Countries*, edited by J. Davis, J. Ossowski, and A. Fedelino. International Monetary Fund.

Baunsgaard, T., M. Villafuerte, M. Poplawski-Ribiero, and C. Richmond. 2012. "Fiscal Frameworks for Resource Rich Developing Countries." Staff Discussion Note, International Monetary Fund.

Bird, R., J. Martinez-Vasquez, and B. Torgler. 2006. "Societal Institutions and Tax Effort in Developing Countries." In *The Challenge of Tax Reform in the Global Economy*, edited by J. Alm and J. Martinez-Vazquez. Springer-Verlag.

Birdsall, N. and A. Subramanian. 2004. "Saving Iraq from its Oil." *Foreign Affairs*, July/August.

Bordo, M.D., C.M. Meissner, and D. Stuckler. 2010. "Foreign Currency Debt, Financial Crises and Economic Growth: A Long-Run View." *Journal of International Money and Finance* 29: 642–65.

Brautigam, D., O. Fjeldstad, and M. Moore. 2008. *Taxation and State Building in Developing Countries*. Cambridge University Press.

Buffie, E.F., A. Berg, C. Pattillo, R. Portillo, and L. Zanna. 2012. "Public Investment, Growth and Debt Sustainability: Putting Together the Pieces." Working Paper 12/144, International Monetary Fund.

Bulte, E. and K. Wick. 2009. "The Curse of Natural Resources." *Annual Review of Resource Economics* 1: 139–56.

Cavalcanti, T.V., K. Mohaddes, and M. Raissi. 2011. "Commodity Price Volatility and the Sources of Growth." Cambridge Working Papers in Economics 1112, University of Cambridge.

Chaaban, J. and W. Mansour. 2012. "The Impact of Remittances on Education in Jordan, Syria and Lebanon." Economic Research Forum Working Paper Series, No. 684, American University of Beirut.

Cherif, R. and F. Hasanov. 2012. "Oil Exporters' Dilemma: How Much to Save and How Much to Invest." Working Paper 12/4, International Monetary Fund.

Chu, K., S. Gupta, B. Clements, D. Hewitt, S. Lugaresi, J. Schiff, L. Schuknecht, and G. Schwartz. 1995. "Unproductive Public Expenditures: A Pragmatic Approach to Policy Analysis." International Monetary Fund Pamphlet Series, No. 48, International Monetary Fund.

Collier, P. and A.J. Venables. 2011. "Key Decisions for Resource Management: Principles and Practice." In *Plundered Nations? Successes and Failures in Natural Resource Extraction*, edited by P. Collier and A.J. Venables. Palgrave Macmillan.

Collier, P. and B. Goderis. 2008. "Commodity Prices, Growth, and the Natural Resource Curse: Reconciling a Conundrum." Working Papers 014, Oxford Centre for the Analysis of Resource Rich Economies, University of Oxford.

Collier, P., F. van der Ploeg, A.M. Spence, and A.J. Venables. 2010. "Managing Resource Revenues in Developing Economies." Staff Papers 57, No. 1: 84–118, International Monetary Fund.

Corden, W.M. 1984. "Booming Sector and Dutch Disease Economics: Survey and Consolidation." *Oxford Economic Papers* 36: 359–80.

Corden, W.M. and J.P. Neary. 1982. "Booming Sector and De-industrialization in a Small Open Economy." *Economic Journal*: 825–48.

Daniel, J. 2001. "Hedging Government Oil Price Risk." Working Paper, International Monetary Fund.

Das, U.S., A. Mazarei, and H. van der Hoorn. 2010. "Economics of Sovereign Wealth Funds: Issues for Policymakers." International Monetary Fund.

Daude, C. and A. Roitman. 2011. "Imperfect Information and Saving in a Small Open Economy." Working Paper No. 60, International Monetary Fund.

Davis, J., J. Owssowski, J. Daniel, and S. Barnett. 2001. "Stabilizing and Saving Funds for Non-Renewable Resources: Experience and Fiscal Policy Implications." Occasional Paper No. 205, International Monetary Fund.

Erden L. and R.G. Holcombe. 2005. "The Effect of Public Investment on Private Investment in Developing Economies." *Public Finance Review* 33: 575–602.

Everest-Phillips, M. 2008. "Business Tax as State-Building in Developing Countries: Applying Governance Principles in Private Sector Development." *International Journal of Regulation and Governance* 8: 123–54.

Fattouh, B. and L. El-Katiri. 2013. "Energy Subsidies in the Middle East and North Africa." *Energy Strategy Reviews* 2: 108–15.

Fattouh, B. and L. Mahadeva. 2014. "Price Reform in Kuwait's Electricity and Water: Assessing the Net Benefits in the Presence of Congestion." Working Paper, Oxford Institute for Energy Studies.

Frankel, J.A. 2010. "The Natural Resource Curse: A Survey." Working Paper 15836, National Bureau of Economic Research.

Gelb, A.H. 1988. *Oil Windfalls: Blessing or Curse?* Oxford University Press.

Gelb, A.H. and S. Majerowicz. 2011. "Oil for Uganda—or Ugandans? Can Cash Transfers Prevent the Resource Curse?" Center for Global Development.

Gillies, A. 2010. "Giving Money Away? The Politics of Direct Distribution in Resource Rich States." Working Paper No. 231, Centre for Global Development.

Guerriero, M. and K. Sen. 2012. "What Determines the Share of Labor in National Income? A Cross-Country Analysis." IZA Discussion Paper 6643, Institute for the Study of Labor.

Gutierrez, E., R. Heinz, T. Homa, and E. Beneit. 2011. "Development Banks: Role and Mechanisms to Increase their Efficiency." Policy Research Working Paper Series 5729, the World Bank.

Harding, T. and A.J. Venables. 2013. "The Implications of Natural Resource Exports for Non-Resource Trade." Discussion Paper 9318, Centre for Economic Policy Research.

Hausmann, R. and R. Rigobon. 2003. "An Alternative Interpretation of the 'Resource Curse': Theory and Policy Implications." Working Paper 9424, National Bureau of Economic Research.

Ismail, K. 2010. "The Structural Manifestation of 'the Dutch Disease': The Case of Oil Exporting Countries." Working Paper 10/103, International Monetary Fund.

Kanj, O. and R. El Khoury. 2013. "Determinants of Non-Resident Deposits in Commercial Banks: Empirical Evidence from Lebanon." *International Journal of Economics and Finance* 5.

194   *The Future of Petroleum in Lebanon*

Laithy, H., K. Abu Ismail, and K. Hamdan. 2008. "Poverty, Growth and Income Distribution in Lebanon." Country Study 13, International Policy Centre for Inclusive Growth.

Magud, N. and S. Sosa. 2010. "When and Why Worry About Real Exchange Rate Appreciation? The Missing Link between Dutch Disease and Growth." Working Paper 10/271, International Monetary Fund.

Manzano, O. and R. Rigobon. 2001. "Resource Curse or Debt Overhang?" Working Paper 8390, National Bureau of Economic Research.

Mehlum, H., K. Moene, and R. Torvik. 2006. "Institutions and the Resource Curse." *Economic Journal* 116: 1–20.

Moss, T. 2011. "Oil-to-Cash: Fighting the Resource Curse through Cash Transfers." Working Paper 237, Center for Global Development.

Nakhle, N. 2011. "Lebanon Real Growth Analysis 1997: 2010." International Monetary Fund.

Rajan, R. and A. Subramanian. 2005. "What Undermines Aid's Impact on Growth?" Working Paper 05/126, International Monetary Fund.

Ross, M.L. 2012. *The Oil Curse: How Petroleum Wealth Shapes the Development of Nations.* Princeton University Press.

Sachs, J. and A.M. Warner. 2001. "The Curse of Natural Resources." *European Economic Review* 45: 827–38.

Sala-i-Martin, X. and A. Subramanian. 2003. "Addressing the Natural Resource Curse: An Illustration from Nigeria." Working Paper, International Monetary Fund.

Takizawa, H., E.H. Gardner, and K. Ueda. 2004. "Are Developing Countries Better Off Spending Their Oil Wealth Upfront?" Working Paper 04/141, International Monetary Fund.

Tornell, P. and P.R. Lane. 1999. "The Voracity Effect." *American Economic Review* 89: 22–46.

Van den Bremer, T. and F. van der Ploeg. 2012. "How to Spend a Windfall: Dealing with Volatility and Capital Scarcity." Oxford Centre for the Analysis of Resource Rich Economies, Research Paper 85, University of Oxford.

Van der Ploeg, F. 2010. "Aggressive Oil Extraction and Precautionary Saving: Coping with Volatility." *Journal of Public Economics* 94: 421–43.

Van der Ploeg, F. 2011. "Natural Resources: Curse or Blessing?" *Journal of Economic Literature* 49: 366–420.

Van der Ploeg, F. and S. Poelhekke. 2009. "Volatility and the Natural Resource Curse." *Oxford Economic Papers* 61: 727–60.

Van der Ploeg, F. and A.J. Venables. 2012. "Natural Resource Wealth: The Challenge of Managing a Windfall." *Annual Review of Economics* 4: 315–37.

Van Wijnbergen, S. 1984. "The 'Dutch Disease': A Disease After All?" *Economic Journal* 94: 41–55.

Van de Walle, D. 1998. "Targeting Revisited." *World Bank Research Observer* 13: 231–48.

Wakeman-Linn, J., C. Aturupane, S. Danninger, K. Gvenetadze, N. Hobdari, and E. Le Borgne. 2004. "Managing Oil Wealth: The Case of Azerbaijan." Discussion Paper, International Monetary Fund.

Non-authored references

Byblos Bank. 2013. "Lebanon This Week." Issue 302, 25 March–6 April.

Credit Libanais. 2012. "The Lebanese Real Estate Sector." Credit Libanais Economic Research Unit Research Update, August.

International Monetary Fund. 2012a. "Lebanon: 2011 Article IV Consultation—Staff Report; Public Information Notice on the Executive Board Discussion; and Statement by the Executive Director for Lebanon." Country Report No. 12/39.

International Monetary Fund. 2012b. "Lebanon: Selected Issues." Country Report No. 12/40.

International Monetary Fund. 2013. "Energy Subsidy Reform: Lessons and Implications."

International Working Group on Sovereign Wealth Funds. 2008. "Sovereign Wealth Funds: Generally Accepted Principles and Practices, 'Santiago Principles.'"

The World Bank. 2012. "Using Lebanon's Large Capital Inflows to Foster Sustainable Long-Term Growth." Poverty Reduction and Economic Management Department, Middle East and North Africa Region, January.

The World Bank. 2013. "Lebanon: Financial Sector Assessment Program (FSAP): Capital Market Development—Technical Note."

World Economic Forum. 2013. "The Global Competitiveness Report 2013–2014."

World Economic Forum. 2014. "The Global Competitiveness Report 2014–2015."

8

Investing Resource Wealth in a Sovereign Development Fund

Sami Atallah, Adeel Malik and Alexandra Tohme

Introduction

The prospect of making a commercial hydrocarbon discovery in the Lebanese offshore has brought with it speculation on the benefits it might reap for the country. Indeed, a substantial amount of oil and gas wealth could transform Lebanon's national economy, but it must be considered that this type of revenue is unique and has its own particular features. First, it is finite. Hydrocarbons are not a renewable resource, therefore the rents are a one-off reward. Second, taking into account the fluctuation of oil prices in the global market, revenues from hydrocarbons are also volatile. Additionally, such revenues usually derive an abnormally large amount of money, begging the question of how this wealth will be distributed across generations and economic sectors, and what kind of investments could reap rewards for the future. Such questions pose a major challenge regarding how to manage resource wealth.

Different political and economic environments have driven some oil-producing states to focus on national economic development, while others with limited absorptive capacity and high-quality infrastructure invest much of their assets abroad. To this end, many resource-rich nations utilize sovereign wealth funds (SWFs) as vehicles to drive public and private investment. SWFs function as an important revenue management entity for hydrocarbon rents and outline parameters for government spending and saving. Their success is largely contingent on the country's ability to ensure that the large amount of profit derived from oil is not vulnerable to elite capture and fiscal mismanagement. That is, SWFs must be well governed internally with strong transparency and oversight principles and embedded within the larger fiscal and budgetary institutions that are also properly managed.

Against this background, Lebanon has two major questions and challenges that it must address. The first concerns what kind of SWF Lebanon should establish and what its investment goals should be in light of its public finance framework. For one, the country has some of the lowest quality infrastructure in the world. It scores poorly across several sectors. For instance, public investment totaled 1.8 percent of state expenditures in 2017, well below the 5 percent in countries with the same level of development. Yet, the challenge does not rest in poor infrastructure or shortage of funds as Lebanon's fiscal management record is considerably weak. The country has suffered from a chronic deficit, and had no national budget from 2005 to 2017. Additionally, Lebanon's poor financial management outcomes are a result of its institutional performance. The World Economic Forum's Global Competitiveness Index ranked Lebanon second-to-last—specifically 139 out of 140 countries—in "wasteful government spending" for fiscal year 2015-16. The inefficiency and weakness of these state institutions and fiscal instruments has led the country down a dangerous path due to precedents that have been set on how it might manage a sudden large inflow of oil revenue. With the prospect of natural gas signaling that a new rent may soon flow into the country, current fiscal and institutional institutions are not up to the task of handling this one-time off rent.

This chapter presents an analytical understanding of SWFs as financial instruments to manage hydrocarbon wealth, and examines the specific characteristics of Lebanon's political economy that help determine the type of domestic needs and institutional policy frameworks that would suit the establishment of such a fund. Overall, this chapter argues that Lebanon's domestic context—facing serious infrastructure and fiscal policy challenges—renders a need for a sovereign development fund (SDF) geared toward socio-economic growth and job creation, and one that demands institutional strengthening, reform, and oversight.

This chapter comprises five sections. Section one offers a brief introduction to SWFs in the global context. In section two, we focus on the management and weakness of SWFs in the Arab region. Section three examines the rationale for developing an SWF in Lebanon. Section four analyzes the political economy of Lebanon's fiscal policy and its potential implications on an SWF. The chapter concludes by laying out an institutional design for an SWF to be successful; specifically, which entity or entities would be tasked with administering the fund and how such a fund could be used as a development vehicle to support domestic economic growth, job creation, and fiscal stability.

Sovereign wealth funds in a global perspective

Increasingly recognized as important state-owned institutional investors, SWFs are playing an ever more important role in the international monetary and financial system. The Organisation for Economic Cooperation and Development (OECD) projected that assets under SWF management could reach $10 trillion by 2015. It is reported that, by the end of year 2009, SWFs managed 1.72 percent of world financial assets, a figure twice the value of those managed by hedge funds (Triki and Faye 2011). The International Monetary Fund (IMF) defines SWFs as "special purpose investment funds or arrangements owned by the general government." Although owned by the state, SWFs involve third parties, typically international financial firms and consultants. The holdings of these funds are generated from current account surpluses, official foreign currency operations, the proceeds of privatizations, fiscal surpluses, and revenues from commodity exports. In recent years, SWFs have grown in number, expanded geographically, and diversified in type. They have become a major source of cross-border investments, including Gulf investments in the Middle East.

As saving and investment vehicles, SWFs gained prominence in the early 2000s when rising oil prices resulted in growing revenues in resource-rich countries. Surging capital account surpluses in these countries led them to direct a growing share of their national wealth toward strategic investments. Typically deployed as institutional mechanisms to save national wealth through foreign and domestic assets, SWFs tend to serve two key purposes: saving wealth for future generations, and providing a buffer against adverse oil price shocks. Traditional SWFs help smooth commodity price volatility and in many countries are incorporated into the central bank in one way or another, while, in others, SWFs retain distinct legal autonomy and independence. Like central banks, these funds can act as a lender of last resort, a buffer against macroeconomic shocks. Indeed, with the recent drop in oil prices, many oil-rich nations are tapping into their reserves from boom years. Although owned by the state, the management of such funds differs in an important respect from the administration of central banks: unlike the latter, SWFs have greater independence and tolerance for high-risk investments, delivering them higher expected returns than central banks (Gieve 2008). SWFs also have longer time horizons (El-Erian 2010).

There is now a vast literature on the form, function, and performance characteristics of SWFs. Differing in type and strategic use, a detailed analysis of these investment vehicles is beyond the scope of this chapter. While fully cognizant of the divergent debates surrounding SWFs, this section provides a brief overview of the principal characteristics of SWFs to frame our subsequent discussion on the desirability and design of a similar fund in Lebanon.

SWFs take many different forms and serve a range of functions. They vary in legal, institutional, and governance structures, but also in objective, need, and strategy. Types of SWFs include: fiscal stabilization funds, savings funds, reserve investment corporations, development funds, and pension reserve funds. The IMF identifies five types of SWFs based on their main objective:

1. Stabilization funds where the primary objective is to insulate the economy from sharp swings in commodity prices
2. Savings funds that are geared toward saving money for future generations
3. Reserve investment corporations that are established to increase return on reserves
4. Development funds that are typically designed to support socio-economic development
5. Contingent pension reserve funds that provide for contingent pension liabilities on the government's balance sheet (International Monetary Fund 2008).

It is clear that the form that these investment funds take in different countries is intimately connected to their functions. A key marker of distinction is an underlying investment strategy. Traditionally, SWF investments are oriented toward foreign markets, in both financial assets and acquisition of companies. A growing part of these investments is now directed toward emerging markets and in non-traditional areas.

200   *The Future of Petroleum in Lebanon*

Some funds are more geared toward meeting local development objectives, and are therefore commonly described as SDFs. This is particularly relevant from Lebanon's perspective, as it faces a key decision about whether the country would benefit more from a fund geared toward external or domestic investments, or a hybrid of the two. If the principal objective of the fund is to save for future generations, as is the case with most SWFs, this can be met through high-return investments abroad. Irrespective of the underlying needs of an economy, such funds invest money in areas and regions with the best return. Others include social, economic, and security objectives in their mandate. Defining the purpose of an investment fund is therefore one of the most important decisions, as it can determine both its form and function. With these broad markers of distinction, we next synthesize the global experiences of SWFs with a focus on funds in the Arab world.

Salient features of Arab SWFs

Some of the earlier experiments in SWFs came from Arab countries in the Gulf. The first states to develop SWFs all maintained certain political economy characteristics that facilitated their inception. SWFs are usually established by countries with sizeable current account surpluses, typically resource-rich nations with abnormally large resource rents. Although many large and resourceful nations, such as Russia and China, have established these saving vehicles, relatively small countries with limited domestic absorptive capacity are particularly well-incentivized to invest their wealth abroad in global markets. In countries rich with natural resources, SWFs provide an additional avenue for diversification of their economies away from hydrocarbons. Arab countries are home to some of the world's largest and oldest SWFs. While Kuwait established the first SWF in 1953, the United Arab Emirates's Abu Dhabi Investment Authority (ADIA) is the largest such fund in the Middle East and third-largest globally (SWF Institute 2014).[1] The oil price boom in the 2000s catapulted many of the Arab SWFs into prominence as important global investors (Behrendt 2008). While several commentaries and reports have appeared on Arab SWFs, there is relatively limited knowledge on the management, operation, and performance of these funds (Figure 8.1).

In general, Arab SWFs are notoriously opaque, providing limited, if any, public disclosure of their assets, investments, and ownership. Even the region's largest and most significant fund, the ADIA, maintains a low public profile, revealing very limited information about its governance, investment strategy, and assets (Behrendt 2008). Secrecy is also strictly maintained within these organizations, even to the extent that one department has little knowledge of what the other is doing.

This brings us to the second key feature: absence of accountability. With limited public disclosure, SWFs can be susceptible to non-transparent deals, conflicts of interest, and limited accountability. This allows for tremendous leeway in setting

[1] As of June 2016, the largest SWFs are Norway's Government Pension Fund and China's China Investment Corporation (CIC), followed by the UAE's ADIA.

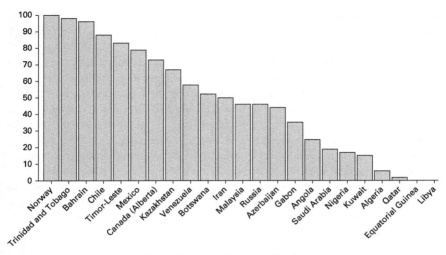

Figure 8.1 Transparency rankings for natural resource funds.
Source: Natural Resource Governance Institute.

boundaries between public and private wealth, and allows for those boundaries to be blurred. Resource fungibility, which makes it possible to mix one pot with another and which is typically held responsible for making foreign aid ineffective, can malign the operation of SWFs too. Additionally, governance structures of these funds leave wide latitude for discretionary decision making. In short, there are few checks and balances. Most Arab SWFs lack clearly-specified withdrawal rules. Even when they do exist, they are rarely enforced in practice. This is most evident in the current low oil price period when most governments in the region are rapidly drawing on their reserves without facing any limitation on such withdrawals.

The third key dimension of Arab SWFs pertains to their investment orientation. Until recently, these funds have predominantly invested in foreign markets, mainly in Western markets (Behrendt 2008). Much of this wealth management is carried out both in-house and by well-established asset management companies. Arab SWFs often engage in international partnerships through global investments. For instance, the Libyan Investment Authority has engaged in deals with British and Italian companies (Wallace 2015). While the Qatar Investment Authority predominantly invests in international markets, it also set up the Qatar–UK Clean Technology Investment Fund with the British government to make venture capital investments of $400 million in clean energy businesses (Behrendt 2009). Over time, SWF investments have relied on more sophisticated instruments and maintained increasingly complex international portfolios. They also represent a prime instrument for acquiring prestige investments and acquisitions abroad, whether in luxury consumer retail, niche technology segments, or bespoke real estate developments. They serve as prime instruments for the external recycling of rents, which adds a significant geo-strategic dimension to their operation. Given the scale of assets under their control, SWF investments can confer meaningful strategic leverage to governments who value these investments not just for their economic, but also geo-political, rates of return. This can draw a wedge between the *de jure* and *de facto* mandates of these funds.

A fourth dimension of SWFs is their dynamic evolution from repositories of surplus incomes and managers of external wealth to increasingly important players in diversification and development projects in domestic and regional markets. While the oil boom during the 2002–8 period expanded financial and economic linkages between Gulf countries and the global economy, the events of 11 September 2001 and the 2007–8 financial crisis made them more risk-averse (Behrendt 2009). Although, with an acute dearth of information, it is difficult to draw definite conclusions on the changing spatial distribution of their investment portfolios, Arab SWFs seem to have increased their exposure to regional markets post-2001. The global financial crisis in 2008 further reinforced this shift by exposing new risks to investments made by these funds. Many SWFs in the region are said to have been severely hit by the financial crisis, with some examples of these losses depicted in Figure 8.2.

Country	Funds	Assets (2007)	Assets (2009)	Assets (current)
Algeria	Fond de Régulation des Recettes	$43b	$60b	$47b
Bahrain	Mumtalakat Holding Company		$14b	$14b
Kuwait	Kuwait Investment Authority	$213b	$169–202.8b	$202.8b
Libya	Libyan Investment Authority	$50b	$65b	$70b
Oman	State General Reserve Fund, Oman Investment Fund	$2b	$8.2b	$8.2b
West Bank/Gaza	Palestine Investment Fund	$0.9b	$0.7b	$4b
Qatar	Qatar Investment Authority	$30–50b	$58–62b	$65b
Saudi Arabia	Public Investment Fund, SAMA Foreign Holdings	$289b	$436.3b	$437.3b
Sudan	Oil Revenue Stabilization Account	$24.6m	$122.4m	$122.4m
United Arab Emirates	ADIA, ADIC, IPIC, ICD, Dubai World, Mubadala, RAKIA, EIA	$250–875b	$408.2–767.9b	$795.1b
Total		**$878–1,523b**	**$1,215–1,617b**	**$1,644b**

Figure 8.2 Financial assets of sovereign wealth funds in Arab countries: 2007–9.
Source: World Bank (2010).

As the value of investments decreased, the foreign assets of the Kuwaiti, Qatari, and UAE governments fell from roughly $1 trillion at end of 2007 to nearly $700 billion at end of 2008 (Setser and Ziemba 2009). The crisis made banks more risk averse. At the same time, domestic investments that were previously considered riskier have since been actively entertained by SWFs. This inward shift is further buttressed by growing social unrest in the region, which has highlighted the need to invest in domestic job creation. This gradual shift represents an expansion of the mandate that now includes investments in strategic development projects, in addition to the usual overseas investment portfolio (Behrendt 2008).

A key example is Abu Dhabi's *Mubadala*, which is playing a more prominent role in the emirate's economic diversification (Behrendt 2008). Established in 2002, it has developed a strong network of international and domestic partnerships in numerous sectors, including renewable energy, aerospace, real estate, health care, technology, and infrastructure services. Long-range development objectives have also begun to figure prominently in the mandate of natural resource funds that were traditionally responsible for managing oil surpluses through sensible investments abroad. Even the traditional worldview on these overseas investments is changing. For example, Saudi Arabia's new development plan, "Vision 2030," has developed the case for a well-diversified global asset portfolio as a means to move toward a post-oil future. It also calls for the establishment of a Public Investment Fund that is predominantly geared toward meeting domestic development needs (Reed 2016).

This brief review of Arab SWFs provides the regional context that a proposed Lebanese fund would be situated in. Lebanon can learn from the Arab experience, avoiding negative lessons in governance and embracing the expanded mandate on development. While Lebanon would do well to avoid the opaque governance structures of Arab SWFs, it could aspire for a greater orientation toward national development objectives. However, before delving into issues of institutional design, it is pertinent to question whether Lebanon needs a conventional natural resource fund and, if so, what type.

The case for a Lebanese sovereign wealth fund

This section focuses on the rationale for creating a dedicated saving instrument in the form of an SWF. Given the growing consensus on the need to create a sovereign fund, this may be a retrospective issue, but one that does need to be considered for at least two reasons. First, it is important to lay out the case for an SWF and its underlying rationale, simply to ensure that Lebanon does not mimic a growingly popular institutional form but also adds the necessary substance that is adapted to its needs. Second, even if an SWF is recommended, it might be needed for reasons that are different from other countries.

In developing the rationale for an SWF, at least four factors are worth highlighting. First, countries that have established such funds typically derive abnormal resource rents whose claimants are both present and future generations. In this context, saving money for future generations is an essential means of achieving inter-generational equity. Second, countries with high resource rents per capita—typically small nations with high levels of natural resource wealth—tend to have limited domestic absorptive capacity, especially if the first generation of domestic infrastructure investments has already been made. This generates a powerful rationale to deploy surplus resources abroad through specialized investment vehicles. Third, SWFs can also help mitigate oil-induced volatility that spills over to the budgetary domain. The excessive fiscal dependence on external rents exposes these countries to boom and bust cycles. In this milieu, SWFs can provide a buffer that helps ride through rough periods.

Finally, and perhaps more importantly, the creation of SWFs is underscored by an important political economy rationale: to insulate national wealth from political struggles, it is necessary to control resource revenues. With short electoral cycles, political incumbents are incentivized to overexploit (or overconsume) resources, thereby saving little for future governments. This is the classic problem of time inconsistency in political economy discussions of fiscal policy. If adequately designed with saving and withdrawal rules that are both clearly defined and well-enforced, SWFs can impose fiscal discipline and help resolve the political incentive problem. As is clear from the preceding discussion, resource-rich countries tend to establish SWFs for a variety of reasons. Some of these may be less relevant for Lebanon, while others deserve more attention. For example, Lebanon is unlikely to enjoy the scale of natural resource rents that are derived by other resource-rich nations of the Middle East. Given that Lebanon does not presently have dependence on resource rents, the issue of oil-induced volatility in budgetary expenditures is also less urgent. Moreover, given the significant developmental needs of Lebanon, especially in infrastructure and job creation, it would be challenging to develop the case for a conventional SWF that is exclusively focused on saving from current resource streams and investing abroad for future generations. In light of this, the traditional reasons for creating an SWF may not be fully applicable to the Lebanese context.

However, the single most important justification for the establishment of an SWF is rooted in political economy. Lebanon has a particularly complicated political economy of fiscal policy, which makes it easy for budgetary processes to feed into distributive politics made by multiple claimants organized around confessional lines. Such distribution of spoils is often described as the price Lebanon has to pay for securing peace after the civil war (Leenders 2012). Regardless of its origins, a clientelistic system exposes public finances to excessive fiscal claims, especially in the absence of any ex-ante rules. While the sovereign fund cannot solve Lebanon's public expenditure mismanagement problems, it can help insulate petroleum resources from the routine politics of spoils that defines Lebanon's political economy. If resource discoveries can lead to struggles for capture of revenues, there is a need to protect them from day-to-day political interference and corruption. This requires checks and balances, which can be built into the institutional design of a sovereign fund. But a well-known lesson in political economy is that rules, no matter how clearly specified, mean little in the absence of a supportive enforcement environment. Such an enforcement environment, in turn, cannot be created without an active constituency that has an existential stake in the maintenance of a rules-based regime.

To summarize, if there is a case for a sovereign fund in Lebanon, it is probably rooted more in political economy concerns than the traditional reasons that motivate the establishment of such vehicles. Problematizing the case for a Lebanese SWF opens a window into deeper questions about the form and function of a possible natural resource fund. Those issues are attended to in the following sections.

The political economy of Lebanese public finance

For Lebanon to optimally benefit from an SWF, there is a need to understand public finance within the historical context of the country's political economy. Lebanon plunged into chronic fiscal deficits soon after the outbreak of the civil war in 1975, when revenues fell sharply while state expenditures on salaries, energy, and subsidies remained intact. Despite the end of the war in 1990, the deficits persisted, even though revenues regained their pre-civil war level of about 20 percent of GDP. In fact, the average Lebanese fiscal deficit represented 13.6 percent of GDP from 1992 to 2016— much higher than the 3 percent average for the MENA region and 2.5 percent for upper middle income countries.[2] Consequently, debt to GDP reached 157.5 percent by the end of 2016, constituting one of the highest ratios in the world (World Bank 2017).[3]

However, deficits in its public finance were not the norm. In fact, looking at periods prior to the civil war, Lebanon had years of fiscal surpluses. After independence in 1943, and until 1958, Lebanon had high surpluses almost every year, averaging 30 percent of spending. Although deficits became more common in the period from 1959 to 1970, the outcome was still average surpluses of 1.1 percent of spending.

To this end, this section examines the challenges Lebanon has faced in managing its public finances, particularly since the end of the civil war. We provide the political and institutional context in which major spending and saving decisions are typically made in Lebanon, focusing primarily on the budgetary institutions responsible for ensuring fiscal discipline and allocating and using resources.

Aggregate fiscal discipline: the size of the deficit

To better understand sources of chronic deficits in its post-war period, it is necessary to consider the period in which Lebanon became independent. The structural shift from high surpluses between 1944 and 1958 to moderate surpluses between 1959 and 1970, and then to high deficits between 1992 and 2016, is attributed to the weakening of the two budgetary institutions responsible for ensuring fiscal discipline. First among them are ex-ante agreements, meaning the ability of coalition partners in the government to agree on limiting the levels of the deficit and spending. Second are informal ex-ante constraints, meaning social norms and economic leanings that influence the decisions of policy makers over the levels of deficit and spending.[4]

---

[2] International Monetary Fund. 2017. OfficeDocument/2006/relationshipsurveys, World Economic Outlook Database.eDhttps://www.imf.org/external/pubs/ft/weo/2017/01/weodata/index.aspx
[3] During this period, debt to GDP peaked at 185 percent in 2006 but managed to come down to 133 percent in 2012 largely due to cyclical rather than structural improvements.
[4] Countries with strong formal ex-ante constraints tend to delegate authority to the Ministry of Finance to limit spending or deficits when negotiating with line ministries. In the case of Lebanon, the Ministry of Finance does not have such prerogatives.

206 *The Future of Petroleum in Lebanon*

In the first two periods (1944 to 1958 and 1959 to 1970), the powerful president—who held executive authority—dominated the ex-ante agreement among decision makers over the level of spending. His power was further enhanced by a political system that constitutionally produced a weak prime minister with vague authority; an incoherent Council of Ministers (COM), which was largely an administrative body reflecting religious and regional balances; and ineffective political parties that rarely competed on economic programs. It was, however, the change in the informal ex-ante constraints from fiscally conservative policies to a welfare ideology, in relative terms, that turned high surpluses into moderate ones. In the 1943–1958 period, the liberal policies of Presidents Michel Khoury and Camille Chamoun called for minimal government intervention and acted as a constraint on spending. However, in the 1958–1970 period, President Fuad Chehab, and later, President Charles Helou, spearheaded developmental projects and institution building, which increased government's role in advancing social welfare.

After the end of the civil war, and especially during President Elias Hrawi's term (1990 to 1998), both the agreements and constraints changed.[5] The new post-Taef political system transferred executive power from the president to the COM. This change severely weakened the ability of decision makers to strike ex-ante agreements that once restricted overspending. This was aggravated by the so-called troika formula in which the president, prime minister, and speaker of the parliament divided power among themselves. Each of the three represented their own respective communities and served the interests of their cronies, at the expense of the institutions over which they presided. In the event of a dispute, Syria intervened as an arbiter. Even when the troika system was replaced, the system of distributing the spoils among community leaders remained intact. Moreover, the economic leanings of the post-civil war elite exacerbated the situation and made the public deficit harder to contain. This was due to the fact that a number of them had been militia leaders who sought to exploit and divide the resources of the state while others were businessmen who sought to maximize profits. Following the assassination of Prime Minister Rafiq Hariri and Syria's withdrawal from Lebanon in 2005, the country became polarized between two political camps: March 8 and March 14. As a result of this deadlock, the country failed to pass a budget over disagreements concerning previous years' fiscal accounts.[6] Consequently, spending was made through treasury advances and ad hoc measures with little fiscal anchor in place.

Several other factors made matters even worse during the post-war period. A larger segment of the budget became autonomous—growing uncontrollably—due to

---

[5] This chapter does not reflect on the period from 1971 to 1991 because the Palestinian presence in the country—especially after 1969 and the civil war period which began in 1975—affected both the distribution of power and the economic situation, hence conflating the sources of the deficit.

[6] While the government submitted the draft budgets for 2006, 2007, 2008, 2009, and 2012, they were not debated in the general parliamentary sessions. As for the budget of 2010, it was debated in the parliament but did not pass because the actual spending and revenue for previous years were not complete. As for the budgets of 2011, 2013, 2014, and 2015, the government did not submit a draft to parliament.

higher salaries, bigger defense budgets, increases in subsidies, and an open-ended reimbursement policy for health services. Spending evolved over the years in such a way that it became rigid, leaving little room for fiscal space to respond to shocks.

The lack of budget comprehensiveness, particularly the exclusion of budgets under the Council for Development and Reconstruction (CDR) (before integrating more recently its operating budget—which is small relative to its overall budget—into the national budget), the Council of the South, the Fund for the Displaced, EdL, as well as those of 61 public agencies, made controlling spending more difficult.

In fact, the public procurement process is infested with corruption. Not only is the procurement law of 1963 outdated, it is neither comprehensive nor does it regulate all aspects of the sector (Lebanon Economic Monitor 2015, WB diagnostic 2016). Furthermore, its rules and guidelines are not properly enforced and the department suffers from a shortage of qualified personnel. A survey of government experts in 2010 indicated that public procurement contracts are granted to firms that provide favorable kickbacks to senior officials (Lebanon Economic Monitor 2015).

According to Leenders (2012), who has studied various cases of corruption in public infrastructure projects such as the purchase of Airbus aircraft for MEA, Beirut port projects, and the waste management contract between the CDR and Sukleen, corruption is prevalent in public projects. More recently, the garbage crisis of 2015 illustrates the extent of corruption. A non-transparent tendering process organized by the government for new waste management contracts culminated in an announcement on 24 August 2015 by the Ministry of Environment naming the winners of the bids, most of whom were seen as having close ties to the political elite.

Even the financing of the deficit was problematic. According to Gaspard (2002), the Lebanese government issued treasury bills with weighted annual yields averaging 18 percent from 1993 to 2002, while only 9 percent would have been adequate. This has effectively cost the treasury an additional $8.5 billion but, once its cumulative effects are taken into account, Gaspard (2002) estimated that $56 billion between 1993 and 2002 went toward interest on public debt.

To make matters worse, the public finance system lacks a serious accountability mechanism. For one, the Court of Accounts—the autonomous watchdog of financial operations—was rendered ineffective and was forced to deny claims of waste in its annual reports. The parliament, which is endowed with oversight power, has failed to exercise its authority. Not only has it not investigated corruption scandals and held the government accountable, until 2018 it facilitated the illegal practice of the government operating without a budget by passing treasury advances rather than forcing it to submit a budget. Even in earlier periods when Lebanon had a budget, the parliament failed to fully exercise its authority when the governing elite agreed on the content and composition of the budget. The parliament has effectively become a partner in the mismanagement of the country's public finances, undermining its own role in the meantime. What makes matters worse is there is no whistleblower or ombudsman's office to facilitate the exposure of corruption or nepotism, let alone regulations that address conflicts of interest or compel public officials to complete income and assets disclosures.

Allocative efficiency: the allocation of budgetary resources

Accentuating these challenges was the inability of budgetary institutions to allocate resources efficiently. This is particularly the case with social spending that suffers from overlapping mandates and duplication of resources. Several public ministries and agencies allocate money to the same sector. For instance, the Ministry of Education, the Office of the Prime Minister, and the Council of the South could allocate resources to public education. This is often the case so spending can be used for clientelistic purposes at a large cost. According to a study by Herera and Pang (2005), Lebanon utilizes 25 percent more input to "produce the same health outcomes than best practices countries" and "13% more input for education."

Furthermore, regional allocations of public resources are driven by political rather than equity considerations. For instance, although North Lebanon has the highest share of population with low satisfaction of basic needs, it has the lowest share of low-income earners who are beneficiaries of social assistance. A government expert survey indicates that only 28 percent of public funds allocated for the poor actually reach that group, while the "rest are pocketed by civil servants, their superiors or kin" (Lebanon Economic Monitor 2015). Salti and Chaaban (2010) go further to show that there is "little association between need and spending." In fact, Salti and Chaaban find "striking conformity between the sectarian composition of the population and each sect's share of public spending." Fiscal allocations can therefore act as political allocations.

Line agencies hardly undertake adequate prior forecasting of operating costs of public investments. There was little cooperation among line ministries, the Ministry of Finance, and the CDR on the long-term affordability of projects. Although the prioritization of programs through objective criteria has improved over the years, economic plans remained at the macro level and spending on programs was rarely subjected to cost–benefit analyses.

For example, the Horizon 2000 economic plan covered most sectors but failed to determine outcomes at the macro and sectoral levels. The allocative efficiency was impeded by the absence of ex-post performance evaluations on major programs. The increase in the autonomy of segments of the budget and the lack of budget comprehensiveness over the years made the allocation of resources harder to achieve since they limited the extent of funds being determined by the budget process. The level of accountability was weak, as there was no explicit sanction against institutions or officials in the event spending levels exceeded projected and approved levels.

Technical efficiency: the use of budgetary resources

Not only did budgetary institutions fail to allocate resources efficiently, they were unable to use these resources productively in the implementation process. Line agencies did not have the autonomy to provide public services. They had no control over the allocation of resources and the recruitment or reallocation of staff. They were constrained by a budgetary control system that relied heavily on input measures. To make matters worse, line agency managers were not held accountable. For instance, there were no performance indicators for public services, projects and activities were not audited, and sanctions were rarely imposed. In addition, the civil service not only suffers from vacancies reaching 70 percent but also is unable to hire and promote public servants on the basis of merit (Le Borgne and Jacobs 2016). Although there had been some improvement in the recruitment and promotion of public servants, the system is still severely plagued by political and sectarian influences. According to an Arab Barometer Survey conducted in 2010–12, 75 percent of respondents stated that "their political affiliation was more important than qualifications and skills" (Lebanon Economic Monitor 2015). For instance, the Civil Service Council, which is responsible for recruiting civil servants, was either pressured to hire full-time employees from the restricted pool of contractual employees and temporary workers, or had been bypassed by ministers in the hiring process. The merit system was also seriously weakened by relatively low salaries. Although salaries for low-level employees were comparable to their private sector counterparts, the discrepancy increased as one moved from low to high-level positions.

For budgetary institutions responsible for ensuring fiscal discipline, allocative and technical efficiencies either deteriorated significantly over the years or were never in place. With large surpluses from 1944 to 1970, Lebanon was able to afford inefficiencies in the allocation and use of resources. However, with persistently high deficits in the post-war era, the challenge of containing the deficit as well as ensuring allocative and technical efficiencies has become a daunting task for the government to undertake.

The issues we have highlighted on the structure and performance of budgetary institutions are tremendously relevant for the proposed SWF. Effectively, the same issues can also mar the performance of a sovereign fund. This raises an important policy question: what sort of institutional design would guard against these political economy risks?

Institutional design

There are three main takeaways from the aforementioned section. First, despite emerging as an important pillar of financial globalization, sovereign funds are still marred by the debate over form versus substance. Global experience suggests that, in many countries, such funds are merely new institutional forms for the global recycling of wealth. The Arab experience, in particular, highlights key areas of weaknesses, including neglect for global best practices in transparency and accountability. Second, the principal justification for a Lebanese SWF lies in the arena of development. We have argued that, unlike traditional SWFs, a Lebanese fund should be more directly geared toward meeting local development needs. Third, and perhaps most importantly, this chapter has thus far highlighted the political economy constraints that define the day-to-day workings of Lebanese fiscal policy. The proposed SWF would have to function in a complicated environment, according to which public spending is mainly driven by demands for distributive politics, especially the need to allocate resources in accordance with the country's fragile consociational arrangement.

While the case for orienting the resource fund toward Lebanese development and addressing political economy constraints is clear, the devil lies in the detail. Crucially, what kind of institutional design would be best able to achieve these objectives? What principles should guide the form and function of an SWF? Can Lebanon learn from global best practices in this regard? In this section, there is an attempt to answer some of these questions. The section begins by emphasizing the need to streamline the development function of the fund. Next, using knowledge of Lebanon's political economy and global best practices, some general principles are proposed that should assist in the institutional design of the fund. Finally, some concrete suggestions are offered toward a possible institutional design.

A sovereign development fund?

Beginning with the development dimension, it is clear that Lebanon would derive greater benefit by orienting its resource fund toward economic development. Whatever the appropriate mix of overseas and domestic investments is, the proposed SWF should be geared toward serving Lebanon's development needs. Rather than establishing a traditional resource fund specializing solely in overseas investments and de-linked from the local development agenda, Lebanon should explicitly link the new institution with economic development. In terms of institutional form, the Lebanese SWF should therefore function more as an SDF. In 2008, the IMF classified "development funds" as part of the SWF community, describing them as vehicles that "typically help fund socio-economic project[s] or promote industrial policies that might raise a country's potential output growth" (International Monetary Fund 2008). Many countries have, since then, begun to adopt and establish such sovereign development funds for the purpose of local development and domestic growth objectives, investing in job-creating industries and underdeveloped sectors. Often, such vehicles are used as a means to unlock capital in regions or sectors that had been previously capital-starved and create greater stability, efficiency, and discipline in those sectors where it is absent (Monk 2013).

These funds manage and utilize resource revenues directly for purposes of national economic development and play an active role in supporting productive efficiency and distributive justice. They do so by making strategic investments in certain sectors and contributing to the development of local financial market capacity. Furthermore, some SDFs work to facilitate technology and knowledge transfer in order to raise the productive capability of local industries that may have previously been neglected, thereby increasing potential returns on local assets (Santiso 2008). Many nations with SDFs ensure that their policies and strategic investments coincide with broader social and education policy objectives. Over time, these funds could work to improve the overall investment climate, serving as a channel between the local government and the international community, helping to crowd-in investment from both local and foreign sources. This is especially significant when foreign investors are reluctant to invest in risky or unstable and underdeveloped markets. Some successful examples include the Korea Investment Corporation, Malaysia's Khazanah Nasional Berhad, the Ireland Strategic Investment Fund (ISIF), and Chile's Economic and Social Stabilization Fund (ESSF).

The main driver behind these smaller investment vehicles is boosting national economic development, employment, and previously neglected areas of the domestic economy. By stimulating sectors that have the potential for job creation and local growth, these SDFs have served as positive vehicles that enhance local capacity and human capital and create industry linkages across sectors for modernization, industrialization, and longer-term economic interest and competitiveness. For example, Malaysia's Khazanah boosted new sectors which spurred a transformation of the Malaysian economy, including in the fields of agro-food, media, education, sustainable development, life-sciences, tourism, and innovation technology. Meanwhile, Ireland's ISIF also has driven strategic industries by unlocking capital and employment in energy, water, infrastructure, real estate, housing, tourism, technology, and finance. Their investment portfolio also includes investment in small and medium-sized enterprises (SMEs), as well as ventures and partnerships with public entities. Like more traditional SWFs, their board members typically comprise representatives from the private sector as well as government ministries. A Lebanese SWF would greatly benefit by considering these examples, particularly the Khazanah in Malaysia, when formulating its own policies.

Focus on public investments

Despite this focus on public investment within Lebanon, the new fund should manage a diversified portfolio consisting of both domestic and foreign assets. However, income streams from these investments could be targeted at priority sectors. Lebanon faces a dire need for public infrastructure and investments in productive sectors that carry the greatest potential for job creation. Since the end of the civil war, economic plans for reconstruction have failed to deliver sustainable growth and equitable development. Post-civil war economic growth was not inclusive, as it benefitted members of the political and business elite at the expense of the rest of the population. The banking and real estate sectors benefitted greatly, whereas productive sectors such as manufacturing and agriculture were at best ignored, if not undermined.

Successive Lebanese governments, irrespective of their political affiliations, privileged the banking and real estate sectors through tax incentives and exemptions, while the manufacturing and agricultural sectors—comprising 37 percent of Lebanon's work force (and predominantly associated with poorer segments of society)—were systematically neglected. The outcome of these policies intensified the concentration of wealth and made a very few people extremely wealthy at the expense of others. According to the Credit Suisse Global Wealth Databook (2014), 0.3 percent of the population owns half of the country's wealth. Precisely, 0.05 percent of Lebanese citizens control $34 billion of bank deposits. In this environment, an SWF mandate that invests in such neglected sectors could provide a tangible means of addressing these challenges.

While there is a clear rationale for scaling up development expenditures, the challenges that this newly established fund will face are: How much to invest? Where to invest? How to invest? Answering these questions is not easy, but this section highlights some general principles in this regard. Infrastructural investments provide a sensible use of the promised gas revenues. Given their economy-wide impact, such investments could carry the biggest reward. This is particularly true for Lebanon, which faces severe infrastructural bottlenecks as a result of weak governance and the clientelistic nature of service provision. Lebanon suffers from poor road networks, costly and unreliable electricity, poor water supply, and expensive and underdeveloped communication infrastructure. In the 2017 Global Competitiveness Report, the World Economic Forum ranked Lebanon at 130 out of 137 countries in terms of quality of overall infrastructure. Defective provision of electricity remains an acute concern for all parts of the economy; on this account, the country ranks at the bottom of the competitiveness table.

It should also be noted that infrastructure spending has declined as a share of GDP in the last decade. Capital spending accounted for only 1.7 percent of GDP and about 5.4 percent of total expenditures in 2016 (Lebanon Economic Monitor 2017). In fact, interest payments accounted for more than one-third of total expenditures, crowding out any expenditure on infrastructure projects. Moreover, key services such as electricity and water are dominated by state-owned monopolies, with limited competition and participation from the private sector. Investment climate surveys have repeatedly flagged the defective provision of electricity infrastructure as the principal constraint for businesses. The provision of a regular and affordable electricity supply would require a major infrastructural intervention, which the proposed SWF could facilitate. Water provision is another core area of concern, which, due to service rationing and unequal provisioning, lies at the heart of geographical disparities and urban fragmentation.[7]

Beyond infrastructure, there are several other deserving areas in which to invest. Lebanon needs to support the creation of specialized manufacturing clusters and micro firms, which often fold a few years after they are founded. There is clearly huge potential for a major development push facilitated by newly acquired resources. Such a development orientation will likely draw a great deal of consensus from citizens and elites alike. However, there are several attendant risks with such investments, which the SWF design must address. First, investments in infrastructure are easy targets for politicians. Political capture of infrastructure projects reduces the efficacy of these investments (NRGI 2015a). Second, there is a danger that SWF investments in infrastructure could substitute for already-limited allocations of capital spending in the budget. It is important that resources from an SWF should complement, rather than substitute for, limited development spending from the budget. Third, SWF investments should explicitly focus on those components of infrastructure where focus on areas of cross-confessional consensus is difficult to forge in Lebanon. For too long, fiscal allocations were designed to maintain a delicate sectarian balance in Lebanon. In reality, economic policies were not simply aimed at privileging one sect over the other but geared to protecting the interests of political and business elites of all sects at the expense of citizens.

---

[7] A significant consequence of poor network supply has been a boom in the practice of digging private wells. Significantly, this informal practice has played an important role in consolidating political allegiances, as political parties have taken up the opportunity to drill wells, using water as a socio-communitarian service, especially in remote areas that lack complete state intervention.

Principles of a good SWF

Based on the information and assertions made above, orienting an SWF toward development is relatively uncontroversial. Ensuring the efficacy of these investments remains a more complicated task. Clearly, Lebanon's underdevelopment is not purely a function of adverse resource endowments. After all, its dilapidated infrastructure sits uneasily against the country's excess banking resources. Even the limited budgetary allocation for capital spending is susceptible to misuse. There are often major discrepancies between reported infrastructure investment by the government and the relevant public debt incurred. There are instances when public infrastructure projects have been diverted through politically linked construction companies, in the absence of either a clear strategy or transparent bidding processes. This reflects the wastefulness in public spending, primarily in investment projects such as roads that cost several times more than they should, garbage collection subjected to over-charging, scandals at the Beirut Port or in telecommunications, and the cancellation of government contracts and compensation worth millions of dollars to companies with ties to politicians' families. The appropriation of water in Lebanon in the wake of liberalization mirrors the economic structures and the confessional system of the country, in ways that have led to inadequate service delivery. Against this backdrop, the most serious challenge that Lebanon's proposed SWF faces is of transparency and accountability of spending. The SWF can only meet its development mandate if it is properly insulated from the spoils of the confessional system.

What principles and practices could help achieve this? There is a need to engage in wide-ranging consultation before the country establishes an SWF. One area where other Arab SWFs are noticeably deficient is public disclosure. Resources accruing to the fund and investment in domestic or overseas assets should be publicly known. While most Arab SWFs provide very limited information on their incoming and outgoing resources and their investment strategy, a Lebanese fund should provide a model of best practices by revealing all relevant information to the public. This would allow adequate oversight by civil society. Accounts should be made publicly accessible at a most disaggregate level. The criteria for project selection and mechanisms for monitoring and accountability should be clearly established. The board should be constituted in a way that satisfies the highest standards of corporate governance. Individuals or instances involving conflict of interest should be avoided. Where possible, the fund should draw on the considerable expertise of the Lebanese diaspora and members of civil society. The best way to ensure that an SWF is saved from political capture is to empower a countervailing constituency that would keep a check on SWF operations.

A good starting point in this regard is to follow the check-list of the Santiago Principles (Annex 1, page 217) that emphasize the transparency, accountability, independence, and commercial orientation of SWFs. The 24 principles proposed by the International Working Group of Sovereign Wealth Funds provide guidance for

---

[8]   For more information refer to http://www.iwg-swf.org/pubs/eng/santiagoprinciples.pdf

SWF operations.[8] Perhaps the three most important ingredients for a successful SWF are: public disclosure, recognition and avoidance of conflicts of interest, and community oversight. In this regard, we offer below some concrete suggestions.

1. *Clarity of mandate*: It is essential that an SWF have a clearly defined mandate so its activities can be judged and evaluated against stated objectives. The goals of a proposed fund should also be well-stated. If Lebanon decides to combine a portfolio of overseas and domestic investments, it may be advisable to conduct these investment activities through separate institutions that are subject to different governance standards.

2. *Withdrawal rules*: A clear and present danger with resource funds in the Middle East is the absence of legally-enshrined constraints on the withdrawal of funds. As a result, political incumbents have an incentive to overuse these funds during lean periods. To address this risk, Lebanon must consider explicit deposit and withdrawal rules. Such fiscal rules should be clearly specified along with exemptions that may accompany exceptional circumstances. Another rule, which is particularly important in the Lebanese context, is to prohibit the use of the funds' assets as collateral to accumulate debt. Detailed investment rules should be set out to guard against such risks, including excessive risk-taking by fund managers.

3. *Ownership*: A lack of ownership can lead to rules being broken. As global experience suggests, rules have little value without enforcement. The key political economy challenge is that those who make the rules have little incentive to ensure that they are enforced. This is understandable. Why would the ruling elite impose constraints on itself when it can easily get away with not delineating or enforcing such rules? The enforcement capacity of any legal regime (including fiscal rules) therefore depends on the existence of a constituency that has an active interest in ensuring that the rules made in good times should be enforced when politicians have the least incentive to enforce them. This is why any saving or development fund would need to have some oversight role for civil society. While conceptualizing an SWF, special attention should be paid to creating multiple independent oversight bodies. One such vehicle could be a civil society commission.

4. *Civil Society Commission*: Any successful SWF needs an initial commitment to transparency, as this can help it gain credibility and legitimacy, particularly in terms of making future decisions, operating in the public interest, and in favor of national development and economic growth. Oversight is needed by multiple actors to ensure that an SWF continues to meet its objectives effectively. A civil society commission should oversee the activities and performance of an SWF and prepare an annual public report made available online. Such a report should disclose operational funds and track spending flows and project implementation. Although lacking any independent enforcement capacity, a commission should be mandated to keep an independent watch over major issues of public interest, including the transparency and monitoring of finances, salaries, spending, and projects. A commission will comprise key civil society actors and experts, none of

whom will be directly connected by family or business partnership with any political stakeholders. A civil society commission would provide a platform for regular communication between the public and the government, and the board of an SWF.

5. *Board*: The Board of Lebanon's SWF should entail provisions that embody the Santiago Principles, including a strict provision on conflicts of interest under which individuals connected to or linked to the Lebanese political establishment or political parties are barred from participating or playing a direct role in the operational management and governance of the fund. The objective is to insulate the fund from the political division of spoils and rent-capture by elites. Whether a board will be housed in the central bank or elsewhere should be decided after a thorough investigation of case studies and Lebanese political structures. Overall, the composition of board members and institutional placement must be based on the Santiago Principles to ensure its autonomy as an independent body that directly serves its mandate and is accountable to a civil society commission and transparent in all its operations and spending, including salaries.

6. *Financial Experts' Committee*: Many SWFs have a financial committee of independent experts on investments, or hire foreign firms to advise on investment decisions and financial operations. Lebanon should utilize its strong diaspora network of financial and investment experts and professionals that are working in financial capitals like London or New York, in order to seek their consultation and capitalize on their expertise for the benefit of the fund. This could result in the creation of a Committee of Lebanese Financial Professionals, whereas professionals of Lebanese origin participate in a bi-annual meeting and are also available for consultation on a needs basis, and can assist in the oversight of sound public financial and investment policies and decisions.

7. *Project Management Unit*: Since some SWF activities are likely to be oriented toward domestic development, there is a need for close coordination with government institutions in charge of fiscal policy. At the same time, public investments carried out by an SWF should be insulated from the day-to-day political challenges affecting fiscal policy operations. One proposal to achieve this is establishing a special Project Management Unit (PMU) that serves as the link between an SWF and planning and budgetary institutions. A PMU can comprise a mix of civil servants and independent professionals, all of whom would complete an application process to select the most qualified candidates to oversee day-to-day and project-basis technical operations. They would coordinate the procurement process of all projects launched by an SWF in line with its mandate along the supply chain to prevent corruption and rent capture and to monitor the implementation of programs. By enforcing the highest standards of professionalism and stringent oversight, a PMU may also have a positive impact on other areas of financial management and state bureaucracy.

Effective management of resource wealth requires both "guardians" who protect the fund and "spenders" who ensure that resources flow into areas carrying the best return.

216   *The Future of Petroleum in Lebanon*

As per the above suggestions, a civil society commission and financial experts committee could be construed as "guardians," whereas a PMU could act as a principal planning and liaison agency for spending money wisely. A financial expert committee could also play a decisive role in directing and overseeing investments.

Conclusion and recommendations

In this chapter, we have discussed the desirability and design of a possible SWF to take advantage of gas revenues that will potentially accrue to Lebanon. Although resource funds have now become a part of the "to do" list for resource-rich countries, we have argued that if there is a case for establishing a Lebanese SWF, it probably lies in a fund oriented toward development. The goal of investing natural resource revenues should be based on development and diversification that results in job creation. This can entail investing in the creation of an enabling environment, such as sustainable infrastructure projects in electricity or waste management, or specific sectors such as eco-tourism or education. Regardless of whether an SWF is primarily oriented toward overseas or domestic investments (or a combination of both), it is important to ensure that its resource revenue management is transparent, guided by fiscal rules and strong oversight, and has an economic mandate grounded in the Lebanese context with equitable benefits and across generations.

To meet these goals, this chapter outlined and recommended a mandate that would support Lebanon in meeting its development objectives, especially in compensating for prolonged neglect in supporting infrastructural investments. Lebanon's hydrocarbon potential has triggered speculation on two extremes. On the one hand, there is positive anticipation of economic growth potential. On the other, there is a fear of the "resource curse" and Dutch disease. Could these revenues represent a "game-changer" for a country grappling with a drastic population increase (by over a quarter in just a few years), deteriorating infrastructure, and unemployment? With one of the highest debt-to-GDP ratios in the world and until recently having lacked a national budget for over 12 years, Lebanon's past fiscal management demonstrates the country's susceptibility to elite capture, wasteful spending, and risk for increased debt and volatility.

One must also consider that natural resources entail development risks in the guise of conflict and instability, turbulent governance, and inefficient spending. Large resource revenues increase expectations for quick returns from a range of actors, including the government, local populations, the private sector, and civil society. While some governments respond by investing in projects with quick tangible returns, it is critical to consider what *types* of project are launched by defining a criteria for projects that bring socio-economic return in the future. As historical experience suggests, wasteful spending on unproductive projects can lead to fiscal crises and deficits. Mexico, Nigeria, and Venezuela suffered this problem as a result of the state's expenditure behavior: overspending on government salaries and vanity projects and underspending on health, education, and other social services (NRGI 2015b). This resulted in debt crises in these countries, weaker state institutions, and a negatively impacted private sector.

To mitigate such risks, this chapter also outlined the importance of principles for credible, transparent, and fiscally responsible institutions by proposing a framework and design that takes into account Lebanon's fiscal policy challenges and political environment. These principles are geared toward creating a transparent fund that operates in full public disclosure and benefits from the oversight of multiple institutions. We have also developed the case for creating effective checks and balances on the fund's managers and backing their work through support (and oversight) from experts. If proper fiscal rules are in place, volatile resource revenues need not translate into volatile government expenditures. Essentially, fiscal rules provide tools for the government to stabilize the amount of revenues that are spent each year. One way of managing this is to adjust and set percentages on how much is spent on capital expenditures (which are onetime allocations, such as building a new bridge or treatment plant) versus recurrent expenditures. If an SWF is simple, legitimate, transparent, and fiscally responsible, it will not only further Lebanon's development but also deliver significant political payoffs. In short, if appropriately designed and supported by all political stakeholders, such an SWF could be turned into an instrument of stability that is insulated from the usual political struggles for distribution of resources in Lebanon.

Annex 1: The Santiago Principles

The Santiago Principles comprise 24 principles, which are as follows:

Principle 1: Sound legal framework: The legal framework for the SWF should be sound and support its effective operation and the achievement of its stated objective(s).

Principle 2: Well-defined mission: The policy purpose of the SWF should be clearly defined and publicly disclosed.

Principle 3: Where the SWF's activities have significant direct domestic macroeconomic implications, those activities should be closely coordinated with the domestic fiscal and monetary authorities, so as to ensure consistency with the overall macroeconomic policies.

Principle 4: Clearly defined withdrawal rules: There should be clear and publicly disclosed policies, rules, procedures, or arrangements in relation to the SWF's general approach to funding, withdrawal, and spending operations.

Principle 5: The relevant statistical data pertaining to the SWF should be reported on a timely basis to the owner, or as otherwise required, for inclusion where appropriate in macroeconomic data sets.

Principle 6: The governance framework for the SWF should be sound and establish a clear and effective division of roles and responsibilities in order to facilitate accountability and operational independence in the management of the SWF to pursue its objectives.

Principle 7: The owner should set the objectives of the SWF, appoint the members of its governing body(ies) in accordance with clearly defined procedures, and exercise oversight over the SWF's operations.

Principle 8: The governing body(ies) should act in the best interests of the SWF, and have a clear mandate and adequate authority and competency to carry out its functions.

Principle 9: The operational management of the SWF should implement the SWF's strategies in an independent manner and in accordance with clearly defined responsibilities.

Principle 10: The accountability framework for the SWF's operations should be clearly defined in the relevant legislation, charter, other constitutive documents, or management agreement.

Principle 11: An annual report and accompanying financial statements on the SWF's operations and performance should be prepared in a timely fashion and in accordance with recognized international or national accounting standards in a consistent manner.

Principle 12: The SWF's operations and financial statements should be audited annually in accordance with recognized international or national auditing standards in a consistent manner.

Principle 13: Professional and ethical standards should be clearly defined and made known to the members of the SWF's governing body(ies), management, and staff.

Principle 14: Dealing with third parties for the purpose of the SWF's operational management should be based on economic and financial grounds, and follow clear rules and procedures.

Principle 15: SWF operations and activities in host countries should be conducted in compliance with all applicable regulatory and disclosure requirements of the countries in which they operate.

Principle 16: The governance framework and objectives, as well as the manner in which the SWF's management is operationally independent from the owner, should be publicly disclosed.

Principle 17: Relevant financial information regarding the SWF should be publicly disclosed to demonstrate its economic and financial orientation, so as to contribute to stability in international financial markets and enhance trust in recipient countries.

Principle 18: The SWF's investment policy should be clear and consistent with its defined objectives, risk tolerance, and investment strategy, as set by the owner or the governing body(ies), and be based on sound portfolio management principles.

The Case for a Lebanese Sovereign Development Fund 219

Principle 19: The SWF's investment decisions should aim to maximize risk-adjusted financial returns in a manner consistent with its investment policy, and based on economic and financial grounds.

Principle 20: The SWF should not seek or take advantage of privileged information or inappropriate influence by the broader government in competing with private entities.

Principle 21: SWFs view shareholder ownership rights as a fundamental element of their equity investments' value. If an SWF chooses to exercise its ownership rights, it should do so in a manner that is consistent with its investment policy and protects the financial value of its investments. The SWF should publicly disclose its general approach to voting securities of listed entities, including the key factors guiding its exercise of ownership rights.

Principle 22: The SWF should have a framework that identifies, assesses, and manages the risks of its operations.

Principle 23: The assets and investment performance (absolute and relative to benchmarks, if any) of the SWF should be measured and reported to the owner according to clearly defined principles or standards.

Principle 24: A process of regular review of the implementation of the Generally Accepted Principles and Practices should be engaged in by or on behalf of the SWF.

References

Authored references

Behrendt, S. 2008. "When Money Talks: Arab Sovereign Wealth Funds in the Global Public Policy Discourse." Carnegie Endowment for International Peace, Carnegie Middle East Center.

Behrendt, S. 2009. "Gulf Arab SWFs—Managing Wealth in Turbulent Times." Policy Outlook, Carnegie Endowment for International Peace.

Collier, P. 2010. "The Political Economy of Natural Resources." *Social Research* 77: 1105–32.

Dixon, A.D. and A. Monk. 2014. "Financializing Development: Towards a Sympathetic Critique of Sovereign Development Funds." *Journal of Sustainable Finance & Investment* 4: 357–71.

El-Erian, M. 2010. "Sovereign Wealth Funds in the New Normal." *Finance and Development*, June.

Gaspard, T. 2002. *A Political Economy of Lebanon, 1948–2002: The Limits of Laissez-Faire*. Brill.

Gieve, J. 2008. "Sovereign Wealth Funds and Global Imbalances." Bank of England Quarterly Bulletin 2008 Q2, June.

Le Borgne, E. and T. Jacobs. 2016. "Lebanon: Promoting Poverty Reduction and Shared Prosperity." The World Bank.

Leenders, R. 2012. *Spoils of Truce: Corruption and State Building in Post-War Lebanon*. Cornell University Press.

Monk, A. 2013. "The Rise of Sovereign Development Funds." *Institutional Investor*, 10 April.

Reed, M. 2016. "Saudi Vision 2030: Winners and Losers." Carnegie Endowment for International Peace.

Salti, N. and J. Chaaban. 2010. "The Role of Sectarianism in the Allocation of Public Expenditure in Postwar Lebanon." *International Journal of Middle East Studies* 42: 637–55.

Santiso, J. 2008. "Sovereign Development Funds: Key Financial Actors of the Shifting Wealth of Nations." Working Paper, OECD Emerging Markets Network, October.

Setser, B. and R. Ziemba. 2009. "GCC Sovereign Funds: Reversal of Fortune." Council on Foreign Relations, Center for Geoeconomic Studies, January.

Triki, T. and I. Faye. 2011. "Africa's Quest for Development: Can Sovereign Wealth Funds Help?" Working Paper Series 142, African Development Bank Group.

Wallace, T. 2015. "Libyan Investment Authority's Case Against Goldman Sachs and SocGen is Back on." The *Telegraph*, 2 July.

Non-authored references

Credit Suisse. 2014. "Global Wealth Databook 2014." Research Institute, October.

International Monetary Fund. 2008. "IMF Survey: IMF Intensifies Work on Sovereign Wealth Funds." March 4.

International Monetary Fund. 2008. "Sovereign Wealth Funds—A Work Agenda." Capital Markets and Policy Development and Review Departments, 29 February.

International Working Group on Sovereign Wealth Funds. 2008. "Sovereign Wealth Funds: Generally Accepted Principles and Practices, 'Santiago Principles'."

Lebanon Economic Monitor. 2015. "The Great Capture." The World Bank.

Natural Resource Governance Institute. 2015a. "The Resource Curse: The Political and Economic Challenges of Natural Resource Wealth." NRGI Reader.

Natural Resource Governance Institute. 2015b. "Revenue Management and Distribution: Addressing the Special Challenges of Resource Revenues to Generate Lasting Benefits." NRGI Reader.

Organisation for Economic Co-operation and Development. 2008. "OECD Guidelines for Recipient Country Investment Policies Relating to National Security." OECD Guidance on Sovereign Wealth Funds, October.

Sovereign Wealth Fund Institute. 2017. "Fund Rankings: Tracking the Activity of Sovereign Wealth Funds, Pensions and Other Public Funds."

The World Bank. 2017. "The World Bank in Lebanon." Overview.

World Economic Forum. 2015. "Global Competitiveness Report 2015–2016."

Impact and Implications

9

Macroeconomic Implications of Windfall Oil and Gas Revenues in Lebanon

Jad Chaaban and Jana Harb[1]

Introduction

The diverse experience of resource-rich countries suggests that natural resource wealth is a mixed blessing. While some countries have been successful in transforming such wealth into sustained economic growth and development, many others have been cursed by it. It is common sense to believe that natural resource abundance could positively contribute to economic progress and poverty reduction. Yet, if not managed properly, riches accrued from natural resources are believed to have undesirable effects on resource-rich economies. These include what is referred to in the literature as "Dutch disease." This widely researched economic phenomenon links increased exploitation and reliance on natural resources with the systematic decline in other economic sectors, specifically agriculture and manufacturing. Resource revenues typically inflate the value of local currency and make other non-resource exports less competitive. At the same time, the economy will be geared toward one sector that absorbs all the resources, labor, and attention of policy makers, which eventually reduces investments in other sectors of the economy. These symptoms are even more dangerous in countries with weak and corrupt institutions, non-democratic regimes, and weak financial systems (Van der Ploeg 2010).

The discovery of potential hydrocarbon resources off the shores of Lebanon raises concerns about the realization of Dutch disease within the economy. This chapter seeks to forecast the potential implications of a resource boom in Lebanon on the economy, especially in light of an ongoing Dutch disease-like scenario within the Lebanese economy.

This chapter first argues that Lebanon may have already been undergoing a Dutch disease episode since the early 1990s. The literature on Dutch disease has demonstrated that this phenomenon may also stem from other large sustained foreign exchange inflows such as foreign aid, remittances, and foreign direct investment, sourced mostly through petrodollar regional income from GCC countries. Since the end of its civil

---

[1] This chapter was originally drafted and published as a paper in 2015. The author's analysis is based on data which was available at the time.

war, Lebanon has been receiving massive capital inflows every year. Using recent macroeconomic annual data, we show that the real exchange rate has appreciated over the past two decades and seems to be caused by substantial foreign inflows into the economy. This period has also been accompanied by a contraction of the agriculture and manufacturing sectors and a distortion of economic activity in favor of the financial and real estate investment sectors.

We then demonstrate that the likely effects of offshore hydrocarbon exploration on the Lebanese economy will be a worsening of current economic outcomes unless deep structural and public policy reforms are implemented. A natural resource boom is simulated by making the following underlying assumption: if appropriate policy responses are not adopted, then the accrued oil and gas windfall revenues will lead to an expansionary fiscal policy through a rise in public spending in light of current fiscal planning, or lack thereof, in Lebanon. Thus, the likely impacts of the resource boom on the Lebanese economy are assessed by forecasting the implications of a rise in the budget deficit on the real and monetary sectors of the economy. Employing a simple time-series cointegration framework, we first estimate a Vector Error Correction model on monthly selected macroeconomic data in order to evaluate the long-run relations as well as short-run dynamics between fiscal and monetary outcomes. The impact of an increase in the budget deficit on these macroeconomic variables is then simulated through Impulse Response Functions by using the estimated parameters of the model. It is found that a permanent positive shock in the budget deficit—an exogenous increase of about 1 percentage point of budget deficit that is sustained over time—causes the real exchange rate to be about 1 percentage point higher at the end of a three-year forecast period. This permanent shock in budget deficit will also lead to an equivalent rise in inflation and decline in real GDP. The results from the estimated model indicate the presence of Dutch disease symptoms following a resource boom. We also simulate alternative policy scenarios to managing windfall revenues, such as the creation of a sovereign wealth fund or investments in infrastructure. These empirical simulations show through a simple macroeconomic adjustment model that fiscal and economic policies in the face of an oil boom play a substantial role in determining the impact of this boom on the economic structure of the country.

This chapter is organized as follows. Section one reviews related theory and evidence. Section two evaluates economic performance in Lebanon in recent decades to assess whether there was already a case of Dutch disease. Finally, section three presents and estimates a dynamic model to forecast the impact of a resource boom on the economy before offering concluding remarks and policy recommendations.

Economics of Dutch disease: theoretical overview and empirical evidence

Theoretical overview

The term "Dutch disease" originated in the 1970s to describe the shrinkage of the manufacturing sector and increasing unemployment in the Netherlands following the discovery of natural gas in the North Sea. Today, it is used to reference a phenomenon in which large inflows of foreign currency cause an appreciation of the real exchange rate and consequent loss of export competitiveness. The theoretical framework for studying Dutch disease was first developed by Corden and Neary (1982), who analyzed the changes in an economy following a boom in the natural resource sector (such as a resource discovery or an increase in the international price of a commodity). Their model is a small open economy consisting of a natural resource sector, a non-resource tradables sector (traditionally agriculture and manufacturing), and a non-tradables sector (traditionally services). The price of tradable goods is set and fixed in the world market while that of the non-traded goods is flexible and domestically determined to attain supply and demand equilibrium in the non-tradables market. They break down the effects of the boom into two principal types: resource movement effect and spending effect. In the short run, reflected by the case where only labor is mobile between all sectors, these two effects combined lead to shrinkage of the non-resource tradables sector and appreciation of the real exchange rate (RER), where RER in this framework is defined as the relative price of non-tradables to tradables.

Resource movement effect

When the resource sector experiences a boom, its demand for labor increases, and is consequently drawn out of the other two sectors. Hence, employment declines in the non-resource tradables sector, which leads to a decline in output in that sector. This shift in labor from the rest of the economy to the booming sector is called direct de-industrialization. Similarly, output in the non-tradables sector falls but now the price of non-tradables must increase in order to eliminate excess demand and reestablish equilibrium in that market. Given that the price of tradables is fixed at the world price, then a rise in the price of non-tradables causes an appreciation of the RER.

Spending effect

A resource sector boom results in an increase in aggregate domestic income, which in turn increases aggregate demand for goods in an economy, including non-tradables. As in the previous case, the price of non-tradables must rise in order to restore market equilibrium, thus raising the level of output in that sector and leading to an appreciation of the RER.

The fall in supplied non-tradables due to the resource movement effect combined with the rise in demanded non-tradables due to the spending effect leads to a final equilibrium with an even higher non-tradables price level. This real appreciation causes demand for labor in that sector to increase and consequently wages to increase as well. The wage increase will now divert more labor away from the non-resource tradables sector and into the non-tradables sector, causing the latter to expand and the former to shrink. This effect on the non-resource tradables sector is called indirect de-industrialization. The overall decline in the output of non-resource tradables, coupled with a rise in domestic demand for these non-resource tradables due to the spending effect and inflexibility of their international price level, leads to an excess domestic demand that can only be satisfied by increasing imports, thus deteriorating the balance of trade.

In summary, a resource sector boom leads to an appreciation of the RER, i.e., a rise in the price of non-tradables relative to the price of tradables, as well as direct and indirect de-industrialization of the non-resource tradables sector, i.e., a fall in sectoral employment and output and a worsening of the balance of trade. The impact of the boom on the non-tradables sector, however, is ambiguous and depends on the relative magnitudes of the two principal effects.

Empirical overview

Empirical evidence on the existence of Dutch disease due to increased foreign exchange inflows is mixed. For instance, Spatafora and Warner (1999) examine the impact of favorable terms-of-trade shocks in 18 oil-exporting developing countries during the period 1965–89. They find evidence of the spending effect with an appreciation of the real exchange rate and an expansion of the non-tradables sector. However, they find no support for the resource movement effect and no contractions in either the manufacturing or the agriculture sector. Hence, they conclude that Dutch disease effects are weak. Similarly, Harvey (1992) studies the economy of Botswana following the discovery of large diamond deposits and finds that it has not suffered from Dutch disease effects. Sala-i-Martin and Subramanian (2003) investigate the "natural resource curse" in Nigeria and find that, although Nigeria's economy has suffered from dismal performance, the adverse impacts following the discovery of oil are a result of waste and corruption stemming from weak institutions, rather than from Dutch disease.

Recent literature, however, has been pointing to the presence of Dutch disease effects stemming from resource windfalls. Ismail (2010) derives from a static model and then empirically tests structural implications of Dutch disease in oil-exporting countries due to a permanent increase in oil prices. Using disaggregated manufacturing sector data for 90 countries over the period 1977–2004, he finds strong evidence for the existence of Dutch disease where a 10 percent increase in the size of oil windfalls decreases value added and output across manufacturing by 3.4 percent and 3.6 percent respectively. Brahmbhatt *et al.* (2010) create a Dutch disease measure by comparing the actual size of the tradables (manufacturing and agriculture) sector to a constructed counterfactual size—i.e., what the size of the tradables sector would have been in the absence of natural resources. Using the Chenery-Syrquin norm to estimate the counterfactual, they create this Dutch disease measure for all resource- and non-resource-rich countries during the period 1975–2005. They find that, on average, resource-rich countries have a tradables sector that is lower than the norm by approximately 15 percentage points of GDP.

From a slightly different angle, Harding and Venables (2013) study the impact of foreign exchange windfalls on trade and balance of payments outcomes. Using panel data on 41 resource exporters for the period 1970–2006, they find that non-resource exports are crowded out by natural resource exports where, on average, one extra dollar of resource revenue decreases non-resource exports by 75 cents and increases non-resource imports by 25 cents. Their findings show that, out of all tradables, manufacturing is the most susceptible to this crowding-out effect—compared to agriculture, food, or services. In addition, this impact is greater in higher income countries and in countries with stronger institutions, which could partly be due to the fact that manufacturing makes up a larger share in total non-resource exports in these countries.

In addition to resource booms, other foreign currency inflows such as Foreign Direct Investment (FDI), foreign aid, and remittances have been shown to induce Dutch disease effects. For instance, to examine whether and what capital inflows cause an appreciation of the real exchange rate, Lartey (2007) develops and estimates static and dynamic autoregressive distributed lag real exchange rate models using data for 16 sub-Saharan African countries for the period 1980–2000. The study finds evidence of Dutch disease effects due to increases in the inflow of both FDI and Official Development Assistance (ODA) with a 1 percent increase in each of the FDI and ODA inflows in a given year causing an appreciation of the real exchange rate by about 0.05 percent and 0.1 percent in the following year, respectively. Similarly, Rajan and Subramanian (2009) find that aid inflows have adverse effects on the manufacturing sector's relative size and growth through the appreciation of the real exchange rate. Estimating a Dynamic Stochastic General Equilibrium model of a small open economy and using data for El Salvador, Acosta *et al.* (2009) find evidence of Dutch disease effects due to an increase in remittances, where the latter causes a fall in labor supply and an increase in demand for non-tradable goods, thus leading to a real exchange rate appreciation and a reallocation of labor from the tradables to the non-tradables sector. Magud and Sosa (2010) review the large empirical literature on Dutch disease and find that overall the evidence points to its existence whereby increased foreign exchange inflows (natural resource booms, sustained foreign aid, remittances, or capital inflows) cause a real exchange rate appreciation, factor reallocation, as well as a reduction in manufacturing output and exports.

Development implications of Dutch disease

A large body of the literature on natural resource booms has debated whether these booms are effectively a blessing or a curse. An increase in natural resource windfalls could have many positive effects on an economy such as higher national income, higher consumption of goods, and greater capabilities to invest in public goods, among others. On the other hand, when a resource boom or more generally a surge in foreign exchange inflows is not managed properly, then the negative indirect effects could very well outweigh the direct positive effects of these windfalls on economic growth and development.

A strand of this literature argues that Dutch disease not only hampers the growth of the non-resource tradables sector but also that of the entire economy, based on the proposition that the tradables sector is typically the source of special growth-enhancing qualities such as learning-by-doing, increasing returns to scale production, and other positive externalities (Brahmbhatt *et al.* 2010, Rajan and Subramanian 2005). Hence, when a natural resource boom depresses the manufacturing sector, it also depresses the productivity and profitability of investments and ultimately slows long-term growth (Sachs and Warner 1999, Gylfason 2000). For instance, Sachs and Warner (1999) developed a model to study the impact of a resource boom on growth and showed that the former can negatively impact the latter through Dutch disease effects when the tradables sector depicts increasing-returns-to-scale (IRS). However, when IRS production is in the non-tradables sector, a resource boom could lead to higher growth. Testing their model empirically on seven countries from Latin America, Sachs and Warner find that resource booms most of the time are associated with declining GDP per capita, although the channels through which this works might not be limited exclusively to Dutch disease. Similarly, looking at 86 countries for the period 1965–98, Gylfason (2001) finds that economic growth and natural resource abundance are inversely related, where a 10 percent point increase in natural resource abundance from one country to another is associated on average with a 1 percent point decrease in per capita GNP growth per year. Magud and Sosa (2010), on the other hand, conclude otherwise. They examine whether Dutch disease has adverse effects on long-term growth by reviewing the theoretical and empirical literature. They do not find strong conclusive evidence suggesting that the tradables sector (manufacturing) enjoys said special growth-enhancing qualities. Consequently, they conclude that Dutch disease does not necessarily reduce overall economic growth because the beneficial effects stemming from the positive wealth effect could potentially outweigh the adverse effects of the disease.

A natural resource boom entails more specialization in the resource sector and less specialization in the non-resource tradables sector through the Dutch disease phenomenon. This, combined with the fact that prices in the world market are more volatile for primary commodities, makes the economy more susceptible to fluctuations, which in turn creates uncertainty for investors and consequently discourages investment and depresses growth (Papyrakis and Gerlagh 2004, van der Ploeg and Poelhekke 2009). Moreover, if natural resources are a major source of income, then volatility in their prices will lead to volatility in revenues and hence volatility in government spending, which further increases macroeconomic volatility and as a result worsens growth performance (van der Ploeg and Poelhekke 2009). Furthermore, volatility in government spending induces volatility in the real exchange rate through the spending effect of Dutch disease (Brahmbhatt et al. 2010). Volatility in the real exchange rate further reduces investment and productivity in the non-resource tradables sector, thus amplifying Dutch disease effects (Gylfason et al. 1999). More generally, real exchange rate volatility can hamper long-term productivity growth in the entire economy, especially in countries with weak financial development (Bacchetta et al. 2006). Servén (2002) empirically tests the relationship between uncertainty in the real exchange rate and private investment and finds that the former significantly and negatively impacts the latter. Moreover, this impact is much larger in countries with a higher degree of trade openness and weaker financial systems.

Natural resource booms could further hinder economic growth through inhibiting investment in human capital. By decreasing the scale of the manufacturing sector, a resource boom (if not coupled with local investments in skilled labor within the resource industry) discourages investment in high-quality education since manufacturing has a higher demand for a high-skilled labor force compared to the expanding resource sector. Hence, both demand and returns to education fall, thereby impeding future growth of any sectors that demand a high-skilled labor force, as well as impeding technological diffusion (Gylfason et al. 1999, Papyrakis and Gerlagh 2004).

Lebanon's economic performance in recent decades: was there already Dutch disease?

There is substantial evidence that the Lebanese economy has been benefiting from massive foreign inflows, originating mostly from expatriates in the GCC, in addition to transfers from GCC governments and private sector entities. A clear link has been established between petrodollar income in the GCC and foreign transfers in the country, either through direct budgetary aid, bank deposits, or foreign direct investments (Berthelemy *et al.* 2007, Finger and Hesse 2009).

The objective of this section is to explore the determinants of RER appreciation in the Lebanese economy in the wake of these transfers, which indirectly point to the impact of oil and gas revenue on the Lebanese economy, through the indirect channels of capital transfers highlighted above. To this end, we compile and evaluate macroeconomic annual data spanning the following fields and variables, for the period 1993–2011.

Macroeconomic indicators

- Real GDP growth in percentage (REAL_GDP—source: United Nations Conference on Trade and Development [UNCTAD])
- Real Exchange Rate year-on-year change percent (RER—based on IMF and Consultation and Research Institute inflation [CRI] data)
- Inflation: year-on-year change in consumer prices percent (INFL—source: CRI)

Foreign inflows:

- Bank deposits of non-residents/GDP percent (DEP—source: Banque du Liban [BDL])
- Migrants' remittances/GDP percent (REMIT—source: UNCTAD)
- Foreign Direct Investment inflows/GDP percent (FDI—source: UNCTAD)
- Trade deficit/GDP percent (TD—source: UNCTAD)

Monetary and fiscal variables

Money supply

- Money and quasi-money M2/GDP percent (M2—source: BDL)
- Public sector revenues/GDP percent (REV—source: Ministry of Finance [MOF])
- Public sector expenditure/GDP percent (EXP—source: MOF)
- Public Deficit/GDP percent (DEF—source: MOF)

Sectoral composition of production

- Agricultural value added as share of GDP percent (VA_A—source: UNCTAD)
- Industrial value added as share of GDP percent (VA_M—source: UNCTAD)
- Services value added as share of GDP percent (VA_S—source: UNCTAD)

Main findings

The annual data confirms that the real exchange rate appreciated during the past two decades. Data for 1993-2011 show fluctuations around a clear upward trend. Inflation and real GDP growth also fluctuated near an annual average of 4.5 percent (Figure 9.1).

RER appreciation, a typical symptom of Dutch disease, seems to be caused by substantial foreign inflows into the Lebanese economy. Non-resident deposits grew at an average annual rate of 8 percent, up from 12 percent of GDP in 1993 to 55 percent in 2011. Remittances and foreign direct investment increased at a slower rate (below 5 percent annual growth) and the trade deficit narrowed until 2002 and then started an upward trend, reaching almost 40 percent of GDP in 2011 (Figure 9.2).

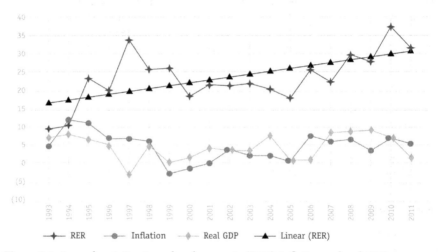

Figure 9.1 Annual variation in real exchange rate (RER), inflation and real GDP.
Source: Authors' calculations.

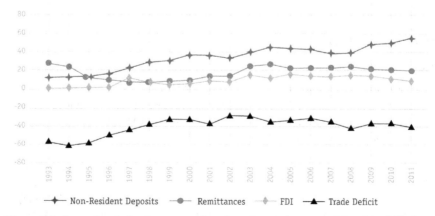

Figure 9.2 Annual variation in non-resident deposits, remittances, FDI and trade deficit.
Source: Authors' calculations.

A simple correlation analysis shows that non-resident deposits and FDI are strongly positively correlated with the real exchange rate in the Lebanese economy. Real GDP growth seems to be correlated with remittances, confirming the high dependence of the economy on private consumption (Table 9.1).

The symptoms of Dutch disease in Lebanon also seem to appear in the monetary and fiscal fields. Money supply has substantially increased over the past two decades as a clear response to increased deposits and higher needs for domestic financing of consumption (Figure 9.3).

Simple correlation relationships for the data at hand show that RER and money supply (M2) are strongly positively correlated, confirming that Dutch disease-type mechanics are at work. The public sector deficit seems to be only correlated with M2, also confirming the linkages between lax fiscal policy and monetary expansion (Table 9.2).

Table 9.1 Macroeconomic correlation matrix

	Non-resident deposits	Remittances	FDI	Trade deficit	RER	Inflation	Real GDP
Non-resident deposits	1.0000						
Remittances	0.3105	1.0000					
FDI	0.7970*	0.3675	1.0000				
Trade deficit	0.7527*	−0.0302	0.7226*	1.0000			
RER	0.5454*	−0.2386	0.5404*	0.3876	1.0000		
Inflation	−0.4427*	0.1433	−0.2918	−0.6730*	0.0145	1.0000	
Real GDP	−0.0868	0.4950*	−0.1229	−0.3756	−0.2353	0.3785	1.0000

*Results are significantly different from zero at the 10 percent level.

Source: Authors' calculations.

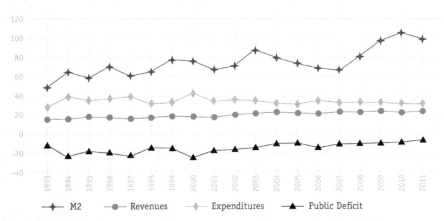

Figure 9.3 Annual variation in M2, revenues, expenditures, and public deficit.
Source: Authors' calculations.

Table 9.2 Correlation matrix real exchange rate (RER), inflation, M2, and public deficit

	RER	Inflation	M2	Public deficit
RER	1.0000			
Inflation	0.0145	1.0000		
M2	0.6022*	−0.2702	1.0000	
Public deficit	0.2855	−0.1083	0.4744*	1.0000

*Results are significantly different from zero at the 10 percent level.

Source: Authors' calculations.

Lastly, the resource movement effects of Dutch disease affecting the Lebanese economy can clearly be seen by examining the sectoral allocation of value added. Agricultural and manufacturing value added as a share of GDP have decreased by 3 percent annually over the period 1993–2011, while the value added of the services sector has increased by 1 percent on an annual basis, reaching more than 80 percent in 2011 (Figure 9.4).

The correlation matrix in Table 9.3 confirms a strong relationship between RER and value added, specifically a positive one for the service sector and a negative one for the manufacturing and agriculture sectors.

The above analysis has demonstrated, using recent macroeconomic data from Lebanon, that the country is already suffering from symptoms of Dutch disease, namely

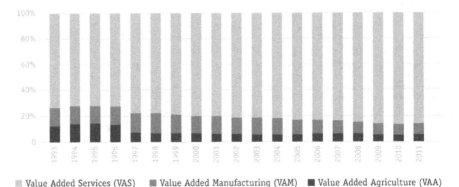

Figure 9.4 Annual variation in sector-level value added.

Source: Authors' calculations.

Table 9.3 Correlation matrix real exchange rate (RER) and value added by sector

	RER	VAS	VAA	VAM
RER	1.0000			
VAS	0.6124*	1.0000		
VAA	−0.5525*	−0.8797*	1.0000	
VAM	−0.5027*	−0.7767*	0.4116*	1.0000

*Results are significantly different from zero at the 10 percent level.

Source: Authors' calculations.

Macroeconomic Implications of Petroleum Revenues 233

through massive sustained foreign inflows received every year (Chami *et al.* 2003, Chaaban 2009). The impact of these inflows (remittances, non-resident bank deposits, and foreign direct investment) on the real and monetary sectors of the economy was explored using simple descriptive statistics. The next section integrates these findings to better forecast the potential implications of an oil and gas revenue boom, in light of ongoing "Dutch disease" within the Lebanese economy.

Dynamic model of windfall oil and gas revenues

The discovery and extraction of oil and gas off the shores of Lebanon would ultimately translate into a boom in revenues for the government, which, under current conditions, including a lack of fiscal planning, could easily translate into an uncontrolled expansionary budget policy. Yet, this should not always be the case, as the government can opt, like in other successful oil revenue management models, to create a sovereign wealth fund to boost local financial reserves and smooth spending. It could also opt for an ambitious energy substitution program with massive upgrades in electricity generation infrastructure by shifting from import-dependent fuel oil production to cheaper and cleaner natural gas produced locally. In this section, we seek to model the impact of these various policy options on the Lebanese economy. This is done by modeling and stimulating the impact of an increase in public revenues following oil and gas exploration on the Lebanese economy, using a simple time-series model applied on monthly available macroeconomic data. We focus on the following variables that will be included in the analysis:

- Budget deficit: defined in this section as public expenditures minus revenues. We apply a moving average based on an annual sliding scale, smoothing for the budget deficit monthly data, in order to capture year-on-year delays in expenditure (as per the Lebanese public fiscal decision making process). This is obtained from the Ministry of Finance.
- Money supply: defined as a money and quasi-money M2 measure as provided by the central bank.
- Real GDP: computed monthly by applying the trend in BDL's monthly Coincident Indicator (CI) to annual real GDP data from the International Monetary Fund World Economic Outlook Database. For instance, Jan 2003 real GDP = annual 2003 real GDP x (share of coincident indicator for Jan 2003/Total coincident indicator for the whole 2003 year). The resulting series is then smoothed for seasonality.
- Trade deficit: defined as imports minus exports. Seasonal smoothing is applied to monthly data to filter seasonal effects. This data is obtained from the central bank.
- Inflation CPI: defined as change (month-on-month) in the Consumer Price Index (CPI) compiled by the Consultation and Research Institute.
- Real exchange rate (RER): computed by using the monthly United States CPI for all urban consumers with 1982–4 as the base. This is obtained from the Federal Reserve Bank of St. Louis. The Lebanese CPI index is used with January 1997 as the base month, in addition to the nominal exchange rate from BDL. RER is computed by rescaling all variables and dividing them by the initial value (i.e., that of January 1997).

234   *The Future of Petroleum in Lebanon*

Table 9.4 Summary statistics for main macroeconomic variables used (monthly data, 1997–2013)

Variable	Number of observations	Mean	Std. dev.	Min	Max
BD: Budget deficit (Bill. LBP)	195	198	78	43	362
M2: Money supply (Bill. LBP)	192	32,933	17,519	13,901	68,749
RGDP: Real GDP (Bill. LBP)	192	2,837	639	2,104	4,058
TD: Trade deficit (Bill. LBP)	189	1,183	530	584	2,414
CPI: Inflation CPI (base = 100 Jan 97)	190	127	20	104	169
RER (base = 100 Jan 97)	190	105	7	92	120

Source: Authors' calculations.

Table 9.4 summarizes the main variables used in the analysis.

Due to the non-stationarity of all variables, we employ a cointegration framework by estimating a Vector Error Correction model (VECM) that aims to capture any long-run relationships between the time series, along with corresponding short-term dynamics (Johansen 1995). We perform Johansen cointegration tests to determine the presence and number of cointegrating relationships, and sequential modified Likelihood Ratio (LR) tests to determine the appropriate lag structure for short-term dynamics (test results in Annex 1).

As in similar models used by Lartey (2008) and Ball *et al.* (2013), the VECM econometric model takes the following reduced form:

$$X_t = r(L)X_t + ce_n + u_t$$

Where X_t is a 6x1 vector of dependent and endogenous variables with

$$X_t = [\Delta\ln(BD)_t, \Delta\ln(M2)_t, \Delta\ln(RGDP)_t, \Delta\ln(TD)_t, \Delta\ln(CPI)_t, \Delta\ln(RER)_t]$$

$r(L)$ is a matrix polynomial in the lag operator, ce_n is the error correction term (lagged one period) derived from the cointegrating vector (estimated using the Johansen procedure), and u_t is the model error. The above model is estimated using four lag structures (as shown by the LR test in Annex 1) and rank = 2 of cointegrating relationships (as shown by the Johansen test). The results obtained with Stata 12 on a sample of 184 monthly data show an overall good fit with most parameter estimates jointly significant (full results in Annex 2).

The model's estimates are then used to simulate the impact of various macroeconomic scenarios that could occur following the development of local oil and gas industries. We focus on the following options:

- Increase in budget expenditures: In this first scenario, the government engages in immediately spending additional revenues from oil and gas. This translates in our framework to a rise in the budget deficit (BD), as public expenditures are increased following the accrual of oil and gas revenues and therefore the budget deficit is assumed to increase. We therefore simulate the impact of an increase in BD on other macroeconomic variables.

- Increase in money supply: In the second scenario, the government creates a sovereign wealth fund that ultimately avoids spending all windfall revenues on general public expenditures, and instead contributes to increasing financial assets over time. This is proxied through a gradual increase in money supply (M2) within our modeling framework.
- Increase in infrastructure and power investments: Under the third and last scenario, we assume that the government engages in a series of public investments that lower the cost of transportation and energy, and therefore boost local production. This is assumed to generate a positive exogenous shock to real GDP (as in Narayan and Smyth 2009), and therefore we proxy the above scenario by an increase in our variable RGDP.

In the simulations we focus on variables of immediate interest: real exchange rate, real GDP, and inflation (CPI). Increases in BD, M2, and RGDP are simulated through Impulse Response Functions (IRFs), commonly used with VAR and VECM models to simulate the dynamic impacts of one variable on others within an integrated model.

Figure 9.5 shows the cumulative impulse response of increasing public expenditure (increase in BD) on RER, CPI, and RGDP. An expansionary fiscal policy through a rise in BD clearly causes a rise in RER and inflation (CPI) and a decline in RGDP. The cumulative impulse responses show the sum of IRFs over a period of 36 months (x-axis). Every IRF causes a 1 percent increase in BD, and we can observe from Figure 9.5 that, within three years of the forecast period, this increase will be matched by an equal decrease in real GDP and a real exchange rate appreciation with a similar magnitude.

This first simulation confirms the Dutch disease theory associated with fiscal expansion following a resource boom (Usui 1997). An increase in budget expenditure mainly on non-tradables (such as services and construction sectors) causes an increase in demand for non-tradable products and services, which results in inflationary pressures and real currency appreciation. This in turn contracts the non-resource tradables sector and causes a decline in GDP.

The second and third simulations (Figures 9.6 and 9.7) show that the alternative policy options of a sovereign wealth fund or an increase in investments in infrastructure (proxied through an exogenous increase in real GDP) would engender a positive macroeconomic effect as real GDP would increase in these two simulations. Notice, however, that these two scenarios also induce an increase in local inflation (CPI) and RER, but these changes are overruled by forecast economic growth. The three simulations clearly point to rejecting outright expenditure expansion as a recommended policy option, and opting instead for more long-term and balanced policy options which have been proven to work in other countries, such as the creation of a sovereign wealth fund and investment in infrastructure that lowers production costs and boosts competitiveness.

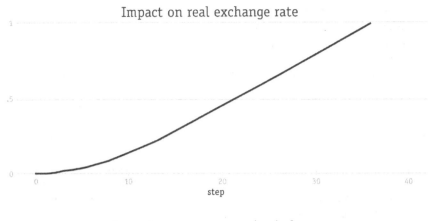
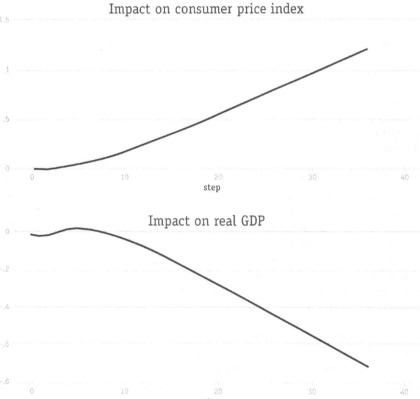

Graphs by irnfame, impulse variable, and response variable

Figure 9.5 Cumulative Impulse Response of an increase in budget deficit.
Source: Authors' calculations.

Macroeconomic Implications of Petroleum Revenues 237

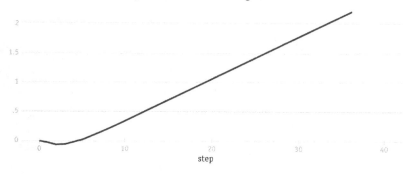

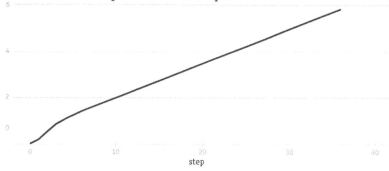

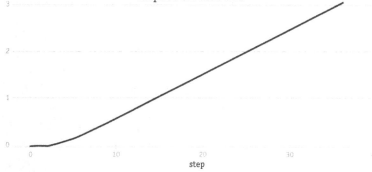

Graphs by irnfame, impulse variable, and response variable

Figure 9.6 Cumulative Impulse Response of an increase in money supply.
Source: Authors' calculations.

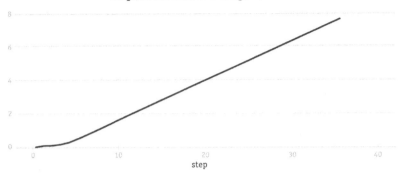

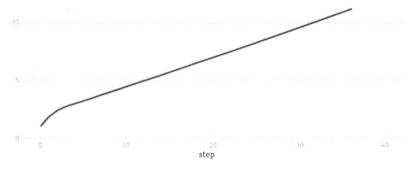

Graphs by irnfame, impulse variable, and response variable

Figure 9.7 Cumulative Impulse Response of an increase in real GDP.
Source: Authors' calculations.

These simulations, although provided here as illustrative of the various policy options available for the Lebanese government to manage its hydrocarbon revenues, clearly show that the level and composition of public expenditure matter when trying to avoid the resource curse. As shown above, the budget expansion following increased hydrocarbon revenues does not necessarily induce the tradables sector to shrink (and therefore inducing a decline in real GDP), as long as the government spends these revenues to strengthen, either directly or indirectly, the tradables sector (like manufacturing and services exports). The empirical findings here also show that adopting a typical expansionary fiscal policy, with a focus on spending more on non-tradables sectors such as construction and services, including higher personnel expenditures, would lead to upward pressure on the real exchange rate. However, by adopting better public financial management and a set of clearly defined and transparent fiscal rules (Elbadawi and Gelb 2010, Schmidt-Hebel 2012), the Lebanese government could avoid the resource curse and invest in the long-term welfare of its citizens. The necessity of adopting a set of fiscal rules aimed at the sustainability of public debt, controlling the size of government, and the contribution to cyclical stability becomes of central importance here (Schmidt-Hebbel 2012).

Conclusion and recommendations

The underperformance of most resource-rich economies is attributed to policy failures in mitigating the potential associated risks of a natural resource boom, one of which is Dutch disease. There is considerable empirical evidence that confirms the theoretical predictions of the Dutch disease phenomenon: in the wake of a natural resource boom, the resulting sudden increase in income leads to increased domestic demand that puts inflationary pressure on the economy and eventually inflates the value of local currency; the traditional export sectors contract while returns to human capital and investments in education decline, potentially harming economic growth.

In light of the recent discovery of potential offshore hydrocarbon resources in Lebanon, it is crucial to investigate the possibility of a Dutch disease realization, especially given the detrimental consequences this discovery could have on the Lebanese economy. This chapter sought to do exactly that. First, our work examines whether the Lebanese economy is already suffering from Dutch disease through massive sustained foreign exchange inflows that have been injected into the economy since the beginning of the 1990s, as a result of channeling of petrodollars into the economy. We find that these inflows have been accompanied by a real exchange rate appreciation as well as contraction of the agriculture and manufacturing sectors, thus indicating the presence of Dutch disease symptoms. Second, our work empirically investigates the impacts of a potential resource boom on the Lebanese economy by simulating a rise in the budget deficit within a cointegrated model of real and monetary indicators, in addition to simulating other more advantageous policy options. The main objective was to determine whether an expansionary fiscal policy would result in real exchange rate appreciation. We estimated a VECM on monthly available macroeconomic data and employed Impulse Response Functions for the simulation. The results show that a permanent increase in the budget deficit by 1 percentage point causes an equal appreciation in the real exchange rate over a three-year forecast period. The results also found adverse impacts on the economy shown by a decline in real GDP. The simulations also clearly showed that economic growth would be achieved through alternative policy options such as a sovereign wealth fund or investments in infrastructure. In summary, results have shown that a resource boom in Lebanon will further exacerbate Dutch disease effects if the country adopts an expansionary fiscal policy, and this could be avoided by adopting best-practice forward looking economic policies.

Despite the gloomy picture these findings paint, the Dutch disease outcome could be avoided if the appropriate policy adjustments are implemented in conjunction with the development of offshore hydrocarbon resources. The successful experiences of a few resource-rich countries have been largely attributed in the literature to their success in managing resource wealth and its associated risks. The optimal response that takes advantage of the boom while mitigating its potential negative implications includes a set of fiscal, monetary, exchange rate, and structural reform policies.

Based on the findings in this chapter, we can see that the fiscal policy a government adopts is critical to determining the actual outcome of the boom. Consequently, choosing an appropriate fiscal policy is a central and necessary policy response for avoiding Dutch disease (van der Ploeg and Venables 2011). Two principal decisions need to be made when designing a fiscal policy response. First, it should be determined how much a government should spend from its resource revenues over time. Second, it should be determined on what the government will spend its resource revenues. Adopting a revenue sterilization policy and accumulating foreign exchange reserves can constrain the spending effect of Dutch disease and as a result curb real exchange rate appreciation. In that respect, the government must resist pressure to enjoy all windfall revenues in the short run and recklessly expand its budget expenditure. On the contrary, it must commit to saving part of the revenue proceeds every period in order to attain a permanent wealth increase (Usui 1997). Deciding how much to save versus how much to spend, though, is not as straightforward. On the one hand, the resource bonanza liberates the (especially, developing) government from its budget constraints and provides a unique opportunity to spend on development and poverty reduction programs. On the other hand, the spending effect of Dutch disease must be constrained in order to shield the economy from adverse impacts. The optimal fiscal rule is one that strikes a balance between these two objectives. This, however, requires that the government has strict fiscal discipline (Brahmbhatt *et al.* 2010), which in turn necessitates political reforms that encourage transparency and accountability in the decision making process.

As for how the windfall revenues should be allocated, the government must be careful not to spend the wealth in a way that increases the domestic aggregate demand for non-tradable goods and services and consequently appreciates the real exchange rate. In that respect, the government must direct its spending toward the non-resource tradables sectors through subsidizing outputs and/or inputs (Usui 1997) or investing in physical and human capital to enhance productivity in these sectors (Brahmbhatt *et al.* 2010). In this case, a budget expansion would not necessarily lead to the non-resource tradables sectors shrinking. Another desirable response would be to use part of the

Macroeconomic Implications of Petroleum Revenues

wealth to repay Lebanon's enormous foreign debt, thereby reducing the absorption of the revenues into the domestic economy.

Key to the above analysis and recommendations is the political economy and institutional setup, especially the role and proper functioning of fiscal institutions. To the extent that the economy is poorly managed and the political economy favors non-transparent and distributive modes of resource allocation, oil- and gas-related rents might lead to a resource curse (Elbadawi and Soto 2012). Within this context, public financial management in Lebanon, as part of the wider scope of financial governance in the country, lacks sufficient transparency in public spending as a result of the absence of a viable system of checks and balances on the state's financials. As is apparent in the controversies concerning the discussion of proposed budget laws, there are several weaknesses in the management and control of public finances. Literature mainly attributes these weaknesses to a lack of specialized support and a shortage in relevant staff resources, all of which hamper the quality of budget work by the executive and budget oversight by the concerned legislative body (World Bank 2005, Gaspard 2006). The burden of public debt on public expenditures greatly narrows the range of possible parliamentary amendments to budget laws. In turn, this straining fiscal environment accentuates underlying weaknesses in the overall control environment that follows budget execution and verification.

Annex 1: Lag order selection and cointegrating rank for VECM model

For a given lag p, the LR test compares a VAR with p lags to one with p-1 lags. The null hypothesis is that all the coefficients on the pth lags of the endogenous variables are zero. To use this sequence of LR tests to select a lag order, we begin by looking at the results of the test for the model with the most lags, which is at the bottom of the table. Proceeding up the table, the first test that rejects the null hypothesis is the lag order selected by this process. An '*' appears next to the LR statistic indicating the optimal lag in Table 9.5 (obtained in Stata 12).

Table 9.5 Selection-order criteria

Sample: 1998m6–2013m9   **Number of obs. = 184**

lag	LL	LR	df	p	FPE	AIC	HQIC	SBIC
0	885.722				2.8e−12	−9.56219	−9.5197	−9.45736
1	2345.09	2918.7	36	0.000	5.4e−19	−25.0336	−24.7362*	−24.2998*
2	2390.97	91.752	36	0.000	4.9e−19*	−25.141*	−24.5886	−23.7781
3	2423.37	64.796	36	0.002	5.1e−19	−25.1018	−24.2945	−23.11
4	2457.05	67.364*	36	0.001	5.2e−19	−25.0766	−24.0144	−22.4558

Endogenous: bd m2 cpi rer rgdp td1.

Exogenous: _cons.

242   *The Future of Petroleum in Lebanon*

Table 9.6 Johansen tests for cointegration

Trend: constant   **Number of obs. = 186**

Sample: 1998m4–2013m9   **Lags = 2**

Maximum rank	Parms	LL	Eigenvalue	Trace statistic	5% critical value
0	42	2339.5069		117.0669	94.15
1	53	2362.998	0.22322	70.0847	68.52
2	62	2377.1793	0.14143	41.7222*	47.21
3	69	2389.8256	0.12714	16.4296	29.68
4	74	2396.6437	0.07069	2.7934	15.41
5	77	2398.0314	0.01481	0.0180	3.76
6	78	2398.0404	0.00010		

In the output in Table 9.6, we use vecrank in Stata 12 to determine the number of cointegrating equations using Johansen's multiple-trace test method. The '*' by the trace statistic at r = 2 indicates that this is the value of r selected by Johansen's multiple-trace test procedure.

Annex 2: Estimation results of the VECM model

Table 9.7 Vector error-correction model

Sample: 1998m6–2013m9   **No. of obs. = 184**
                                                 AIC = −25.11042

Log likelihood = 2444.159   **HQIC = −24.16146**

Det(Sigma_ml) = 1.17e–19   **SBIC = −22.76911**

Equation	Parms	RMSE	R-sq.	chi2	P > chi2
D_bd	21	.114778	0.1668	32.43713	0.0528
D_m2	21	.026721	0.4030	109.3717	0.0000
D_cpi	21	.013098	0.2243	46.84294	0.0010
D_rer	21	.013289	0.1771	34.85943	0.0293
D_rgdp	21	.027646	0.2331	49.24528	0.0005
D_td1	21	.082014	0.4116	113.3183	0.0000

References

Authored references

Acosta, P., E. Lartey, and F. Mandelman. 2009. "Remittances and the Dutch Disease." Working Paper 2007-8a, Federal Reserve Bank of Atlanta.

Bacchetta, P., K. Rogoff, P. Aghion, and R. Rancière. 2006. "Exchange Rate Volatility and Productivity Growth: The Role of Financial Development." *Journal of Monetary Economics* 56: 494–513.

Macroeconomic Implications of Petroleum Revenues

Ball, C., C. Lopez, and J. Reyes. 2013. "Remittances, Inflation and Exchange Rate Regimes in Small Open Economies." *The World Economy* 36: 487–507.

Berthelemy, J., S. Dessus, and C. Nahas. 2007. "Exploring Lebanon's Growth Prospects." Policy Research Working Paper No. 4332, The World Bank.

Brahmbhatt, M., O. Canuto, and E. Vostroknutova. 2010. "Dealing with Dutch Disease." Economic Premise Note Series, No. 16, The World Bank.

Chaaban, J. 2009. "The Impact of Instability and Migration on Lebanon's Human Capital." In *Generation in Waiting: The Unfulfilled Promise of Young People in the Middle East,* edited by N. Dhillon and T. Yousef. Brookings Institution Press.

Chami, R., C. Fullenkamp, and S. Jahjah. 2003. "Are Immigrant Remittance Flows a Source of Capital for Development?" Working Paper 03/189, International Monetary Fund.

Collier, P., F. van der Ploeg, M.M. Spence, and A.J. Venables. 2010. "Managing Resource Revenues in Developing Economies." Staff Papers 57: 84–118, International Monetary Fund.

Corden, W.M. and P.J. Neary. 1982. "Booming Sector and De-industrialization in a Small Open Economy." *Economic Journal* 92: 825–48.

Elbadawi, I. and A. Gelb. 2010. "Oil, Economic Diversification, and Development in the Arab World." Policy Research Report 35, Economic Research Forum.

Elbadawi, I. and R. Soto. 2012. "Resource Rents, Political Institutions and Economic Growth." Documentos de Trabajo 413, Instituto de Economia, Pontificia Universidad Católica de Chile.

Gaspard, D.T. 2006. "Towards an Organic Budget Law for Lebanon: A Reform Strategy-Institutional and Technical Perspective." Beirut.

Gylfason, T. 2000. "Resources, Agriculture, and Economic Growth in Economies in Transition." Working Paper Series 313, Center for Economic Studies, Munich.

Gylfason, T. 2001. "Natural Resource, Education and Economic Development." *European Economic Review* 45: 847–59.

Gylfason, T., T. Herbertsson and G. Zoega. 1999. "A Mixed Blessing: Natural Resources and Economic Growth." *Macroeconomic Dynamics* 3: 204–25.

Finger, H. and H. Hesse. 2009. "Lebanon-Determinants of Commercial Bank Deposits in a Regional Financial Center." Working Paper 09/195, International Monetary Fund.

Harding, T. and A.J. Venables. 2013. "The Implications of Natural Resource Exports for Non-Resource Trade." Oxford Centre for the Analysis of Resource Rich Economies, Research Paper 103, University of Oxford.

Harvey, C. 1992. "Botswana: Is the Economic Miracle Over?" *Journal of African Economies* 1: 335–68.

Ismail, K. 2010. "The Structural Manifestation of the 'Dutch Disease': The Case of Oil Exporting Countries." Working Paper 10/103, International Monetary Fund.

Johansen, S. 1995. *Likelihood-Based Inference in Cointegrated Vector Autoregressive Models.* Oxford University Press.

Lartey, E. 2007. "Capital Inflows and the Real Exchange Rate: An Empirical Study of Sub-Saharan Africa." *Journal of International Trade and Economic Development* 16: 337–57.

Lartey, E. 2008. "Capital Inflows, Dutch Disease Effects, and Monetary Policy in a Small Open Economy." *Review of International Economics* 16: 971–89.

Magud, N. and S. Sosa. 2010. "When and Why Worry About Real Exchange Rate Appreciation? The Missing Link between Dutch Disease and Growth." Working Paper 10/271, International Monetary Fund.

Narayan, P.K. and R. Smyth. 2009. "Multivariate Granger Causality between Electricity Consumption, Exports and GDP: Evidence from a Panel of Middle Eastern Countries." *Energy Policy* 37: 229–36.

Papyrakis, E. and R. Gerlagh. 2004. "The Resource Curse Hypothesis and its Transmission Channels." *Journal of Comparative Economics* 32: 181–93.

Rajan, R. and A. Subramanian. 2005. "Aid and Growth: What Does the Cross-Country Evidence Really Show?" Working Paper 05/127, International Monetary Fund.

Rajan, R. and A. Subramanian. 2009. "Aid, Dutch Disease, and Manufacturing Growth." *Journal of Development Economics* 94: 106–18.

Sachs, J. and A. Warner. 1999. "The Big Push, Natural Resource Booms and Growth." *Journal of Development Economics* 59: 43–76.

Sala-i-Martin, X. and A. Subramanian. 2003. "Addressing the Natural Resource Curse: An Illustration from Nigeria." Working Paper 9804, National Bureau of Economic Research.

Schmidt-Hebbel, K. 2012. "Fiscal Institutions in Resource-Rich Economies: Lessons from Chile and Norway." Working Paper 682, Economic Research Forum.

Servén, L. 2002. "Real Exchange Rate Uncertainty and Private Investment in Developing Countries." The World Bank.

Spatafora, N. and A. Warner. 1999. "Macroeconomic and Sectoral Effects of Terms-of-Trade Shocks: The Experience of the Oil Exporting Developing Countries." Working Paper 99/134, International Monetary Fund.

Usui, N. 1997. "Dutch Disease and Policy Adjustments to the Oil Boom: A Comparative Study of Indonesia and Mexico." *Resources Policy* 23: 151–62.

Van der Ploeg, F. 2010. "Natural Resources: Curse or Blessing?" Working Paper No. 3125, Category 9: Resource and Environment Economics, Centre for Economic Studies.

Van der Ploeg, F. and S. Poelhekke. 2009. "The Volatility Curse: Revisiting the Paradox of Plenty." Working Paper No. 2616, Category 6: Fiscal Policy, Macroeconomics and Growth, Centre for Economic Studies.

Van Der Ploeg, F. and A.J. Venables. 2011. "Harnessing Windfall Revenues: Optimal Policies for Resource-Rich Developing Economies." *Economic Journal* 121, 551: 1–30.

Van der Ploeg, F. and A.J. Venables. 2013. "Absorbing a Windfall of Foreign Exchange: Dutch Disease Dynamics." *Journal of Development Economics* 103: 229–43.

Non-authored reference

The World Bank. 2005. "Lebanon: Public Expenditure Reform Priorities for Fiscal Adjustment, Growth and Poverty Alleviation."

10

How Will Oil Affect Lebanon's Export Opportunities?

Zeina Hasna

Introduction

Lebanon's industrial sector has not been operating at full capacity. The Lebanese economy's dependence on the service sector has increased the country's vulnerability to exogenous shocks and political instability that have long plagued both itself and the region. Despite the gloomy outlook of Lebanon's industrial sector, its GDP per capita steadily increased from 1995 to 2012, while its exports per capita almost tripled over the same period (Bustos and Yildirim 2016). This demonstrates that there is a lot of untapped potential in the Lebanese industrial sector, primarily at the exports level.

A closer look at Lebanon's industrial policy through the product space reveals that, despite Lebanon's not-so-diversified economy, it still has a bright outlook as it is well positioned to make products that can further add to the country's overall complexity level. However, this optimistic outlook concerning Lebanon's diversification might be at stake in light of the potential oil and gas discovery off Lebanon's shore, particularly as recent research warns of possible adverse effects stemming from the exploitation of natural resources.

The themes of strengthening exports and diversification have been lent increasing importance in literature on growth and trade. For instance, over the past few decades, there has been an increase in income disparity across countries. Although some countries in the Arab world registered high growth rates at the beginning of the century, they now have one of the lowest per capita growth rates in the world (Bustos and Yildirim 2016). This is attributed to the fact that economic growth at the beginning of the century was not accompanied by a structural transformation required to diversify Arab economies (Hidalgo *et al.* 2007, Hausmann *et al.* 2007). Therefore, challenges remain, not only in how to encourage economic growth but also concerning how to best manage growth so it is inclusive and sustainable. As such, many studies have emerged demonstrating the urgency of diversification to ensure economic stability and prosperity. Economic diversification is a key sign that countries are going through structural changes, which is crucial for development, particularly as diversification renders countries resilient to idiosyncratic shocks that otherwise would

246   *The Future of Petroleum in Lebanon*

be more damaging if the economy were concentrated in a few sectors (Kalemli-Ozcan *et al.* 2003).

Until recently, research on growth strategies was not focused on diagnosing constraints to a country's economic growth, even though such research could help formulate solutions suited to each country's economic needs. Conventional theories adopted the "fundamentals view of the world," stating that patterns of specialization are determined by a country's fundamentals—its endowments of physical and human capital, labor, natural resources, and institutions. A number of papers have addressed these issues by looking more closely at the evolution of export patterns along the development process. However, Hausmann, Hwang, and Rodrik (2007) argue that, in the presence of externalities, specialization patterns are not fully determined by endowments, can display path dependence, and hamper economic growth. They consequently proposed a measure of the technology content of exports based on the average income level of exporters of the same product. This measure associates each traded good with a productivity level. Based on that, Hausmann, Hwang, and Rodrik proposed another measure, the economic complexity index (ECI), which measures the productivity level associated with a country's specialization pattern. They showed that economic complexity correlates positively with future growth. The authors visualized their concept through the "product space," which presents a given country's exports in visual form based on their sophistication.

In light of the recent oil and gas discovery off Lebanon's coast, this chapter primarily examines how oil might influence export diversification and offers recommendations on how Lebanon's export basket can be revived before the country embarks on a period of resource extraction. This chapter undertakes a worldwide comparative study, looking at the interplay between oil abundance and export diversification in 95 countries over 18 years, while simultaneously considering major determinants of export diversification proven through previous studies.

This chapter is structured as follows. Section one reviews literature on the importance of diversification, while section two provides the framework of this chapter's econometric analysis. Section three presents the results of an economic analysis of the effects of oil abundance on export diversification in Lebanon. The chapter concludes by revisiting Lebanon's industrial sector and presenting policy recommendations.

Literature review

Seminal works produced by classical economists Adam Smith (1776) and David Ricardo (1817), among others, argue that countries should specialize in producing goods in which they have a comparative advantage. However, trade in the second half of the twentieth century has different patterns than those propagated by classical trade theory. Prebisch (1950) and Singer (1950) were among the first to challenge the trade specialization hypothesis as they associated export concentration with lower levels of development. They argue that trade specialization confined developing countries to the production of primary products in exchange for consumer and investment goods

How Will Oil Affect Lebanon's Export Opportunities? 247

produced in developed countries. The Prebisch–Singer hypothesis therefore propagates a more varied export basket for developing countries to boost their income growth.

Many studies emerged afterward in favor of the Prebisch–Singer hypothesis, namely Sachs and Warner (1995), Gylfason (2004), and De Ferranti *et al.* (2002), who show through cross-country regressions that export specialization is associated with slow growth, particularly when the concentration of exports is that of primary products. This spurred the notion that poor countries, or countries at an economic disadvantage, should diversify away from primary commodities on account of their low value added, slow productivity growth, and minimal contribution to the economy's overall growth. Additionally, it also encouraged modifying the composition of their exports to include products characterized by technology spillovers and high productivity growth (Cadot, Carrere, and Strauss-Kahn 2011). With economic diversification, each country should progress toward the production and exportation of products in which it has productive knowledge, pushing the country on a path of economic development (Hausmann and Klinger 2006, Hwang 2006). After all, countries become what they produce: wealthy countries produce "rich-country products," and poor countries produce "poor-country products" (Hausmann, Hwang, and Rodrik 2007).

Commodity concentration, or market concentration more generally, causes instability in export revenue that can eventually harm growth. Commodity concentration makes countries vulnerable to volatility in market prices brought on by fluctuations in foreign exchange revenues or by trade shocks, apart from the adverse effects it has on employment and investment. With diversification, investment risks spread over a wider set of economic sectors that in turn boost income (Acemoglu and Zilibotti 1997). This occurs in line with the literature on volatility and growth, which states that countries should avoid dependence on a small number of products as this reduces the state's ability to offset, at least partially, fluctuations in some export sectors or exposure to idiosyncratic (sectoral) shocks (Love 1986). This is complemented by the work of Ramey and Ramey (1994), which argues that countries with more volatility have lower growth rates. Additionally, Kalemli-Ozcan *et al.* (2003) illustrate that a higher variance of gross domestic product resulting from specialized output with uninsured production risk entails a welfare loss that in turn outweighs the potential benefits of industrial specialization. De Ferranti *et al.* (2002) validate the above by employing the case of Latin America and showing that its highly concentrated structure of export revenues is leading to economic volatility and thus lower growth rates. Hammouda *et al.* (2010) also show that in the case of African economies, export and product diversification improve countries' total factor productivity and in turn boost economic growth. Therefore, diversifying commodities in the export base helps maintain economic stability in export receipts, upgrades value added, and overcomes growth constraints that in turn enhance long-term growth.

Despite the common belief that diversification of economic activities rises monotonically with income, Imbs and Wacziarg's seminal work (Imbs and Wacziarg 2003) demonstrates that this is not necessarily the case, by showing a non-monotone path of production and employment as functions of per capita income. In fact, they proved that sectoral diversification increases with income level until it reaches a certain level of income, but, beyond this benchmark, countries re-concentrate their production structure, whether measured by employment or value added. Therefore, countries display patterns of re-specialization at higher levels of income per capita. Koren and Tenreyro (2007) confirm the existence of a U-shaped relationship between the concentration of production and level of development using a different dataset. While Imbs and Wacziarg, and Koren and Tenreyro, conclude that sectoral diversification follows a U-shaped pattern, Klinger and Lederman (2004) prove, by looking at export data, that the pattern also holds for export diversification. Klinger and Lederman find that the number of new export products follows an inverted U-curve in income: as income increases, export diversification increases as well. It is only beyond a high level of income that further income growth is associated with concentration and less diversification (Klinger and Lederman 2004). These findings are confirmed by Cadot, Carrere, and Strauss-Kahn (2011), as they found a hump-shaped relationship between export diversification and economic development. Klinger and Lederman also built upon Hausmann and Rodrik (2003) to investigate a causal link between market failures and insufficient diversification. They concluded that opening up new export markets is an entrepreneurial gamble that, if successful, is quickly imitated. The authors also show that poor institutions appear empirically to compound the problem, lending support to the Hausmann–Rodrik view (Hausmann and Rodrik 2003).

In conclusion, the literature asserts the importance of diversification on a country's development and economic stability. Therefore, any country aiming to create inclusive growth must first diversify its economy.

Framework of analysis

Motivation

Economists have long warned of the potential adverse effects of natural resources. The pivotal work of Sachs and Warner (1995) spurred the so-called "resource curse paradox" by contrasting the poor macroeconomic performance of resource-rich countries with the economic prosperity of resource-poor countries. By using the ratio of natural resource exports to GDP as a measure of resource wealth, the authors emphasized that export dependence on primary products can be harmful. This compliments diversification literature discussed earlier supporting the importance of diversification away from primary commodities.

Extensive literature on the economics of natural resources later emerged showing the various channels through which resources can be a curse. The most commonly analyzed channels for a resource curse are the Dutch disease phenomenon (Corden and Neary 1982, Corden 1984, Gylfason, Herbertsson, and Zoega 1999), overconfidence and neglect of human resources (Gylfason 2001), and rent-seeking activities upon a natural resource discovery (Lane and Tornell 1996, Torvik 2002). Moreover, if countries fail to diversify their economies prior to a resource boom, they will grow dependent on their resource sector and thus become vulnerable to commodity prices, and this volatility will adversely affect growth (Ramey and Ramey 1994, van der Ploeg and Poelhekke 2010, Bacchetta et al. 2006). Also, a boom in a resource sector would necessitate the reallocation of capital and human resources from non-resource sectors (especially the high-tech manufacturing sector) to the low-tech resource sector (Cavalcanti *et al.* 2011). Once resources are depleted, those with high-tech skills would have already lost out on experience needed in the non-resource sectors. Consequently, it would be very expensive to reallocate and invest in human and physical capital in the more high-tech, non-resource sectors again, thus leading to adverse effects on economic growth in the long run.

On the other hand, some countries have become growth winners due to their resource wealth, including but not limited to: Norway, Botswana, Canada, the United States, and Australia. The aforementioned countries challenge the resource curse hypothesis and show that non-renewable resource endowments can indeed be blessings. Research by Esfahani, Mohaddes, and Pesaran (2013), Alexeev and Conrad (2009), and Cavalcanti, Mohaddes, and Raissi (2011) demonstrates that oil wealth has positive effects on growth and development. Brunnschweiler and Bulte (2008) show that oil abundance has positive effects on growth and on institutional quality, which further demonstrates that resources can be blessings not only from an economic perspective, but from a social one too. However, what is common among all growth winners is the adoption of a solid industrial policy that helped those countries deal with windfall resource revenues. Natural resource supply is ultimately limited and by the time resources are depleted, countries do not want their non-resource sectors to have shrunk to non-redeemable extents. This is where economic diversification policies are needed to render oil revenues a blessing as opposed to a curse.

The literature reviewed thus far has addressed the resource curse paradox by analyzing the effect of oil on income growth or income per capita. However, to the best of the author's knowledge, none of this literature has examined the impact of oil resources on export diversification in a cross-country study. The following sub-sections aim to bridge the two strands of literature by examining the effect of oil abundance on export diversification while controlling for income and other determinants of export diversification touched upon in the literature.

In order to look at the role of oil abundance in influencing export diversification, this chapter uses two econometric approaches to carry out an empirical investigation. First, the chapter compares different functional forms in the context of parametric and semi-parametric estimations to determine which form fits the data best. Second, the chapter presents results obtained using various econometric techniques (POLS, FE, RE[3]), while accounting for potential endogeneity of specialization by implementing an instrumental variable approach.

In all the approaches employed, results prove robust to a wide array of checks, demonstrating that oil abundance influences export concentration positively, or equivalently, influences export diversification negatively. Further estimations will demonstrate that this effect decreases as countries' wealth increases.

Data description

To empirically test the effects of oil reserves on export diversification, a balanced panel cross-country dataset of 95 countries (53 of which have oil reserves) from 1990 to 2007 was used including the following variables: the Theil index as the measure of export diversification, oil reserves value as a share of GDP, investment as a share of GDP, trade openness as a share of GDP, lack of price stability, government final expenditure as a share of GDP, logarithm of income per capita, logarithm of income per capita squared, population growth, and the logarithm of distance closest to the three most important trading cities: New York, Rotterdam, and Tokyo. The macroeconomic variables are chosen in line with existing growth literature (see for instance Cavalcanti, Mohaddes, and Raissi 2014, Salti 2008) to account for macroeconomic trends. Income squared is taken into consideration because many papers have examined non-linear patterns between income and diversification. Therefore, income squared as a regressor captures some of this non-linearity. Moreover, log distance from the closest market (New York, Rotterdam, and Tokyo) and population growth are chosen in line with Parteka and Tamberi's paper on empirical determinants of export diversification (Parteka and Tamberi 2011). The choice of population growth as a proxy for the geo-demographical country size can also be found in New Trade Theory (Dixit and Norman 1980, Helpman and Kurgman 1985). Tables 9, 10, and 11 in the annex provide a list of all 95 countries in the sample, a list of 53 oil-rich countries, and a description of data variables and their sources.

There are several concentration indices that basically measure inequality between export shares. The most frequently used concentration indices are those used in income-distribution literature: Herfindahl, Gini, and Theil. For the purpose of this study, and for the availability of data given the size of the dataset employed and the time span, this chapter will adopt the International Monetary Fund Theil index as an index of specialization. The lower bound of the Theil index is zero while the upper limit is ln(m), where m is the number of sectors (industries). The index is positively related to the overall level of specialization—the greater its value, the higher the specialization in exports (this chapter uses diversification and specialization as antonyms, so higher values of Theil index indicate a less diversified export basket and vice versa). The Theil index is calculated using the following formula:

$$T = \frac{1}{n}\sum_{k=1}^{n}\frac{x_k}{\mu}ln\left(\frac{x_k}{\mu}\right) \qquad where \; \mu = \frac{\sum_{k=1}^{n}x_k}{n},$$

x_k is the trade value in export line k, and n is the total number of export lines

Furthermore, the Theil index has two components: the extensive and intensive margins. According to Besedeš and Prusa (2011), the extensive margin involves establishing new partners and markets, while the intensive margin involves having relationships survive or persist and deepening existing relationships. In other words, the extensive margin can be thought of as horizontal diversification, as in diversification by addition of new product lines, and the intensive margin as vertical diversification entailing diversification of export values within active product lines (Hummels and Klenow 2005, Cadot *et al.* 2011).

While this chapter examines the effect of oil abundance exclusively on the overall Theil index and not on the extensive and intensive margins, it is important to consider the extensive and intensive margins of a few countries in the employed dataset to gain a better understanding of their export structures. Table 10.1 presents the summary statistics of the Theil index and its components for all 95 countries. In all three measures, variability "between" is much higher than "within," which means that there is greater variability in the degree of specialization between countries in this chapter's sample but not a big variability around each country's sample mean. In other words, cross-country variation is greater than within-country variation. This is expected since diversification is closely related to countries' economic structures and requires a considerable amount of time to adjust, hence the small variation around countries' sample means. Moreover, there is greater cross-country variability at the intensive margin than at the extensive margin ("between" variability of the intensive margin is 0.90 compared to 0.51 of the extensive margin). This demonstrates that the intensive margin plays a larger role in the variability of the overall index, indicating that countries differ more in the quality of their existing export lines than in the quantity of lines. This comes in line with the Hausmann–Rodrik view that countries are what they produce and export.

To better illustrate cross-country variability in diversification patterns, Table 10.2 shows countries exhibiting the highest and lowest values of the three measures in year 2007.

Table 10.1 Summary statistics for Theil index, extensive and intensive margins obtained with SITC-4 data

Variable		Mean	Std. Dev.	Min	Max	Observations
Theil Index	overall	3.161077	1.133629	1.28583	5.9913	N = 1710
	between		1.092684	1.430741	5.561563	n = 95
	within		0.3209876	1.522203	4.686093	T = 18
Extensive	overall	0.4379385	0.5409664	−0.045783	2.7882	N = 1710
Margin	between		0.5126332	0.0058397	2.322892	n = 95
	within		0.180183	−0.8268237	1.750782	T = 18
Intensive	overall	2.723139	0.9430644	1.23956	5.80353	N = 1710
Margin	between		0.8988026	1.351496	5.537957	n = 95
	within		0.2992663	1.301369	4.467805	T = 18

Source: International Monetary Fund and author's calculations.

Table 10.2 Summary statistics for Theil index, extensive and intensive margins obtained with SITC-4 data in 2007

Variable	Mean	Std. Dev.	Min-Country		Max-Country		Observations
Theil Index	3.1315	1.164433	1.44676	Italy	5.9913	Sudan	95
Extensive Margin	0.34554	0.4910209	−0.036329	El Salvador	2.3749	Gabon	95
Intensive Margin	2.78595	1.022846	1.39157	Greece	5.79538	Sudan	95

Source: International Monetary Fund and author's calculations.

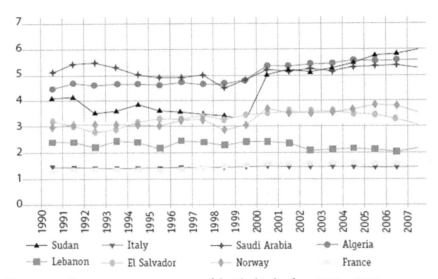

Figure 10.1 Cross-country comparisons of the Theil index from 1990 to 2007.

The evolution of the Theil index of some countries, including Lebanon, is presented in Figure 10.1.

It is noteworthy that countries known for their oil abundance, such as Saudi Arabia and Algeria, exhibit high Theil indices, indicating a high level of export specialization, while developed countries, such as Italy and France, known for their advanced industrial sectors, exhibit low specialization trends. Also, it is important to note Lebanon's not-so-poor diversification status, which will be examined further below.

Figures 10.2a, 10.2b, 10.2c, and 10.2d examine Italy, Norway, Lebanon, and Saudi Arabia further by looking at the extensive and intensive margins as well.

For the four countries represented in Figures 10a–d, there is more concentration at the intensive margin than at the extensive margin. The intensive margins are highest in Norway and Saudi Arabia, which means that the two countries concentrate on a few product lines. Given their oil wealth, this could mean that Norway and Saudi Arabia probably concentrated on oil-related products, leading to less diversified statuses in comparison to Lebanon and Italy (this will be investigated empirically in the following sub-section). However, Norway does significantly better than Saudi Arabia at the extensive margin, showing that it exports a much wider range of goods. Meanwhile, in the case of Lebanon, results seem comparatively promising, as it exhibits a relatively diversified extensive margin, which demonstrates that Lebanon exports a wide variety of goods.

In order to measure oil wealth, this chapter constructs a variable of the real value of oil reserves as a percentage of GDP. Previous papers have typically used the ratio of natural resource exports to GDP as a measure of resource wealth, as demonstrated by

How Will Oil Affect Lebanon's Export Opportunities?   253

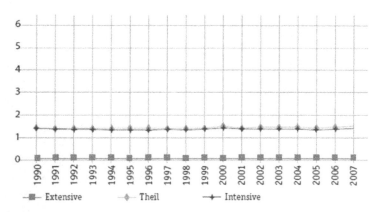

Figure 10.2a

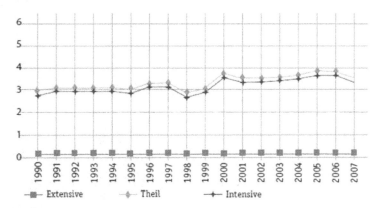

Figure 10.2b

Figure 10.2 Extensive and intensive margins for a) Italy, b) Norway, c) Lebanon, and d) Saudi Arabia.

Sachs and Warner (1995). However, Brunnschweiler and Bulte (2008) clearly demonstrate that the above ratio actually measures resource dependence and not resource abundance. Resource dependence, similar to market concentration discussed earlier, is considered an unfavorable topic in the literature, as it is associated with poor economic diversification and performance (Arezki and van der Ploeg 2007). For this purpose, the measure constructed for this study is that of oil abundance and is calculated for country i in year t as follows:

$$Oil\ reserves\ GDP_{it} = \frac{Oil\ reserves_{it} * Real\ Price\ per\ barrel_{2015\ USD}}{Real\ GDP_{i\ 2005\ USD}} * \frac{USA\ CPI_{2005}}{USA\ CPI_{2015}} * 100$$

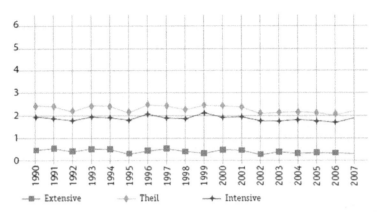

Figure 10.2c

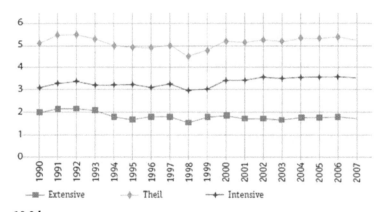

Figure 10.2d

Figure 10.2 *continued*

It is important to measure oil reserves as a share of GDP so that the effect of oil reserves can be comparable across countries. For example, 165 billion barrels of oil a year in the US will have a different effect on the economy than the same amount would on Ecuador due the massive differences in respective GDPs.

Table 10.3 presents the summary statistics of oil wealth for the 53 and 95 oil-rich countries in our sample.

Similar to specialization patterns, variability in oil wealth is much greater between countries rather than within. Therefore, it is expected that cross-country variability in specialization patterns and oil wealth play a major role in explaining the interplay between oil and export diversification internationally.

How Will Oil Affect Lebanon's Export Opportunities? 255

Table 10.3 Summary statistics for oil abundance for 53 and 95 oil-rich countries

Variable		Mean	Std. Dev.	Min	Max	Observations
Oil	overall	882.7157	3015.78	0.0805536	32368.53	N = 946
Abundance	between		2879.774	0.1645985	19810.04	n = 53
	within		941.6287	−6824.746	15197.99	T-bar = 17.8491
Oil	overall	501.1628	2312.352	0	32368.53	N = 1668
Abundance	between		2185.188	0	19810.04	n = 95
	within		708.9699	−7206.299	14816.44	T-bar = 17.5579

Source: Author's calculations.

The impact of oil revenues on export diversification

This section examines the impact of oil revenues on export diversification in Lebanon using econometric methods.

Econometric methodology

The basic model has the following form:

$$Theil\ index_{it} = \alpha + f(Oil_{it}) + \varepsilon_{it}$$

where the Theil index is a measurement of export specialization, oil represents oil abundance, and ε is the regression error term. Since many studies have shown that there could be a nonlinear relationship between income per capita and export diversification (Cadot et al. 2011, Imbs and Wacziarg 2003), this chapter considers different functional forms associated with oil abundance. Therefore, f(.) is a function that can take several forms. In its analysis, this chapter considers the linear, quadratic, and logarithmic forms.

Linear Model: $Theil_{it} = \alpha + Oil_{it} + \varepsilon_{it}$

Quadratic Model: $Theil_{it} = \alpha + Oil_{it} + Oil^2_{it} + \varepsilon_{it}$

Logarithmic Model: $ln(Theil)_{it} = \alpha + ln(Oil)_{it} + \varepsilon_{it}$

Each model can be enriched by including controls that influence diversification either directly or indirectly and country-specific fixed effects. So the full version of the model has the following form:

$$Theil\ Index_{it} = \alpha + f(Oil_{it}) + \sum_{k-1}^{K} \beta_k X_k + D_i + \varepsilon_{it}$$

with K = total number of explanatory variable considered

256   *The Future of Petroleum in Lebanon*

where X is a set of explanatory variables other than oil abundance which are likely to contribute to the process of diversification and D_i is country-specific fixed effects. The enriched models are presented below:

Linear Model: $\qquad Theil_{it} = \alpha + Oil_{it} + \sum_{k-1}^{K} \beta_k X_k + \varepsilon_{it}$

Quadratic Model: $\qquad Theil_{it} = \alpha + Oil_{it} + Oil_{it}^2 + \sum_{k-1}^{K} \beta_k X_k + \varepsilon_{it}$

Logarithmic Model: $\qquad ln(Theil)_{it} = \alpha + ln(Oil)_{it} + \sum_{k-1}^{K} \beta_k X_k + \varepsilon_{it}$

The econometric methodology consists of two main approaches. In the first approach, ordinary least squares estimation is used to test various functional forms of oil abundance. In the second approach, this chapter defers to the linear model but uses various estimation techniques to prove robustness. Fixed effects (FE), to control for country-specific unobservable characteristics, and random effects (RE) are employed. Finally, instrumental variables, also known as two-stage least squares (2SLS), are used to address the potential endogeneity of regressors.

Results

The complete econometric methodology will first be implemented on the sample of 53 oil-rich countries. The same techniques are then applied to the larger sample for robustness.

In line with the econometric methodology described earlier, this chapter begins by exclusively examining the relationship between export diversification and oil abundance. Later, explanatory variables and country fixed effects will be added.

Oil abundance is introduced in various forms: Linear (model 1), quadratic (model 2), and logarithmic (log-log model 3).

Table 10.4 presents the ordinary least squares estimates of the three models. Column 1 presents the linear model and shows that oil abundance has a positive and significant effect on export specialization whereby a one standard deviation increase in oil abundance increases specialization by 0.54 percent. It is noteworthy that the effect of oil abundance on export specialization reflects the marginal effect that country-specific changes in oil abundance have on country-specific changes on export specialization.

Column 2 runs the quadratic model and shows that oil still has a positive significant effect on export specialization whereby a one standard deviation increase in oil abundance increases export specialization by 1.82 percent. More importantly, the negative and significant quadratic formulation suggests that a reversal of the trend might be plausible. This could occur if countries used their oil wealth wisely and became more developed by using extra revenues from oil abundance to improve their productive structures and diversify their export baskets.

Column 3 runs the logarithmic model or log-log model. The log-log model is distinctive from the rest as it allows for the estimated coefficient to be interpreted as elasticity. Results show that the elasticity between oil abundance and the Theil index is 0.078, such that a 1 percent increase in oil abundance increases the Theil index by

Table 10.4 Functional forms

	(1) Linear	(2) Quadratic	(3) Log-log
Oil	0.000180***	0.000603***	
	(1.81e–05)	(8.24e–05)	
Oil^2		−2.13e–08***	
		(4.96e–09)	
ln(Oil)			0.0782***
			(0.00399)
Constant	2.763***	2.600***	0.679***
	(0.0348)	(0.0409)	(0.0209)
Observations	946	946	946
R-squared	0.211	0.365	0.308

In all the regressions, the dependent variable is the Theil index. Estimations are carried through pooled ordinary least squares with robust standard errors. Standard errors are reported in parenthesis. Symbols ***, **, * denote significance at the 1 percent, 5 percent, and 10 percent levels respectively.

Source: Author's calculations.

0.078 percent. Therefore, specialization does occur in contexts of high oil abundance. All three regressions implemented robust standard errors to account for heteroskedasticity in the error terms.[1]

Table 10.5 repeats the same estimation techniques for the enriched models, i.e. with the inclusion of the explanatory variables referenced earlier. The first three columns run the enriched linear, quadratic, and log-log models respectively. Results still show that oil abundance has a significant and positive effect on export specialization. However, all three estimates of oil abundance are now slightly smaller in magnitude, which demonstrates that the exclusion of explanatory variables in Table 10.4 slightly biased the results upward, thus emphasizing the explanatory power that they have. In column 4, the linear model is adopted again but with the addition of an interaction term that is the product of oil abundance and income per capita. The interaction term is significant and negative, meaning that while oil abundance has a positive effect on export specialization, the effect becomes smaller as countries become wealthier (have higher income per capita). In other words, oil encourages export specialization more in poorer countries. This is consistent with natural resource theory, which posits that oil is perceived as a curse in poorer countries with less capabilities to diversify and weaker manufacturing sectors generally (Salti 2008).

In all four regressions, the explanatory variables have consistent and significant effects on export specialization. Increases in investment and government expenditure encourage export diversification. A lack of price stability also encourages diversification, as it can be a tool to stabilize export revenues amid price volatility. Increasing national income has a positive effect on diversification, though a trend reversal is possible as indicated with the squared income variable. Moreover, an increase in population

---

[1] The Breusch–Pagan/Cook–Weisberg test for heteroskedasticity reports a p-value of 0.000, which rejects the null of no heteroskedasticity in the three regressions.

258   *The Future of Petroleum in Lebanon*

Table 10.5 Functional forms continued

	(1) Linear	(2) Quadratic	(3) Log-log ln	(4) Linear with interaction term
Oil	0.000166***	0.000575***		0.000759***
	(1.46e–05)	(4.29e–05)		(0.000266)
Oil2		−2.24e–08***		
		(2.27e–09)		
ln(Oil)			0.0488***	
			(0.00394)	
Investment	−0.0153***	−0.0107**	−0.00339*	−0.0137**
	(0.00560)	(0.00498)	(0.00175)	(0.00545)
Trade openness	0.00489***	0.00299***	0.00101***	0.00456***
	(0.000990)	(0.000823)	(0.000321)	(0.000969)
Lack of price stability	−0.343***	−0.323***	−0.157***	−0.367***
	(0.0722)	(0.0678)	(0.0226)	(0.0755)
Government expenditure	−0.0218***	−0.0117*	0.00207	−0.0215***
	(0.00735)	(0.00640)	(0.00232)	(0.00699)
ln(GDPpc)	−0.595*	−0.912***	−0.166	−0.585*
	(0.314)	(0.281)	(0.101)	(0.311)
ln(GDPpc)2	0.0217	0.0407**	0.00532	0.0227
	(0.0184)	(0.0165)	(0.00590)	(0.0184)
Population growth	0.304***	0.231***	0.119***	0.268***
	(0.0650)	(0.0502)	(0.0229)	(0.0594)
ln (Market distance)	0.0385	0.0739**	0.0204	0.0617*
	(0.0356)	(0.0303)	(0.0142)	(0.0340)
Oil*ln(GDPpc)				−6.49e–05**
				(2.82e–05)
Constant	7.379***	8.116***	2.168***	7.146***
	(1.157)	(1.050)	(0.382)	(1.136)
Observations	895	895	895	895
R-squared	0.568	0.658	0.602	0.588

In all the regressions, the dependent variable is the Theil index. Estimations are carried through pooled ordinary least squares with robust standard errors. Standard errors are reported in parenthesis. Symbols ***, **, * denote significance at the 1 percent, 5 percent, and 10 percent levels respectively.

Source: Author's calculations.

growth increases export specialization. According to the monopolistic competition view, larger countries have the capacity to produce a wider set of goods. Finally, an increase in distance from major markets decreases export diversification. This is the case because the further countries are from major markets, the greater the barriers to trade and thus the less incentivized countries are to diversify.

The general result is that, independent of the functional form, oil abundance always influences export specialization positively and significantly, thus influencing export diversification negatively and significantly. However, the enriched models show that oil abundance is not the only determinant of export specialization. Other characteristics of countries matter and should be taken into account while analyzing export specialization patterns.[2]

While the regressions in Tables 10.4 and 10.5 present significant and robust results, they fail to account for country fixed effects, which may cause omitted variable bias and render estimates inconsistent. Therefore, the chapter adheres to the linear model but uses various estimation techniques, such as FE, RE, and 2SLS that serve as further robustness checks. The new techniques yield consistent results with oil abundance having a positive and significant effect on export specialization. The results are presented in Annex 1.

In conclusion, after conducting a wide array of robustness checks, results consistently show that oil abundance has a significant positive effect on export specialization, or, equivalently, a significant negative effect on export diversification. The results therefore pose a threat to countries about to embark on oil discoveries. The next section looks closely at Lebanon's industrial structure and concludes with recommendations on how Lebanon can diversify its export basket before it extracts its resources and falls into the specialization trap.

The case of Lebanon

Lebanon's industrial sector at a glance

Lebanon's economy has been dependent on its service sector that has kept its industrial sector underperforming for decades. From 2000 to 2015, the value added of the service sector reached 68.3 percent of nominal GDP, while that of the industrial sector averaged only 17.4 percent (Harake et al. 2016, 25–41). The dependence on the service sector has also rendered the economy vulnerable to exogenous shocks and political instability.

However, despite the industrial sector not operating at full capacity, Atallah and Srour (2014) show that Lebanon's exports per capita actually increased from $282 in 2000 to $785 in 2009 and that the share of industrial exports out of total exports increased from 37 percent in 2000 to 57 percent in 2007 (Atallah and Srour 2014).

Moreover, Lebanon's economic complexity index (ECI)—a measure of the country's productive knowledge reflected through the complexity of its export basket—although oscillating from 1995 to 2014, has followed an overall inclining trend (Figure 10.3). This overall increase in ECI shows a significant improvement in Lebanon's exports' complexity. This should provide a positive outlook for Lebanon's industrial sector according to Hidalgo, who believes that "what a country produces matters more than how much value it extracts from its products" (Hidalgo 2009).

---

[2] It is noteworthy that the same econometric methodology is rerun on the sample of 95 countries. Results prove robust, showing a positive and significant effect of oil abundance on export specialization. However, the marginal effect of oil is now smaller in magnitude given that the standard deviation of oil abundance in this sample is smaller as a result of the inclusion of forty-two oil-deprived countries.

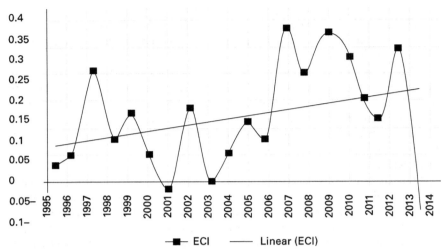

Figure 10.3 Lebanon's ECI evolution from 1995 to 2014.
Source: Atlas of Economic Complexity.

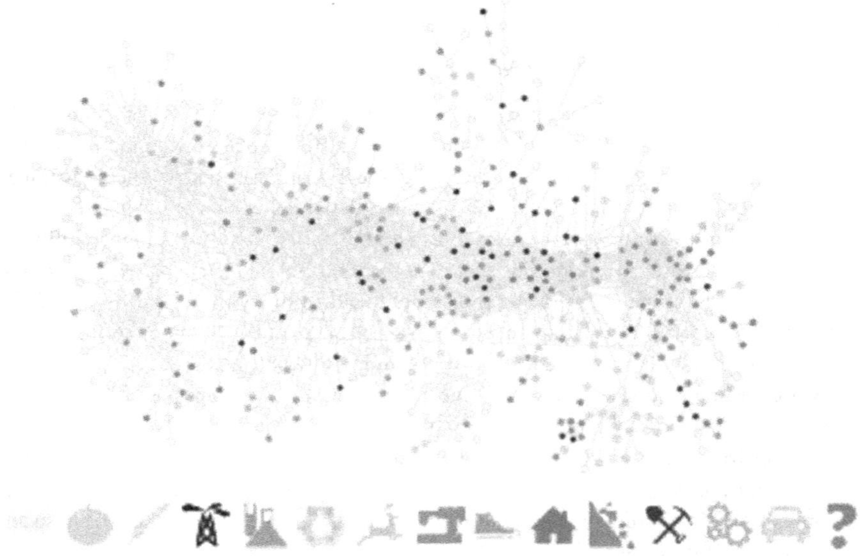

Figure 10.4 Lebanon's product space in 2012.
Source: The Observatory of Economic Complexity.

While Lebanon's product space in 2012 (Figure 10.4) is not indicative of a great deal of diversification, it shows that some of the products that Lebanon exported in that year—particularly machinery, chemicals, and construction materials[3]—were in the

[3] It is noteworthy that Lebanon has been adding new products and these three industries have increased the overall level of complexity.

vicinity of more complex products (i.e. products more central in the product space). This suggests that Lebanon has the capabilities and productive knowledge to move into producing more complex and higher value added products, which would positively impact Lebanon's future growth prospects.

However, Atallah and Srour (2014) show that surges in Lebanese exports and sophistication were mainly driven by external factors rather than by modernization of the industrial sector. Therefore, despite the improvements listed above, the Lebanese industrial sector is still placed to benefit from upgrading, in particular on account of the fact that diversification prospects are at risk. Apart from the expected problems that could arise and hinder diversification such as coordination and market failures (Atallah and Srour 2014), the picture becomes bleaker should Lebanon embark on a period of resource extraction prior to strengthening its industry. Therefore, a coherent industrial policy is the first step toward strengthening Lebanon's industrial sector and ensuring sustainable and inclusive growth.

A way forward for Lebanon

Lebanon is about to embark on a period of resource exploration and its diversification is at stake given the effects oil reserves are estimated to have on export diversification. Consequently, the formulation of a coherent industrial policy should be considered to support the industrial sector and enhance diversification to weather the possible resource dependence curse.

Using the Hausman–Rodrik view as a departure point and the product space as an analytical tool, Bustos and Yildirim (2016)—while aiming to diversify Lebanon's export basket—identify "strategic products" that are most attractive to the country based on two categories: distance and sophistication. The distance of an item from the products currently produced depicts the ease of conquering such a product. The shorter the distance from a particular product, the easier it is to make this product since the country would already have most of the capabilities needed to produce it. On the other hand, product sophistication (or equivalently product complexity) represents how much the country's overall complexity and diversification prospects would improve upon making this product. Bustos and Yildirim explain that, "by considering the tradeoff between existing productive knowledge (distance), complexity of a new product, and future diversification possibilities that the new productive knowledge will bring, a country is more likely to be successful in diversifying its product space" (Bustos and Yildirim 2016). Following this optimization strategy, the authors conclude with a list of strategic products that Lebanon should diversify into. The products are fully listed in Table 10.6 and mostly span the machinery, chemical, and textile clusters.

Making new products requires a combination of public and private inputs. If new products are made, then new capabilities need to emerge. This cannot occur on its own due to market failures. Therefore, the government must intervene and provide necessary inputs for the production of these new items. In fact, Bustos and Yildirim (2016) show that, based on Lebanon's current productive knowledge, the country has a parsimonious industrial policy which is set to benefit from government support in providing public inputs such as infrastructure and regulations on existing industries (Bustos and Yildirim 2016).

262 *The Future of Petroleum in Lebanon*

The aforementioned factors necessitate the rise of a strong public–private process aimed at assisting existing industries in Lebanon in order for them to improve their productivity, expand to nearby opportunities, and diversify their production set. With such a strategy, Lebanon would be less likely to fall into the resource dependence trap.

Conclusion and recommendations

This chapter has investigated the effect of oil on export diversification. The results presented herein suggest that oil abundance has a positive significant effect on export specialization. Results are alarming for countries with weak productive bases and about to become resource-rich, which is potentially the case in Lebanon.

The chapter has also examined the Lebanese export sector using the product space methodology and concluded that export diversification is the first step in supporting the Lebanese industrial sector given Lebanon's position in the product space and existing productive knowledge. With diversification, Lebanon will reduce its vulnerability to external shocks as investments are distributed over a wider set of sectors/products. Also, more exports and larger foreign direct investment will strengthen Lebanon's balance of payments which, if imbalanced, could threaten the country's prosperity (Harake *et al.* 2016).

As a result, the country is well placed to benefit from a coherent industrial policy that will revive its long-neglected industrial sector by diversifying into more complex products and thus ensure sustainable and inclusive growth. The challenge that remains, however, is establishing such an industrial policy in a country with a weak institutional setup. Rodrik (2004) warns that "What stands in the way of coherent industrial policy is the willingness of governments to deploy it, not their ability to do so."

Annex 1

This annex extends the analysis of the linear model using various estimation techniques as presented in Tables 10.7 and 10.8.

Looking at Table 10.7, the regression in column 1 uses a fixed-effects estimator to control for time-invariant country-specific unobservable characteristics, including aspects pertaining to social and human capital that are consistent over time but may influence the diversification process. The FE[4] estimates in column 1 are aligned with earlier findings showing that oil has a positive and significant effect on export specialization, whereby a one standard deviation increase in oil abundance increases export specialization by 0.12 percent. Column 2 repeats the regression of column 1 but includes time effects[5] to control for global common shocks such as oil prices.

---

[4] Under fixed effects estimation, log (market distance) is omitted because it is time-invariant.
[5] The time-year effects are significantly different from zero.

Table 10.6 More functional forms

HS4	Product name	RCA-2012	Distance	PCI	Target rank	W. Trade	Top Importers	Top Exporters
8419	Machinery, plant or laboratory equipment involving a change of temperature such as heating, cooking, roasting	0.6	0.9	3.7	1	37 B	USA CHN DEU	DEU USA CHN
3004	Medicaments, packaged	0.9	0.9	1.5	2	331 B	USA DEU BEL	DEU USA CHE
2105	Ice cream	0.4	0.8	0.6	3	3 B	GBR FRA DEU	DEU FRA BEL
1601	Sausages	1.0	0.9	1.4	3	4 B	GBR DEU JPN	DEU USA ITA
8424	Mechanical appliances for dispersing liquids or powders; fire extinguishers; spray guns; steam or sand blasting machines	0.4	0.9	3.5	5	17 B	USA CHN DEU	CHN DEU USA
3922	Baths, shower baths, sinks, washbasins, bidets, lavatory pans, seats, and covers	1.0	0.9	1.3	6	3 B	DEU FRA GBR	CHN DEU ITA
8530	Electric signal, safety and traffic controls, railways, waterways, parking, or airfields	0.6	1.0	3.7	7	2 B	USA CHN DEU	DEU SWE ESP
8416	Furnace burners for liquid fuel	0.4	1.0	4.0	8	2 B	CHN RUS FRA	DEU ITA CHN
8481	Appliances for thermostatically controlled valves	0.3	1.0	4.3	9	82 B	USA CHN DEU	CHN DEU USA
9402	Medical, surgical, dental, or veterinary furniture	1.0	0.9	3.5	10	3 B	USA DEU RUS	CHN DEU USA
8716	Trailers and semi-trailers	0.4	0.9	1.1	11	22 B	CAN USA DEU	DEU USA CHN
8434	Milking and dairy machines	0.4	0.9	2.5	12	2 B	DEU FRA BLR	DEU NLD SWE
3005	Wadding, gauze, and bandages	0.2	0.9	1.1	13	7 B	USA DEU FRA	CHN USA DEU
5402	Synthetic filament yarn	0.0	0.9	0.1	14	18 B	TUR USA CHN	CHN TWN IND

(*Continued*)

Table 10.6 Continued

HS4	Product name	RCA-2012	Distance	PCI	Target rank	W. Trade	Top Importers	Top Exporters
2309	Preparations of a kind used in animal feeding	0.0	0.9	0.4	14	23 B	DEU USA JPN	NLD USA FRA
6108	Women's undergarmnets	0.5	0.8	-2.4	16	11 B	USA JPN DEU	CHN IND KHM
3105	Mineral or chemical fertilizers, mixed	0.4	0.8	-0.9	16	24 B	IND BRA THA	RUS USA CHN
5911	Textile fabric for card clothing, technical use	0.3	1.0	3.8	18	4 B	USA DEU CHN	DEU USA CHN
9404	Mattress supports; articles of bedding	0.6	0.8	-1.1	18	13 B	USA JPN DEU	CHN POL DEU
8432	Agricultural, forestry machinery for soil preparation	0.2	0.9	1.5	20	8 B	USA FRA RUS	DEU USA ITA
8536	Apparatus protecting electrical circuits for < 1k volts	0.7	0.9	2.3	21	84 B	USA CHN HKG	CHN DEU JPN
8403	Central heating boilers	0.1	1.0	3.2	22	7 B	DEU GBR FRA	DEU ITA FRA
6406	Parts of footwear	0.4	0.8	-2.2	23	7 B	ITA DEU RUS	CHN ITA IND
8413	Pumps for liquids	0.6	0.9	2.9	23	62 B	USA DEU CHN	DEU USA CHN
8538	Parts for use with apparatus for protecting electrical circuits	0.8	1.0	3.2	25	32 B	CHN USA MEX	DEU CHN JPN
8431	Parts for use with hoists and excavation machinery	0.3	0.9	0.9	26	59 B	USA DEU CHN	CHN DEU USA
6306	Tarpaulins, awnings, and sunblinds	0.5	0.8	-2.4	26	3 B	USA DEU FRA	CHN DEU PAK
6104	Women's suits	0.9	0.8	-3.6	28	27 B	USA DEU JPN	CHN TUR VNM
2101	Extracts of coffee, tea, or mate	0.9	0.8	-1.3	28	8 B	USA DEU RUS	DEU BRA MYS
2402	Cigars	0.4	0.8	-2.0	31	22 B	ITA FRA JPN	DEU NLD POL
6106	Women's shirts	0.9	0.8	-3.7	31	6 B	USA DEU GBR	CHN TUR BGD
8705	Special purpose motor vehicles	0.9	0.9	-0.8	31	14 B	CAN RUS USA	DEU USA CHN
6305	Sacks and bags, used for packing goods	0.6	0.8	-4.1	33	4 B	USA JPN DEU	CHN IND TUR

2306	Cotton seed oilcake	0.9	0.8	−1.6	34	7 B	USA NLD ESP	CAN UKR IDN
6107	Men's undergarments	0.8	0.8	−3.6	35	6 B	USA JPN GBR	CHN IND VNM
6201	Men's overcoats, not knit	0.1	0.8	−2.9	36	12 B	USA JPN DEU	CHN VNM ITA
9028	Gas, liquid, or electricity supply or production meters	0.1	0.9	1.7	38	6 B	USA DEU GBR	CHN USA MEX
6110	Sweaters, pullovers, sweatshirts, etc.	0.8	0.8	−4.0	38	50 B	USA JPN DEU	CHN BGD ITA
4012	Retreaded or used pneumatic tires of rubber	0.4	0.9	1.5	38	3 B	USA DEU FRA	LKA DEU CHN
1604	Prepared or preserved fish	0.8	0.8	−3.0	40	16 B	USA JPN ITA	THA CHN ECU
4011	New pneumatic tires, of rubber	0.6	0.9	0.7	40	86 B	USA DEU FRA	CHN JPN DEU
6202	Womens overcoats, not knit	0.5	0.8	−2.6	43	14 B	USA JPN DEU	CHN VNM ITA
8512	Electrical lighting or signaling equipment used for motor vehicles	0.2	1.0	3.8	43	19 B	DEU USA CHN	CHN DEU JPN
8514	Industrial or laboratory electric furnaces	0.8	1.0	3.0	43	5 B	CHN USA KOR	DEU JPN USA
8507	Electric storage batteries	0.6	0.9	−1.2	45	32 B	USA CHN HKG	CHN JPN KOR
8433	Harvesting or agricultural machinery	0.1	1.0	3.8	45	20 B	FRA DEU USA	USA DEU CHN
6102	Women's overcoats	0.4	0.8	−4.0	47	3 B	USA DEU GBR	CHN VNM KHM
8546	Electrical insulators of any material	0.0	0.9	1.9	48	3 B	USA CHN DEU	CHN DEU ITA
5903	Textile fabrics impregnated with plastics	0.4	0.9	1.6	49	9 B	CHN USA MEX	CHN KOR DEU
8409	Parts suitable for use with spark-ignition engines	0.4	1.0	4.6	49	67 B	USA DEU GBR	DEU JPN USA

K = thousand, M = million, B = billion

Source: Bustos and Yildirim 2016.

Table 10.7 Fixed and random effects

	(1) FE	(2) FE	(3) FE Robust	(4) RE	(5) RE Robust	(6) RE Robust
Oil	3.95e–05***	3.56e–05***	3.56e–05	5.15e–05***	5.15e–05**	5.28e–05**
	(1.19e–05)	(1.22e–05)	(2.80e–05)	(1.16e–05)	(2.62e–05)	(2.67e–05)
Investment	0.000333	0.000831	0.000831	0.000665	0.000665	–0.00244
	(0.00255)	(0.00258)	(0.00899)	(0.00256)	(0.00893)	(0.00872)
Trade openness	0.00544***	0.00680***	0.00680**	0.00643***	0.00643**	0.00478**
	(0.00101)	(0.00109)	(0.00299)	(0.000923)	(0.00250)	(0.00235)
Lack of price stability	–0.100**	–0.152***	–0.152	–0.118**	–0.118	–0.100
	(0.0467)	(0.0475)	(0.0931)	(0.0469)	(0.0876)	(0.0768)
Government expenditure	0.00470	0.00243	0.00243	0.00505	0.00505	0.00214
	(0.00531)	(0.00532)	(0.0264)	(0.00527)	(0.0252)	(0.0248)
ln(GDPpc)	–1.580***	–1.803***	–1.803*	–1.578***	–1.578**	
	(0.375)	(0.373)	(0.927)	(0.359)	(0.763)	
ln(GDPpc)2	0.0933***	0.120***	0.120*	0.0845***	0.0845*	
	(0.0223)	(0.0230)	(0.0645)	(0.0213)	(0.0482)	
ln(Initial GDPpc)						–0.300**
						(0.138)
Population growth	–0.0279	–0.0578***	–0.0578	–0.0256	–0.0256	–0.00702
	(0.0185)	(0.0193)	(0.0487)	(0.0186)	(0.0432)	(0.0388)
ln(Market distance)	—	—	—	0.413***	0.413**	0.216
				(0.120)	(0.176)	(0.138)
Constant	9.477***	10.30***	10.30***	6.821***	6.821**	3.834**
	(1.605)	(1.608)	(3.587)	(1.759)	(3.331)	(1.813)
Time fixed effects	No	Yes	Yes	—	—	—
Observations	895	895	895	895	895	895
Number of cid	53	53	53	53	53	53
R-squared	0.088	0.134	0.134	0.3811	0.3811	0.3899

In all the regressions, the dependent variable is the Theil index. Standard errors are reported in parentheses. Symbols ***, **, and * denote significance at the 1 percent, 5 percent, and 10 percent levels respectively.

Table 10.8 Instrumental variables

	(1) 2SLS	(2) FE IV	(3) RE IV	(4) RE IV
Oil	0.000166***	4.47e−05*	6.40e−05***	7.01e−05***
	(1.09e−05)	(2.40e−05)	(2.16e−05)	(2.16e−05)
Investment	−0.0203***	0.00861**	0.00771**	0.00119
	(0.00597)	(0.00387)	(0.00377)	(0.00350)
Trade openness	0.00510***	0.00958***	0.00962***	0.00638***
	(0.00100)	(0.00144)	(0.00120)	(0.000965)
Lack of price stability	−0.404**	−0.0433	−0.0523	−0.0357
	(0.159)	(0.0660)	(0.0662)	(0.0661)
Government expenditure	−0.0201***	0.0168**	0.0174**	0.0108
	(0.00766)	(0.00722)	(0.00702)	(0.00675)
ln(GDPpc)	−0.552**	−2.374***	−2.215***	
	(0.273)	(0.426)	(0.396)	
ln(GDPpc)2	0.0188	0.126***	0.114***	
	(0.0162)	(0.0244)	(0.0231)	
ln(Initial GDPpc)				−0.325***
				(0.0917)
Population Growth	0.305***	−0.0401**	−0.0345*	−0.00478
	(0.0343)	(0.0195)	(0.0194)	(0.0186)
ln(Market distance)	0.0335	−	0.329***	0.198
	(0.0371)		(0.123)	(0.131)
Constant	7.627***	12.88***	9.839***	3.554**
	(1.163)	(1.839)	(1.914)	(1.629)
Observations	888	888	888	888
R-squared	0.566	0.2424	0.3869	0.4021

In all the regressions, the dependent variable is the Theil Index. Standard errors are reported in parenthesis. Symbols ***, **, and * denote significance at the 1% 5%, and 10% levels respectively.

Results are consistent and significant and reveal that a one standard deviation increase in oil abundance increases export specialization by 0.11 percent. Column 3 repeats the regression of column 2 but corrects for standard errors clustered at the country level. The effect of oil is consistent in sign but no longer significant. Column 4 runs a random effects model and shows that the marginal effect of oil abundance is still positive and significant but now higher at 0.16 percent. The effect does not change upon correcting for clustered standard errors in column 5. The Hausmann test prefers the Random Effects Model reporting a p-value of 0.4006, which fails to reject the null that RE is consistent. This demonstrates that country-fixed effects play a major role in describing cross-country variability in specialization patterns. This is not surprising since country-fixed effects refer to structural characteristics of countries' economies that barely change over time, which also are the essential determinants of countries' export baskets.

In column 6, using the preferred RE model, income and income squared variables as proxies of countries' development are replaced with the logarithm of income in 1990. Controlling for initial income captures the differences in levels of development between countries while being less endogenous to export diversification than income per capita and its square. Regression still delivers a positive and significant effect of oil on export specialization, whereby a one standard deviation increase in oil increases specialization by 0.16 percent. It is important to note that the effect of initial income is consistent with income per capita in prior regressions. This is expected since both variables proxy for development.

Finally, RE and FE models fail to control for possible simultaneity between variables in this model. In fact, it might be possible that there is reverse causation in the model whereby a decrease in export specialization—equivalently an increase in export diversification—can enhance development and increase national income that might incentivize the state to engage in oil exploration or extraction missions, eventually increasing oil abundance. Therefore, this chapter uses instrumental variables by considering lagged values as instruments for oil abundance and the controls employed,[6] except for population growth and market distance that are strictly exogenous to the dependent variable. Table 10.8 presents the results accordingly.

Columns 1, 2, and 3 report the two-stage least squares (2SLS), FE-IV, and RE-IV estimates, respectively, and display a consistent positive significant effect of oil on export specialization. Results show that a one standard deviation increase in oil abundance increases export specialization by 0.5 percent in column 1, 0.13 percent in column 2, and 0.19 percent in column 3. Column 4 repeats the regression of column 3 but uses initial income as a proxy for development, and shows a marginal effect of oil of 0.21 percent. As expected, when implementing IV, the marginal effect of oil abundance on export specialization is larger than in non-instrumented regressions.

After trying various functional forms and various estimation techniques, results unanimously show that oil has a positive and significant effect on export specialization and equivalently a negative and significant effect on export diversification.

---

[6] The choice of lagged values as instruments is inspired by Barro and Sala-i-Martin (1995).

Annex 2

Table 10.9 All countries in the sample

Among top 80 countries with oil exports (in the world)	OECD*	Other countries
Algeria	Australia	Bangladesh
Argentina	Austria	Benin
Australia	Canada	Bolivia
Belize	Chile	Burundi
Brazil	Denmark	Central African Republic
Cameroon	Finland	Costa Rica
China	France	Cyprus
Colombia	Germany	El Salvador
Republic of Congo	Greece	Haiti
Cote d'Ivoire	Iceland	Honduras
Denmark	Ireland	Hong Kong
Ecuador	Israel	India
Egypt	Italy	Jamaica
France	Japan	Jordan
Gabon	Mexico	Kenya
Ghana	New Zealand	Laos
Greece	Norway	Lebanon
Guatemala	Poland	Macau
Indonesia	Portugal	Malawi
Ireland	South Korea	Mali
Israel	Spain	Malta
Italy	Sweden	Mauritius
Malaysia	Switzerland	Morocco
Mauritania	Turkey	Mozambique
Mexico	United Kingdom	Nepal
Mongolia	United States	Nicaragua
New Zealand		Pakistan
Niger		Panama
Norway		Paraguay
Peru		Senegal
Philippines		Sierra Leone
Poland		Singapore
Romania		South Africa
Saudi Arabia		Syria
South Korea		Tanzania
Spain		The Gambia
Sudan		Togo
Sweden		Uganda
Thailand		Uruguay
Trinidad and Tobago		Zambia
Tunisia		
Turkey		
United Kingdom		
United States		
Vietnam		
Yemen		

Annex 3

Table 10.10 Sample of countries empirically investigated

Among top 80 countries with oil exports (in the world)		OECD*	Other countries
Algeria	Malaysia	Australia	Bangladesh
Argentina	Mexico	Austria	Benin
Australia	New Zealand	Canada	Bolivia
Brazil	Norway	Chile	India
Cameroon	Peru	Denmark	Jordan
China	Philippines	France	Morocco
Colombia	Poland	Germany	Pakistan
Republic of Congo	Romania	Greece	South Africa
Cote d'Ivoire	Saudi Arabia	Israel	Syria
Denmark	Spain	Italy	
Ecuador	Sudan	Japan	
Egypt	Thailand	Mexico	
France	Trinidad and Tobago	New Zealand	
Gabon	Tunisia	Norway	
Ghana	Turkey	Poland	
Greece	United Kingdom	Spain	
Guatemala	United States	Turkey	
Indonesia	Vietnam	United Kingdom	
Israel	Yemen	United States	
Italy			

* Refers to the Organization for Economic Cooperation and Development.

Annex 4

Table 10.11 Description of variables

Variable	Definition and Construction	Source
Theil Index	IMF measures of export	International Monetary Fund
Extensive Theil Index	diversification using COMTRADE	The Diversification Toolkit
Intensive Theil Index	Bilateral trade flow data at the 4-digit SITC (Rev. 1) level	Export Diversification and Quality Databases (Spring 2014)
Inflation rate	Annual percentage change in CPI	Own construction using data from World Development
Lack of price stability	Log (100+inflation rate)	Indicators (2015) and International Country Risk Guide
Investment	Fixed Capital Formation's share of GDP	Own construction using data from UN National Accounts Main
Trade Openness	Imports and Exports' share of GDP	Aggregates Database (2014) and
Government expenditure	General government final consumption expenditures as a share of GDP; proxy for government burden	World Development Indicators (2015)

How Will Oil Affect Lebanon's Export Opportunities?   271

Table 10.11 Continued

Variable	Definition and Construction	Source
Oil Reserves	Real value of oil reserves as a share of GDP	Own construction using oil data (reserves, production, prices) from US Energy Information Administration, Real GDP from UN National Accounts Main Aggregates Database and CPI data from US Inflation Calculator
Logarithm of income per capita	Log(GDP/capita) expressed in constant 2005 USD	World Bank Development Indicators (2015)
Population growth	Growth rate of total population	Own construction using data from UN National Accounts Main Aggregates Database (2014)
Distance to the closest market	Log of the distance closest to Rotterdam, New York, Tokyo	Courtesy of Dr. Aleksandra Parteka for sharing her dataset

References

Acemoglu, D. and F. Zilibotti. 1997. "Was Prometheus Unbound by Chance? Risk, Diversification, and Growth." *Journal of Political Economy* 105: 709–51.

Alexeev, M. and R. Conrad. 2009. "The Elusive Curse of Oil." *Review of Economics and Statistics* 91: 586–98.

Arezki, R. and F. van der Ploeg. 2007. "Can the Natural Resource Curse Be Turned Into a Blessing? The Role of Trade Policies and Institutions." Working Paper, International Monetary Fund.

Atallah, S. and I. Srour. 2014. "The Emergence of Highly Sophisticated Lebanese Exports in the Absence of an Industrial Policy." Policy Brief, Lebanese Center for Policy Studies.

Bacchetta, P., K. Rogoff, P. Aghion, and R. Rancière. 2006. "Exchange Rate Volatility and Productivity Growth: The Role of Financial Development." *Journal of Monetary Economics* 56: 494–513.

Barro, R. and S.I. Martin. 1995. *Economic Growth.* Massachusetts Institute of Technology Press.

Besedeš, T. and T.J. Prusa. 2011. "The Role of Extensive and Intensive Margins and Export Growth." *Journal of Development Economics* 96: 371–9.

Brunnschweiler, C.N. and E.H. Bulte. 2008. "The Resource Curse Revisited and Revised: A Tale of Paradoxes and Red Herrings." *Journal of Environmental Economics and Management* 55: 248–64.

Bustos, S. and M. Yildirim. 2016. "Lebanon's Manufacturing Sector: Inaction and Untapped Potential." Policy Paper, February.

Cadot, O., C. Carrère, and V. Strauss-Kahn. 2011. "Export Diversification: What's Behind the Hump?" *Review of Economics and Statistics* 93: 590–605.

Cadot, O., C. Carrère, and V. Strauss-Kahn. 2013. "Trade Diversification, Income, and Growth: What Do We Know?" *Journal of Economic Surveys* 27: 790–812.

Cavalcanti, D.V., V. Tiago, K. Mohaddes, and M. Raissi. 2011. "Growth, Development and Natural Resources: New Evidence Using a Heterogeneous Panel Analysis." *The Quarterly Review of Economics and Finance* 51: 305–18.

Cavalcanti, D.V., V. Tiago, K. Mohaddes, and M. Raissi. 2015. "Commodity Price Volatility and the Sources of Growth." *Journal of Applied Econometrics* 30: 857–73.

Corden, W.M. 1984. "Booming Sector and Dutch Disease Economics: Survey and Consolidation." *Oxford Economic Papers* 36: 359–80.

Corden, W.M., and J.P. Neary. 1982. "Booming Sector and De-Industrialisation in a Small Open Economy." *The Economic Journal* 92: 825–48.

De Ferranti, D., G.E. Perry, D. Lederman, and W.E. Maloney. 2002. "From Natural Resources to the Knowledge Economy: Trade and Job Quality." The World Bank.

De Piñeres, S.A.G. and M.J. Ferrantino. 2000. *Export Dynamics and Economic Growth in Latin America: A Comparative Perspective*. Ashgate Publishing.

Dixit, A. and V. Norman. 1980. *Theory of International Trade: A Dual, General Equilibrium Approach*. Cambridge University Press.

Esfahani, H.S., K. Mohaddes, and M.H. Pesaran. 2013. "Oil Exports and the Iranian Economy." *The Quarterly Review of Economics and Finance* 53: 221–37.

Gylfason, T. 2001. "Natural Resources, Education, and Economic Development." *European Economic Review* 45: 847–59.

Gylfason, T. 2004. "Natural Resources and Economic Growth: From Dependence to Diversification." Discussion paper 4804, Centre for Economic Policy Research.

Gylfason, T. 2008. "Development and Growth in Mineral-Rich Countries." Faculty of Economics and Business Administration, University of Iceland.

Gylfason, T., T.T. Herbertsson, and G. Zoega. 1999. "A Mixed Blessing." *Macroeconomic Dynamics* 3: 204–25.

Hammouda, H.B., S.N. Karingi, A.E. Njuguna, and M.S. Jallab. 2010. "Growth, Productivity and Diversification in Africa." *Journal of Productivity Analysis* 33: 125–46.

Harake, W. and V. Mulas. 2016. "Lebanon Economic Monitor: A Geo-Economy of Risks and Rewards." The World Bank.

Hausmann, R., C. Hidalgo, D.P. Stock, and M.A. Yildirim. 2014. "Implied Comparative Advantage." Harvard University.

Hausmann, R., J. Hwang, and D. Rodrik. 2007. "What You Export Matters." *Journal of Economic Growth* 12: 1–25.

Hausmann, R. and B. Klinger. 2006. "Structural Transformation and Patterns of Comparative Advantage in the Product Space." Harvard University.

Hausmann, R. and D. Rodrik. 2003. "Economic Development as Self-Discovery." *Journal of Development Economics* 72: 603–33.

Helpman, E. and P.R. Krugman. 1985. *Market Structure and Foreign Trade: Increasing Returns, Imperfect Competition, and the International Economy*. Massachusetts Institute of Technology Press.

Hidalgo, C. 2009. "The Dynamics of Economic Complexity and the Product Space over a 42 Year Period." Working Paper, Center for International Development.

Hidalgo, C., B. Klinger, A.L. Barabási, and R. Hausmann. 2007. "The Product Space Conditions the Development of Nations." *Science* 317: 482–7.

Hummels, D. and P. Klenow. 2005. "The Variety and Quality of a Nation's Exports." *American Economic Review* 95: 704–23.

Hwang, J. 2006. "Introduction of New Goods, Convergence and Growth." Department of Economics, Harvard University.

Imbs, J. and R. Wacziarg. 2003. "Stages of Diversification." *American Economic Review* 93: 63–86.

Kalemli-Ozcan, S., B.E. Sørensen, and O. Yosha. 2003. "Risk Sharing and Industrial Specialization: Regional and International Evidence." *The American Economic Review* 93: 903–18.

Klinger, B. and D. Lederman. 2004. "Discovery and Development: An Empirical Exploration of 'New' Products." The World Bank.

Koren, M. and S. Tenreyro. 2007. "Volatility and Development." *The Quarterly Journal of Economics* 122: 243–87.

Lane, P.R. and A. Tornell. 1996. "Power, Growth, and the Voracity Effect." *Journal of Economic Growth* 1: 213–41.

Love, J. 1986. "Commodity Concentration and Export Earnings Instability: A Shift from Cross-Section to Time Series Analysis." *Journal of Development Economics* 24: 239–48.

Mehlum, H., K. Moene, and R. Torvik. 2006. "Institutions and the Resource Curse." *The Economic Journal* 116: 1–20.

Michaely, M. 1977. "Exports and Growth: An Empirical Investigation." *Journal of Development Economics* 4: 49–53.

Parteka, A. and M. Tamberi. 2008. "Determinants of Export Diversification: An Empirical Investigation." Dipartimento di Economia Quaderno di Ricerca, Universita Politecnica delle Marche.

Parteka, A. and M. Tamberi. 2011. "Export Diversification and Development-Empirical Assessment." Working Paper, Dipartimento di Scienze Econo-miche e Sociali, Universita Politecnica delle Marche.

Prebisch, R. 1950. "The Economic Development of Latin America and Its Principal Problems." United Nations Department of Economic Affairs.

Ramey, G. and V.A. Ramey. 1994. "Cross-Country Evidence on the Link between Volatility and Growth." National Bureau of Economic Research.

Ricardo, D. 1891. *On the Principles of Political Economy and Taxation*. G. Bell & Sons.

Rodrik, D. 2004. "Industrial Policy for the Twenty-First Century." Harvard University.

Sachs, J.D. and A.M. Warner. 1995. "Natural Resource Abundance and Economic Growth." National Bureau of Economic Research.

Salti, N. 2008. "Oil Greasing the Wheels: When Do Natural Resources Become a Blessing?" Working Paper No. 439, Economic Research Forum.

Sharma, A. and T. Panagiotidis. 2005. "An Analysis of Exports and Growth in India: Cointegration and Causality Evidence (1971–2001)." *Review of Development Economics* 9: 232–48.

Singer, H.W. 1950. "The Distribution of Gains between Investing and Borrowing Countries." *The American Economic Review* 40: 473–85.

Smith, A. 1776. "An Inquiry into the Wealth of Nations." Strahan and Cadell.

Theil, H. 1972. *Statistical Decomposition Analysis. With Applications in the Social and Administrative Sciences*. North-Holland Pub. Co.

Torvik, R. 2002. "Natural Resources, Rent Seeking and Welfare." *Journal of Development Economics* 67: 455–70.

11

Strengthening Environmental Governance of the Oil and Gas Sector in Lebanon

Ricardo Khoury and Dima Al Haj

Introduction

Offshore oil and gas activities present environmental challenges due to their remote and harsh operating environment and the vulnerability of marine ecosystems in which they take place. Much of the innovation in the offshore petroleum sector focuses on overcoming these challenges. As Lebanon is a potential emerging offshore oil and gas producer, it must be prepared to address environmental challenges that are intrinsic to the sector.

In many respects, the Lebanese environmental governance system meets international standards. However, there are various gaps that need to be addressed to ensure the Lebanese government is prepared to manage the environmental risks associated with offshore oil and gas activities. Existing legislation covers the majority of environmental issues related to the oil and gas sector. However, some requirements are not covered, such as the management and disposal of drill cuttings and fluids, produced water, and NORM wastes, which are the main pollutant streams that arise from the offshore petroleum sector. Decrees that cover these issues need to be issued and supported by specific guidelines that the oil and gas sector will be required to follow. Also, the limits, conditions, and procedures for issuing different types of environmental permits have yet to be specified. With regard to environmental impact assessment (EIA) studies, it is imperative that an agreement be reached on whether an EIA (or at least an initial environmental examination [IEE]) will be required for the exploration phase, and particularly for exploratory drilling activities, which can have significant environmental impacts if not properly managed. Mishandling of this issue could lead to major delays in the exploration phase.

Most identified gaps can be overcome by completing the environmental legislation framework through issuing additional necessary decrees and other official decisions that clearly delineate the roles of relevant Lebanese institutions in environmental management and strengthen the capacity of these institutions, in particular that of the Ministry of Environment (MOE).

276 *The Future of Petroleum in Lebanon*

In an effort to best examine these issues, this chapter has been divided into four sections.[1] Section one describes environmental risks associated with exploration and extraction of petroleum in the Lebanese offshore. International best practices in environmental regulation of the oil and gas sector are outlined in section two. Section three offers an overview of the existing environmental governance system in Lebanon. The chapter ends with a set of conclusions and recommendations.

Environmental threats and risks

The main environmental threats that may arise from offshore exploration and production are described in this section. Potential environmental effects and risks that occur throughout the exploration and production phases are illustrated in Figures 11.1 and 11.2.

Prospecting and exploration phase

Seismic surveys and exploratory drilling during the exploration phase can each have a significant effect on Lebanon's offshore environment.

Effects of noise from seismic and drilling activities on marine animals

During seismic exploration activities, the main environmental threats include the impact of noise generating activities. Sound is readily transmitted underwater and there is potential for noise produced by seismic sources to have adverse effects on marine animals. The use of underwater sound is important for many marine mammals (e.g. seals, whales, and dolphins), as they use sound to navigate, communicate, and forage effectively. The introduction of additional noise into the marine environment could potentially (through masking effects) interfere with these animals' ability to determine the presence of predators, food, and underwater land features and obstructions (Richardson *et al.* 1995). It could therefore cause short-term behavioral changes and, in more extreme cases, there is a risk of temporary or permanent auditory trauma to marine mammals within a range of several hundred meters of a typical air gun array, particularly if they swim beneath the array.

The animals most likely to be affected by sound produced from a seismic survey are baleen whales, beaked whales, and seals, as it is believed that most toothed whale species are less affected by sound frequencies used in seismic operations (Evans 1998, Gordon *et al.* 2004).

Additionally, underwater noise may also cause behavioral changes in other animals such as fish and cephalopods. The behavioral response exhibited by fish is to move away from seismic survey sound sources temporarily. Research indicates that such

---

[1] Supplementary annexes breaking down the environmental protection regime of the United States, Norway, Ireland, the United Arab Emirates, and Qatar and describing Lebanon's environmental protection regime are available on LCPS's website via the following link: https://www.lcps-lebanon.org/publications/1464090554-ricardo-dima_eng_web.pdf

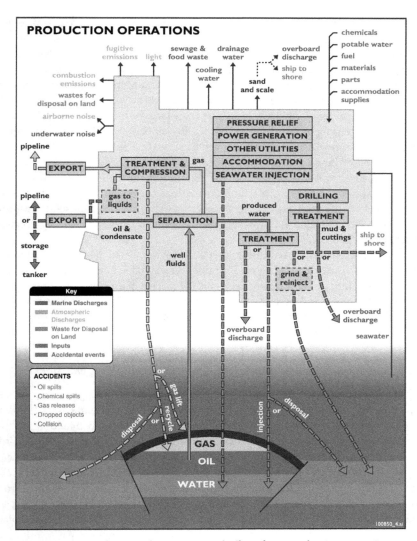

Figure 11.1 Sources of potential environmental effects from production operations.
Source: Hartley Anderson Limited (2001).

movements are short-lived and that fish stocks will most likely return to the targeted area after completion of the survey. Research also indicates that larval fish and eggs can be killed within two meters of a detonating air gun source (Coull et al. 1998).

During exploratory drilling, sound levels originating from offshore installations are dependent on platform type. Semi-submersible installations may generate more radiated sound than fixed installations when using thrusters to maintain position. Little information has been published on which sources and propagation processes are most significant in generating sound from installations, although sound generated

278   *The Future of Petroleum in Lebanon*

during drilling operations—by the drill bit itself, the drill string, or riser—does not appear to be a significant source (NCE 2007).

Vessels used to support offshore operations are also a source of sound that radiates from propellers/thrusters and internal machinery. The characteristics of sound generated by shipping are determined by ship size, mode of propulsion, operational characteristics, speed, and other factors (NCE 2007). In addition, rigs will be visited several times a week for personnel transfers. Low-flying helicopters may increase localized underwater noise levels. In such instances, a majority of the sound will be reflected off the sea surface. Only animals immediately below aircraft will therefore be affected.

Individual drilling operations only occur for a short time. During these drilling operations, noise will be generated as the drill moves through the seabed strata, in addition to noise produced by machinery vibrations and generator noise. On a semi-submersible rig, the drilling machinery and generators are located on solid platforms above water, where sound is lost as it transmits through the air and the rig flotation structure (Richardson *et al.* 1995).

Low frequency noises from drilling wells and all associated vessels will add to the ambient noise in an exploration area. The impact of generated noise is difficult to assess due to uncertainties in how noise affects specific marine mammals, in addition to the distances that noise will be transmitted. It is estimated that such underwater noise could elicit a response from some individual marine mammals if they pass within one kilometer of a drilling rig.

Risks to human health and the environment from atmospheric emissions

Exhaust emissions from ships include air pollutants, greenhouse gases, and ozone-depleting substances that entail risks to human health and the environment. The impacts of these potential emissions are generally mitigated by the open and dispersive environment offshore. Shipping in general is built and operated according to standards that preclude significant impacts on the health of their crews, while other environmental receptors (e.g. flora and fauna) tend to be sparsely distributed and/or transient in the local area. The main sources of atmospheric emissions from drilling activity will be from drilling rigs and associated vessels, as well as aircraft support. Drilling rigs typically are powered by diesel engines that emit air pollutants including CO, NOx, SOx, particulate matter (PM), volatile organic compounds (VOCs), and greenhouse gases, primarily $CO2$. Support vessels and helicopters will also emit air pollutants from the combustion of diesel fuel (vessels) and aviation fuel. Also, in the event that drilling is successful and hydrocarbons are discovered, atmospheric emissions may additionally include those arising from the combustion of produced hydrocarbons during well testing.

Impacts on fishing, shipping activities and sub-sea features due to the presence of survey vessels and drill and support vessels

Survey vessels have limited capability to avoid other vessels. Acquisition of 2D seismic data requires the towing of a single streamer from 3 kilometers to 12 kilometers in length at about 5 meters depth. Surveys operate in a grid pattern and therefore require a turning area at the end of each line. Three dimensional seismic surveys, however, tow a number of streamers in parallel and the length of streamers are shorter than those used in 2D seismic surveys, about three kilometers in length. In both cases, while the survey is being conducted, survey vessels are limited in their ability to take evasive action with respect to other shipping. Fishing vessels will be unable to operate in the vicinity of a seismic survey and will therefore lose access to grounds in the survey area for the duration of the survey.

The presence of drill and support vessels may interfere with other sea users. During exploratory drilling, the exclusion zone that surrounds a drilling rig is patrolled by a safety standby vessel. This will lead to the temporary loss of fishing access and will require other vessels to avoid the area. Interference with other sea users (especially the fishing industry) due to the physical presence of a rig, vessels, and subsea equipment, should be expected. Supply vessels and helicopters will ferry goods and personnel to and from the drilling rig, leading to an increase in vessel traffic in the region.

Seismic survey and exploratory drilling activities may interfere with subsea benthic communities, archaeological sites, and infrastructure. Some types of seismic surveys involve a limited amount of sea floor disturbance. The extent of sea floor disturbance should be minimal, and in most cases impacts are negligible.

In order for exploration drilling to take place, a drilling rig is towed into position over a well site by towing vessels and anchored into position by the same vessels. Depending on the type of drilling rig used, sea floor sediments could be disturbed during installation and removal of drilling rigs. After a drilling rig is removed, anchor scars will likely remain on the sea bottom for months to years. The anchor scars will eventually disappear as sediments are redistributed by currents and benthic organisms. The main concern with regard to potential impacts is the placement of anchors in areas where protected benthic communities, coral communities, and areas of special marine biodiversity importance exist. Underwater archaeological sites and submarine infrastructure may be susceptible to physical damage if not identified and avoided prior to initiation of activities.

Drilling operations may also impact the seascape value. While seismic survey activities will not be distinguishable from other normal shipping activities, drilling operations will be. The visibility of the rig from the shore depends on its proximity to the shore and on other factors such as sea and weather conditions.

Migrating birds can become disoriented by light sources at night. Birds may use offshore structures for resting, feeding, or as temporary shelter from inclement weather. Evidence indicates that migrating birds can become disoriented when encountering a steady artificial light source at night, likely as a result of a disruption in their internal magnetic compass used for navigation. Birds can become "trapped" when a light source enters their zone of influence at night. This phenomenon can cause birds to circle the light source for hours, increasing the risk of collision with the lighted structure, decreasing fat reserves, and potentially interrupting migration.

Effects of exploratory drilling operations on seawater quality

Routine discharges during seismic surveys and exploratory drilling typically include treated sewage and domestic wastes (including food waste), deck drainage, and bilge and ballast water. These are subject to the International Convention for the Prevention of Pollution from Ships (MARPOL) regulations. Such discharges may affect concentrations of suspended solids, nutrients, and chlorine, in addition to generating biological oxygen demand. These discharges are expected to be diluted rapidly in the open sea but discharges in sensitive areas must be avoided.

During drilling of exploration and appraisal wells, drill cuttings and spent drilling muds require disposal. Cuttings and particulate material from water-based muds used to drill the top hole section(s) are typically deposited on the seabed near the wellhead. A small quantity of the cement used to secure the first set of casings in the borehole is also deposited in the same location. Cuttings generated from subsequent sections of a well are contaminated with residual drilling muds and associated chemicals.

Most of the discharged material will end up as deposits on the seabed, where the main potential for environmental impact occurs. Additionally, discharges from caissons create plumes of suspended fine sediment, which may cause localized chemical changes as sediment settles through the water column. The impacts of drilling discharges on both the seabed and its associated fauna, as well as on marine organisms in the water column, must be considered. Chemicals are added to drilling muds and to cement used to secure well casings. Drilling rigs and ships also carry contingency chemicals that might be used in the event of an abnormal occurrence. The potential for such chemicals to be toxic to marine organisms when discharged therefore needs to be assessed and policies need to be put in place to avoid significant negative impacts. In many jurisdictions, when oil-based mud or synthetic-based mud is used, no discharge is allowed into the sea and onshore disposal is required.

Accidental events associated with the oil industry

The risk of accidental hydrocarbon and/or chemical spillage into the sea is one of the main environmental concerns associated with oil industry developments. Spilled oil and chemicals at sea can have a number of environmental and economic impacts, the most noticeable of which affect seabirds and marine mammals. The actual impacts depend on many factors, including the volume and type of oil or chemical spilled, and sea and weather conditions.

Oil may enter the marine environment during seismic operations as a result of accidental streamer rupture or collision with another vessel. The most likely scenario is spillages of several hundred liters of kerosene-like oil entering the environment from a streamer becoming disconnected while deployed. However, seismic survey vessels may have numerous streamers deployed containing several thousand liters of oil each and the potential for larger volume spills cannot be ruled out. A worst-case scenario would entail accidental collision with another vessel and a complete loss of fuel inventory and streamer reservoir.

Strengthening Oil and Gas Environmental Governance

During exploration and appraisal drilling, there is a risk of spillage of oil (fuel/crude), and spillage or leakage of chemicals. Drilling accidents are usually associated with unexpected blowouts of liquid and gaseous hydrocarbons from a well as a result of encountering zones with abnormally high pressure. No situations other than tanker oil spills are as frequent or severe as drilling accidents. Broadly speaking, two major categories of drilling accidents should be distinguished. One covers catastrophic situations involving intense and prolonged hydrocarbon gushing. These occur when the pressure in a drilling zone is so high that usual technological methods of well muffling are not sufficient. The probability of such extreme situations is relatively low, with some oil experts estimating it at one incident per ten thousand wells. The other group of accidental situations includes regular, routine episodes of hydrocarbon spills and blowouts during drilling operations. These accidents can be controlled rather effectively (in several hours or days) by closing the well with the help of blowout preventers and by changing the density of the drilling fluid. Accidents of this kind often do not receive considerable media coverage or public attention but their ecological hazard and associated environmental risks can be rather considerable, primarily due to their regularity, leading ultimately to chronic impacts on the marine environment.

Hydrocarbon spills

When oil is released into a marine environment, it undergoes a number of physicochemical changes, some of which assist in the degradation of the spill, while others may cause it to persist. These changes are dependent upon the type and volume of oil spilled, and prevailing weather and sea conditions (Figure 11.1). Evaporation and dispersion are the two main mechanisms that remove oil from the sea surface. Following a hydrocarbon spill, evaporation is the initial predominant mechanism of reducing an oil mass, as light fractions (including aromatic compounds such as benzene and toluene) evaporate quickly. If spilled oil contains a high percentage of light hydrocarbon fractions—such as diesel—a large portion of the spilled oil will evaporate relatively quickly in comparison to heavier (crude) oil. The evaporation process is enhanced by warm air temperatures and moderate winds and can produce considerable changes in the density, viscosity, and volume of the spill.

After light fractions have evaporated from a slick, the degradation process slows down and natural dispersion becomes the dominant mechanism in reducing slick volume. This process is dependent upon sea surface turbulence, which in turn is affected by wind speed. Water soluble components of the oil mass will dissolve in seawater, while immiscible components will either emulsify and disperse as small droplets in the water column (an oil-in-water emulsion) or, under certain sea conditions, aggregate into tight water-in-oil emulsions, often referred to as "chocolate mousse." In practice, usually only one of the two processes will take place or be dominant. Thick (large) oil slicks tend to form water-in-oil emulsions, whereas thin (smaller) slicks tend to form oil-in-water emulsions that usually disappear due to natural dispersion.

When a water-in-oil emulsion ("chocolate mousse") is formed, the overall volume of such a water-in-oil emulsion increases significantly, as it may contain up to

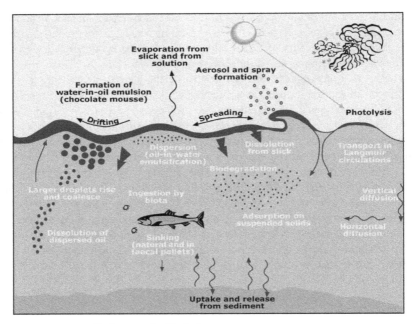

Figure 11.2 Fate and behavior of spilled oil at sea.
Source: ERT (Scotland) Ltd, IOSEA1, Ireland (2006).

70 percent or 80 percent water. This chocolate mousse will form a thick layer on the sea surface, reducing slick spreading and inhibiting natural dispersion. By diminishing the surface area available for weathering and degradation, these chocolate mousses will be difficult to break up using dispersants. In their emulsified form, with drastically increased volume, they can cause complications for mechanical recovery devices as well.

Wind and surface current speed and direction are the main parameters affecting where a slick travels. A slick will travel in the same general direction as surface water currents and a prevailing wind drives a slick downwind at 3 to 4 percent of wind speed.

Spill modeling in the oil and gas industry is undertaken as a matter of course as there is usually a requirement, prior to drilling, that an Oil Spill Contingency Plan (OSCP) be prepared. For crude oil spills, modeling must be based on the expected characteristics of the crude, i.e. heavy/light, which are determined by the reservoir the crude originated from. Therefore, site-specific modeling should be undertaken where drilling is expected to take place in an oil bearing formation. The OSCP produced for all drilling operations will specify the level of spill response equipment and facilities present both offshore and onshore.

Factors important to determining oil spill impacts and recovery rates include the type of oil, the thickness of shore deposits, climate and season, biological and physical characteristics of the area, relative sensitivity of species and communities, and type of clean-up response. A summary of impacts arising from oil spills is provided below.

- Plankton: Short-term effects have been recorded in the industry. However, serious impacts on planktonic organisms have not been observed in the open sea. The main impact is considered to be through initial acute toxicity, while long-term effects have been reduced, possibly due to the high reproductive rates and immigration from outside an affected area.
- Benthos: Effects on benthos include acute toxicity and possible organic enrichment. Offshore impacts are likely to be minimal and influenced by water depth and local hydrography. Shallow inshore areas and the shoreline are susceptible to heavy mortalities if coated with fresh crude oil. Recovery times are variable, dependent on many environmental factors, and may be in the region of one to ten-plus years.
- Fish and cephalopods: Adult fish tend to avoid impacted areas, however, populations moving back into an affected area may take some time to recover. Eggs and larvae in shallow areas may suffer heavy mortalities under fresh slicks, particularly if dispersants are used. There is no evidence that offshore fish populations have been significantly affected by a spill. Spills that affect spawning migration of fish into rivers can affect populations in subsequent years.
- Mammals and reptiles: It has been rare for cetaceans to be affected following a spill. They are able to avoid affected areas and are not believed to be susceptible to the physical impacts of oil emulsion, specifically lowering their resistance to the cold. Respiratory problems may be caused by volatile hydrocarbon fractions, for example in seals, which are susceptible to oiling and the contamination of food sources, particularly in coastal areas surrounding their colonies. Impacts on marine turtles are considered to be similar to those for cetaceans but if nesting beaches are polluted, they may be significantly affected.
- Birds: Potential fatalities of offshore species may arise, although this tends to be dependent on species present at the time of the spill. Birds are sensitive to physical fouling of feathers and toxicity by ingestion.
- Archaeology: Historic wrecks and archaeological sites in sheltered shallow water on the coast may be at risk from large hydrocarbon spills. An OSCP should take the location of these sites into account when adopting a response strategy. Impacts on coastal archaeology are associated with smothering and damage from cleanup operations.
- Fisheries and mariculture: Fish exposed to oil may become tainted by oil-derived substances. This is of particular concern in caged fish and shellfish. Major spills can result in a loss of fishing days and exclusion zones and bans on certain species may be enforced which last several years. Media coverage together with public perception can also damage fisheries and lead to a loss of market confidence that can hurt fishing businesses, even those located in areas unaffected by the spill.
- Tourism: Coastal tourism is vulnerable to the effects of major oil spills. The impact would be influenced by a number of factors including media coverage and public perception. When an oil spill occurs, not only are tourist destinations directly affected in areas where the spill has flooded land and washed up on beaches, but the tourism industry also faces serious reputational impacts. Public perception strongly influences people's decisions about whether to visit and spend time in a particular community.

Chemical spills

The environmental implication of a chemical spill is largely dependent on the type of chemical involved, the size and location of the spill, and weather conditions at the time. The actual hazard presented by a spill will depend on exposure concentration, which is determined by the quantity and rate of spillage as well as dilution and dispersion rates. These factors will differ according to whether the spill takes place at the sea surface or seabed.

The dilution and dispersion of a sea surface spill will depend on the sea state at the time: larger waves will be more effective at dispersing the spill than calm sea states. An oil spill is generally diluted as it sinks and will be moved by tidal currents and wave activity. Diluted chemicals are also carried with the body of ambient seawater and gradually disperse and degrade. Although it may be detectable within a circle of a tidal motion, a spill will only be toxic within a very limited area and for a short period of time.

The fate of a spill at seabed level will depend on the properties of a chemical. If a chemical is denser than seawater it may spread over the seabed and become mixed within the substrate, causing potential harm to benthic communities. A lighter chemical will leach into the water column and be dispersed with currents.

Gas blowouts

A gas blowout occurs when a drilling pipe encounters a shallow or a deep pressurized gas zone or an over-pressured rock layer in the subsurface without being prepared to counter the pressure. This allows the gas or the fluid from the rock layer to enter the drilling pipe and flow toward the surface. Any gas zone penetrated before a blowout preventer (BOP) has been installed is known as a shallow gas blowout.

Based on an OGP 2010 report, blowout frequency during exploration drilling for deepwater HPHT wells (high pressure/high-temperature) is 1 in every 526 wells drilled, and in the case of deepwater the frequency is 1 in every 3,226 wells drilled for offshore operations of North Sea standard and 1 in every 714 wells drilled for offshore operations not of North Sea standard (OGP 2010). While potentially dangerous, there are few studies available on gas interactions with the marine environment. Naturally occurring gas blowouts have been linked to gas hydrates and form a potential natural geohazard in the marine environment.

Atmospheric emissions may occur as a result of a blowout in an emergency situation. Emissions would be reservoir specific and are likely to contain a large proportion of methane (CH_4) with smaller amounts of volatile organic compounds. In the unlikely event of an explosion and hydrocarbons burn, combustion products including carbon dioxide (CO_2) and carbon monoxide (CO) will be emitted.

During development and production phase

Development drilling, the presence of production facilities, and accidents have the potential to present a threat to both wildlife and humans.

Atmospheric emissions entail risks to human health and the environment

The main sources of atmospheric emissions from the operation of rigs will be from power generation on a platform and associated vessels and support aircraft. Platform equipment are typically powered by diesel engines or natural gas that emit air pollutants including CO, NOx, SOx, PM, VOCs, and greenhouse gases such as CO_2 and CH_4.

Another source of emissions related to oil production is the associated gas brought to the surface, which is disposed of at offshore facilities by venting or flaring into the atmosphere. This practice is now widely recognized to be a waste of a valuable resource, as well as a significant source of GHG emissions. However, flaring or venting is also an important safety measure used on offshore oil and gas facilities to ensure gas and other hydrocarbons are safely disposed of in the event of an emergency, power or equipment failure, or other plant upset condition.

Sub-sea features, birds, fishing and shipping activities may be impacted by the physical presence of production facilities and support vessels

Sea floor-disturbing activities during installation of production facilities will re-suspend bottom sediments, crush benthic organisms, and produce turbidity. The impacts of facility installation will depend on the type of facility selected for a particular project. Physical impacts on the sea bottom may occur in connection with installing pipelines, cables, and platforms, including platform legs and anchoring.

The main concern with regard to potential impacts is the placement of structures in areas where sensitive benthic communities, coral communities, and areas of special marine biodiversity importance exist. Production facilities typically remain in place for a long period of time and the physical presence of platforms will attract pelagic fish. Noise and lights may cause minor behavioral changes in marine mammals and sea turtles (e.g., attraction or avoidance). Benthic communities may be affected by sloughing of organic debris from platforms and by the physical presence of pipelines on the sea floor.

The visibility of a platform from the shore depends on its proximity to the shore and on other factors such as sea and weather conditions. Platforms typically are visible from shore at distances of 5–16 kilometers. On a clear night, lights on top of offshore structures can be visible at a distance of approximately 32 kilometers.

Similar to impacts during exploratory drilling, the presence of platforms and support vessels may interact with shipping and marine transport. The movements of support vessels may lead to a slight increase in vessel activity in the region during the operation period.

Drilling discharge effects on sea floor and sea water quality

Impacts during development drilling would be qualitatively similar to those during exploratory drilling (discussed earlier). However, because numerous wells would be drilled at each production location, the real extent and severity of benthic impacts would be greater than for exploratory drilling.

The impact of the discharge of drilling wastes will primarily affect the seabed rather than the sea surface or water column. Drilling fluids and cuttings will accumulate on the sea floor if discharged directly, resulting in changes in bottom contours, grain size, Barium concentrations, and concentrations of other metals. Impacts on benthic communities from discharges of mud and cement may occur in the immediate vicinity of each well (within approximately 50 meters), and will likely recover within months or a few years. Routine discharges during operations typically include produced water, well workover and completion fluids, treated sewage and domestic wastes, deck drainage, and other discharges. Produced water refers to water found in reservoirs along with oil or gas. When oil or gas is extracted, produced water is associated with it. Entrained within the water are hydrocarbons that, as much as possible, are removed from the water prior to any discharge. As the volume of hydrocarbons found in a reservoir decreases over the life of the field, the volume of produced water generally increases.

Produced water includes formation water, condensed water, brine, injection water, and other technological wastes, which usually consist of oil, natural hydrocarbons, inorganic salts, and technological chemicals. The discharge of produced water accounts for the greatest portion of wastes arising from offshore oil and gas production operations. Produced water, having been in contact with various rock strata at elevated pressure and temperature, contains many soluble components including Barium and the radioactive intermediates of the Uranium and Thorium decay series. As the water is produced, temperature and pressure decreases, creating conditions in which Barium and radionuclides can co-precipitate inside separators, valves, and pipework, forming an insoluble naturally-occurring radioactive material (NORM) scale. Some of the soluble radionuclides and particles of NORM scale will pass through the system and be discharged with produced water. Similarly, some particulate scale and soluble radionuclides will be entrained with the exported oil by pipeline and discharged from the onshore terminal.

Additional miscellaneous discharges typically occur from numerous sources on an offshore platform. Examples include workover and completion fluids (brines), sanitary and domestic waste, deck drainage, uncontaminated freshwater and seawater used for cooling and ballast, desalination unit discharges, BOP fluids, and boiler blowdown discharges. These discharges are required to meet MARPOL requirements.

Accidental events

The risk of accidental hydrocarbon and/or chemical spillage into the sea is one of the main environmental concerns associated with oil industry developments. Spilled oil and chemicals at sea can have a number of environmental and economic impacts, the most conspicuous of which are on seabirds and marine mammals. The actual impacts depend on many factors, including the volume and type of oil spilled and sea and weather conditions. During the production phase, there is a risk of oil spillages (fuel/crude) and spillage or leakage of chemicals. The impacts from accidental events during the operation phase are similar to those during drilling operations (discussed earlier).

Abandoning oil fields

Impacts from platform decommissioning are dependent on the type of facility removed and the proposed decommissioning plan. If explosive charges are used for platform removal, then there is a risk of impacts to fish, marine mammals, and sea turtles. The large amounts of different types of waste that will result from the removal of a structure may have a significant impact on existing waste management infrastructure in the country and result in the spread of pollution on land.

Naturally occurring radioactive substances in scale, sludge, and other deposits on oil and gas platforms may be found in different parts of the processing equipment, including valves, wellheads, risers, separators, hydrocyclones, and piping. They may also be present in subsea systems and pipelines that convey hydrocarbons to the processing installation they are linked to. The same applies to wellhead platforms.

Also, the disposal of large amounts of marine fouling will pose an environmental threat whether disposed of offshore or on land. Decommissioning of offshore installations can complicate fishery operations and the aquaculture industry more generally, including fish farming. For fisheries, any problems are largely related to the offshore phase of decommissioning and include restrictions on access to select areas.

International best practices in environmental management in the oil and gas sector

Different environmental management systems for offshore petroleum activities are adopted worldwide. The main aspects of environmental management in the offshore petroleum industry in the US, Norway, Ireland, United Arab Emirates, and Qatar are presented below. These have been categorized in terms of environmental regulatory authority, main environmental legislation, environmental risk assessment, environmental permits, monitoring, enforcement and assurance mechanisms, and emergency preparedness and response.

Environmental regulatory authority

Throughout the world, petroleum producing states have government agencies—each with its own prerogatives and authority—which oversee extractive operations. By assessing such agencies in different countries, it is possible to compare and better assess the environmental regulatory regime in Lebanon.

The United States has three agencies responsible for overseeing extractive operations: the Bureau of Safety and Environmental Enforcement (BSEE), the United States Coast Guard (USCG), and the United States Environmental Protection Agency (EPA). The BSEE, formerly under the Minerals Management Service,[2] has several

---

[2] Bureau of Safety and Environmental Enforcement. 2016. United States Department of the Interior. http://www.bsee.gov/

288 *The Future of Petroleum in Lebanon*

functions which include the development and enforcement of safety and environmental regulations; permitting offshore exploration and production; oil-spill response and training; and environmental compliance programs. It has the authority to inspect, investigate, and produce evidence; levy penalties; cancel or suspend activities; and oversee safety, response, and removal preparedness. The second agency, USCG, is responsible for protecting the public, environment, and US economic and security interests in all maritime regions. Finally, the EPA has as a primary responsibility to enforce environmental regulations concerning air quality, water quality, and waste in the Outer Continental Shelf.

In Norway, the Norwegian Environment Agency (NEA) is responsible for managing Norwegian nature and preventing pollution. The NEA monitors the state of the environment, conveys environment-related information, oversees and guides regional and municipal authorities, cooperates with relevant industry authorities, acts as an expert advisor, and assists in international environmental efforts.

The main agency for environmental protection and policing in Ireland is the Environmental Protection Agency. Its primary responsibilities include environmental licensing, enforcement of environmental laws, monitoring, and reporting environment-related activities.[3]

The de-facto regulator of health, safety, and environment (HSE) matters in the oil and gas industry in Abu Dhabi is the Abu Dhabi National Oil Company (ADNOC). ADNOC has established a Memorandum of Understanding with the Abu Dhabi Environment Agency (EAD), whereby the EAD only interferes where projects may affect protected areas. In other UAE emirates, each municipality's environmental department acts as the environmental regulator.

And finally, in Qatar, the Ministry of Environment is the ultimate authority responsible for environmental management.[4] It reviews and approves all EIA studies prepared by oil and gas companies in Qatar and monitors their implementation by issuing permits to build and operate.

It can be concluded that in all benchmark states except for Abu Dhabi in the UAE, environmental regulatory authority is independent from the oil and gas licensing authority. This is essential to ensure the independence of the opinion of the environmental regulatory authority, that environmental measures are implemented, and to avoid conflicts of interest.

Environmental legislation

The main pieces of legislation related to the offshore oil and gas industry in the US are the National Environmental Policy Act (NEPA), 30 CFR 250/550 "Oil and gas and Sulphur operations in the Outer Continental Shelf" (includes requirements for pollution prevention), and 40 CFR "Protection of the environment" under the EPA, Clean Water Act, and Clear Air Act. Such legislation in Norway includes the Petroleum

---

[3] Environmental Protection Agency, Ireland. http://www.epa.ie
[4] Qatar. Ministry of Municipal and Environment. http://www.mme.gov.qa/cui/index.dox?siteID=2

Activities Act, Pollution Control Act,[5] Product Control Act, HSE regulations comprising the framework regulation, management regulation, facilities regulation and activities regulation, and general pollution and waste regulations. In Ireland, environmental legislation comprises the Petroleum and Other Minerals Development Act, Protection of the Environment Act, Dumping at Sea Act, Waste Management Act, and Petroleum Safety Act. The Federal Environmental Law, Federal Petroleum Resources Conservation Law, UAE Cabinet Regulation for the Protection of Maritime Environment, and local environmental regulations as dictated in every emirate are the main legislation applicable to the offshore oil and gas industry in Abu Dhabi. Moreover, ADNOC has issued several codes of practice, including those on the environment, to be implemented by oil and gas companies. In Qatar, general laws apply to the offshore oil and gas industry, which include the Natural Resources Law, Environmental Protection Law, and Law on Exploitation and Protection of Marine Life. The MOE has also recently issued a modern law for the management of NORM wastes.

General environmental legislation applies to the oil and gas sector in all benchmark countries, yet specific petroleum sector legislation includes certain environmental provisions and requirements such as those related to flaring and venting.

Environmental risk assessment

Environmental studies, whether environmental impact statements, environmental area assessments, or EIAs are required for all phases of oil and gas operations.

In the US, the NEPA requires federal agencies to incorporate environmental considerations into their planning and decision making. The NEPA process consists of an evaluation of the environmental effects of a federal undertaking, which then either is determined to have no significant environmental impact, or requires an environmental assessment or environmental impact statement. Under Norwegian law, strategic environmental assessment must be carried out before new areas for petroleum activities can be opened. This process is carried out by the resource authority, Ministry of Petroleum and Energy, and NPD. Furthermore, environmental authorities (NEA) may need additional assessment and information as part of the application process under the Pollution Control Act before issuing the pollution permit for exploration and production drilling. In Ireland, a strategic environmental assessment and environmental area assessment are compulsory during the exploration phase, and an environmental impact statement is required during production. Similarly, EIAs must be undertaken for oil and gas projects in the UAE, and in Qatar, an EIA is required before undertaking any kind of development projects or other industrial activities that may have a harmful impact on the environment.

Environmental permits

Although the nature of permits differs across countries, they all cover air emissions, flaring, and venting; discharges at sea; and waste management, and are generally granted by the environmental regulatory authority.

---

[5] Norwegian Ministry of Climate and Environment. 1981. *Pollution Control Act*. 13 March.

In the US, a new or modified exploration or development oil and gas operation requires several permits, including a local land use development permit, drilling permit, and an operating permit. To obtain these permits, projects must comply with certain federal and state emissions regulations, such as the National Emission Standards for Hazardous Air Pollutants and the Clean Water Act (CWA). Under the CWA, all discharges of pollutants to surface waters (including oceans) must be authorized by a permit. In April 2012, the EPA passed rules to address air emissions from oil and gas activities, which dictate that oil and gas well operators reduce air emissions. The Pollution Control Act in Norway requires a pollution permit by the NEA, which includes requirements related to emission limits, discharges, use of chemicals, handling of waste, and emergency preparedness requirements, among others. Gas flaring and venting is regulated by the Petroleum Act, under which the level of gas flaring and venting cannot exceed the quantities determined by the Ministry of Petroleum and Energy (MPE). The permit in Ireland is an Integrated Pollution Prevention and Control License, issued by the EPA. The License covers all emissions from the facility and its environmental management. In the UAE, the Federal Environmental Law lists obligations regarding emissions, including discharge obligations; obligations regarding the handling, transportation, and disposal of hazardous substances and wastes; and burning of any fuel or other substances in oil and gas operations. The Federal Petroleum Resources Conservation Law sets out requirements for dealing with associated gas in the production of oil. Moreover, an environmental permit is generally linked to the approval of an EIA study. Permits for each project in Qatar are granted by the MOE and address all issues involving environmental impact, including permitted emissions and discharges during the extraction and processing of oil and gas. The permit is primarily issued as a result of an EIA study and in the form of a consent to operate (CTO) which is renewed on a yearly basis. The CTO is only renewed if the MOE finds that the operator is complying with environmental requirements based on the findings of an audit and review of the operator's environmental reports.

Monitoring/enforcement/assurance mechanisms

Generally, the environmental regulatory authority monitors compliance by conducting audits and inspections and issuing reports. Scheduled and unannounced inspections are conducted to ensure compliance with license conditions and environmental requirements. Authorities either issue reports of noncompliance or certificates of compliance/consent to operate.

The Outer Continental Shelf Lands Act in the US authorizes and requires the BSEE to carry out both an annual scheduled inspection and a periodic unscheduled (unannounced) inspection of all oil and gas operations on the Outer Continental Shelf (OCS). Additionally, industry self-inspections are required by regulation, and third party reviews for deepwater or novel structures. In Norway, the NEA monitors compliance through audits, inspections, checking annual reports, and assessing environmental monitoring programs, in addition to imposing sanctions when needed. Compliance at activity level in Ireland is monitored by the DCENR, while the EPA

Strengthening Oil and Gas Environmental Governance

monitors changes in the environment and adherence to the conditions of the IPC license. The Office of Environmental Enforcement is a dedicated office within the EPA dealing with the implementation and enforcement of environmental legislation. In the UAE, the ADNOC HSE department conducts self-monitoring in Abu Dhabi, while the environmental departments in other emirates conduct inspections. Finally, in Qatar, the MOE conducts inspections and issues/renews consent to operate certificates.

Emergency preparedness and response

Operators are required to submit oil spill response plans that act as a first layer of environmental protection. These plans should be formulated in line with national oil spill response plans prepared by competent authorities. In most cases, emergency response and cleaning required at a national level are led by coastguard authorities.

The primary responsibility for oil spill response efforts in the US lies within the USCG, while the BSEE is responsible for planning (i.e. reviewing preparations) for potential oil spills on the OCS. Operators are required to submit oil spill response plans for approval by the bureau. The EPA and USCG are the main bodies that coordinate national contingency plan preparedness and response activities. In Norway, the Petroleum Safety Authority (PSA) is responsible for all preventive measures related to emergency accidents and major accidents affecting the environment. The Norwegian Environmental Authority (NEA) is tasked with setting out emergency preparedness requirements in pollution permits, comprising an emergency preparedness plan that includes detection time for oil in water, type of equipment, and use of dispersant chemicals. Operators coordinate their own as well as contractors' emergency preparedness plans. The Norwegian Clean Seas Association for Operating Companies (NOFO) is responsible for oil spill response, planning, and preparedness on behalf of companies[6] and the Norwegian Coastal Administration is responsible for the operational side of such clean-ups.[7] Emergency preparedness in Ireland is the operator's obligation, while oil spill preparedness and response is that of the Irish Coast Guard. Local authorities are responsible for the shoreline response under the oversight of the Irish Coast Guard. Oil spill preparedness and response in Abu Dhabi is the task of the Supreme Petroleum Council and ADNOC, while in Qatar, it is that of Qatar Petroleum's Oil Spill and Emergency Response Department (OS&ERD). This department also monitors operations and provides support if needed. Oil spill and clean-up operations are carried out by the Doha Port Management.

Existing environmental governance system in Lebanon

A detailed review of existing environmental governance systems for offshore petroleum activities in Lebanon is presented in the sub-sections below.

---

[6] Norwegian Clean Seas Association for Operating Companies. "Our Operation: Dimensioned Oil Recovery Preparedness in Norway." https://www.nofo.no/en/our-operation/
[7] Norwegian Coastal Administration. http://www.kystverket.no/en

Environmental regulatory authority

The MOE is the main body responsible for environment protection and management in Lebanon. The role of the MOE in the oil and gas sector is explicitly defined in the 2010 Offshore Petroleum Resources Law (OPRL)[8] and the Petroleum Activities Regulations (PAR) Decree No. 10289/2013. The ministry is tasked with supervising the conduct of petroleum activities and ensuring its overall compliance with environmental standards and regulations. In Article 60, the OPRL grants the MOE the authority to "supervise; control environmental matters related to petroleum activities; coordinate with other concerned authorities; and take initiatives or measures deemed necessary to minimize negative impacts that petroleum activities may have on local communities and the environment." Other provisions in the OPRL and the PAR refer to the MOE, particularly in relation to an EIA report and other environmental concerns including monitoring and site inspection.

Different departments of the MOE will be involved with petroleum activities, particularly the Department of Natural Resources Protection, Department of Ecosystems, Department of Chemical Safety, Department of Air Quality, Department of Integrated Environmental Systems, and the Department of Monitoring and Statistics, among others.

The new petroleum sector will require capacity building of existing departments at the MOE to cater to new requirements introduced by the petroleum sector. The need to establish a dedicated department for oil and gas should be assessed against empowering specific departments in the existing structure. At the very least, the capacity of a dedicated team from the MOE needs to be strengthened, particularly in the areas of EIAs, mitigation and monitoring, environmental audits and inspections of oil and gas facilities and assets, and environmental emergency preparedness and response.

Another primary stakeholder in environmental management of petroleum activities in Lebanon is the Lebanese Petroleum Administration (LPA). The LPA was established on 4 December 2012, to be the regulatory body in charge of managing the petroleum sector in Lebanon. The Quality, Health, Safety, and Environment Department of the LPA is responsible for all matters related to the quality of operators' systems and the extent of their adherence to the conditions of health, safety, and environment, in addition to studying applications for licenses, studying plans on quality of performance, monitoring preparedness for addressing accidents and emergencies, monitoring the compliance of operators with regulations, assessing the impact of operations on occupational and environmental health, and monitoring facilities to ensure compliance with environmental, health, and safety standards.

Other stakeholders involved in the environmental management of the petroleum sector include the Council of Ministers (COM); Ministry of Energy and Water (MEW); Committee for Field Emergencies for Energy and Water; National Emergency Response Committee (NERC); National Council for Environment; Ministry of Public Works and Transport (MOPWT); Ministry of Defense (Lebanese Navy); Lebanese Ministry of Finance (Lebanese Customs); Lebanese Standards Institution—LIBNOR;

---

[8] Lebanese Parliament. 2010. Offshore Petroleum Resources Law. Law 132, 24 August.

Disaster Risk Reduction (DRR) (within the COM); Lebanese Atomic Energy Commission (LAEC); and the Chemical, Biological, Radiological, and Nuclear (CBRN) National Team.

The above indicates that there are various authorities that have specific roles in environmental protection in Lebanon, although the main competent authority is the MOE. A clear distribution of roles is critical to avoiding major environmental impacts that arise from oil and gas operations.

Main legislation

Lebanon has ratified various conventions related to the protection of the environment and marine environmental resources. The MOE or MOPWT (depending on the convention in question) is the focal point for maritime conventions and protocols while the MOE is the focal point for other environmental conventions. In the event of discoveries of hydrocarbons in offshore Lebanon, activities in the Mediterranean Sea are expected to increase significantly, making implementation of the requirements of these conventions more challenging and resource-intensive. Effective coordination between both ministries is key to properly implementing these conventions.

Existing legislation including general environmental regulations and signed conventions—in addition to the OPRL and the PAR—covers a majority of environmental issues. However, there are some requirements that existing legislation does not cover such as the management and disposal of drill cutting and fluids, produced water, and NORM wastes, which are the main pollutant streams that arise from the offshore petroleum sector.

Additionally, some requirements referred to in existing legislation have yet to be specified or issued via decrees, such as:

- A decree to determine which industrial institutions require a permit for releasing emissions into the air and to specify the mechanism for granting a permit, which is referred to in Decree No. 2275/2009 (role of the Department of Air Quality)
- A decree to specify the list of materials permitted for discharge into the sea, which are referred to in Article 30 of Law No. 444/2002
- COM decrees mentioned in Articles 40 and 44 of Law 444/2002 related to dangerous or hazardous wastes
- Standards for the management of solid waste streams expected from the oil and gas sector (pursuant to ISWM Draft Law)
- Application of MOE Decision No. 99-1/2013, which sets the guidelines for submitting information on greenhouse gas emissions by companies and industrial and commercial institutions.

Environmental risk assessment

The requirement of conducting environmental studies for petroleum activities is stipulated in different legislative texts, namely: Law No. 444/2002 (Article 21); Law No. 690/2005 (Article 2); Offshore Petroleum Resources Law (OPRL) Law No. 132/2010

(Article 7.2, Article 29.1, Article 29.3, Article 32, Article 47.3); EIA Decree No. 8633/2012; the Petroleum Activities Regulations (PAR) Decree No. 10289/2013 (Article 43, Article 54, Articles 59/61); and the Exploration and Production Agreement (EPA) Annex 2 of Decree 43/ 2017 (Article 17).

The OPRL and the PAR require an EIA for development, production, transportation, storage, utilization, and decommissioning activities, but do not explicitly require an EIA for exploration activities. Also, the OPRL stipulates that the procedures, requirements, and conditions related to the EIA study shall be stipulated by a COM decree. The LPA has undertaken a pre-qualification process for International Oil Companies (IOCs) whereby HSE was one of the main criteria used in the pre-qualification process. This was done to ensure that pre-qualified companies have the necessary experience to manage the health, safety, and environmental risks associated with deep-offshore operations.

According to the EIA Decree, the MOE verifies whether a project falls within the domain of Annex 1 or Annex 2 of the decree or is located in an area listed in Annex 3, in addition to the likelihood of a significant impact on that area. If the proposed project falls in the domain of Annex 1, it will be subject to an "EIA" study. If it falls in the domain of Annex 2, it will be subject to an "IEE." If the proposed project is classified in the domain of Annex 2 of the decree and located in an area listed in Annex 3—or if it may have a significant environmental impact on that area—the project will be subject to an EIA study. If the project does not fall within the domain of Annex 1 or Annex 2 but is located in an area listed in Annex 3 where it may have a significant environmental impact, it will be subject to an IEE. Additionally, the minister of environment, based on an informed review, may request an IEE or an EIA report for the project regardless of its classification.

Oil and gas pipelines, tanks, refineries, drilling, and extraction of oil and gas are listed in Annex 1 of the EIA decree and thus require an EIA. However, exploration is not listed in the annexes of the decree. According to Annex 3, sensitive areas include: areas classified, by laws or decrees, as specifically protected areas, natural environment protected areas, natural forests or wetlands, important bird areas, public parks, natural scenery sites, touristic and historic sites, archaeological locations, river banks, springs, and/or holy places; areas that are habitats of endangered species; watersheds; and sea beaches, river waterways, and springs.

Since marine water is a habitat of many endangered species, and coastal areas are considered sensitive areas, oil and gas exploration activities may be subject to an IEE or EIA, even if not explicitly listed in Annex 1 or Annex 2 of the EIA decree. Additionally, the minister of environment may request an IEE or an EIA report for the project regardless of its classification.

Coordination between the minister of energy and water and minister of environment is essential to ensure an effective EIA process for oil and gas activities in offshore Lebanon. Regarding this, two points are particularly important:

- Deciding whether a new decree on an EIA specific to oil and gas activities should be issued as allowed by Article 29.3 of Law 132/2010. It is the authors' opinion that the requirement for a new EIA decree specific to oil and gas activities was included in Law 132/2010 due to the absence of an EIA decree when preparing the law. Nevertheless, this requirement is no longer needed after the EIA decree was issued in 2012 (Decree No. 8633/2012) and the EIA decree provides the necessary framework for a robust environmental assessment for oil and gas activities. The Petroleum Activities Regulations (PAR) Decree No. 10289/2013 also set some requirements for EIA studies and referred the EIA decree with regard to the content of EIA studies. Given the lack of clarity in EIA requirements for each stage of oil and gas development, it might be preferable to issue a sector-specific decree for an EIA in the offshore oil and gas sector to clarify EIA requirements for each stage of oil and gas exploration and production activities.

- Agreeing on whether an EIA (or IEE) shall be required for the exploration phase, and particularly for exploratory drilling activities. While the Offshore Petroleum Resources Law and Decree 10289 do not explicitly require it, provisions for such impact assessments are still required by Law 444 and the EIA decree. The legislation is subject to interpretation and mishandling of this issue could lead to major public opposition and delays in the exploration phase. The authors strongly advise that, as Lebanon opens its waters for the first time for exploration activities, detailed environmental assessment studies be conducted, including comprehensive environmental baseline studies (in particular marine and deep water studies) and modeling of discharges as applicable in line with recommendations made in the Strategic Environmental Assessment study that is also required by Law 132.

Environmental permits

Requirements for environmental permits which apply to offshore oil and gas activities are stipulated in several legislative texts.

The Environment Protection Law No. 444/2002 requires a permit for discharge into territorial waters (Article 3.1), a prior permit that sets limits for all types of pollutant releases from the facility (Article 42), and a prior permit for the import, handling, or disposal of dangerous/hazardous chemicals (Article 44).

Decree No. 2275/2009 stipulates that the Department of Air Quality at the MOE is responsible for determining the industrial institutions that require a permit for releasing emissions into the air and specifying the mechanism for granting the permit. The Department of Urban Environmental Protection is responsible for determining the industrial institutions that require a permit for wastewater discharge and specifying the mechanism for granting the permit. Decree 15512/2005 stipulates that the minister of public health is entitled to issue the necessary permits for the use, exploitation, entry, and exit of ionizing radiation, all in accordance with scientific studies and assessments of the Lebanese Atomic Energy Commission (LAEC).

The PAR and the OPRL require permits for flaring and venting (excluding emergency flaring or venting). The application for the permit shall include justifications for venting or flaring, a description of the facility, and the amounts, composition, and timing of venting and flaring. The permit shall be granted by the minister of energy and water based on the opinion of the LPA in coordination with the MOE.

296 *The Future of Petroleum in Lebanon*

The Environmental Compliance Decree No. 8471/2012 and decisions 202-1/2013, 539-2015, and 540/2015, in addition to others issued pursuant to it, require that industrial establishments apply for a three-year renewable environmental compliance certificate (ECC). Although the requirements for different types of permits are included in Lebanese legislation, the limits, conditions, and procedures for issuing these permits have yet to be specified. This must be considered a priority as oil and gas activities should not be initiated in the absence of specific environmental permitting procedures.

Monitoring/enforcement/assurance mechanisms

Assurance mechanisms including monitoring, inspection, auditing, and investigation are stipulated in the OPRL, Petroleum Activities Regulations (PAR) Decree No. 10289/2013, and in the Environmental Protection Law No. 444/2002. The main stakeholders involved are the LPA, MOE, and MEW. Responsibilities and mechanisms for environmental monitoring, auditing, inspection, and reporting shall be defined between different stakeholders. This can be achieved by signing memoranda of understanding (MoUs) between the LPA and concerned ministries, particularly the MOE.

Emergency preparedness and response

Lebanon is party to several international conventions that require the establishment of measures for dealing with offshore pollution incidents, either nationally or in cooperation with other countries. Such conventions include:

- IMO International Convention on Oil Pollution Preparedness, Response, and Cooperation
- ILO, C174—Prevention of Major Industrial Accidents Convention
- 2002 Emergency Protocol of the Barcelona Convention

Conclusion and recommendations

In many ways, the Lebanese environmental governance system should be considered to meet international standards. However, there are various gaps that need to be addressed to ensure the Lebanese government is prepared to manage the environmental risks associated with offshore oil and gas activities. A National Oil Spill Contingency Plan is being prepared by the LPA to organize environmental emergency responses related to activities from the petroleum sector.

In terms of environmental regulatory authority

In line with international best practices, the main environmental regulator for the oil and gas sector in Lebanon (the MOE) is independent from the oil and gas licensing authority.

Although the role of the MOE in the oil and gas sector is explicitly defined in the OPRL and in several provisions of the Petroleum Activities Regulations (PAR) Decree

No. 10289/2013, there are gray areas that need to be better defined. These include responsibilities and mechanisms for environmental monitoring, auditing, inspection, and reporting. This can be achieved by signing MoUs between the LPA and the MOE. Other entities have specific environmental management roles such as the MOPWT, which is the focal point of important international conventions related to the environment (notably MARPOL) or LAEC, which has specific authority over radioactive materials including NORM. MoUs between the MOE and these agencies are encouraged to ensure responsibilities are clearly delineated and to promote coordination and cooperation.

With regard to the capacity of institutions, existing ones do not currently have the needed capacity to deal with the requirements of the petroleum sector. Training need assessment studies should be performed for institutions that have an environmental role in the petroleum sector, and required training and capacity building should be implemented. The needed equipment for monitoring changes in environmental indicators/parameters should be made available. The Norwegian government is currently supporting the LPA in building the capacity of relevant stakeholders in the oil and gas sector, including the MOE, through the Oil for Development Program.

It is also recommended that an institutional assessment be conducted to evaluate the feasibility and need of establishing a dedicated oil and gas service or department at the MOE, and possibly at other ministries with specific environmental management roles, such as the Ministry of Public Works and Transport.

The use of third parties for EIA reviews, inspection, and auditing should be seriously considered, especially in the short term until existing institutions gain the capacity to conduct such work. In this case, it is recommended that procedures to pre-qualify competent firms be put in place.

In terms of environmental legislation

Existing legislation—including general environmental regulations and signed conventions, in addition to the OPRL and the PAR—covers the majority of environmental aspects related to the oil and gas sector. However, there are some requirements that existing legislation does not cover, such as the management and disposal of drill cutting and fluids, produced water, and NORM wastes, which are the main pollutant streams that arise from the offshore petroleum sector. Legislative action that covers these aspects should be carried out—or possibly in the form of decrees— and sampling procedures should also be set, which could take the form of decisions made by the MOE.

Additionally, some requirements referred to in existing legislation, such as those referenced in section 3, have yet to be specified or issued by decrees. It is highly recommended that specific limits and targets regarding GHG emissions be established, along with specific guidelines for the oil and gas sector. The Sustainable Oil and Gas Development in Lebanon project (SODEL), managed by the United Nations Development Programme (UNDP), is supporting the LPA and relevant stakeholders including the MOE, in order to strengthen the legal framework in line with the requirements of the oil and gas sector.

In terms of environmental risk assessment

With regard to EIA studies, it should be decided whether a new EIA decree specific to oil and gas activities should be issued as allowed by Article 29.3 of Law 132/2010. Given the lack of clarity in EIA requirements throughout the exploration and production stages, it is recommended that sector-specific EIA guidelines providing clear guidance for impact assessment studies to operators, in line with prevalent legislation, be issued.

For example, it is important to agree on whether an EIA (or IEE) will be required for the exploration phase, and particularly for exploratory drilling activities. According to international best practice, it is recommended that an EIA be required since environmental impacts from exploratory drilling can be significant if not properly managed. Mishandling of this issue could lead to major public opposition and delays in the exploration phase. It is recommended that operators submit an EIA scoping report along with their exploration plan, followed by a detailed EIA study to be approved by the MOE prior to operators being granted a drilling permit.

In terms of environmental permits

Although requirements for different types of permits are included in Lebanese legislation, the limits, conditions, and procedures for issuing these permits have yet to be specified.

According to existing legislation, different ministries have roles in issuing related permits. The MOE can issue emissions permits, the MOPWT can authorize disposal in territorial waters and under the seabed in territorial waters, the minister of public health issues permits related to ionizing radiation, and the MEW can issue flaring and venting permits.

It is recommended that MoUs be signed between these ministries to establish a permitting system that clearly sets responsibilities and procedures. Moreover, the MOE should be responsible for issuing discharge permits, emissions permits, and waste disposal permits. The discharge limits stipulated in the permit can be specific to the drilling/operation geographic location. General discharge limits at sea may apply to areas that do not contain sensitive receptors (such as important marine eco-systems or areas approximate to fisheries), while more stringent limits apply to important/sensitive areas. With regard to flaring and venting permits, they shall be reviewed by the MOE before being issued by the MEW as stipulated in the PAR.

In terms of monitoring/enforcement/assurance mechanisms

Responsibilities and mechanisms for environmental monitoring, auditing, inspection, and reporting should be defined among different stakeholders. This can be achieved by signing MoUs between the LPA and concerned ministries, especially the MOE. While the LPA can be responsible for monitoring and inspection at the activity level, the MOE should be empowered to monitor the state of the environment and should conduct regular and unannounced audits and inspections to ensure compliance with the requirements of granted permits and the environmental management plans proposed in EIA studies. Additionally, the MOE should issue annual compliance reports, and the option of using a third party for inspection should be considered.

In terms of emergency preparedness and response

It is necessary to develop a detailed guidance document for emergency preparedness and response which specifies emergency procedures and roles and responsibilities for different tiers of emergencies. The LPA is working toward the development of a National Oil Spill Contingency Plan in coordination with all relevant stakeholders. Mechanisms for increased transboundary cooperation in environmental management must also be established.

Annex 1: Organizational structure of the MoE

Source: Republic of Lebanon. Ministry of Environment.

Annex 2: Organizational structure of the LPA

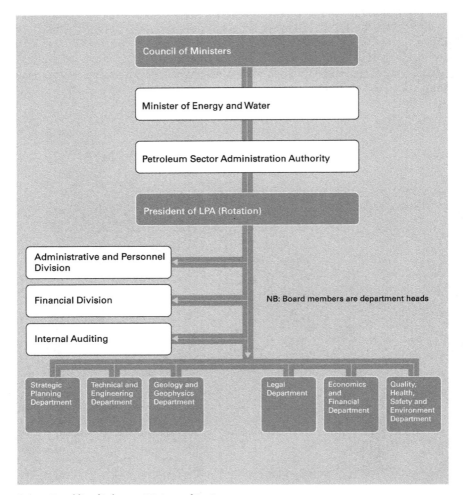

Source: Republic of Lebanon. Ministry of Environment.

References

Authored references

Coull, K.A., R. Johnstone, and S.I. Rogers. 1998. "Fisheries Sensitivity Maps in British Waters." United Kingdom Offshore Operators Association.

Evans, P.G.H. 1998. "Biology of Cetaceans of the North-East Atlantic (in Relation to Seismic Energy)." In *Proceedings of the Seismic and Marine Mammals Workshop, London, 23–25 June 1998*, edited by M.L. Tasker and C. Weir. United Kingdom Offshore Operators Association.

Strengthening Oil and Gas Environmental Governance 301

Gordon, J.C.D., D. Gillespie, J. Potter, A. Frantzis, M. Simmonds, R. Swift, and D. Thompson. 2004. "A Review of the Effects of Seismic Survey on Marine Mammals." *Marine Technology Society Journal* 37.

Richardson, W.J., C.R. Greene, C.I. Malme, and D.H. Thomson. 1995. *Marine Mammals and Noise.* Academic Press.

Non-authored references

Bureau of Ocean Energy Management. 2016. "What is the Environmental Impact Statement (EIS) Process?" United States Department of the Interior.

Bureau of Ocean Energy Management. 2016. "When to Prepare an Environmental Assessment." United States Department of the Interior.

ERT (Scotland) Ltd. 2006. "Irish Offshore Strategic Environmental Assessment 1 for Offshore Exploration Licensing in the Slyne, Erris and Donegal Basins, (IOSEA 1), Petroleum Affairs Division, Ireland." June.

International Association of Oil and Gas Producers (IOGP). 2010. "Risk Assessment Data Directory, Blowout Frequencies." IOGP Report No. 434-02. Prepared for Joint Industry Program on E&P Sound and Marine Life.

Irish Department of Communications, Climate Action and Environment. 2015. *Petroleum (Exploration and Extraction) Safety Act 2015.* 22 July.

Noise Control Engineering, Inc. 2007. "Review of Existing and Future Potential Treatments for Reducing Underwater Sound from Oil and Gas Industry Activities, Report 07-001." Prepared for Joint Industry Program on E&P Sound and Marine Life.

Norwegian Environmental Agency. 2017. "Hazardous Waste." 12 December. http://www.environment.no/topics/waste/avfallstyper/hazardous-waste/

Norwegian Petroleum Directorate. 1997. *Regulations to Act Relating to Petroleum Activities, Section 6b, Impact Assessment Programme.* 27 June

United Kingdom Department of Trade and Industry. 2001. "An Overview of Offshore Oil and Gas Exploration and Production Activities." Hartley Anderson.

United States Environmental Protection Agency. 2016. "Controlling Air Pollution from the Oil and Natural Gas Industry." https://www.epa.gov/controlling-air-pollution-oil-and-natural-gas-industry

United States Environmental Protection Agency. 2010. *National Pollutant Discharge Elimination System (NPDES) Permit Writers' Manual.* Water Permits Division, Office of Wastewater Management. Washington D.C.

Public Input

12

What Do Lebanese Citizens Want From Oil and Gas Revenues?

Sami Atallah, Daniel Garrote Sanchez, Zeina Hawa, Leslie Marshall and Laura Paler

Introduction

In a country that has long been heavily dependent on its neighbors to meet its energy needs, the prospect of major oil and gas discoveries off Lebanon's coast is both exciting and daunting. Although natural resources and other types of windfall revenue generally promise economic growth, development, employment, and better welfare for citizens, a multitude of examples have shown that these resources are neither necessary nor sufficient to spur and sustain national prosperity and progress. In fact, the opposite is generally true. If mismanaged, a large amount of natural resources may lead to multiple negative outcomes such as slower economic growth, weaker transparency and accountability, a less diversified economy, and resource dependency, to name a few. An abundance of resources can also increase inequality and exacerbate corruption, as Caselli and Michaels (2013) observed in Brazil through the distribution of oil revenues to municipalities.

While countries such as Norway and Botswana have successfully managed to utilize their resources to create better welfare for their citizens, many others have failed to avoid the resource curse. The legal framework and institutions that regulate Lebanon's oil sector become especially important in this respect. Windfall revenues can be a point of concern due to the scale of the income they generate, the "external" nature of that income (income that is not derived from domestic production), and because that income directly builds up in the government treasury without the involvement or scrutiny of citizens (Ross 2012). Furthermore, in societies where political representation is structured along sectarian lines and political patronage defines the mode of operation for most political groups, windfall revenues strengthen the ability of leaders to expand and intensify their political support through the provision of goods and services without the need to raise tax revenue.

In Lebanon in particular, the prospect of oil and gas production raises concerns about its potential to undermine the country's political and economic systems. Given Lebanon's disappointing track record in delivering quality public services and combating corruption, and its chronically gridlocked political process, the risks of rendering the sector another outlet for corruption—one with high levels of "unearned" income—are considerable (Leenders, Chapter 3 in this volume). Furthermore, political representation in Lebanon is structured and institutionalized along confessional lines (Cammett 2014, Salloukh *et al.* 2015). Political organizations with confessional orientations often directly provide or facilitate access to social services, given the state's inadequate public service provision and its failure to provide basic social safety nets. Filling in for the state, such parties and organizations become key suppliers of social services, giving rise to a situation in which clientelism and patronage allow them to maintain political support. This clientelism, combined with the confessional nature of these parties, in turn propagates the politics of sectarianism (Cammett 2014). From the perspective of balanced regional and national development, relying on political organizations to determine where and how social spending is allocated also results in an inefficient and unjust distribution of welfare and resources, even though it cuts across sectarian lines. In this way, welfare distribution is often not congruent with development objectives or economic need, as needier areas receive much less public investment than areas where development is higher and poverty is less widespread (Salti and Chaaban 2010).

The current political system—entailing electoral laws, confessionalism, and corruption—also hinders the capacity of the public to be an effective monitoring tool and its ability to properly reward or sanction politicians for their actions. The situation becomes infinitely more dangerous with a natural resource sector promising sizable national revenues, as it is argued in rentier state literature that windfall revenues relieve social pressure and free politicians from greater public accountability (Paler 2013), making room for misuse and rampant corruption in the sector. It is clear that public participation and consultation, as well as strong public accountability, keep the government in check and lead to improved welfare for citizens. Public participation is a delicate, complex, and nuanced subject, and for it to be meaningful and effective, several steps and criteria need to be fulfilled. As a start, the public needs to be informed. Additionally, people's needs and preferences need to be understood and measured.

To this end, this chapter attempts to capture an initial snapshot of public opinion, needs, and preferences regarding the management of revenues generated by the oil and gas sector. It examines the public's attitudes toward and aspirations for the nascent oil and gas sector in Lebanon, but its findings and implications go beyond the scope of the sector. The disconnect between government planning and citizens' needs may reduce opportunities for citizens to benefit properly from these resources. This provides a rationale for a survey that invites the public to begin engaging with and thinking about the sector. A survey allows us to understand how much the public already knows about oil and gas, and allows for citizens to voice their thoughts on spending priorities, concerns, and expectations with respect to the sector and what it means for them, their communities, and Lebanon. This is crucial as we do not already have a clear understanding of what people—other than political elites—actually think of the Lebanese petroleum sector. In sum, this chapter focuses on four main sets of questions encompassing the following. What are the general attitudes of Lebanese citizens regarding the impact of the oil and gas sector? What are peoples' general preferences on how to allocate future potential revenues? Are there discernable variations in attitudes toward preferences on and engagement with oil- and gas-related issues, and what individual and geographical characteristics explain these differences? Finally, do economic or confessional factors influence people's preferences on oil and gas revenue allocation in the sector?

The results on citizens' perceptions show that Lebanese are moderately optimistic about the prospective benefits of oil and gas rents on their households, although they predict that political elites will benefit more. A wide range of individual citizen characteristics such as sect, education, and political networks, as well as features of districts where they live, shape these perceptions. Individual and regional factors also explain the variation in citizens' preferences concerning which sectors should be allocated petroleum revenues and how to do so. Different regions seem to have different priorities, with the Bekaa demanding more cash transfers, the North more infrastructure, and the greater Beirut area other long-term investments such as the creation of a sovereign wealth fund (SWF). In general, geographical variations on sectoral preferences are based on needs and the relative availability of services.

Additionally, people's preferences over how oil revenues should be distributed geographically are primarily shaped by their level of economic conservatism, political networks, sectarian affiliation, and the level of development of their own districts of residence. On the whole, people want future oil revenues to be distributed to districts that are home to citizens of the same sect and similar development levels as their own areas of residence. Additionally, some people who are more economically conservative or politically connected are resistant to revenue redistribution. Furthermore, a regional oil revenue allocation experiment fails to show clear and robust effects on distribution information when information about sect or development of a district is provided.

This chapter proceeds as follows. Section one offers a brief description of the national survey used in the study. Section two presents results on people's perceptions of the impact that the oil and gas sector will have on their households, the political elite, their confessional group, and on Lebanon as a whole. In sections three through five, we analyze the public's preferences for petroleum revenue distribution across three levels: by function, by sector, and by region (including an experiment that assesses the impact of information on allocation decisions), while examining how these preferences vary according to individual and regional characteristics. This chapter concludes with a set of recommendations.

Survey methodology

To explore the issue of citizens' perceptions, preferences, and behaviors regarding the oil and gas sector, an original, national-level survey of 2,496 randomly selected adult citizens (aged 18 to 65) across Lebanon was conducted from December 2015 to March 2016. Details on the sampling strategy can be found in Annex 1 of this chapter. Design and post-survey weights were used to enable generalization of the sample to the

308 *The Future of Petroleum in Lebanon*

population in all analyzes below (unless otherwise noted). Annex 1 provides details on how the weights were constructed.[1]

The survey on which this chapter is based is nationally representative in a way that resembles the Lebanese population in its confessional, gender, and educational background, and other socio-economic background composition. Among the working age population (using weights) in Lebanon, one-third of respondents are young (from 18 to 29 years old), compared to nearly half being of prime age (from 30 to 55 years old), and over one-fifth above 55 years old (Table 12.1). In Lebanon, females represent 52 percent of the population compared to 48 percent males. The majority of citizens reside in Mount Lebanon (36 percent), followed by the Northern regions (22 percent), and the South (19 percent including Nabatiyeh). The confessional breakdown is

Table 12.1 Descriptive statistics of the sample and the Lebanese population

	Variable	Sample (unweighted data)	Population (weighted data)
Gender	Male	51%	48%
	Female	49%	52%
Sect	Christian	39%	39%
	Sunni	26%	28%
	Shia	26%	25%
	Druze	9%	7%
	Other	1%	1%
Region	Beirut	5%	11%
	Beqaa	20%	13%
	Mount Lebanon	26%	36%
	North	22%	22%
	South	27%	18%
Age	Youth (17–29)	38%	33%
	Mid-age (30–54)	43%	46%
	Elder (+55)	19%	21%
Education	Below secondary education	31%	38%
	Secondary education	42%	38%
	Above secondary education	27%	24%
Income	Less than $667	14%	27%
	Between $667 and $1,333	39%	46%
	More than $1,333	47%	27%

Source: Survey of Public Opinion in Lebanon, LCPS (2016).

---

[1] Weighting is especially important in our analysis as there was a significant amount of unit non-response in the survey; about 60 percent of those initially sampled did not consent to participate. We attribute this to the fact that the survey was long and some parts were sensitive in nature. To compensate for non-responses, we construct post-survey weights using population estimates from the Arab Barometer III survey. We use the Arab Barometer III as a reference dataset because it is a nationally representative survey that is widely used by academic and policy researchers to draw inferences about the population (for details, see http://www.arabbarometer.org/).

as follows: about 40 percent are Christians, 28 percent Sunnis, 25 percent Shia, and 7 percent Druze. Regarding the education profile, 38 percent of the working age population have low levels of education (below secondary school), another 38 percent have secondary schooling, and 24 percent have completed tertiary education. Finally, more than one-quarter of Lebanese households have an income below $667 per month (low-income), a figure only slightly above the poverty line ($3.84 per day per person). The majority of households have an income ranging from $667 to $1,333, while only 27 percent of families have an income higher than $1,333.

Through 82 core questions and a set of embedded experiments, the survey aims to understand people's economic, political, and confessional opinions and identities, and the association between these factors and their attitudes toward the oil and gas sector, its governance, and the prospects of realizing its potential benefits in the form of increased public welfare. The full structure of the survey is provided in Annex 1.

Peoples' perceptions of the impact of oil rents

One of the key issues the survey examines is peoples' perceptions of the oil and gas sector and the extent to which they think they will benefit from it. To this end, this section examines their views, taking into account their level of education, confessional background, economic ideologies, how politically connected they are, as well as the socio-economic and political characteristics of the districts they reside in.

Lebanese think political elites will benefit more than ordinary citizens

The prospect of future oil revenues is viewed by Lebanese citizens with a certain degree of optimism. According to the survey results, about three-quarters of the Lebanese population think that oil revenues will have a net positive impact on their households.[2] The majority of respondents expect to receive moderate benefits, although a significant portion believe that they will end up worse off (about one-quarter). While citizens have similar views on the impact that new revenues will have on their households and their confessional group, they expect, in general, greater gains for the country and political elites. An overwhelming 90 percent expect an improvement for Lebanon as a whole and its leaders in particular. When looking exclusively at who is going to strongly benefit from petroleum revenues, we see that more than double the number of adult citizens expect a very positive effect for politicians (~70 percent) compared to the same outcome for their own families or confessional group (~30 percent). Therefore, citizens not only exhibit mild optimism about how much their families and those close to them can benefit from future oil and gas extraction, but also feel that other groups in the country are going to benefit more, in particular political elites and those connected to elites (Figure 12.1).

---

[2] This is calculated by summing all respondents that either expect the prospective petroleum revenues to have a "somewhat positive" or a "very positive" impact on their households.

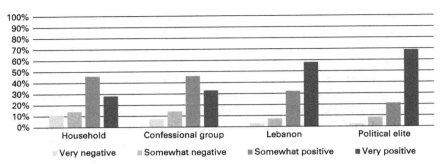

Figure 12.1 Citizens' perceptions of the net impact of oil revenues.
Source: Survey of Public Opinion in Lebanon, LCPS (2016).

There is more optimism among the less educated, Christians, those who are politically connected, and economic conservatives

The previous section demonstrated that, among Lebanese, there is a widespread perception that oil rents will be primarily distributed vertically, with people at the top benefiting the most, while there is less optimism about the impact on other individuals who are not connected to political elites. Apart from this vertical dimension, individuals have different expectations about how much they are going to benefit from petroleum revenues, depending on their socio-economic background (which can be considered a more horizontal dimension). It is therefore important to analyze which socio-economic characteristics influence those expectations, and the relative importance of each of them. In order to examine how key characteristics correlate with beliefs about who will benefit the most from future oil revenues, we constructed a series of multivariate regression models. Specifically, we consider how factors such as level of education, income, employment status, gender, marital status, political connections, confession, social and economic values, and district of residence are associated with beliefs about who—whether one's household or confessional group, the country as a whole, or political elites—will benefit from future oil and gas revenue.[3]

The results of the analysis show how respondents' perceptions are shaped by their personal characteristics. First, higher educated individuals have more critical views on the impact of petroleum revenues regarding their families and their confessional group. A person with a college degree is 22 percent less likely to expect positive outcomes for their family compared to a person who did not finish secondary school and who, otherwise, has identical characteristics (same income, confession, and gender, among others). Second, when asked about the impact on political elites, those differences disappear, and lower- and higher-educated respondents have similar views

---

[3] Tables 12.10 and 12.11 (in Annex 1 and 2) provide a more detailed explanation of the econometric methods and variables used, as well as the regression results of the models. Technically speaking, we run separate regressions, which we take as our outcome variables beliefs about who (household, confession, the country, political elites) will benefit from oil revenues and include the characteristics listed above as independent variables.

What Do Lebanese Citizens Want From Oil and Gas Revenues? 311

on how the elite will benefit from petroleum production and sale. The difference in perceptions between expected benefits for citizens' households and political elites provides some insight about what Lebanese think the distribution of revenues across different segments of society will be. Taking into account the two previously referenced results, it can be inferred that more educated citizens are more skeptical about the realization of fair revenue distribution and believe political elites will receive a relatively larger share of new sources of income.

Another explanatory characteristic is the situation of respondents in the labor market. Compared to those employed in the private sector, self-employed Lebanese, public sector employees, and those who are unemployed have more negative expectations about the impact of petroleum revenues on their households. These results might point at a specific channel through which petroleum extraction can benefit citizens: jobs. Within a framework of insiders and outsiders in the labor market,[4] those who are already in the system would expect to benefit more. We observe some of those signs, as those employed in the private sector think they will benefit more than those who do not have formal private-sector jobs (unemployed and self-employed, who are mostly working in the informal economy). The more skeptical views among public employees denote either a lack of trust in a system with which they are particularly familiar, or a perception that petroleum jobs are going to benefit those working in the private sector and will offer less benefit to those in the public sector.

The confession of respondents also shapes their perceptions about the net impact of oil revenues in Lebanon. Compared to both Sunnis and Shias, Christians think their families and confessional group will benefit more. Interestingly, Christian respondents' expectations do not exceed those of Muslims when asked about the impact on the country as a whole or on political elites. Therefore, it seems that Christians, compared to Muslims, are more optimistic about the impact oil revenues will have on their group as a whole. Sectarian differences might be associated with differences in media coverage and public signaling among different political groups, specifically whether they show support or optimism, or raise concerns. In this regard, the active and leading role of the Free Patriotic Movement party (FPM), which has traditionally held the office of the Ministry of Energy and Water (MEW), might lead Christian Lebanese to believe that oil rents can be particularly beneficial for their communities.

Two additional characteristics strongly influence citizens' perceptions on this issue: whether they are politically connected, and how economically conservative they are. The survey accounts for Lebanese political networks and individuals' connections to them by asking how easy it would be for respondents to ask a politician, *zaim*, or other key public figures for specific services such as access to electricity, healthcare, or jobs. In theory, one would expect that those who are more politically connected would be more optimistic about potential benefits from oil extraction as they would have easier access to new revenues or items resulting from the collection and allocation of new revenues. Regarding economic orientations, we define economic conservatives as

---

[4] Insiders refers to those who already have jobs compared to those who are outside the labor market (outsiders).

those who oppose redistribution of income through taxation. In general, they are wealthier and would expect higher benefits for their households if the government does not implement a strong redistribution system.[5] In line with these two hypotheses, the empirical results show that politically connected individuals and economic conservatives both believe their households will benefit more compared to those who are not connected or economically conservative. On the flip side, they actually expect worse outcomes for the country as a whole than do non-connected, liberal citizens. These two results combined suggest that the politically connected and economic conservatives foresee an unequal distribution of benefits stemming from petroleum revenues, according to which they expect to benefit more than other segments of the population.

To better understand these initial findings, we analyze the interactions between economic views and political networks, controlling for other socio-economic characteristics. Respondents are divided into four groups: politically connected and economic conservative, politically connected and economic progressive, not politically connected and economic conservative, and neither connected nor conservative. We see that, regardless of their economic inclinations, connection to political networks leads to more optimistic expectations about reaping the benefits of oil rents (Table 12.2). Among those who are politically connected, beliefs about how much their household will benefit are not affected by whether the respondent is an economic conservative or progressive. However, among those who are not politically connected, economic conservatives are more optimistic than economic progressives. The results imply that even economic conservatives who are not politically connected believe they will benefit more because they anticipate that the government will not allocate revenues in a manner that targets lower-income citizens. This would be the case, for instance, if the government were to establish an SWF to improve macroeconomic stability rather than issuing cash handouts that could reach a broader spectrum of the population and, in particular, the poor.

Table 12.2 Interactions between political connections and economic values on the net impact of oil rents

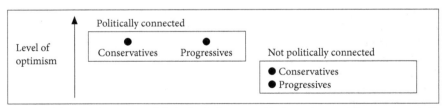

Note: Higher dots/boxes mean statistically higher levels of optimism. If the dots are horizontal, there are no statistically significant differences. These results are based on the standard multivariate regression that controls for other socio-economic and regional characteristics and includes interactive terms between economic preferences and political networks.

Source: Author's production.

[5] In this case, as it is a revenues windfall and not an increase in taxation, economic conservatives should be somewhat less opposed to redistribution (Dunning 2008). However, the analysis in the next sections show how "economic conservatives" want to allocate oil funds differently than "economic progressives" and, in particular, they want to allocate less funds to cash transfers.

Therefore, more optimistic expectations among conservatives might be tied to the lack of strong redistributive policies in Lebanon, at least in the public sector.

Citizens in districts with less poverty, higher levels of homogeneity, that are more politically competitive, and with a higher share of local politicians in ministerial positions have more positive views

Apart from the individual characteristics of respondents described above, there are strong regional disparities with respect to people's perceptions. Citizens from the same sect and similar socio-economic background have different expectations depending on where they live in Lebanon.

Regional variations (Figure 12.2) in citizens' perceptions on the net impact of oil rents on their households shows regional variations (controlling for individual socio-economic characteristics of citizens) regarding expected impact on respondents'

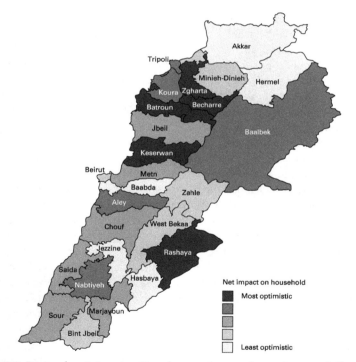

Figure 12.2 Regional variations in citizens' perceptions on the net impact of oil rents on their households.

Note: Darker colors show more optimistic views on the impact of oil rents. The results are based on average results at the district level after controlling for differences in socio-economic characteristics of their residents. The district-level differences are captured by dummy variables on multivariate regressions.

Source: Produced by authors based on data findings in Survey of Public Opinion in Lebanon, LCPS (2016).

households, where a darker blue denotes more positive expectations.[6] Greater optimism is observed in northern coastal districts in the areas of Batroun, Keserwan, Becharre, and Zgharta, which are mainly Christian areas located near one of the potential exploration and petroleum extraction zones. More surprising is optimism in the Druze inland district of Rachaya. Conversely, respondents in Akkar and Hermel—regions that are among the poorest in the country—are the most pessimistic.

Different factors that extend beyond the individual characteristics of respondents can account for regional differences in attitudes. For example, the prevalence of poverty in a region might lead its residents to feel that they are more excluded from economic development. This feeling, in turn, could lead them to be skeptical about the benefits their district, and in particular their households, could receive from a new economic opportunity such as petroleum extraction. Similarly, not only the presence of poverty but the broader level of economic development of each region (such as quality of infrastructure, availability of health and education centers, factories and job availability, etc.) can shape perceptions of exclusion or inclusion from the system and thus the likelihood of benefiting from future revenue windfalls.

Another potential factor could be the political structure in a given district. Theoretically, there can be a link between political competition and level of public service provision. Cammett and Issar (2010) show how, in districts with a higher degree of political competition, political parties reach out not only to in-group voters but also to out-group voters as a strategy to mobilize the electorate. Therefore, the different characteristics of electoral districts affect the ways parties establish patronage and clientelistic networks. Minority groups living in more politically competitive districts are more likely to be optimistic about oil revenues compared to those living in non-politically competitive ones, as they might expect greater benefits in the form of public services. More generally, the broader inclusion of citizens in politically competitive districts might lead to more positive expectations.

Previous studies also highlight the relationship between ethnic–religious divisions and the provision of public services. Alesina, Baqir, and Easterly (1999) show that the share of spending on public goods across geographic units in the United States is inversely related to ethnic fractionalization, and Miguel and Gugerty (2005) and Banerjee *et al.* (2005) find similar results for Kenya and India, respectively. Living in more heterogeneous districts that receive fewer or worse public services (education, roads, health, etc.) could lead residents to express less optimistic views regarding the extent to which they believe oil rent distributions will benefit their households.

Finally, the capacity of leaders in each district to influence policy decisions at the national level and negotiate the regional split of economic benefits of oil could also affect citizens' perceptions of local benefits for their households. In order to test the relevance of these factors in the Lebanese context, we draw from other LCPS databases at the district level, including: the prevalence of poverty, level of political competitiveness, level of ethnic homogeneity (measured by the percentage of citizens from the

---

[6] The numbers on which this figure is based are the results of the regression for each district dummy variable. Although not directly meaningful, the differences in these numbers are significant, and can be read as darker colors showing more optimistic views on the net impact of petroleum rents.

What Do Lebanese Citizens Want From Oil and Gas Revenues? 315

Table 12.3 District-level determinants of geographical variations in citizens' perceptions

Dependent variable: Net impact of oil by region		
Variables	Coefficient	Significance
Poverty Index	−0.09	(**)
Homogeneity	1.04	(***)
Ministers/Voters	0.18	(***)
Political Competition	0.22	(**)

Note: One star (two/ three) shows that the results are statistically significant at the 10 percent level (5 percent/ 1 percent).[8]

Source: Authors' production.

majoritarian sect), and capacity of local politicians to influence the national arena (measured by the number of members of parliament [MP] from each district that are also ministers).[7] To analyze their impact we (a) correlate these factors with regional variations in attitudes (dummy variables at the district level) and (b) replace district-level dummies with these four district-level variables. In both cases, and after controlling for all individual-level characteristics, all four key district-level characteristics have a significant impact on the perceptions of individuals, in line with the theoretical hypothesis (Table 12.3). First, citizens from districts with a higher prevalence of poverty—regardless of their personal income—are less likely to be optimistic about the economic impact of petroleum revenues on their households. Thus, people in neglected areas seem to think that they will continue to be neglected when potential revenues are distributed at the national level. Second, citizens in districts with more influential politicians at the national level expect a more positive impact from oil revenues. The level of influence of local politicians is approximated by the number of members of parliament of each district that have also been ministers from 2009 to 2016. Third, the higher the percentage of citizens from one sect a district has (i.e. the higher the level of sectarian homogeneity), the more optimistic they are about oil extraction. Finally, as expected, people living in more politically competitive districts have higher expectations about the potential benefits of oil rents.

Revenue allocation by function

The Lebanese government can opt for different schemes to manage public revenues from the oil and gas sector, each with different implications for the country and Lebanese citizens. One option that has been discussed is channeling new funds toward

---

[7] We use the number of ministerial appointments originating from each district as a proxy for influence of politicians in the district over national politics, as politicians in these positions have more direct access and higher ability to shape policy decisions.

[8] This simple regression is based on 26 observations that include each district, which is a very small number. However, when we include the four district-level variables instead of dummy variables in the general multivariate regression (2,496 observations), the results show similarly significant effects.

316 *The Future of Petroleum in Lebanon*

improving Lebanon's weak public finances, which could reduce the public debt, cut interest rates, and improve the country's economic stability. Another option is creating an SWF to manage oil reserves and preserve a more equitable allocation between current and future generations. Finally, the government could use revenues to increase its current spending in different forms, by increasing the budget for public employees (either by increasing its size or by raising their salaries), creating a development bank to provide loans to private-sector entrepreneurs and small and medium enterprises (SMEs), investing in public goods such as improvements in public infrastructure (such as roads, schools, hospitals, electric system, etc.), or directly transferring money to citizens, in particular to those who are most disadvantaged (cash transfers). In line with these alternatives, the survey asks respondents about their preferences in terms of allocating petroleum revenues to cash transfers, public salaries, public investment, a development bank, the central bank, public debt payment, and an SWF. This section explores citizens' preferences and how those preferences differ according to their socio-economic characteristics and place of residence.

Citizens want the government to spend petroleum revenues through different channels, mainly through public investment

When asked about their preferences regarding where to allocate oil revenues, an overwhelming majority of citizens would not choose to spend it all on a single scheme, but rather through a wide array of channels. On average, Lebanese would invest 30 percent of total funding on needed infrastructure projects across the country, followed by 15 percent on direct cash transfers, 13 percent on public wages, and about 10 percent each on creating a development bank, paying the public debt, creating an SWF, and depositing resources in the central bank. About one-quarter of citizens would not send oil resources to the central bank, invest in a development bank, or issue cash payments to citizens; only 5 percent would not invest in infrastructure projects altogether (Figure 12.3). Therefore, it appears that, above all other schemes, Lebanese think it is most important to improve public infrastructure. This is consistent with the poor condition of infrastructure in the country: according to the Global Competitiveness Report of the World Economic Forum (2016), Lebanon ranks 117th out of 138 countries in quality of infrastructure.

Vulnerable groups, those more in favor of redistribution, Muslims and non-politically connected people favor more cash transfers

Research shows that different socio-economic characteristics of citizens shape their preferences on government spending allocation (Eismeier 1982, Jacoby 1994). In the context of oil revenue management in a developing country, Amoako-Tuffour (2011) observes differences in preferences across regional and socio-economic cleavages. Therefore, it seems pertinent to analyze different individual and regional characteristics to better understand factors that shape the preferences and priorities of Lebanese citizens regarding how to channel revenue windfalls. Based on multivariate econometric models, this section studies factors that determine citizens' preferences on how much to allocate to different functions, based on both the individual socio-economic

What Do Lebanese Citizens Want From Oil and Gas Revenues?

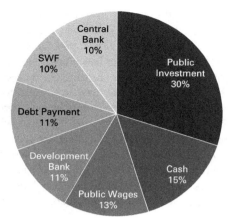

Figure 12.3 Where do Lebanese want to allocate oil revenues?
Note: The results use weighted data to represent the population statistics.
Source: Survey of Public Opinion in Lebanon, LCPS (2016).

characteristics of citizens (such as level of education, income, employment status, gender, marital status, political networks, sect, social and economic values) and the places where they live (district of residence in Lebanon). Tables 12.10 and 12.12 provide further explanations for the econometric methods and variables used, as well as the regression results of the models.

Young Lebanese (below 29 years old) prefer to allocate a greater amount of revenues to an SWF compared to older Lebanese. This observation is consistent with the fact that this particular scheme is an inter-generational transfer for the future, meaning that, apart from altruistic considerations, young citizens are more likely to benefit from future revenues. To compensate, youth would like to spend less on remunerating public sector employees, as public sector jobs are predominantly occupied by older citizens.

Regarding income levels of respondents, wealthier Lebanese favor setting aside a higher share of oil rents to pay for public debt as well as to increase public salaries, while reducing the allocation to a development bank that provides loans to the private sector. As wealthier people have less credit constraints, it seems logical that they would place less value on the option of a loan provision. At the same time, given lower financial constraints and needs, they are more likely to recognize the fragility of public finances as a main concern. For their part, particularly vulnerable groups are more inclined to receive sizable transfers in the form of cash, in exchange for lower public debt payments, suggesting more liquidity constraints. Furthermore, religion (and confession) stands out as a major factor, with Christians preferring to reduce the amount of cash transfers to Sunni, Shia, and Druze communities. Instead, they opt to channel more funds to a development bank.

Economic values also shape citizens' preferences. Economically conservative citizens are less in favor of cash transfers and more inclined to approve of oil rents being managed through an SWF. As cash transfers are an important instrument of redistribution, economic values might explain why conservatives wish to allocate fewer funds to transfers compared to those with more progressive views. An alternative explanation could be the declining marginal utility of additional money for conservatives who are, on average, better off and thus less in need of cash.

Level of trust is another relevant variable that is often mentioned in the literature on citizens' preferences about government distribution. We approximate trust as the gap between respondents' expectations about the extent to which they feel their households and the political elites are going to benefit from oil rents. The smaller the gap, the more trust they have in government to distribute wealth. Similar to economic conservatives, those who have more trust in a just and egalitarian distribution of benefits have less need to receive revenues in the fastest and most direct manner (cash transfers), and are willing to invest more in long-term projects with the expectation of future benefits.

A more detailed focus on relative preferences regarding cash transfers reveals interesting relationships between income, sect, and political networks. Table 12.4 shows the results of the same multivariate regression including interaction terms between income, sect, and political networks.[9] The results show that more politically connected people want, on average, to allocate fewer funds to cash transfers,

Table 12.4 Oil revenue allocation to cash transfers: interactions between sect, income, and political networks on preferences over cash transfers

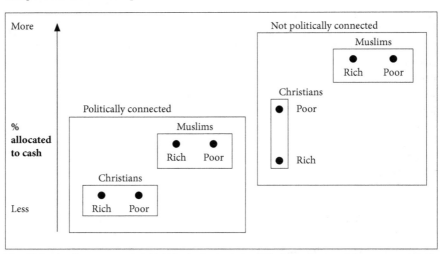

Note: Higher dots/boxes mean statistically higher levels of optimism. If the dots are horizontal there are no statistically significant differences. These results are based on multivariate regression that controls for other socio-economic and regional characteristics and includes interactive terms between sect, income, and political networks.

Source: Authors' production.

[9] The type of regression used (non-linear) makes the coefficients not directly interpretable but we are able to observe whether there are statistically significant differences.

which might be explained by their ability to reap the benefits of oil rents through different means. Among citizens without connections to political networks, wealthier Christians are less interested in cash transfers than poorer Christians, while income does not appear to determine how much Muslims would like to be channeled through cash. When taking into consideration only those who are politically connected, the level of wealth does not lead to significantly different appetites for cash transfers for either Christians or Muslims. This finding highlights how being politically connected trumps other differences such as income, as even poor but politically connected citizens reduce their preference for cash transfers to levels similar to wealthier and connected ones. In sum, when lacking easy access to politicians, poorer Lebanese seem to face more liquidity constraints and would therefore prefer to receive more cash transfers. Poorer but politically connected citizens, having easier access to rent-seeking through political connections, are not as in favor of cash transfers because they do not exhibit the same cash constraints as non-politically connected poor individuals.

More infrastructure in the North, more cash in the Bekaa, and more transfers to a sovereign wealth fund in Mount Lebanon

Apart from disparities in the individual background of respondents, regional factors affect how citizens view oil rent distribution (Figure 12.4). Econometric analysis, controlling for the previously mentioned socio-economic characteristics of individuals, shows a tale of three regions with very different priorities: the North, the Bekaa, and Mount Lebanon. People residing in the North, and in particular in the more remote district of Akkar, would redistribute more funds through public investments. Citizens in Akkar would set aside a higher share than the 30 percent that the average Lebanese citizen would allocate for this type of investment, demonstrating a preference for funding the construction and upkeep of roads, hospitals, and other infrastructure and services in the area. Similar findings, although less acute, seem to appear in some districts in the South such as Sour.

In the eastern districts of Bekaa, citizens prioritize cash transfers more than in other regions. This region stands out as the least financially developed in Lebanon, with only 7 percent of total bank branches, 7 percent of banking credit, and 8 percent of bank deposits, compared to a resident population of about 17 percent of the Lebanese population.[10] This higher prevalence of a cash economy might increase demand for cash among its population, even after taking into consideration other factors such as disparities in income.

Finally, Mount Lebanon residents would allocate relatively more funds to institutions such as an SWF or the central bank. As this is a relative measure and not an absolute one, this result might point either to a stronger preference for this type of institution or to less cash and infrastructure needs given the more developed state of the region.

---

[10] Data from Central Administration Statistics of Lebanon for the year 2013.

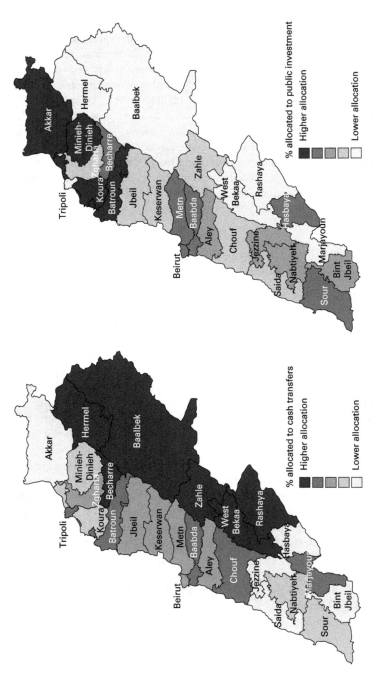

Figure 12.4 Regional variations in citizens' preferences regarding to which government function more rents should be distributed.

Left: Percentage allocated to cash transfers. Right: Percentage allocated to public investment.

Note: Darker colors show a relatively higher allocation of funds through a specific instrument or function. The results are based on district level dummy variables on multivariate regressions after controlling for those individual socio-economic characteristics.

Source: Produced by authors based on data findings in Survey of Public Opinion in Lebanon, LCPS (2016).

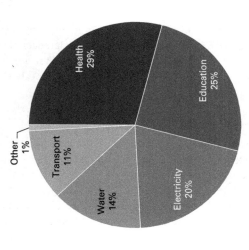

Figure 12.5 Where do citizens want to allocate oil rents?

Note: The results use weighted data to represent the population statistics.

Source: Survey of Public Opinion in Lebanon, LCPS (2016).

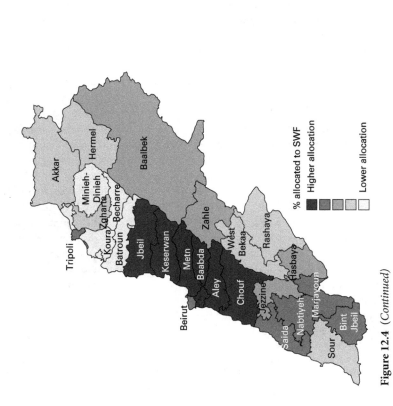

Figure 12.4 (*Continued*)

Percentage allocated to an SWF.

Revenue allocation by sector

The previous section demonstrated that nearly half of all oil rents would be spent on public investment and public wages if such decisions were based on the preferences of Lebanese citizens. However, this does not demonstrate toward which economic sectors citizens would channel funds. In this section we focus on potential revenues allocated to public investment and public wages and analyze sectoral preferences.[11]

Lebanese prioritize investing oil revenues in health, education, and electricity

The survey asks respondents to allocate public funds into the following sectors: education, health, electricity, water, transportation, or other. According to the survey, respondents prefer spending 29 percent of funds on health (this could take the form of construction of facilities, public health professionals' salaries, or purchases of materials and equipment). The second-most prioritized sector is education (Figure 12.5), with 25 percent of proposed funds allocated, followed by electricity with 20 percent. The remaining 30 percent is split between allocations to the water and transportation sectors.

Shias and youth would spend less funds on health, while more educated citizens would invest more in education

Similar to the types of schemes, the choice of sectoral allocation of oil rents is not uniform across socio-economic and regional cleavages. Once again, in this section we use multivariate econometric models to determine which individual and regional factors impact the proportion of public funds that citizens would channel to each of the five economic sectors. Tables 12.10 and 12.13 provide further explanations about the econometric methods and variables used, as well as the regression results of the models.

Elderly citizens, who are more likely to face health problems, place a stronger focus on improving the public health system compared to youth, while also favoring a reduction of funding for transportation and water. More educated Lebanese, all other characteristics being equal, want to spend more public funds on improving the education system, suggesting that they place a higher value on education.

Regarding sect, Christians show more interest in health and less in electricity provision compared to Shias. Studies (Cammett and Issar 2010) show how parties target specific communities with welfare programs, in particular the Shia community. Of the more than 3,000 health centers in Lebanon, more than half are provided by partisan agencies that prioritize their coreligionists. Shia agencies in particular have developed a network of health support systems, which translates into a lower pressing need from the Shia community to increase funding in the sector. Meanwhile, Druze prefer that the government spend more funds on transportation given that large portions of the community reside in mountainous and remote areas.

---

[11] The other functional schemes (cash transfers, sovereign wealth funds, central bank, development bank, and debt payments) cannot be allocated to any of the public sectors as they are either transferred to the private sector (families or firms) or not currently spent.

Another key characteristic is employment status. Lebanese who do not work (the inactive and even more so the unemployed) would use relatively more funds to improve electricity connections and less on health, compared to employed people. This does not mean that they value health services less than employed people do, but rather that they have relatively more pressing needs regarding electricity provision. Vulnerable populations—such as the unemployed—might have relatively better informal support systems in the form of access to and affordability of healthcare,[12] while electricity connectivity requires a more centralized investment through public institutions.

Regional variations on sectoral allocation: Lower demand of social services in regions that have affordable supply

The findings from our multivariate regressions reveal the importance of district-level variables in explaining preferences on sectoral allocation of funds, even after taking into consideration other personal characteristics (Figure 12.6). Lebanese living in districts in the South, regardless of their sect or social status, demand more and better electricity and transport infrastructure. This is in line with the latest World Bank Enterprise Survey, which shows that among all regions, the South has the most hours of electricity cuts per day (about eleven hours, compared to three hours per day in Beirut).[13] Also, about 30 percent of companies in the South find transportation to be a binding constraint on running their businesses, while in other regions the share is significantly lower (between 11 percent and 18 percent). Unsurprisingly, then, residents in the South prioritize sectors that are the least developed in their region, while not allocating that many resources to health and education.[14] Interestingly, districts with a majority Shia population, not only those in the South, demand significantly less funds for health, again pointing to a well-developed health support system provided by Shia-party affiliated agencies. On the opposite side, most Druze and Christian majority districts prioritize health. Therefore, not only Christians, but also residents of Christian-majority districts—whether they are Christians or not—want more health services, and the opposite appears to be the case in Sunni- and Shia-majority districts. Although partisan welfare and health centers are strategically located where constituents live, it also seems that other sectarian groups within the same districts benefit from these welfare services (Cammett and Issar 2010).

In Lebanon's northern districts and Baalbek, citizens would channel more resources into education. Behind this choice lies the nature of the education system in the North—a region with higher illiteracy rates, a high share of the national youth population, and more pressing demands for public services—which is characterized by the low availability of private schooling. Finally, residents of Beirut and Mount Lebanon demand comparatively more resources for the water sector and (but less clear)

---

[12] These comprise religious and political welfare organizations that can target their vulnerable constituents.

[13] World Bank (2015).

[14] As described in Figure 12.9 later in the section, Shia districts, including those in the South, demand less resources for healthcare as Shia welfare agencies seem to better provide and cover the health needs of their populations.

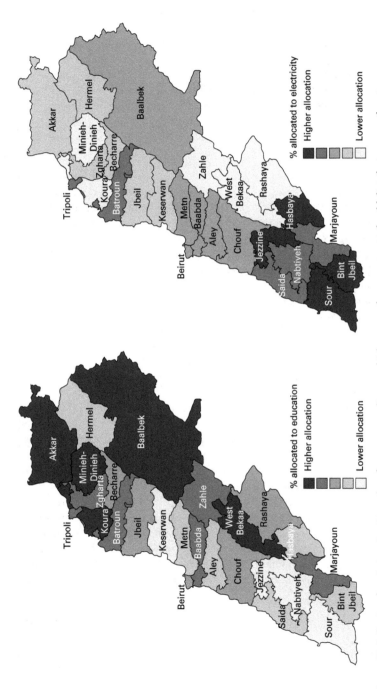

Figure 12.6 Regional variations in citizens' preferences regarding to which sectors the government should distribute more oil rents.

Left: Percentage allocated to education. Right: Percentage allocated to electricity.

Note: Darker colors show a relatively higher allocation of funds to a specific sector. The results are based on district level dummy variables on the multivariate regressions after controlling for those individual socio-economic characteristics.

Source: Produced by authors based on data findings in Survey of Public Opinion in Lebanon, LCPS (2016).

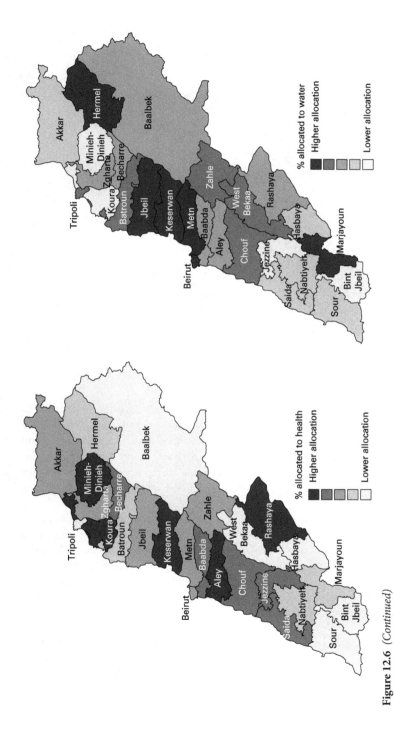

Figure 12.6 (*Continued*)

Left: Percentage allocated to health. Right: Percentage allocated to water.

Figure 12.6 (*Continued*).
Percentage allocated to transportation.

healthcare (as previously mentioned), while demanding less improvements in transportation facilities. Although there are major instances of traffic congestion in the Beirut metropolitan area, these districts have a better developed network of roads and transportation than more outlying areas. By contrast, water scarcity in the capital has been a major concern in recent years, an issue that is currently being addressed by a World Bank project that aims to provide a more constant supply of water even during the peak months of summer.

A key factor that could explain observed variations in sectoral preferences across districts (Figure 12.6) is the relative scarcity (supply) of each service in the area, as the previous analysis initially suggested. In order to quantitatively analyze demands for specific services or sectors, we merge geographical disparities in the relative allocation of funds to health services with the availability of health centers per district using the Cammett and Issar (2010) database to approximate the supply side of healthcare. An initial hypothesis is that, in districts with a greater supply of healthcare centers, people are less willing to allocate funds to health compared to districts that have less centers. However, Figure 12.7 shows there is no clear correlation between the two: if anything, there is a slightly positive relation between the two. This points to other dimensions that extend beyond the number of health clinics in the area. A more refined hypothesis would be that, in districts with more affordable healthcare

What Do Lebanese Citizens Want From Oil and Gas Revenues?   327

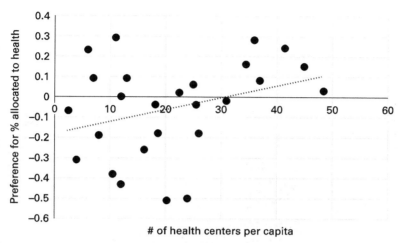

Figure 12.7 Regional preference for spending on health and the supply of clinics per capita.

(which entails not only supply but also the accessibility and price of health services), people would be less willing to allocate funds for health compared to districts that have less centers.

Figure 12.8 shows the presence of healthcare centers by type of organization or agency, divided between public clinics, private sectarian agencies (political or religious agencies pertaining to any of the sectarian groups), non-partisan for-profit private organizations, and non-partisan non-profit organizations. The map of district-level health supply per population looks quite different depending on the type of institution. While, overall, there are more healthcare centers per capita in the Greater Beirut/Mount Lebanon area, Saida and the Bekaa have two of the highest rates of private for-profit (and non-partisan) clinics, Zahle stands out in the number of partisan clinics, and Nabatiyeh for the number of public clinics. Therefore, we see relevant regional variations in the type of healthcare that is available in each district.

When taking into consideration different types of health centers, a clear pattern emerges which points to the issue of affordability. On the one hand, the more for-profit clinics in a district, the more citizens in that district think that it is important to allocate future revenues from petroleum revenues to healthcare (Figure 12.9). This could be due to the substitute nature of different types of health agencies and the lack of pro-bono agencies, meaning prices may be too high for many disadvantaged citizens in the area. Conversely, the availability of healthcare provided by Shia agencies reduces citizens' need to allocate more funds to health, suggesting that these agencies have non-profit interests that target particularly vulnerable groups and facilitate access to healthcare for all segments of the population. This pattern is only observed for Shia clinics, while it is not significantly present for Christian, Sunni, or Druze healthcare agencies. Living in Shia-majority districts reduces the proportion of funds that citizens would like to allocate to health by 15 percentage points. More visually, the

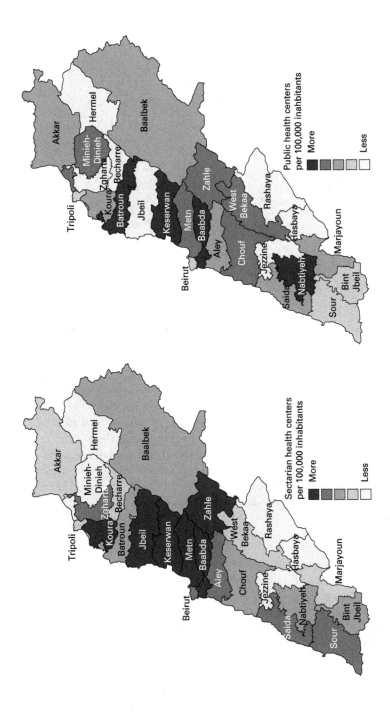

Figure 12.8 Supply of health centers by district and type of institution.

Left: Number of private sectarian health centers per 100,000 residents

Right: Number of public health centers per 100,000 residents

Note: Darker colors show a relatively higher number of health centers per population.

Source: Cammett and Issar (2010).

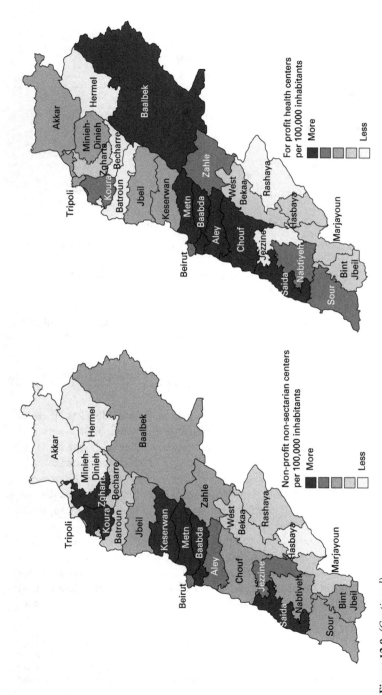

Figure 12.8 (*Continued*)

Left: Number of non-profit non-sectarian health centers per 100,000 residents.

Right: Number of for-profit health centers per 100,000 residents

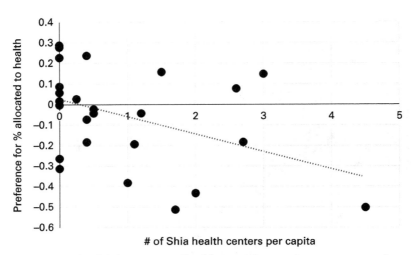

Figure 12.9 Supply of different types of healthcare and regional variations on preference for health.
Source: Produced by authors based on data findings in Survey of Public Opinion in Lebanon, LCPS (2016).

lower panel of Figure 12.9 shows the negative relationship between the number of Shia clinics per district and residents' willingness to allocate future funds to health.

Revenue allocation by region

The third layer of preferences focuses on allocations to various districts. There is significant regional variation in preferences concerning allocation, both in terms of how future revenue from oil and gas should be used (whether it should be spent, transferred to citizens, invested, or saved), and regarding in which sectors investment should be made. A number of factors, such as the availability of existing services, the quality of these services, and liquidity, development, and poverty levels in a district, contribute to this variation and highlight that investment (of oil revenue or any other public funds) should be tailored at the local level.

In this section, respondents were asked how they would prefer to distribute future oil revenues across Lebanon's 26 districts.[15] A first look at average allocations shows varying levels of revenue allocated to different districts (Figure 12.10). Beirut alone, for example, received almost 12 percent of allocations, even though it is the richest, most developed administrative district, and also considerably smaller in area than other

---

[15] This was originally done as an experiment according to which respondents were also randomly assigned to receive different amounts of information about each district, namely information about the level of economic development in the district and/or the majority sect living in that district. We find that the information had no effect on how participants allocated the revenue, therefore, in this analysis we pool the data.

What Do Lebanese Citizens Want From Oil and Gas Revenues?   331

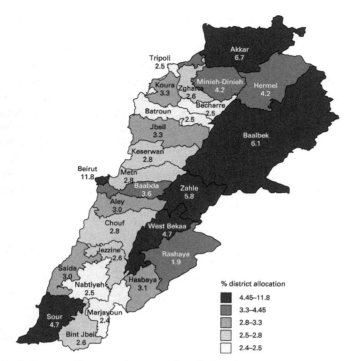

Figure 12.10 Average allocations (percent of total oil and gas revenue) to each district (weighted).

Source: Produced by authors based on data findings in Survey of Public Opinion in Lebanon, LCPS (2016).

districts. Administrative Beirut's population ranges from 7 percent to 12 percent of Lebanon's total resident population (according to different sources),[16] which means that the allocation of funds to Beirut according to population distribution is about average or slightly above average. The Bekaa (West Bekaa, Zahle, Baalbek, and Hermel) and the North (Akkar and Minnieh-Dannieh) received relatively higher allocations (4 percent to 7 percent) compared to other districts. Most of these districts (apart from West Bekaa and Zahle) are categorized as poor and underdeveloped, and many of them have medium-sized populations relative to other districts.

If the baseline assumption for equal distribution is equal revenue per capita allocated to each district, we compare allocations received by each district's population. Equal distribution is not necessarily fair, equitable, or desirable, and to achieve effective, holistic, and balanced development, different districts require different types and levels of investment that address regional disparities. Equitable distribution would therefore

---

[16] Central Administration of Statistics, http://www.cas.gov.lb/index.php/demographic-and-social-en/population-en and LCPS survey data based on weighted population according to the Arab Barometer survey data (Annex 2).

take into account needs and current development levels and not follow a "one person, one dollar" spending policy.

Figure 12.10 offers a clearer picture of distribution by population size. Beirut's allocation compared to its population becomes relatively proportional. Parts of the North and the Bekaa still exhibit higher-than-average allocation compared to their populations (Akkar, Koura, Hermel, Baalbek, Becharre, Hasbaya, Rashaya, and West Bekaa). Most of these areas (apart from Becharre, Koura, and West Bekaa) have below-average levels of development and high levels of poverty (Figure 12.11). Several parts of Mount Lebanon and Saida exhibit low allocations compared to their relatively large populations, but these areas also have higher levels of development and less poverty. From an equity standpoint, the average distribution of revenue compared to population distribution seems generally fair, with poorer and less developed districts receiving a higher-than-average share compared to their populations. There are some exceptions, with Zgharta, Saida, and the Chouf (all with medium development and poverty levels) receiving lower-than-average allocations, compared to districts like Koura and West Bekaa (both wealthier and more developed) receiving relatively high allocations.

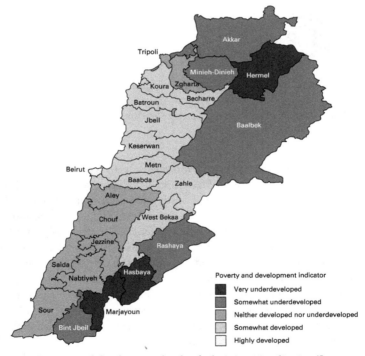

Figure 12.11 Poverty and development levels of administrative districts.[17]
Source: Produced by authors based on data findings in Survey of Public Opinion in Lebanon, LCPS (2016).

[17] Poverty and Development Index, UNDP (2004).

The requirements for what constitutes equity are layered and multi-faceted, meaning that pinning down what balanced development looks like at a practical level is often a challenge due to intrinsic differences in regions' geographic, demographic, cultural, and economic characteristics. When observing this pattern of revenue allocation among ordinary citizens, distribution preferences somewhat resemble what would be considered equitable or balanced distribution that accounts for disproportionate levels of development and poverty, and targets these regional disparities. Traditionally, development projects have unevenly focused on Beirut and Mount Lebanon, with the rest of the country receiving secondary attention. Additionally, the distribution of public funds in Lebanon has largely been channeled in a manner that primarily addresses political concerns or sectarian balance, as opposed to public spending that responds to needs and contributes to development (Salti and Chaaban 2010). This public spending arrangement has accentuated regional disparities and become a tool for fueling clientelism and garnering electoral support.

Even though it appears some form of redistribution is occurring—with poorer districts receiving generally more per capita than wealthier districts—this does not necessarily mean that people on the whole are concerned with redistribution and that economic factors play a prominent role in their allocation decisions. In fact, the mechanisms, motivations, and thought processes that lead to this final allocation result are unclear. One likely explanation is that when people distribute revenue, they regard all districts as similar entities, rather than as entities with varying population sizes, especially since population sizes are largely unknown. This leads to a situation in which—even if unintentional—the respondent can allocate more per capita to districts with lower populations, many of which are poor districts. If we compare population size with average allocation per capita, we find that this is generally the case (Figure 12.12). This could also explain why wealthier, smaller districts, such as Batroun, Koura, West Bekaa, and Becharre (all of whose populations are less than 2 percent of Lebanon's total resident population) also receive higher-than-average allocations per capita. It may also explain why medium to wealthy large districts, like Metn, Baabda, Chouf, Saida, and Tripoli (all of whose populations are more than 5.5 percent of Lebanon's total) receive lower-than-average allocations per capita.

People allocate significantly more revenue to their own districts first, and to districts of their same sect second

We then examine variations in allocations according to individual and regional characteristics to understand factors that affect people's allocations to each district. In this case, we expect that where people are from and where people live will impact their allocation preferences, and, in particular, the level of development and poverty exhibited in people's own districts. Additionally, we consider other identity-based factors such as sect, strength of sectarian identity, and economic conservatism.

Hermel, a poor, underdeveloped and remote district with a predominantly Shia population, received 4.2 percent of total petroleum revenue in the allocation exercise.

Figure 12.12 Average allocations (percent of total oil and gas revenue) to each district divided by population size (weighted).

Note: Darker colors mean a higher relative allocation compared to population size. Lighter colors are a relative under-allocation.

Source: Produced by authors based on data findings in Survey of Public Opinion in Lebanon, LCPS (2016).

Using econometric regressions (Annex 2.4), we analyze the effect of multiple independent variables on allocations to Hermel, controlling for demographic characteristics such as age, gender, education level, marital status, and employment status. The characteristics we focus on are: level of economic conservatism, one aspect of which is the extent of support for public fund redistribution (pro re-allocation); strength of political networks and ease of access to benefits and services from politicians, particularly of the same sect; level of trust in the political system and public institutions and their ability to address the level of development and poverty in one's own district of residence; and the sectarian affiliation of the individual.

When observing factors that affect allocations to Hermel (Annex 2.4 for details on regression results), we see that the level of trust in public institutions, level of economic conservatism, strength of political networks, and respondents' respective sects all play a significant role in allocations toward Hermel. The more economically conservative a respondent is, the lower the allocation to Hermel, which is in line with resistance to public redistribution to poorer areas. Similarly, the more politically

What Do Lebanese Citizens Want From Oil and Gas Revenues? 335

connected a respondent is, the lower the allocations to Hermel. We would expect those who are politically connected—regardless of their socio-economic condition—to not be as concerned with public spending and public redistribution of funds to regions that are more in need. This is likely due to a combination of factors, among them that a politically connected respondent is already receiving benefits and services through their political connections. Additionally, it could be due to politically connected respondents understanding the clientelistic game and recognizing that most services are in fact received through political connections and not through public services, in addition to their lower level of trust in governmental institutions to redistribute funds. When it comes to sect, Sunnis are significantly less likely than Shia to allocate funds to Hermel, which is a predominantly Shia district. No significant results emerge with Christian and Druze respondents. Regarding district development and poverty, if Beirut is excluded, the more developed the district a respondent lives in, the less likely he or she is to allocate to Hermel, a poor and underdeveloped district. This suggests some resistance to reallocation from respondents in wealthier districts. We also see that people from Hermel are significantly more likely to allocate to Hermel compared to others. When looking at other districts for comparison, this appears to be a strong recurring pattern of preferences for more allocation toward one's own district.

Other districts are examined to discern existing allocation patterns (results presented in Annex 2.4). There appears to be a strong recurring pattern of preferences for more allocation toward one's own district in almost all cases. It is difficult to draw further conclusions based solely on district-by-district allocations, so districts are grouped in different ways to capture preferences. We first look at allocations to poor districts in general. One issue to consider is that individuals may allocate more to poor districts because they happen to live in a poor district and are allocating more toward their district. To account for this, we control for respondents' own districts of residence in the analysis.[18] We also examine allocations to wealthy districts, allocations to districts according to sectarian majority, and allocations to poor districts of a different sect to understand the socio-economic and/or sectarian factors that may contribute to allocation patterns. The main results of this analysis are presented in Table 12.5. In brief, people prefer allocating more revenue toward their own districts, and their next best option is generally allocating more toward districts where residents are primarily of the same sect as them.

Of particular interest are extreme allocators, or people who allocate 0 percent to certain types of districts. These individuals can often provide insight into what the rest of society believes or how it behaves. Building on the findings in Table 12.6, we look at extreme allocators regarding poor districts, districts of other majority sects

---

[18] The same analysis was done (on allocations to poor districts), excluding districts of origin rather than districts of residence. This is because a significant portion of the population live in areas different than their areas of origin, and there are generally still strong ties to people's districts of origin and interest in investment in people's areas of origin, including through foreign remittances. The results hold almost exactly the same compared to when respondents' districts of residence were excluded, suggesting that people regard their districts of residence and of origin in a similar way.

336   *The Future of Petroleum in Lebanon*

Table 12.5 Districts categorized by majority sect and development and poverty level

Districts (Excluding Beirut)	Majority Sect*					
Development Level	Sunni	Shia	Christian	Druze	Christian/Druze	Total
Poor	2	4	0	1	1	8
Medium	2	2	2	1	1	8
Rich	1	0	8	0	0	9
Total	5	6	10	2	2	25

* A district's majority sect is the predominant sectarian/confessional affiliation of 60% or more of the population in that district. In some districts there is no clear majority sect (i.e the population of one sectarian group is between 50% and 60%), such as the case of Chouf and Hasbaya.

Source: Produced by authors based on data findings in Survey of Public Opinion in Lebanon, LCPS (2016).

Table 12.6 The effect of various individual and regional characteristics on respondents' likelihood to allocate to certain types of districts

Allocations to: (District type)	Statistically significant Factors
Poor Districts (excluding districts respondents live in)	– Those with middle or high education levels are more likely to allocate – Those who are economically conservative are less likely to allocate – Those who are politically connected are much less likely to allocate – Interestingly, those with more trust toward government institutions are less likely to allocate to poor districts; We would expect this to be the opposite, as more trust entails believing in the ability of the government to provide adequate public services and redistribute public funding fairly – People from poorer districts are much more likely to allocate to poor districts than people from wealthier districts
Districts with Druze, Christian, Shia, or Sunni Majority	In general, respondents are more likely to allocate to districts of their own sect. (example: other sects are significantly less likely to allocate to Druze majority districts compared to Druze respondents)
Districts of different sect (excluding districts respondents live in)	– High correlation between respondent sect and district majority sect – Druze, Sunni, and Shia are significantly more likely than Christians to allocate to districts of a different sect. This is likely due to the composition of districts and fact that there are several more Christian majority districts than there are of other sects (Table 12.5), and Christian respondents have less options of districts of other sects to allocate to, making their allocations to other districts lower in total
Poor districts of different sect (excluding districts respondents live in)	– Those who are economically conservative are less likely to allocate – Those who are politically connected are much less likely to allocate – Interestingly, those with more trust toward government institutions are less likely to allocate to poor districts – People from poorer districts are much more likely to allocate to poor districts of a different majority sect than people from wealthier districts – High correlation between respondent sect and district sect

Source: Produced by authors based on data findings in Survey of Public Opinion in Lebanon, LCPS (2016).

(non-co-sectarian districts), and poor districts of other majority sects. We first look at poor districts and districts of other majority sects separately to determine where there are stronger results and which factors people more often take into consideration. These provide insight on the "othering" phenomenon,[19] both from a socio-economic perspective and from a sect perspective.

Sectarian considerations are significant in allocation decisions and generally override other considerations

We find that 16.2 percent of the population was not willing to allocate revenues to poor districts, which is significant given that eight of the 26 districts, or roughly one-third, are poor and underdeveloped. Additionally, 16.2 percent of individuals were not willing to allocate revenue to districts that are of a different sect than their own. This finding is even more revealing given that there are many options available for people to allocate to non-co-sectarian districts (a Christian respondent has 13 non-Christian majority districts that can be allocated to; a Druze respondent has 21 non-Druze majority districts; a Shia and a Sunni have 19 and 20 respectively). This might point to an active decision on the part of the population to provide funds only to districts that are from their own sect. Even though the proportion of people who choose not to allocate revenue to poor districts and to districts of other sects is similar, the fact that there are significantly more districts from a different majority sect than districts that are poor (Table 12.7) suggests that on the whole people feel more strongly about not allocating revenue to districts of other sects than they do about not allocating revenue to poor districts. Finally, roughly one-quarter of the population is not willing to allocate revenue to poor districts of a different majority sect.

Table 12.7 Non-co-sectarian districts available for allocation as a respondent from a particular sect

Non co-sectarian districts (options for allocation)	Poor	Medium	Rich	(excluding Beirut)	
As a Christian respondent	7	5	1	out of 13	Non-Christian Districts
As a Sunni respondent	6	6	8	out of 20	Non-Sunni Districts
As a Shia respondent	4	6	9	out of 19	Non-Shia Districts
As a Druze respondent	6	6	9	out of 21	Non-Druze Districts
	out of 8	out of 8	out of 9		
		Non Co-sectarian Districts			

Source: Produced by authors based on data findings in Survey of Public Opinion in Lebanon, LCPS (2016).

---

[19] The phenomenon of portraying or mentally labelling someone or something as fundamentally different or alien, and creating separate entities in which one group is seen as "us" and the other as "them" or "not one of us."

338 *The Future of Petroleum in Lebanon*

Allocation experiment: Providing information has no clear effect on decision making in revenue allocation

A pattern can be observed by examining respondents' allocation preferences to individual districts. Sectarian affiliation, the development and poverty levels of districts allocated to, and respondents' district of residence stand out as significant predictors of people's allocation decisions. To understand these relationships further, we focus on sect and development levels as primary factors, and introduce an integrated experiment that attempts to measure how people weigh sectarian and economic considerations when making allocation decisions. The experiment entails introducing variations on the map where respondents are asked how they would distribute future revenue from the oil and gas sector to Lebanon's 26 districts. Respondents were randomly assigned to receive one of four versions of the map: the control group received a basic map of Lebanon with labeled districts; a treatment group received additional information on the majority confession in each of the districts (sect information); another treatment group received additional information on the development levels of each of the districts (economic information); and a final treatment group received both additional sect and economic information.[20]

Through the experiment, we sought to understand how information affects people's thought processes and decision-making in revenue allocation. The goal of the experiment is to understand how information about the majority confession in a district and/or the level of economic development affect preferences over how future oil revenue is allocated. We focus specifically on examining how much people allocate to less developed, poor districts where the majority sect is different from theirs (henceforth referred to as poor non-co-sectarian districts—for example, a Christian respondent's allocation to a poor predominantly Shia district). This factor provides the clearest tradeoff between sect-based and development-based decision making in revenue allocation. It provides a measure of how much people would allocate to areas on the basis of need, rather than according to sectarian considerations.

Table 12.8 Extreme allocators according to district type

District Type (all excluding districts that respondents live in)	Percent of Respondents who allocate 0% of revenue (weighted)	Districts Available for Allocation
Poor	16.2	8
Of a different majority sect	16.2	13, 20 or 19 or 21 depending on majority sect (Table 12.5)
Poor non co-sectarian	24.5	7, 6 or 4 depending on majority sect (Table 12.5)

Source: Produced by authors based on data findings in Survey of Public Opinion in Lebanon, LCPS (2016).

[20] For details on the experiment and how the randomization was implemented, see Annex 2.

Analysis through econometric regressions produces no robust results, meaning that there is no conclusive evidence that providing information about sect and poverty levels has a clear effect on behavior and decision making in revenue allocation. Different methods were used,[21] with some producing no evidence of an effect, and with one case showing a small effect on allocations. In that case, the results showed a pattern where development and economic treatment caused a statistically significant but small increase in the share allocated to poor non-co-sectarian districts. However, the receipt of development information only had an effect on increased allocation to poor non-co-sectarian districts when sectarian information was not received. The respondents who received both sectarian information and development information behaved similarly to the group that did not receive any information, as allocations to poor non-co-sectarian districts were reduced to levels similar to the group that did not receive any information. This suggests that sectarian considerations play a larger role than economic considerations when people make allocation decisions, which is in line with what other findings point toward as shown in Table 12.5. However, the lack of robust results across different specifications demonstrates that preferences on geographical allocation of revenues are persistent, and providing specific information does not significantly alter those preferences.

Conclusion and recommendations

There is general optimism regarding the potential impact of Lebanon's petroleum sector, but there are strong beliefs that political elites will benefit most. People want to allocate revenues through diverse mechanisms but with a strong emphasis on public investment, which reflects the poor state of infrastructure in the country. Sectoral allocations are primarily concentrated on health, education, and electricity. Regional allocations to different districts are diverse and on the whole appear equitably distributed when taking into account population and development levels, though the driving factors behind people's decision making are layered, with a good proportion of people choosing not to allocate to poor districts or districts where the majority of people are from a different sect.

People's preferences vary significantly depending on the socio-economic characteristics of the population as well as geographical disparities regarding where they reside. Among different individual characteristics, sect-related factors play an important role. Muslims are less optimistic about the future impact and benefit of the petroleum sector overall, and they also prefer to channel more revenue through cash transfers. Additionally, the geographical distribution of sectarian welfare agencies affects how people from different sects allocate funds, and this also results in positive spillovers for minorities in areas where these agencies are concentrated. Lastly, people are generally prone to allocating more funds to districts of their own sect, and this factor has a larger weight than other considerations such as district development levels.

There are also stark regional differences in how people view the future impact of the oil and gas sector and how they choose to allocate potential revenues. First, the level of

---

[21] These include linear and binary regression with weighted and non-weighted data.

340 *The Future of Petroleum in Lebanon*

optimism in a particular district is heavily influenced by its level of development, its degree of homogeneity, its political competitiveness, and the influence of local politicians at the national level. Second, the geographic availability of services affects the instruments through which and the sectors to which people prefer to allocate potential revenue. Finally, people generally allocate more to their own districts, with the next best option being allocation to districts of the same sect.

There is no clear evidence that providing basic information on the sectarian or development characteristics of districts plays a significant role in influencing people's allocation decisions, though patterns of sectarian considerations overriding economic considerations exist. This means that, in this case, providing such basic information might not be the best tool to influence people's decisions, especially regarding issues of inequality in development. This could have implications on knowledge or awareness campaigns that use information to shed light on development-related issues or try to influence people away from sectarianism. Though the map information experiment produced no clear evidence of an effect, this does not mean that other types of information would not be more effective. While the aim of this experiment was to investigate how sectarian and development considerations affect people's preferences over the distribution of future oil revenues, future experiments could examine how providing more information on the petroleum discovery itself or plans for public spending affect preferences.

Finally, the main takeaway from these findings concerns the importance of using measurable and evidence-based data to inform the policy making process. Studies and survey results like these, which hold a wealth of information about the observed preferences of a mostly representative sample of the Lebanese population, have the potential to be utilized to create and adapt policies that genuinely answer to people's varying needs and attempt to improve livelihoods through people-driven development. If the intention is there, policy makers can use this process of dissecting and analyzing data on public opinion to properly understand people's preferences, the differences in their needs, and how these vary between different regions and among people from different backgrounds. They can then tailor government policies to these needs, not just within the governance of the oil and gas sector but in the broader domain of public service provision. Considering the nascent state of the oil and gas sector, an opportunity has arisen to utilize the development of the sector as a model or framework for public participation in the policy making process. This raises two important questions. How much of a say can and should the general public have in the oil and gas sector's formation? Additionally, what are the best ways to meaningfully involve the public given that the sector is specialized and novel?

Annex 1: Questionnaire and methodology of the survey

Questionnaire

The survey is divided into five main sections and includes three main groups of experiments:

- Section 1 deals with the random selection of a respondent at the level of the household.
- Section 2 includes all baseline questions, or the pre-experiment questions that capture demographic information, information on political networks and politics, oil and gas (including a map experiment), information on confession, and economic conditions of the respondent and household.
- Section 3 includes the information experiment, where respondents are randomly assigned to receive between one and three pieces of information which tackle the following topics: (1) economic and social inequality in Lebanon; (2) the divergence of economic preferences between people who belong to the same sect but are in different economic classes; and (3) examples of successful or hopeful national political movements that have overcome traditional sectarian politics and brought different people together under common economic interests and demands. The third piece of information (political movements) was received by all respondents, but framed in two different ways. The first version focused on the movements as cross-sectarian, combining people from different sects and societal groups together. The second version emphasized the common economic concerns that brought people together and framed the movements as socio-economic in nature.
- Section 4 includes the outcome questions that measure the effect of the information treatments on people's responses and preferences. These questions look into issues such as self-categorization, distance between different confessional and economic groups, as well as support for sectarian versus programmatic politics.
- Finally, section 5 includes the behavioral outcomes, which measure people's real willingness to take political action and real preferences for programmatic politics as opposed to the current sect-based political system and way of thinking. The outcomes comprise the opportunity to sign a petition and the opportunity to join a Facebook group. For each of these behavioral outcomes, two versions were randomly assigned: a public one, which asks respondents to provide their names that will be publically visible to their social circles and political leaders; and a private one which allows respondents to take action while protecting their identity. Adding a public vs. private dimension, the behavioral outcomes also become treatments in themselves, in that they measure preference falsification regarding which political systems people prefer.

Sampling

The data in this study come from a nationally representative sample of 2,496 adult Lebanese citizens (18 to 65 years of age) fielded from December 2015 to February 2016. Respondents were selected through stratified random sampling. First, primary sampling units (primarily villages in rural areas and cities or neighborhoods in urban areas) were classified on the basis of population size and predominant sect. Primary Sampling Units (PSU) that had fewer than 2,000 people were classified as "small," PSUs with 2,001–35,000 people were classified as "medium," and PSUs with more than 35,000 people were classified as "large". Information on the predominant sect in each

PSU was obtained from Information International (II), the professional Beirut-based survey firm that implemented the survey, with assistance from LCPS. We then grouped PSUs into strata on the basis of their district, the PSU population category, the predominant sect, and whether or not the PSU was in the capital of that district.[22] PSUs were randomly sampled within strata using simple random sampling. All in all, the final sample consists of 2,496 respondents in 195 PSUs.

Households (and individuals within households) were randomly sampled within PSUs, with one respondent per household. The number of respondents in each PSU was determined by the PSU population category. We sampled eight households in "small" PSUs, 16 households in "medium" PSUs, and 32 households in "large" PSUs.[23] II sampled households within PSUs following their standard procedures. They first divided each PSU into neighborhoods based on local information and then selected households using systematic random sampling in each selected neighborhood according to the number of buildings in the neighborhood. One challenge with this method is that there is a lack of reliable data in Lebanon on the number of households within each neighborhood, making it difficult to know with confidence the probability that a household was selected within its PSU strata. We address how we deal with this below.

Within sampled households, respondents were selected using simple random sampling. To achieve a similar number of men and women in the sample, a target sex was set for each household. Individuals were eligible for sampling if they belonged to the target sex, were Lebanese citizens, were a member of the household (defined as "a group of people that typically live and eat together and in most cases form a common decision-making unit"), and were between the ages of 18 and 65. Individuals were then selected by randomly selecting a month of the year and then selecting the person born earliest in that month (in case no one is born in that month, the field workers moved on to the next month). This method was used after piloting showed that fully enumerating a list of all eligible individuals within a household and sampling from that list drew too much suspicion from respondents. If a sampled household or individual was not at home, a follow-up was conducted. Enumerators took the next household or respondent on the list if no one was available after the second contact or if a household/respondent refused to provide consent.

Randomization in the map experiment

The map experiment involved two treatments. All survey respondents were randomly assigned at the individual level (blocking on PSU) to an "economic" treatment or control group, where those in the treatment group received information on the economic status of each district (ranging on a five-point scale from 1, "rich and

---

[22] We excluded PSUs and strata that had fewer than 200 people and that were in insecure areas, which were predominantly Hezbollah-controlled areas. In total we excluded 194 PSUs, reducing our eligible PSUs from 1,017 to 823.

[23] These numbers were set based on our block random assignment needs for a different component of this project.

well-developed," to 5, "very under-developed"). All survey respondents were also independently randomly assigned to "sectarian" treatment or control groups, where those in the treatment group received information on the majority confession in each district and those in the control group did not. The experiments were implemented following a 2x2 factorial design, which yielded four possible experimental conditions: (1) a control group that only received a map of the districts and a list of district names; (2) a sectarian only group that received information on the sectarian status of the district; (3) an economic group that received information on the economic status of the district; and (4) a group that received both sectarian and economic information.

Generalizing to the population

For both the survey data and petition results we aim to generalize from the sample to the population, which requires weighting the sample. One option for weighting would involve using our survey design weights, specifically weighting by the inverse of the probability of selection.[24] However, there are two challenges to this approach. First, as described above, it is very hard to obtain accurate information on the number of households within a PSU or neighborhood because of the population density in many urban PSUs and because reliable official information on populations is not maintained in Lebanon (there has been no official census in Lebanon since 1932). While we construct probabilities based on the PSU population and estimated household size using our data, these estimates should be treated with caution. Second, approximately 60 percent of the sampled households or respondents refused to take part in the survey, which we attribute to the length of the survey and the sensitivity of some of the subject matter. While this is a better response rate than in many public opinion surveys in other countries, it still suggests that our sample could be systematically different from the population.[25]

A common procedure in such cases is to use post-survey weight adjustments, such as post-stratification weighting or calibration/raking, to generalize from the sample to the population. Regardless of the method used, post-survey weight adjustments aim to bring the sample closer to known population totals. The key to post-survey weighting is the existence of a high-quality reference dataset, such as a census or general population survey, with population totals for observable (typically demographic) characteristics. As discussed above, in the case of Lebanon, no census has been conducted since 1932 and (to our knowledge) there are few general population surveys on which to draw. We decided to use data from the Arab Barometer III survey (conducted in Lebanon in July 2013) as our reference. The Arab Barometer III is a nationally representative survey that is widely used by academic and policy researchers to draw population inferences.[26]

---

[24] The probability a PSU was selected within a strata × the probability a household was selected within a PSU × the probability that an individual was selected within a household.

[25] For instance, Rosenfeld, Imai, and Shapiro (2016) report that the American Association for Public Opinion Research's Response Rate 3 was 5.3 percent. Response rates for Pew Research Polls typically range from 5 to 15 percent in the United States. See http://www.pewresearch.org/methodology/u-s-survey-research/our-survey-methodology-in-detail/

[26] For details, see http://www.arabbarometer.org/

Table 12.9 Population demographics before and after weights are applied

	Arabbarometer Population Estimates				Our Survey Population Estimates			Our Survey Population Estimates after Post-stratification		
	mean	*lower ci*	*upper ci*	*N*	*mean*	*lower ci*	*upper ci*	*mean*	*lower ci*	*upper ci*
Panel A: Region										
Beirut	0.11	0.09	0.13	1200	0.09	0.06	0.11	0.09	0.06	0.12
Mout Lebanon	0.39	0.36	0.42	1200	0.36	0.32	0.39	0.34	0.30	0.37
North	0.22	0.19	0.24	1200	0.23	0.20	0.26	0.22	0.18	0.25
Beqaa	0.12	0.10	0.14	1200	0.15	0.13	0.17	0.16	0.13	0.18
South	0.11	0.09	0.12	1200	0.12	0.10	0.14	0.13	0.11	0.16
Nabatieh	0.06	0.05	0.08	1200	0.06	0.05	0.06	0.07	0.06	0.08
Panel B: Demographics										
Age (18–66)	39	38	40	1117	37	36	38	39	38	40
Female	0.51	0.48	0.54	1200	0.49	0.46	0.52	0.51	0.47	0.55
Secondary education (=1)	0.52	0.49	0.55	1200	0.65	0.61	0.68	0.52	0.48	0.56
Married (=1)	0.59	0.56	0.62	1200	0.57	0.53	0.60	0.62	0.58	0.66
Panel C: Confession										
Sunni	0.27	0.25	0.30	1200	0.33	0.29	0.36	0.27	0.24	0.31
Shia	0.27	0.24	0.30	1200	0.23	0.21	0.26	0.27	0.24	0.30
Maronite Christian	0.26	0.23	0.28	1200	0.29	0.25	0.32	0.26	0.22	0.29
Druze	0.08	0.06	0.09	1200	0.07	0.05	0.08	0.08	0.06	0.10
Panel D: Employment and wealth										
Income (scale 1–15)	4.90	4.82	4.97	864	5.53	5.46	5.60	5.57	5.48	5.65
Employed	0.65	0.62	0.68	1200	0.49	0.45	0.52	0.65	0.62	0.68
HH own computer	0.78	0.76	0.81	1196	0.67	0.63	0.70	0.65	0.61	0.68
HH owns a car	0.69	0.66	0.71	1200	0.93	0.91	0.94	0.92	0.91	0.94

What Do Lebanese Citizens Want From Oil and Gas Revenues? 345

While there might also be valid concerns about the accuracy of population estimates derived from the Arab Barometer, we take this step to bring our sample closer to the distribution of demographic characteristics from a well-known and widely used data source.

We use entropy balancing to construct post-survey weights. Entropy balancing is increasingly used as a reweighting method to achieve covariate balance between "treatment" and "control" groups in observational studies (Hainmueller 2012). As discussed by Hainmueller (2012), however, entropy balancing can also be used to adjust survey design weights so that sample moments match the known population moments (see also Hainmueller and Xu 2013). Entropy balancing is comparable to other traditional post-survey weighting schemes, including post-stratification and calibration/raking. The advantages of entropy balancing include the ability to incorporate survey design weights as base weights and to obtain exact balance between sample and population moments (up to three moments) and for a large number of covariates (Watson and Elliot 2016). For our analysis we balance on the first moment (the mean) and trim one observation that achieved excessive weight.

Table 12.9 shows the population proportions for 18 key variables as estimated in the Arab Barometer data (column 1) and our data (column 2). This comparison suggests that our survey has a higher proportion of individuals who have at least a secondary

Details on methodology

Table 12.10 Summary table of multivariate regressions with dependent and independent variables

Explanatory variables (down)	Dependent variables (right)	(a) Citizens' perceptions on net impact of oil revenues	(b) Citizens' preferences on revenue allocation by function	(c) Citizens' preferences on revenue allocation by sector	(d) Citizens' preferences on revenue allocation by district
Individual characteristics		X	X	X	X
Age		X	X	X	X
Gender		X	X	X	X
Education		X	X	X	X
Income		X	X	X	X
Labor market status		X	X	X	X
Marital status		X	X	X	X
Confession		X	X	X	X
Economic views (conservative vs progressive)		X	X	X	X
Political networks		X	X	X	X
Regional characteristics		X	X	X	X
Dummies for each district		X	X	X	
Dummies for district development level					X

education (65 percent compared to 52 percent) and a lower proportion of people who are employed (49 percent compared to 65 percent). Our estimated population proportions for the main confessions (Sunni, Shia, and Maronite Christian) also differ slightly. We correct for these differences by using the Arab Barometer data to post-stratify our results, with the results after post-stratification weighting presented in the column to the far right. We check the robustness of our results by using these post-stratification weights.

Definition of variables

Age: split into youth (18–29), mid-age (30–55), and old (55–65).
Gender: male or female.
Household income: split into poor (below average income) and rich (above average income).
Labor market status: employed (self-employed, public employee, or private employee), unemployed or outside the labor force (students or inactive).
Marital status: single, married, divorced, widowed.
Sect: Shia, Sunni, Christian, or Druze.
Economic views: conservative or progressive, based on whether they are in favor of or against using taxes to redistribute money to the poor.
Political networks: based on how easy it is for citizens to ask relevant figures (*zaim*, religious leaders, etc.) for help when searching for jobs or accessing different services.

Annex 2: Regressions and details

Perceptions of the net impact of petroleum revenues on citizens' households

Dependent variable: Net impact of oil revenues (1: very negative; 2: somewhat negative; 3: somewhat positive; 4: very positive) on: (a) citizens' families; (b) citizens' sects; (c) Lebanon; (d) the political elites; and (e) overall.
Regression analysis: As the dependent variable has more than two categories (from 1 to 4) that have a meaningful sequential order (the higher the number the more optimistic about the impact of oil revenues), ordered probit regressions are used.

Additional regressions on allocation of revenue by function

Dependent variable: Proportion of funds (between 0 percent and 100 percent) allocated to: cash, public wages, public investment, public debt payments, development bank to grant loans to small and medium enterprises SMEs (small and medium enterprises), sovereign wealth fund, and central bank.
Regression analysis: Generalized linear models from the binomial family.

Additional regressions on allocation of revenue by sector

Dependent variable: Proportion of funds (between 0 percent and 100 percent) allocated to: education, electricity, health, transportation and water.
Regression analysis: Generalized linear models from the binomial family.

Additional regressions on allocation of revenue by region

The following tables show the results of regressions on the allocation of revenue to different districts according to several independent variables that characterize respondent background and regional differences. The analysis is based on binomial regressions (since the allocation responses are fractions that vary between zero and one) and several factors are controlled for, including age, gender, education, income, employment, and marital status. The results show which characteristics or factors are statistically significant and play a role in people's allocation decisions.

Table 12.14 looks at regression results on allocations to a selection of districts to get an initial understanding of important characteristics that affect allocations. The districts chosen represent mostly poor districts of the four different majority sects, and Zahle was added as a comparatively rich district to observe if any differences arise.

Table 12.15 looks at regression results on allocations to districts according to their majority sect to understand whether clear sect-related patterns exist.

The third table (Table 12.16) looks at regression results on allocations to poor districts and rich districts to understand whether clear patterns exist when classifying districts by level of development and poverty.

The fourth table (Table 12.17) looks specifically at regression results on allocations to poor districts whose majority sect is different from respondents' (poor non-co-sectarian districts) to understand the trade-off between sectarian considerations and development considerations in allocations.

Table 12.11 Regression results for perceptions on impact

Socio-economic characteristics	VARIABLES	Overall Impact	Impact on household	Impact on sect	Impact on Lebanon	Impact on pol. elites
AGE	midage	−0.149	−0.0961	−0.151	−0.212*	−0.0367
		(0.104)	(0.127)	(0.118)	(0.122)	(0.132)
	old	−0.120	0.00313	−0.173	−0.324**	−0.190
		(0.135)	(0.157)	(0.150)	(0.155)	(0.167)
GENDER	female	−0.0349	−0.0696	−0.0262	0.0578	−0.0577
		(0.0913)	(0.0955)	(0.0994)	(0.109)	(0.111)
EDUCATION	mid-education	−0.239**	−0.205*	−0.202	−0.282**	0.0770
		(0.113)	(0.119)	(0.124)	(0.118)	(0.137)
	high-education	−0.250**	−0.228*	−0.247*	−0.232*	−0.0129
		(0.119)	(0.130)	(0.132)	(0.136)	(0.142)
INCOME	Income	0.0332	0.0343	0.0214	0.0163	−0.0990
		(0.0502)	(0.0580)	(0.0539)	(0.0561)	(0.0648)
LABOR MARKET STATUS	self-employed	−0.466***	−0.516***	−0.386***	−0.417***	−0.130
		(0.116)	(0.126)	(0.129)	(0.131)	(0.135)
	unemployed	−0.425**	−0.385**	−0.348*	−0.547**	−0.193
		(0.198)	(0.179)	(0.202)	(0.259)	(0.258)
	inactive	−0.0620	−0.0866	−0.0300	−0.0577	0.361**
		(0.127)	(0.143)	(0.135)	(0.138)	(0.147)
	student	0.0805	0.0171	0.137	0.0913	−0.0786
		(0.160)	(0.170)	(0.178)	(0.158)	(0.187)
	public employment	−0.315**	−0.283**	−0.463***	−0.0996	−0.307
		(0.131)	(0.122)	(0.153)	(0.159)	(0.232)
MARITAL STATUS	single	−0.0635	0.0320	−0.0722	−0.229	0.166
		(0.112)	(0.130)	(0.121)	(0.140)	(0.139)
	divorced	0.395	0.0688	0.615**	0.650**	0.432*
		(0.313)	(0.408)	(0.273)	(0.269)	(0.251)
	widowed	0.0633	−0.0696	0.325	0.0693	0.456
		(0.208)	(0.212)	(0.273)	(0.268)	(0.399)

Table 12.11 (Continued)

Socio-economic characteristics	VARIABLES	Overall Impact	Impact on household	Impact on sect	Impact on Lebanon	Impact on pol. elites
SECT	christian	0.333***	0.311**	0.346***	0.194	−0.0528
		(0.115)	(0.132)	(0.127)	(0.134)	(0.139)
	sunni	0.0858	0.153	0.0592	−0.0442	−0.444***
		(0.117)	(0.124)	(0.132)	(0.154)	(0.146)
	druze	0.291	0.249	0.310	0.272	−0.467*
		(0.188)	(0.203)	(0.239)	(0.234)	(0.252)
ECONOMIC VIEWS	econ. conservative	0.151**	0.279***	0.196**	−0.161*	−0.0518
		(0.0741)	(0.0785)	(0.0797)	(0.0848)	(0.0927)
SOCIAL VIEWS	social conservative	0.0201	0.0457	0.0512	−0.0499	−0.162**
		(0.0521)	(0.0558)	(0.0549)	(0.0563)	(0.0695)
POLITICAL NETWORKS	political networks	0.310	0.478**	0.337	−0.205	0.153
		(0.202)	(0.209)	(0.206)	(0.212)	(0.252)
	Econ Cons * Pol Net	−0.194*	−0.216**	−0.231**	0.0225	−0.112
		(0.107)	(0.110)	(0.114)	(0.120)	(0.134)
Observations		2,440	2,440	2,440	2,440	2,440

Robust standard errors in parentheses.

*** $p<0.01$, ** $p<0.05$, * $p<0.1$.

Table 12.12 Regression results on revenue allocation by function

VARIABLES	(1) cash	(2) wage	(3) investment	(4) pay debt	(5) development bank	(6) sov. wealth fund	(7) central bank
midage	0.0384	0.153*	−0.111	0.0674	−0.0217	0.000982	0.0173
	(0.132)	(0.0781)	(0.0831)	(0.0899)	(0.116)	(0.0807)	(0.0972)
old	−0.183	0.241**	0.113	0.145	−0.0333	−0.241**	−0.144
	(0.160)	(0.100)	(0.149)	(0.125)	(0.136)	(0.0942)	(0.117)
female	−0.134	−0.0684	0.0639	0.118	−0.0656	0.0644	0.0309
	(0.103)	(0.0647)	(0.0769)	(0.0784)	(0.0826)	(0.0639)	(0.0786)
midedu	0.217	−0.0197	0.00646	−0.171*	−0.158	0.0908	−0.0150
	(0.137)	(0.0770)	(0.0985)	(0.0916)	(0.102)	(0.0741)	(0.0995)
higedu	0.0564	0.116	0.0301	0.152	−0.260**	−0.0493	−0.172
	(0.159)	(0.0836)	(0.100)	(0.111)	(0.123)	(0.101)	(0.113)
Income	−0.0135	0.106***	−0.0309	0.0909**	−0.115**	−0.0535	0.0184
	(0.0618)	(0.0322)	(0.0424)	(0.0409)	(0.0482)	(0.0380)	(0.0431)
selfemp	0.178	−0.0100	0.0327	0.0690	0.0259	−0.0755	−0.315***
	(0.143)	(0.0765)	(0.101)	(0.0905)	(0.106)	(0.0781)	(0.0966)
unemp	−0.258	−0.227	0.106	−0.0650	0.152	0.174	0.0827
	(0.222)	(0.144)	(0.129)	(0.131)	(0.177)	(0.129)	(0.130)
inactive	−0.0138	−0.0259	0.224*	−0.0125	0.131	−0.233**	−0.303***
	(0.163)	(0.0838)	(0.125)	(0.108)	(0.123)	(0.0965)	(0.103)
student	−0.132	0.177*	−0.134	0.0671	0.157	0.0640	−0.0281
	(0.200)	(0.106)	(0.128)	(0.109)	(0.149)	(0.0917)	(0.121)
pubemp	−0.828***	0.122	0.364***	0.0819	0.381*	−0.396**	−0.559***
	(0.232)	(0.116)	(0.0990)	(0.129)	(0.194)	(0.163)	(0.191)
single	−0.178	0.00392	0.150	0.0536	0.121	−0.197**	−0.0413
	(0.146)	(0.0864)	(0.0964)	(0.110)	(0.127)	(0.0894)	(0.102)

Table 12.12 (Continued)

VARIABLES	(1) cash	(2) wage	(3) investment	(4) pay debt	(5) development bank	(6) sov. wealth fund	(7) central bank
divorced	0.141	0.0379	0.206	−0.270*	−0.128	−0.248	−0.0163
	(0.281)	(0.131)	(0.218)	(0.139)	(0.192)	(0.178)	(0.224)
widowed	0.855***	−0.446	0.174	−0.939***	−0.407	−0.267	−0.329
	(0.298)	(0.310)	(0.182)	(0.257)	(0.288)	(0.242)	(0.256)
chris	−0.356***	−0.0446	−0.0187	0.103	0.233*	0.0851	0.0843
	(0.136)	(0.0853)	(0.103)	(0.0983)	(0.139)	(0.0898)	(0.0987)
sunni	0.145	0.182*	−0.202*	−0.0297	0.187	−0.0621	−0.0702
	(0.149)	(0.0948)	(0.112)	(0.122)	(0.148)	(0.104)	(0.121)
druze	0.0499	0.200*	−0.165	0.113	0.272	−0.131	−0.0670
	(0.258)	(0.117)	(0.154)	(0.138)	(0.180)	(0.120)	(0.128)
trust	−0.0850*	−0.0266	0.0285	−0.00639	0.0558	0.00398	0.0686*
	(0.0515)	(0.0309)	(0.0347)	(0.0318)	(0.0413)	(0.0308)	(0.0391)
ecocons	−0.435***	−0.174***	−0.0136	−0.104**	0.540***	0.115***	0.0541
	(0.0809)	(0.0502)	(0.0455)	(0.0436)	(0.0461)	(0.0376)	(0.0476)
polnet	−0.366***	0.00911	−0.0179	0.118	0.0478	0.161**	0.0709
	(0.100)	(0.0759)	(0.102)	(0.0812)	(0.0814)	(0.0640)	(0.0779)
Constant	−1.962***	−2.144***	−0.274	−2.419***	−2.520***	−2.210***	−2.325***
	(0.367)	(0.211)	(0.303)	(0.284)	(0.284)	(0.253)	(0.273)
Observations	2,426	2,426	2,426	2,426	2,426	2,426	2,426

Robust standard errors in parentheses.

*** $p<0.01$, ** $p<0.05$, * $p<0.1$.

352 *The Future of Petroleum in Lebanon*

Table 12.13 Regression results on revenue allocation by sector

VARIABLES	(8) Education	(9) Electricity	(10) Health	(11) Transport	(12) Water
midage	−0.0985	−0.0485	0.150***	0.0635	−0.0693
	(0.0642)	(0.0598)	(0.0580)	(0.0749)	(0.0619)
old	−0.0822	−0.0115	0.222***	−0.178*	−0.155**
	(0.0807)	(0.0873)	(0.0813)	(0.100)	(0.0750)
female	−0.0644	0.0329	0.00856	0.0300	0.0301
	(0.0506)	(0.0525)	(0.0533)	(0.0583)	(0.0531)
midedu	0.198***	−0.211***	0.0210	−0.0418	−0.0983
	(0.0608)	(0.0789)	(0.0608)	(0.0701)	(0.0604)
higedu	0.269***	−0.197**	−0.0729	−0.0467	−0.0468
	(0.0759)	(0.0859)	(0.0690)	(0.0920)	(0.0671)
Income	−0.0160	0.00109	−0.0279	0.0498	0.0483
	(0.0316)	(0.0451)	(0.0405)	(0.0340)	(0.0294)
selfemp	−0.000568	0.0976	−0.138*	−0.00188	0.114*
	(0.0690)	(0.0693)	(0.0727)	(0.0790)	(0.0667)
unemp	0.0726	0.236**	−0.258**	−0.0498	0.159
	(0.120)	(0.103)	(0.105)	(0.104)	(0.107)
inactive	−0.00753	0.179**	−0.116	0.114	−0.0184
	(0.0731)	(0.0844)	(0.0776)	(0.0919)	(0.0749)
student	0.0568	0.183*	−0.0596	−0.207**	0.0687
	(0.0912)	(0.0938)	(0.0869)	(0.0903)	(0.0870)
pubemp	0.0407	0.184*	−0.0853	−0.00740	−0.131
	(0.0894)	(0.109)	(0.0537)	(0.113)	(0.104)
single	−0.0559	0.00435	0.0355	0.139*	−0.0965
	(0.0659)	(0.0659)	(0.0617)	(0.0791)	(0.0660)
divorced	−0.0445	−0.0508	0.193	−0.195	0.0385
	(0.113)	(0.0979)	(0.138)	(0.128)	(0.154)
widowed	−0.157	0.0287	0.124	−0.564**	0.0974
	(0.208)	(0.228)	(0.244)	(0.259)	(0.249)
chris	0.0542	−0.123*	0.158**	−0.00114	−0.133**
	(0.0669)	(0.0698)	(0.0666)	(0.0861)	(0.0630)
sunni	0.0589	−0.100	0.0785	−0.00660	0.0624
	(0.0789)	(0.102)	(0.0816)	(0.101)	(0.0958)
druze	−0.00328	−0.0245	−0.0219	0.215*	−0.0647
	(0.0965)	(0.102)	(0.0936)	(0.116)	(0.0874)
trust	−0.00464	0.0227	−0.0287	0.0772**	0.0463**
	(0.0223)	(0.0304)	(0.0263)	(0.0300)	(0.0215)
ecocons	−0.0229	−0.00720	0.0277	0.160***	−0.0461
	(0.0296)	(0.0379)	(0.0339)	(0.0343)	(0.0324)
polnet	−0.0143	0.0259	0.0921	0.0157	−0.151**
	(0.0575)	(0.0957)	(0.0643)	(0.0627)	(0.0597)
Constant	−0.653***	−1.492***	−0.957***	−2.659***	−2.064***
	(0.198)	(0.256)	(0.208)	(0.221)	(0.178)
Observations	2,429	2,429	2,429	2,429	2,429

Robust standard errors in parentheses.

*** $p<0.01$, ** $p<0.05$, * $p<0.1$.

Table 12.14 Multivariate binomial regression results on allocations to particular example districts and the independent factors that affect these allocations

District	Hermel		Minnieh-Dannieh		Hasbaya		Zgharta		Zahle	
Independent Variables	Coef.	P Value	Coef.	P Value	Coef.	P Value	Coef.	P Value	Coef.	P Value
Middle Aged	−0.2	0.332	−0.3	0.045	−0.2	0.282	−0.3	0.147	−0.4	0.225
Old	−0.1	0.666	−0.1	0.718	0.0	0.944	0.1	0.617	−0.4	0.399
Female	−0.1	0.428	−0.1	0.746	0.1	0.221	−0.1	0.469	0.2	0.329
Mid Education	0.3	0.122	0.6	0.063	0.0	0.714	0.2	0.494	−0.1	0.573
High Education	0.3	0.117	0.4	0.108	0.0	0.977	−0.5	0.090	−0.2	0.442
Income	0.0	0.686	0.0	0.863	0.0	0.562	0.1	0.168	−0.2	0.077
Self-employed	0.4	0.027	0.2	0.318	0.3	0.079	−0.6	0.016	−0.1	0.803
Unemployed	0.3	0.207	0.2	0.550	−0.1	0.707	0.2	0.593	−1.3	0.008
Inactive	0.3	0.129	0.5	0.058	−0.1	0.693	−0.5	0.047	−0.8	0.014
Student	−0.5	0.064	−0.1	0.855	−0.1	0.482	0.2	0.486	−0.8	0.134
Public Employee	0.0	0.895	0.1	0.727	0.0	0.977	0.0	0.959	−0.9	0.098
Single	−0.1	0.487	−0.2	0.267	0.2	0.161	−0.2	0.277	0.0	0.980
Divorced	0.4	0.653	−2.0	0.000	0.8	0.193	0.8	0.084	−0.5	0.387
Widowed	0.1	0.825	−0.8	0.269	−0.4	0.446	0.3	0.544	0.9	0.065
Christian	−0.4	0.378	−0.4	0.192						
Sunni	−0.2	0.030			−0.4	0.041	−0.7	0.005	0.7	0.014
Shia			−0.1	0.833	0.1	0.517	−0.2	0.328	0.7	0.013
Druze	−0.2	0.522	−0.1	0.742	0.7	0.000	−0.4	0.116	0.7	0.015
Trust	−0.2	0.005	−0.2	0.020	0.0	0.406	−0.1	0.153	0.1	0.267
Econ Conservatism	−0.2	0.093	0.0	0.827	−0.1	0.276	0.2	0.076	0.5	0.000
Pol. Networks	−0.5	0.020	−0.1	0.585	−0.2	0.149	−0.5	0.025	0.7	0.006
District Development										
High	−2.2	0.000	1.5	0.006	−1.2	0.002	−1.0	0.076	0.9	0.103
Medium	−1.5	0.003	1.4	0.006	−0.6	0.038	−0.8	0.128	0.5	0.076
Low	−1.5	0.007	1.5	0.004	−0.1	0.637	−0.6	0.193	1.1	0.001
Very Low	−1.1	0.055	1.2	0.051	0.3	0.231	−1.6	0.009	1.7	0.000

Significant at the 10% confidence level

Significant at the 5% confidence level

Significant at the 1% confidence level

Table 12.15 Multivariate binomial regression results on allocations to districts according to their majority sect

District	Shia Majority Districts		Christian Majority Districts		Druze Majority Districts		Sunni Majority Districts	
Independent Variable	Coef.	P Value	Coef.	P Value	Coef.	P Value	Coef.	P Value
Middle Aged	−0.32	0.038	−0.17	0.251	−0.06	0.69	−0.33	0.073
Old	−0.17	0.417	−0.16	0.464	−0.04	0.869	−0.25	0.261
Female	0.16	0.168	0.08	0.492	0.14	0.279	−0.23	0.141
Middle Education	0.26	0.039	−0.11	0.385	−0.07	0.626	0.28	0.148
High Education	0.16	0.347	−0.37	0.031	−0.04	0.841	0.45	0.015
Income	−0.15	0.029	−0.05	0.46	0.02	0.846	−0.05	0.539
Self-employed	0.04	0.782	−0.16	0.307	0.29	0.063	0.22	0.23
Un-employed	0.31	0.157	−0.45	0.038	−0.11	0.646	−0.15	0.562
Inactive	−0.24	0.179	−0.41	0.038	0.01	0.977	0.77	0.002
Student	−0.08	0.703	−0.20	0.32	−0.10	0.641	0.34	0.187
Public Employee	0.02	0.941	−0.34	0.27	−0.16	0.591	−0.27	0.148
Single	−0.36	0.013	−0.06	0.643	0.21	0.187	−0.04	0.86
Divorced	−0.72	0.254	−0.20	0.789	0.64	0.261	0.75	0.454
Widowed	0.49	0.338	0.38	0.359	−0.51	0.164	−0.54	0.338
Christian	0.80	0			−1.16	0	−0.69	0.003
Sunni	−0.09	0.58	−0.50	0.004	−0.75	0.007		
Shia			−0.10	0.542	−0.72	0.001	−0.36	0.046
Druze	0.03	0.851	−0.01	0.925			−0.72	0
Trust	0.08	0.162	0.05	0.446	0.08	0.281	−0.19	0.015
Econ. Conservatism	0.04	0.606	0.18	0.008	0.12	0.131	−0.19	0.013
Pol. Networks	−0.20	0.137	0.01	0.959	−0.08	0.583	−0.36	0.008
District Development								
High	−0.06	0.891	−0.64	0.074	−0.05	0.915	0.80	0.014
Medium	−0.61	0.076	0.08	0.79	−0.08	0.742	0.36	0.183
Low	−0.45	0.213	0.64	0.041	−0.05	0.848	0.40	0.16
Very Low	−0.54	0.153	0.45	0.16	0.58	0.057	0.10	0.808

What Do Lebanese Citizens Want From Oil and Gas Revenues? 355

Table 12.16 Multivariate binomial regression results on allocations to districts according to their levels of poverty and development, also taking into account the districts that people are from or the districts that people live in, and that personal allocations to these districts may be biased and above average compared to other districts

District	Poor Districts		Poor Districts (excl dist respondent is from)		Poor Districts (excl dist respondent lives in)		Rich Districts	
Independent Variable	Coef.	P Value	Coef.	P Value	Coef.	P Value	Coef.	P Value
Middle Aged	−0.28	0.052	−0.30	0.013	−0.34	0.008	0.47	0.003
Old	−0.18	0.448	−0.02	0.907	−0.01	0.954	0.27	0.199
Female	−0.03	0.823	−0.05	0.682	0.00	0.980	0.03	0.829
Middle Education	0.18	0.220	0.23	0.097	0.24	0.095	−0.35	0.016
High Education	0.29	0.134	0.29	0.081	0.32	0.090	−0.25	0.142
Income	−0.10	0.151	0.04	0.500	0.04	0.478	0.09	0.251
Self-employed	0.31	0.035	0.24	0.072	0.32	0.037	−0.07	0.635
Un-employed	0.30	0.170	0.28	0.186	0.27	0.203	0.04	0.861
Inactive	0.28	0.129	0.16	0.374	0.18	0.369	−0.17	0.345
Student	0.16	0.383	0.03	0.822	0.08	0.672	0.05	0.784
Public Employee	0.05	0.878	−0.10	0.685	0.08	0.790	0.12	0.656
Single	−0.23	0.110	−0.19	0.156	−0.25	0.068	0.20	0.229
Divorced	−0.89	0.026	0.62	0.464	0.53	0.545	0.88	0.090
Widowed	−0.17	0.650	−0.37	0.257	−0.50	0.143	0.22	0.582
Sunni	0.08	0.635	−0.15	0.297	−0.06	0.725	0.06	0.707
Shia	−0.08	0.618	0.15	0.307	0.15	0.320	0.11	0.483
Druze	0.24	0.161	0.26	0.068	0.21	0.174	−0.10	0.542
Trust	−0.14	0.025	−0.12	0.028	−0.12	0.031	0.08	0.186
Econ. Conservatism	−0.09	0.218	−0.11	0.059	−0.15	0.030	−0.03	0.703
Pol. Networks	−0.40	0.001	−0.30	0.005	−0.38	0.001	0.48	0.000
District Development								
High	1.16	0.000	−0.39	0.124	−0.66	0.004	−0.76	0.016
Medium	−0.55	0.035	0.42	0.037	0.10	0.592	0.47	0.052
Low	−0.35	0.209	0.68	0.001	0.39	0.050	0.58	0.022
Very Low	−0.08	0.804	0.85	0.002	0.62	0.015	0.45	0.145

Table 12.17 Multivariate binomial regression results on allocations to districts whose majority sect is different from theirs (i.e. sum of allocations of Christian respondents to non-Christian districts, Sunni respondents to non-Sunni districts, Shia respondents to non-Shia districts, and Druze respondents to non-Druze districts), and to poor non-co-sectarian districts

District	Districts whose majority sect is different from respondents'		Poor districts whose majority sect is different from respondents'	
Independent Variable	Coef.	P Value	Coef.	P Value
Middle Aged	−0.32	0.022	−0.32	0.005
Old	−0.06	0.745	0.06	0.789
Female	0.05	0.666	−0.05	0.6
Middle Education	−0.16	0.216	0.16	0.252
High Education	−0.08	0.538	0.28	0.15
Income	−0.09	0.239	0.02	0.706
Self-employed	−0.13	0.34	0.16	0.179
Un-employed	−0.74	0.001	0.11	0.601
Inactive	−0.16	0.37	0.12	0.515
Student	−0.34	0.078	−0.19	0.324
Public Employee	−0.30	0.143	0.15	0.641
Single	0.22	0.093	−0.08	0.487
Divorced	0.12	0.875	1.10	0.147
Widowed	−0.66	0.089	−0.52	0.119
Sunni	0.64	0	1.06	0
Shia	0.72	0	0.61	0.006
Druze	1.32	0	1.05	0
Trust	0.03	0.585	−0.11	0.041
Econ. Conservatism	0.16	0.011	−0.13	0.053
Pol. Networks	−0.13	0.281	−0.34	0.006
District Development				
High	−0.85	0.013	−0.51	0.055
Medium	−0.22	0.44	0.36	0.068
Low	−0.13	0.662	0.66	0.001
Very Low	0.31	0.315	1.01	0

References

Authored references

Alesina, A., R. Baqir, and W. Easterly. 1999. "Public Goods and Ethnic Divisions." *Quarterly Journal of Economics* 114: 1243–84.

Amoako-Tuffour, J. 2011. "Public Participation in the Making of Ghana's Petroleum Revenue Management Law." Natural Resource Charter Technical Advisory Group.

Banerjee, A., L. Iyer, and R. Somanathan, 2005. "History, Social Divisions, and Public Goods in Rural India." *Journal of the European Economic Association* 3: 639–47.

Cammett, M. 2014. *Compassionate Communalism*. Cornell University Press.

Cammett, M. and S. Issar. 2010. "Bricks and Mortar Clientelism, Sectarianism and the Logics of Welfare Allocation in Lebanon." *World Politics* 62: 381–421.

Caselli, F. and G. Michaels. 2013. "Do Oil Windfalls Improve Living Standards? Evidence from Brazil." *Applied Economics* 5: 208–38.

Dunning, T. 2008. *Crude Democracy: Natural Resource Wealth and Political Regimes.* Cambridge University Press.

Eismeier, T. 1982. "Public Preferences about Government Spending: Partisan, Social, and Attitudinal Sources of Policy Differences." *Political Behavior* 4: 133–45

Hainmueller, J. 2012. "Entropy Balancing for Causal Effects: A Multivariate Reweighting Method to Produce Balanced Samples in Observational Studies." *Political Analysis* 20: 25–46.

Hainmueller, J. and Y. Xu. 2013. "Ebalance: A Stata Package for Entropy Balancing." *Journal of Statistical Software* 54.

Jacoby, W. 1994. "Public Attitudes toward Government Spending." *American Journal of Political Science* 38: 336–61.

Miguel, E. and M.K. Gugerty. 2005. "Ethnic Diversity, Social Sanctions, and Public Goods in Kenya." *Journal of Public Economics* 89: 2325–68.

Paler, L. 2013. "Keeping the Public Purse: An Experiment in Windfalls, Taxes, and the Incentives to Restrain Government." *American Political Science Review* 107: 706–25.

Rosenfeld, B., K. Imai, and J. Shapiro. 2016. "An Empirical Validation Study of Popular Survey Methodologies for Sensitive Questions." *American Journal of Political Science* 60: 783–802.

Ross, M. 2012. *The Oil Curse: How Petroleum Wealth Shapes the Development of Nations.* Princeton University Press.

Salloukh, B., R. Barakat, J. Al-Habbal, L. Khattab, and S. Mikaelian. 2015. *The Politics of Sectarianism in Postwar Lebanon.* Pluto Press.

Salti, N. and J. Chaaban, 2010. "The Role of Sectarianism in the Allocation of Public Expenditure in Postwar Lebanon." *International Journal of Middle East Studies* 42: 637–55.

Watson, S. and M. Elliot. 2016. "Entropy Balancing: A Maximum-Entropy Reweighting Scheme to Adjust for Coverage Error." Technical Report, The Cathie Marsh Center for Census and Survey Research.

Non-authored references

International Energy Agency. 2012. "Lebanon: Balances for 2012." www.iea.org/statistics/statisticssearch/report/?year=2012&country=LEBANON&product=Balances

International Monetary Fund. 2014. "Subsidy Reform in the Middle East and North Africa." http://www.imf.org/external/pubs/ft/dp/20141403/mcd.pdf

The World Bank. 2015. "Enterprise Survey." http://www.enterprisesurveys.org/data

World Economic Forum. 2016. "The Global Competitiveness Report 2016-2017."

Index

3D seismic data, 2, 23, 31, 155

Arab Barometer Survey, 209, 343, 345–6

Banque du Liban (Central Bank of
    Lebanon), 71, 85–6, 92, 180, 183,
    186, 199, 215, 229, 233, 316, 319,
    322, 346

civil society organization(s), 5–6, 40, 58–9,
    64, 68, 79, 87, 89–90, 92
clientelism, 4–5, 68, 108, 306, 333
concentration indices 246–50, 252–3
    Theil, 250–2, 255–8
corruption, 52, 56–8, 63–92, 102, 110–14,
    121–3, 159, 173–8, 188–91, 204,
    207, 215, 226
    risks of, 64, 66, 79
Cyprus
    National Hydrocarbon Company, 30
    (Cypriot) basin, 21
    offshore, 130–1
    petroleum fiscal regime, 144–6

Dutch disease, 175–6, 248
    empirical overview, 226–8
    theoretical overview, 224–6

economic complexity index (ECI), 246,
    260
Electricité du Liban, 82, 157–8, 186, 207
Eni, 3, 37, 70, 74, 107
environment, effects of drilling on
    development and production phase,
    284–6
    prospecting and exploration phase,
    276–84
environmental impact assessment, 275
environmental management
    emergency response, 291
    legislation, 288–9

monitoring, enforcement, assurance
    mechanisms, 290–1
permits, 289–90
regulatory authority, 287–8
risk assessment, 289
exclusive economic zone (EEZ), 23, 25,
    30–1, 155
exploration and production agreement
    (EPA)
    bidding, 91–2
    contract, 91–2
export specialization
    impact in Lebanon, 259–62
    impact of oil, 255–9
Extractive Industries Transparency Initiative
    (EITI), 58, 66–7, 77, 90, 114

Gazprom, 74
Global Corruption Barometer 2016, 67

healthcare, 42, 68, 173, 203, 311, 323,
    326–7, 330

initial environmental examination, 275,
    294–5, 298
international oil companies, 73, 80–3, 88–91
    non-operating, 73–7, 80, 91
    pre-qualified, 54, 91
Israel
    offshore law, 132
    petroleum fiscal regime, 146–7

Lebanese Petroleum Administration
    (LPA), 2–3, 7, 48–50, 54, 57,
    70–5, 79–82, 89–91, 101–6, 109,
    112, 114, 134, 149, 292–9
Lebanon
    block delineation, 77–8
    Constitutional Council, 4
    Court of Accounts, 72–3, 91, 207
    Decree 9882, 70, 73, 75

Decree 10289, 70, 78–80
Dutch disease, 229–39
environmental governance, 291–6
imports, gas 156–61
Ministry of Energy and Water (MEW),
2, 30–1, 37–9, 45, 49, 51, 53, 58,
68, 71–9, 90–1, 104, 106, 109, 157,
159, 161, 173, 292, 296, 298, 311
Ministry of Environment (MOE), 275,
289–99
Offshore Petroleum Resources Law
(OPRL), 2, 8, 43–6, 50–8, 69, 71,
82–3, 97, 105, 128–9, 134–5, 141,
144, 151, 292–7
petroleum export, 155–69
LNG options, 167–8
pipeline exports, 162–6
petroleum fiscal regime, 141–4
petroleum policy, 45
sovereign wealth fund, 203–5
Levantine Basin, 19, 21, 23–32, 155, 173–4
Leviathan Field, 24, 29, 30, 131–3, 167

model contract, 70, 76

national hydrocarbon law
Cyprus, 129–31
Israel, 131–4
national oil company 97–116
commercial downstream, 109–10
commercial upstream, 106–9
governance framework, 112–15
mandate, 103–11
Petoro, 104–6
Qatar Petroleum, 98
Saudi Aramco, 98
state equity shares, manager of, 104–6
natural gas liquids, 26–7
Noble Energy, 24, 130–2
Norway
Norwegian Oil for Development
Program, 71
Norwegian Petroleum GeoServices, 2
Novatek, 3, 37, 70, 74

oil and gas rights, allocation of, 122–34
biddable parameters, 125–7
block delineation, 127–8
licensing, 123

Palestine, 19, 24, 29, 30, 132, 185
Parliament of Lebanon
Committee on Public Works, 57
petroleum fiscal regime, types of 136–51,
137–9
petroleum systems, 16–17
product space, 245–6, 260–2

R-factor, 126, 129, 139–48, 151
resource curse, 3–4, 10, 39, 51, 65,
174–9, 216, 226, 239–41,
248–9, 305
resource value chain, 38–9, 51
revenue management and allocation,
173–91
accumulation of foreign assets, 183
cash transfers, handouts, 180–1
debt repayment, 182–3
increase public spending, 181–2
public lending to the private sector,
182

Sovereign Wealth Fund (SWF), 197–217
civil society, role of, 213–16
institutional design, 209–15
types of, 198–203
Survey of Public Opinion in Lebanon,
LCPS (2016)
impact of oil rents, perceptions of,
309–15
methodology, 307–9
revenue allocation by function,
315–21
revenue allocation by region, 330–9
revenue allocation by sector, 322–30
Syria, 21, 23–5, 31, 160, 162–6, 169, 185,
206

Taef Accord, 4, 41, 68–9, 73, 113, 206
Total, 3, 37, 70, 74, 130
Transparency International Corruption
Perceptions Index 2016, 67
treasury bills, 85, 207

United States Geological Survey (USGS),
26

World Economic Forum's Competitiveness
Index, 111

CPSIA information can be obtained
at www.ICGtesting.com
Printed in the USA
LVHW080000240721
693495LV00015B/902